The Separatist Conflict in Sri Lanka

The book provides a detailed historically-based analysis of the origin and evolution of the civil conflict in Sri Lanka over the struggle to establish a separate state in its Northern and Eastern provinces. This conflict between the Sri Lankan government and the secessionist LTTE (Liberation Tigers of Tamil Eelam) is one of the world's most intractable contemporary armed struggles. The internationally banned LTTE is considered the prototype of modern terrorism. It is known to have introduced suicide bombing to the world, and recently became the first terrorist organization ever to acquire air power.

The 'iron law of ethnicity' – the assumption that cultural difference inevitably leads to conflict – has been reinforced by the 9/11 attacks and conflicts like the one in Sri Lanka. However, the connections among ethnic difference, conflict, and terrorism are not automatic. This book broadens the discourse on the separatist conflict in Sri Lanka by moving beyond the familiar bipolar Sinhala versus Tamil ethnic antagonism to show how the form and content of ethnicity are shaped by historical social forces. It develops a multipolar analysis which takes into account diverse ethnic groups, intra-ethnic, social class, caste and other variables at the local, regional and international levels.

Overall, this book presents a conceptual framework useful for comparative global conflict analysis and resolution, shedding light on a host of complex issues such as terrorism, civil society, diasporas, international intervention and secessionism.

Asoka Bandarage is currently a professor at Georgetown University. She has taught at Yale, Brandeis and Mount Holyoke, and is the author of *Colonialism in Sri Lanka; Women, Population and Global Crisis* and publications on South Asia, global political economy, ethnicity, gender and population.

The Separatist Conflict in Sri Lanka

Terrorism, ethnicity, political economy

Asoka Bandarage

iUniverse, Inc.
New York   Bloomington

The Separatist Conflict in Sri Lanka
Terrorism, ethnicity, political economy

iUniverse books may be ordered through booksellers or by contacting:

iUniverse
1663 Liberty Drive
Bloomington, IN 47403
www.iuniverse.com
1-800-Authors (1-800-288-4677)

Because of the dynamic nature of the Internet, any Web addresses or links contained in this book may have changed since publication and may no longer be valid.

ISBN: 978-1-4401-5561-1 (pbk)
ISBN: 978-1-4401-5562-8 ebk)

Printed in the United States of America

iUniverse rev. date: 7/15/2009

Dedicated to the Sri Lankan people

Mind Without Fear

Where the mind is without fear and the head is held high;

Where knowledge is free;

Where the world has not been broken up into fragments by narrow domestic walls;

Where words come out from the depth of truth;

Where tireless striving stretches its arms towards perfection;

Where the clear stream of reason has not lost its way into the dreary desert sand of dead habit;

Where the mind is led forward by thee into ever-widening thought and action –

Into that heaven of freedom, my Father, let my country awake.

Rabindranath Tagore

Contents

Illustrations

Figures

Maps

Tables

Acknowledgments

My thanks to all the colleagues, student assistants, friends and family who have supported me in the writing and completion of this book. I must mention at least several persons by name: Ambassador Shirin Tahir-Kheli and Dr. Tom Keaney who invited me to spend a year at the Foreign Policy Institute at the School for Advanced International Studies at Johns Hopkins University on a Ford Fellowship in 2002–2003 during the early stage of this work; Carole Sargent, Director of the Office of Literary and Scholarly Publications at Georgetown University who guided me through the publication process; Meredith Sprengel and Rachel Tucker, my student research assistants who helped with data collection and collation until the very end; editor Peter Whitten, who facilitated the difficult task of reducing what was a much longer manuscript to its present length; artist Sushila Mallawaarachchi who helped with graphic design, Dorothea Schaefter, Associate Editor at Routledge for taking on this project and to her and editors Suzanne Chilestone, Tom Bates, Philippa Mulberry and Allie Waite for their patience and continuing support. Thanks also to my parents Mrs. Tilaka and Dr. D.S. Bandarage, my siblings (Rohan, Wasantha, Dammika, Chandana, Chanaka), to Jaime Babson and to all my teachers, especially Mr. S.N. Goenka. Last, but not least, thanks to my son, Maithri for his patience, tolerance and love during my long preoccupation with this book.

Abbreviations

ACSLU	Australian Center for Sri Lankan Unity
ACTC	All Ceylon Tamil Congress
AI	Amnesty International
AIADMK	All India Anna Dravida Munnetra Kazhagam
AMDP	Accelerated Mahaweli Development Program
CFA	ceasefire agreement
CJC	Criminal Justice Commission
CNC	Ceylon National Congress
CPA	Center for Policy Alternatives
CSO	civil society organization
CWC	Ceylon Workers' Congress
DJV	Deshapremi Janatha Viyaparaya (Patriotic People's Movement)
DK	Dravida Kazhagam
DMK	Dravida Munnetra Kazhagam (Dravidian Progress Federation)
EPDP	Eelam People's Democratic Party
EPRLF	Eelam People's Revolutionary Liberation Front
EROS	Eelam Revolutionary Organization of Students
FCE	Foundation for Co-Existence
FETNA	Federation of Tamil Sangams of North America
FP	Federal Party
GOSL	Government of Sri Lanka
HRC	Human Rights Commission
IC	international community
ICCPR	International Covenant on Civil and Political Rights
ICES	International Center for Ethnic Studies
ICG	International Crisis Group
ICJ	International Commission of Jurists
IIGEP	International Independent Group of Eminent Persons
IMF	International Monetary Fund
INGO	International Non Government Organization
INPACT	Initiative for Political and Conflict Transformation
ISGA	Interim Self Governing Authority
ITAK	Illankai Thamil Arasu Kadchi (Sri Lanka Tamil State Party)

JHU	Jathika Hela Urumaya (National Sinhala Heritage Party)
JSS	Jathika Sevaka Sangamaya (National Workers Association)
JVP	Janatha Vimukthi Peramuna (People's Liberation Front)
LSSP	Lanka Sama Samaja Pakshaya (Lanka Equal Society Party)
LTTE	Liberation Tigers of Tamil Eelam
MDMK	Marumalarchi Dravida Munnetra Kazhagam
MEP	Mahajana Eksath Peramuna (People's United Front)
MIRJE	Movement for Inter-Racial Justice and Equality
MOU	Memorandum of Understanding
NAT	Norwegians Against Terrorism
NEPC	North East Provincial Council
NGO	non-governmental organization
NJC	National Joint Committee
NLSSP	Nava Lanka Sama Samaja Party (New Lanka Equal Society Party)
NORAD	Norwegian Agency for Development Cooperation
NPC	National Peace Council
PA	People's Alliance
PFLP	Popular Front for the Liberation of Palestine
PICAR	Program on International Conflict Analysis and Resolution (Harvard University)
PLO	Palestine Liberation Organization
PLOTE	People's Liberation Organization of Tamil Eelam
PRAA	People's Revolutionary Red Army
PTA	Prevention of Terrorism Act
P-TOMS	Post-Tsunami Operational Management Structure
R2P	Responsibility to Protect
RAW	Research and Analysis Wing (India)
SAARC	South Asian Association for Regional Cooperation
SCOPP	Secretariat for Coordinating the Peace Process
SEDEC	Social and Economic Development Centre
SLES	Sri Lankan Ekiya Sanvidhanaya (Association for a United Sri Lanka)
SLFP	Sri Lanka Freedom Party
SLMC	Sri Lanka Muslim Congress
SLMM	Sri Lanka Monitoring Mission
SLUNA	Sri Lanka United National Association of Canada
SPUR	Society for Peace and Unity and Human Rights in Sri Lanka
SSA	Social Scientists Association
STF	Special Task Force
TELO	Tamil Eelam Liberation Organization
TMVP	Tamileela Makkal Viduthalai Pulikal (Tamil Peoples Liberation Tigers)
TNA	Tamil National Alliance
TRO	Tamil Rehabilitation Organization

TUF	Tamil United Front
TULF	Tamil United Liberation Front
UCPF	Up-Country People's Front
UNF	United National Front
UNHCR	United Nations High Commission for Refugees
UNICEF	United Nations Children's Fund
UN(O)	United Nations (Organization)
UNP	United National Party
UPFA	United People Freedom Alliance
USCR	United States Country Reports
USIP	United States Institute of Peace
UTHR	University Teachers for Human Rights (Jaffna)
WAPS	World Alliance for Peace in Sri Lanka
YMBA	Young Men's Buddhist Association

Introduction

Sri Lanka, resplendent island at the southern tip of India, land of ancient cultures and mélange of people, is the only country in the world to have an honorific title – Sri – before its name. It is also the oldest electoral democracy in Asia and one of the first developing countries in the world to promote universal free health-care and education. In 2007, Sri Lanka had the highest score on the Human Development Index in South Asia.[1]

Yet in recent decades Sri Lanka has become home to one of the world's most intractable wars and the longest running conflict in Asia. The armed struggle between the Sri Lankan government and the secessionist LTTE (Liberation Tigers of Tamil Eelam, also known as the Tamil Tigers) has turned Sri Lanka into 'one of the most dangerous places on earth'.[2] A vicious territorial struggle has been going on in the northern and eastern regions, while the entire island is threatened by suicide bombings and other deadly attacks. Since 1983, 70,000 people – the majority of them Tamil, Sinhalese and Muslims civilians – have been killed due to the conflict.[3] The actual figures may be much higher than this official estimate, especially if the 40,000–60,000, mostly Sinhala youth, who were killed in the JVP (Janatha Vimukthi Peramuna) insurgency in the late 1980s is also included. Of course, the extent of devastation and human suffering caused by the conflict is immeasurable by statistical quantification.

Over the course of the Sri Lankan secessionist war, the LTTE – banned in the US, Canada, UK, the EU, India, and Malaysia as a terrorist organization – has emerged as a 'most lethal and well organized terrorist group in the world' and a proto-type of global terrorism.[4] According to the FBI, LTTE's ruthless tactics have 'inspired terrorist networks worldwide including Al Qaeda in Iraq'. The LTTE 'perfected the use of suicide bombers; invented the suicide belt; pio-neered the use of women in suicide attacks;... assassinated two world leaders [former Indian Premier, Rajiv Gandhi and Sri Lankan President Premadasa] – the only terrorist organization to do so'.[5] The LTTE is the first militant group to acquire air power. Its attack against Sri Lanka's World Trade Center was the largest terrorist assault in the world prior to the attacks on New York and Wash-ington on 11 September 2001.[6] It is also known for its extensive reliance on forced conscription of child soldiers and women suicide bombers. The Tamil Tigers are believed to have killed more civilians from the Tamil, Sinhalese, and

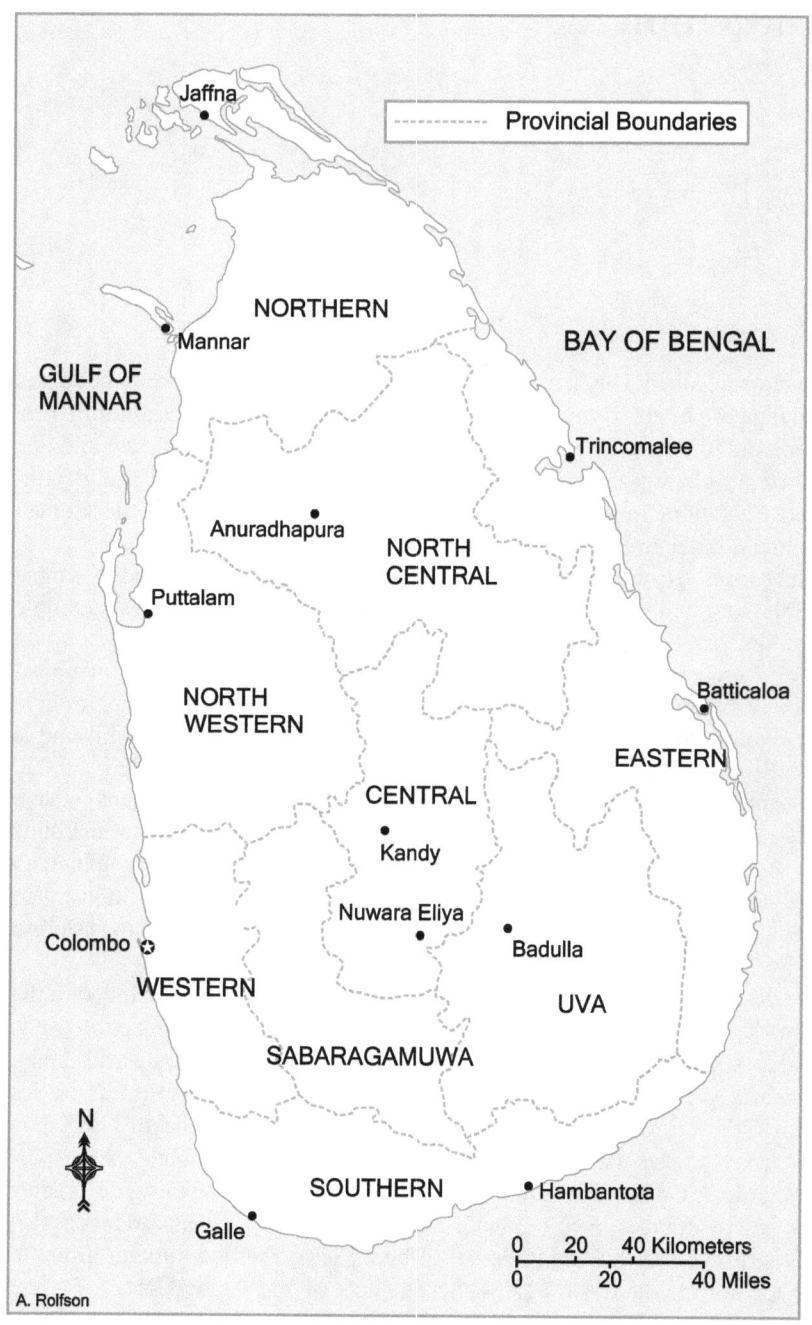

Map I.1 Sri Lanka: provinces (source: Asoka Bandarage, *Colonialism in Sri Lanka: The Political Economy of the Kandyan Highlands, 1833–1886* (Berlin: Mouton, 1983) p. xiv).

Table I.1 Population of Sri Lanka by ethnicity, 1921–2001 (percentages)

Ethnic group	1921	1931	1946	1953	1963	1971	1981	2001*
Sinhalese	67.0	65.3	69.4	59.3	71.0	72.0	74.0	74.5
Sri Lankan Tamil	11.5	11.2	11.0	10.9	11.0	11.2	12.7	11.9
Indian Tamil	13.4	15.4	11.7	12.0	10.6	9.3	5.5	4.6
Sri Lankan Moor	6.3	5.6	5.1	6.3	6.5	6.7	7.0	8.3
Others	1.8	2.5	1.6	1.4	0.9	0.8	0.8	0.7

Sources: Sri Lanka Department of Census and Statistics, 1921–1981; Sri Lanka Population and Housing Census, 2001.

Note
* Estimated population. Census was not completed in the Northern and Eastern Provinces except for Ampara District.

Muslim communities than the Sri Lankan armed forces, although numbers are not available.[7]

The LTTE, claims to be the 'sole representative' of all Sri Lankan Tamils and blames the Sinhala (anglicized as Sinhalese)-dominated Sri Lankan government for alleged discrimination and acts of state terrorism against the island's Tamil minority.[8] The LTTE has vowed never to give up its struggle until the realization of its goal of an independent Tamil state of Eelam in the north and east of Sri Lanka, which it claims as belonging to the 'traditional Tamil Homeland'. While there is no historical evidence for this claim, different maps have been put forward to justify the Tamil separatist demand for the Northern and Eastern provinces, which together constitute about one-third of the island's land mass and two-thirds of its coastline (Map I.1 and Eelam in Map I.2). The Sri Lankan government has been fighting since the early 1970s to preserve the island's territorial integrity and sovereignty against the armed separatist struggle. Over the course of the conflict, charges of human rights violations have been brought against the Sri Lankan government by the local and international peace lobby. Recent aid embargos and international pressures on the government to accept United Nations intervention have greatly exacerbated tensions over self-determination and sovereignty.[9]

While a large body of writing exists on the Sri Lankan conflict, it is conceptually limited. It portrays the conflict largely as either (1) a terrorist problem between an extremist secessionist group and the Sri Lankan state, or (2) a primordial and intractable ethnic problem between the Sinhala majority and the Tamil minority. Many studies have focused on the so-called hegemony of Sinhala Buddhist nationalism, generally depicting the Sinhala majority as a monolithic aggressor and the Tamil minority as a monolithic victim.[10] Others have examined post-independence language, employment, and land settlement policies and concluded that they gave rise to legitimate Tamil grievances, ethnic conflict, and the demand for a separate Tamil state.[11] The various peace initiatives that have been put forward, including the Indo-Sri Lanka Treaty imposed by India in 1987 and the peace initiative facilitated by Norway in 2002, have also conceptualized the conflict in dualistic ethnic terms as a contest between the

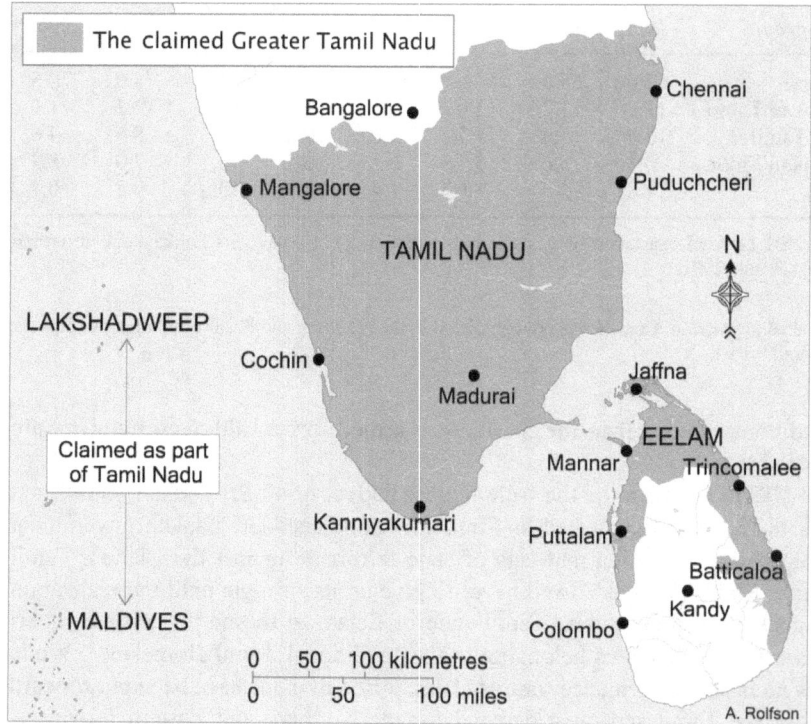

Map I.2 The claimed Greater Tamil Nadu (source: Research Division, Tamil Nadu Liberation Front (www.globalsecurity.org/military/world/para/ltte-maps.htm, accessed 10 September 2008).

Sinhala government and the Tamil rebels. This limited perception has led to the marginalization of a number of groups, such as Tamil dissidents opposed to the Tigers, the Muslims, and Sinhalese of the contentious Eastern Province, and Sinhala opposition parties and groups. Thus large segments of all of Sri Lanka's communities, whose support is crucial to conflict resolution, became mere 'outliers' and potential 'spoilers' of peace processes.[12]

Beyond ethnic dualism

Much of the long pre-colonial history of Sri Lanka was characterized by ethno-religious pluralism and co-existence over antagonism and conflict. Assimilation of the many pre-historic tribal and linguistic groups with colonists mostly from South as well as North India produced the island's present day populations.[13] The majority of the people speak Sinhala, an Indo-Aryan language and a derivative of Pali, the language of the Buddhist scriptures. A minority speak Tamil, a Dravidian cognate language spoken widely in South India. The Sinhala ethno-linguistic group which evolved in Sri Lanka has no counterparts in India or elsewhere in the world, whereas the Tamils have a large community of co-ethnics in India. The Sinhalese and Tamils, however, are not two exclusive groups with entirely 'separate historical pasts' as asserted by extremist nationalists. Caste, not language or religion, was the basis of social stratification in pre-colonial society. Multilingualism was common; Tamil language was included in the monastic education of Sinhala Buddhist monks.[14] The division of Sinhala and Tamil into two separate Aryan and Dravidian racial groups by European Orientalists is not historically valid either for Sri Lanka or India.[15] There has been tremendous inter-mixture between Sinhala and Tamil populations as well as the Muslims who are considered an ethno-religious group in Sri Lanka. Sri Lanka is characterized by religious diversity: in 1981, Buddhists, Hindus, Muslims and Christians were 69.3 percent, 15.5 percent, 7.6 percent and 7.6 percent of the island's total population respectively.[16]

Binary analyses built on the duality of 'Self versus Other' have been used historically to depict relations between cultural groups. Thus, White versus Black; East versus West – and myriad ethno-religious dualisms, such as, Islam versus Christianity, Tutsi versus Hutu, Serb versus Croat, Hindu versus Muslim, Sinhala versus Tamil – have upheld differences as if they are essentialist and immutable (Figure I.1). The 'iron law of ethnicity' – the assumption that cultural difference inevitably leads to conflict – has been reinforced by the 9/11 attacks, proliferating 'us. versus them' polarizations across the world.[17] However, the connections among ethnic difference, conflict, terrorism, and secessionism are not automatic. Narrow interpretations of cultural identity and models of conflict resolution built on ethnic dualism contribute to ethnic polarization and inhibit sustainable peace. Studies that explore how the form and content of ethnicity are shaped by political and economic forces are urgently needed to demystify ethnicity as well as religious identity and to improve both the analysis and processes of conflict resolution.[18]

Bipolar analysis

A key element in the Sri Lankan separatist conflict that has received relatively little attention is the intra-ethnic conflicts and killings within the Tamil and the Sinhalese communities. It is believed that the Tamil Tigers have killed more Tamils than the Sri Lankan armed forces, especially given the fratricidal wars among Tamil militant groups since 1985. Likewise, the Sri Lankan security forces had killed more Sinhalese than Tamils by the end of the 1980s, particularly when it suppressed the JVP

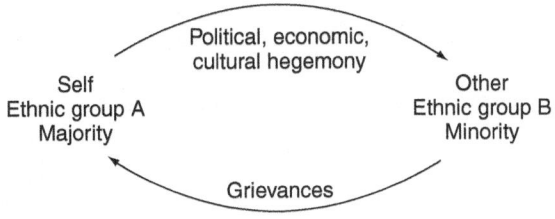

Figure I.1 Asymmetric bipolar conflict model.

insurgency that arose against the 1987 Indo-Sri Lanka Peace Accord, which was introduced to resolve the Tamil separatist conflict.[19] Within the Tamil community there are major differences between northern Jaffna Tamils, the Eastern Batticoloa Tamils, the hill country Indian Tamils, and the Colombo Tamils. There is also an oppressive Tamil caste system that includes so-called untouchables who make up a disproportionately large number of the LTTE cadres.[20]

Despite these differences and inequities, the dominant Sinhala versus Tamil dualism projects Tamils and Sinhalese as two homogeneous categories. On the Tamil side, it is the 'partial and often partisan view' of the northern, especially Jaffna peninsula Tamils that is often identified as the Sri Lankan Tamil perspective. This is largely due to the fact that the Tamil diaspora in the West is drawn largely from that conflict-ridden region of the island. The leadership of the LTTE, also drawn mostly from the Jaffna peninsula, is largely Catholic rather than Hindu, as are most Tamils. The diaspora influence has prevented the international community from understanding 'the diversities and intricacies' within Tamil communities.[21] Moreover, the Tamil Tigers who claim to be the 'sole representative of Tamils' have turned Sri Lankan Tamils, on the island and in the diaspora, into a 'silent majority' presenting the LTTE position as the only Tamil perspective .[22]

Electoral politics has contributed to a vibrant multi-party democracy among the Sinhalese, but the entrenched party rivalry, especially between the two major political parties, UNP (United National Party) and the SLFP (Sri Lanka Freedom Party), has undermined a unified approach to eradicating terrorism and a political solution to the separatist conflict.[23] Sinhalese society also has caste and deep-rooted class divisions in addition to the regional difference between the Kandyans and the low-country populations and the religious division between the majority Buddhists and minority Christians introduced by European colonialism. The Muslims are generally left out of the dominant discourse on the Sri Lankan separatist conflict, yet they are a distinct and important island-wide community and the largest group in the Eastern Province. But, like the Sinhalese and the Tamils, they too have internal divisions, there being at least four regional Muslim groups based in Colombo, the East, Kandy and Mannar and division between Moors and Malays – 97 percent and 3 percent of all Muslims respectively.[24] The Eurasian community known as the Burghers have also been an important community since colonial times, although due to widespread emigration to the West, their numbers in Sri Lanka are very small today.

A few recent academic works on Sri Lanka have pointed out the intra-ethnic divisions within the Sinhala and Tamil communities, helping to broaden the analysis of the Sri Lankan conflict.[25] However, even those studies, because of their continued focus on ethnicity, tend to reinforce the idea of the Sri Lankan separatist conflict as simply an ethnic struggle. Even works that attempt to move beyond ethnicity have largely remained within the globally dominant identity-based discourse which focuses on culture and consciousness.[26] Most analyses depict a static Sinhala–Tamil antagonism throughout history or outdated representations of the conflict that reflect realities in the early 1980s, when the armed separatist conflict began.[27]

A multipolar approach

This book seeks to develop a broader analysis of the Sri Lankan conflict by examining multiple ethnic and religious groups and by focusing on intra-ethnic, social class, caste, regional and other divisions as they pertain to the separatist conflict. While each of these dimensions has been separately explored, this treatise seeks to synthesize earlier studies and provide a more comprehensive, historically-based social structural analysis. In so doing, it seeks to broaden the global discourse on ethno-religious conflict beyond ethno-dualism and identity politics toward a framework that takes into account both the inherent unity (nonduality) between groups as well as the socio-economic inequalities and hierarchies at the local, regional, and international levels (Figure I.2). This work recognizes vast political, demographic, and other changes that have transpired since the early 1980s and the possibility of change in identities and positions within groups and in their relations with each other. For example, over the course of the conflict the Sinhala polity has shifted away from the Sinhala Buddhist ideological position toward a more inclusive and pluralist stance. Tamil groups have evolved dissident positions despite LTTE attempts to suppress them. India and members of the international community have also moved in recent years from sympathy for the LTTE to opposition to its terrorism.[28]

The dominant ethnically based approaches portray the Sri Lankan conflict as a purely domestic conflict, when in fact it has been a regional South Asian conflict from the very beginning. Moreover, it has increasingly become an international conflict with serious implications for peace and security across the world. This book demonstrates that the Sri Lankan conflict is neither just a terrorist problem, nor a primordial ethnic confrontation. Rather, it is a complex political-economic conflict perpetuated by the confluence of factors in an

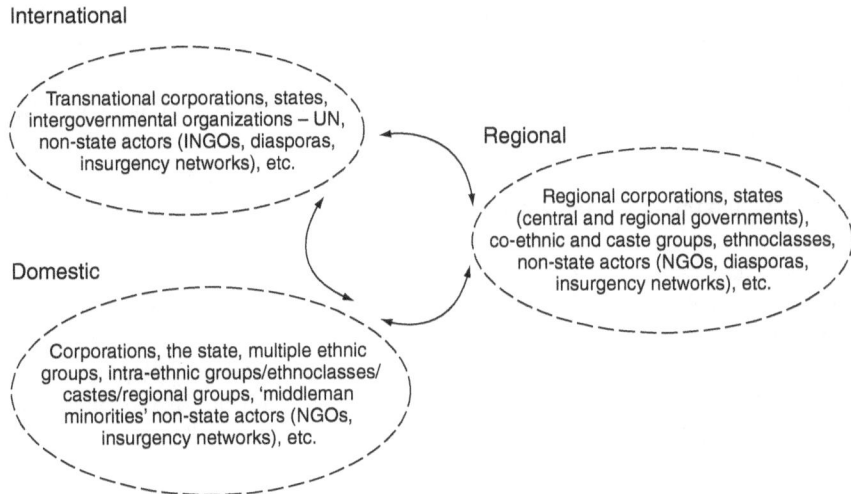

Figure I.2 Multipolar model: levels and actors.

increasingly globalized world. Within this perspective, ethnic groups are not seen as inherently antagonistic towards one another merely by reason of the differentiation along cultural lines. Rather, conflicts are seen to emerge in the context of changes in economic and political structures and the unequal distribution of wealth and power between groups at the local, regional and international levels.[29] The Sri Lankan conflict, like many other 'ethnic' conflicts around the world, emerged with democratization and the shift of power from privileged minorities to the majority who had been marginalized under colonial rule.[30] In addition to exploring the intersection of ethnicity with social class, caste and other social groupings in Sri Lanka, this study explores South Indian Tamil nationalism and strategic concerns of India in the regional context and the Sri Lankan diaspora, INGOs, Norway and other actors in the international context as they pertain to Sri Lanka's separatist conflict.

Scope of the book

The origin and evolution of Sri Lankan Tamil separatism predates the 1970s. However, discussions of the long pre-colonial history, including the Sinhala Buddhist heritage of the north and the east, or a detailed analysis of the colonial period are beyond the scope of this book. An overview of the British colonial period, when forms of ethno-religious competition and stratification that continue down to the present were established, and the early years of Independence is presented in Chapter 2 as historical background. The study of the modern Sri Lankan conflict begins in Chapter 3 with the Sinhala youth struggle in 1971, which reveals the common class-based grievances that gave rise to Tamil youth militancy a few years later. The chapter explores how the connection between Tamil moderate elites and militant youth and South Indian Tamil nationalism gave rise to an ethno-regional separatist movement instead of a class struggle, as was the case with the Sinhalese. Subsequent chapters, in which the conflict is presented chronologically, discuss the internationalization of the separatist struggle in the context of globalization, political authoritarianism, and communal violence. They explore the roles of the diaspora-insurgency network, the international community, including NGOs and the human rights lobby. The book concludes by raising critical questions regarding international intervention, separatism, and the future of peace, justice, and pluralism in Sri Lanka.

Much of the information provided in this work is not new. Unlike the author's earlier book, *Colonialism in Sri Lanka*,[31] which was based on primary sources, this volume relies on quantitative and qualitative sources that are readily available and on the secondary literature in the English language. The chapters of the book are organized historically, and the materials in each are presented within a political-economic perspective, upholding the overall thesis of the work: the multipolar nature of the Sri Lankan separatist conflict.

1 Conceptual frameworks
Broadening the discourse

The choice of analytical frameworks shapes, if not determines, the understanding as well as the resolution of conflicts.[1] Much of contemporary media, as well as academic analyses of global conflicts, rarely moves beyond the frames of reference of terrorism and ethnicity.

The terrorist problem

Terrorism is commonly defined as premeditated political violence by non-state actors and aimed at civilians to instill fear in broader target populations.[2] It is important to distinguish between legitimate national liberation movements and indiscriminate terrorism in which innocent populations are targeted – a distinction made even by the quintessential revolutionary Che Guevara.[3]

The September 2001 attacks in New York and Washington DC, and the subsequent bombings in Madrid and London, have led to the identification of terrorism as the fundamental cause of global insecurity and the 'war on terror' as the world's number one priority. There is no question that the spread of terrorism needs to be stopped in order to protect life and liberty around the world. Terrorism is directed against civilians: it is a massive violation of human rights. However, as many liberals and progressive critics point out, the fight against terror is begetting state terror, widespread human rights violations, and infringements on civil liberties and democratic freedoms around the world.[4] Indeed, the protection of human rights – the right to life, freedom of expression, and due process of law – is fundamental. Elimination of the outward manifestation of terrorism without respect for human rights could lead to global authoritarianism. Ultimately, it is necessary to find non-violent solutions and move beyond simplistic dualisms, such as 'good versus evil' and 'us versus them', including culturally and ethnically based dualisms that underlie the law and order anti-terrorist approach.

The ethnic problem

Those who search for the root causes of global conflicts, as well as terrorism, attribute them overwhelmingly to ethnicity, commonly defined as shared culture derived from inherited group identities, such as, language, religion, tribe and region.[5] Most scholarly approaches to ethnicity fall into two broad categories: primordialism and contextualism:

- *Primordialism* assumes that blood ties and ascriptive group identities always claim the deepest of human attachments and form the basis for conflict. This inherently conservative approach which sees ethnicity as a fixed, biological phenomenon is repudiated by liberal and radical theorists advancing more contextual approaches.
- *Contextualism* posits that 'Self' and 'Other' are fluid – not fixed – categories, and argues that there are dangers in essentialist interpretations of culture and ethnicity.[6] Embraced more commonly by liberals (and radicals), contextualism emphasizes the changing nature of ethnic identity seeing it as a socially constructed phenomenon that is also available for instrumental use. Cultural markers are frequently manipulated by ideologues, and cultural categories are 'available for instant manipulation by those … seeking power'[7] – the 'ethnic entrepreneurs'.

As Benedict Anderson suggests, many of the primordial identities, nations and traditional homelands espoused by various ethno-nationalist groups are only 'imagined communities' formulated in response to modern circumstances rather than primordial entities based on historical facts.[8] The traditional Tamil homelands thesis manufactured by the Sri Lankan Tamil elites is a case in point.

Despite basic differences between conservative/primordialist and liberal/contextualist perspectives, there is a growing consensus that ethno-religious conflict (and the terrorism that it can spawn) has replaced Communism as the main threat to global security and prosperity in the post-Cold War period. The 'iron law of ethnicity' has been reinforced by 9/11 and on-going conflicts such as the one in Sri Lanka. The tendency of both conservatives and liberals is to treat ethnicity as the independent variable and to take identity politics as the 'basic point of departure'.[9] In many ways, therefore, the 'new identity discourse' perpetuates the very bipolar ethno-religious stereotypes and polarizations it seeks to transcend.[10] Even Edward Said's popular concept of Orientalism inadvertently reinforces the binary opposites: Occidental and Oriental, oppressor and oppressed.[11] Such concepts tend to reproduce the good versus evil dualism often attributed to conservative primordialists. They also tend to perpetuate *majority* and *minority* as fixed immutable categories.

The term 'minority', commonly used to identify groups characterized by 'hereditary membership', was derived from the European experience. It identified groups that had been subordinated during the rise of nationalism and the emergence of nation states in the late eighteenth and early nineteenth centuries.[12] According to the widely used definition by sociologist Joseph Gittler, 'Minority groups are those whose members experience a wide range of discriminatory treatment and frequently are relegated to positions relatively low in the status structure of a society'.[13] Minority carries a negative connotation of inferiority.

The terms majority and minority do not necessarily pertain to numerical size but to inequality in prestige, privilege, and power. Accordingly, numerical superiority does not ensure the dominant majority status and numerical inferiority does not always relegate a group to the subordinate minority status.[14] It is, rather, a concept pertaining to power. With the introduction of electoral democracy and the empowerment of numerical majorities, many numerical minorities that were privileged groups under European colonialism, such as the Sri Lankan Tamils, have struggled to obtain international recognition by establishing new states in which they would become majorities. In a global context where only the 'unsuccessful aspirants to statehood' seem to remain as minorities, there is increasing competition between local ethnic elites over recognition of right to self-determination and separate sovereign states.[15]

Ethnically based approaches to social conflict have led to the proliferation of ethnically based solutions. Liberalism favors negotiated political settlement based on education and legal frameworks as the means of conflict resolution, with the military option as a last resort. Yet liberal conflict resolution strategies, which claim to advance multiculturalism and reconciliation, can also appease terrorism, reinforcing ethnic polarization and separation instead. In this regard, it is useful to consider how the classical liberal approach to individual rights has been transformed in the contemporary era of identity politics. Human rights activism, which emerged originally to defend individual civil and fundamental rights, has become associated with the protection of group rights, especially ethnic minority rights. The confluence of terrorism, local minority nationalisms. and international intervention on human rights grounds is contributing to political fragmentation and 'partitioning ethnic groups' as the 'only viable way to maintain peace and stability'.[16]

There is now a thriving discipline known as 'partition theory' in the western academic establishment and international relations field in particular. Its core assumption is that if the 'security dilemma' arising from distrust and violence between ethnic opponents cannot be resolved by other means, then separation of groups into 'defensible, mostly homogenous regions' is the only credible solution to civil war, notwithstanding population transfers that may be entailed.[17] In other words, minorities will be 'victimized unless they are partitioned'.[18] But partition is not a magic formula for so-called 'ethnic conflicts', and some theorists argue that deepening globalization will reinforce territorial integrity and only a few of the on-going national liberation struggles seeking to establish new states will succeed.[19] As Timothy Sisk, of the United States Institute for Peace has pointed out, 'Secession only serves to rearrange majorities and minorities and rarely solved the problem of multi-ethnic societies, and the issue of who genuinely represents any group is not resolved'.[20]

The real world: multipolarity

Most societies are not bipolar entities characterized by one majority and one minority group. Majority and minority themselves are not fixed categories.

When the analysis is broadened beyond the state as the unit of analysis and when regional and international contexts are incorporated, the minority–majority positions are frequently reversed, as in the Sri Lankan case where the Sinhalese are the majority on the island, but the Tamils are a much bigger majority region-ally and globally.

Most societies are also multi-ethnic entities constituting of a hierarchy of groups with several or more groups occupying competing positions. Furnivall's 'plural society' theory points out that hierarchical integration of ethnic groups within colonial economies created almost caste-like, ethnically based divisions of labor providing the basis for social conflict after the end of authoritarian colo-nial rule.[21] Formulations such as the theory of 'middleman minorities', which takes into account the intermediary positions held by ethnically distinct groups such as traders, creditors, and so on, are useful in transcending the simplistic minority and majority dichotomy. As sociologist Edna Bonacich and others have noted, being mostly immigrants and regarded as outsiders, the 'middleman minorities' are frequently the subject of 'host hostility' of those at the bottom of the socio-economic structure, especially so, during economic downturns.[22] Muslims and Indian Tamils in Sri Lanka have been placed in such circumstances during the colonial and post-independence periods.

In considering the question as to who genuinely represents a given ethnic group and the issue of democratic representation, Milton Gordon's 'ethclass' concept is useful. Gordon pointed out that social participation is not defined either along ethnic or class lines, but, mostly along sub-group lines intersecting ethnicity and social class.[23] Gordon's ethclass (or ethnoclass) concept developed in relation to immigration in early twentieth century United States has wide applicability to other societies. In caste based societies such as Sri Lanka, inter-ests of ethnocastes emerging from the intersection of ethnicity and caste have been significant in the emergence and perpetuation of conflicts, especially the Tamil separatist conflict. Whether one uses the terms ethclass/ethnoclass/ethno-caste or not, it is necessary to understand conflict in relation to the intersection of ethnicity and class, caste, as well as region, age and so on. It is also important to explore how and why elite classes are able to mobilize the lower classes along ethnic lines undermining class based mobilization that could cut across ethnic divides.

Political-economic approaches

Ethnic-based, bipolar frameworks mitigate against analyses that see 'vast inequities in wealth' not cultural difference as the central problem.[24] To explore the class character of conflict, however, is not to deny 'operational significance' of ethnic factors or to reduce culturally based attachments and political mobil-ization to a simplistic Marxist notion of 'false consciousness'. To comprehend the complexity of global conflicts, it is necessary to move beyond the classical conservative, liberal, and Marxist approaches and carefully examine particular cases, delineating processes of local, regional and global social change that are contributing to economic inequality and culturally based political violence. Social structural approaches which explore how historical changes shape 'the form and content of ethnicity'[25] are needed to demystify both terrorism and ethnicity and to deepen the processes of conflict resolution and respect for human rights.

Advancing a social constructivist approach to ethnicity and conceptualizing ethnicity as a variable, rather than a fixed factor, Charles Keyes has argued that ethnic change needs to be viewed as a 'dialectical process' precipitated by 'radical changes in the political-economic contexts in which people live'.[26] Likewise, Paul Brass has attributed elite competition which constitutes the 'basic dynamic precipitating ethnic conflict' to 'broader political and economic environments' rather than 'the cultural values of the ethnic groups in question'.[27] 'Protracted', and seemingly domestic 'ethnic' conflicts like the one in Sri Lanka cannot be understood apart from the processes of political-economic and cultural globalization and the collective impact of external factors. As Donald Horowitz has argued 'the emergence of [ethnic] separatism is not generally a function of international relations. Yet, to grow in strength, a movement may require outside help'.[28] The recent theoretical framework put forward by Ted Gurr is particularly useful for understanding the confluence of domestic and international political-economic processes which produce so-called ethnic conflicts. It identifies political opportunity structures and resource mobilization at the international level, including doctrines of nationalism, regional and global ethnic networks, contagion of ethno-political conflict and external political and material support.[29] Relative deprivation and group mobilization, the two dimensions generally associated with the rise of identity based conflict, then, need to be conceptualized within a global perspective.[30]

Amy Chua has explained the rise of ethnic conflicts in the current era in relation to globalization of markets and the export of electoral democracy. She argues that the extension of the vote to the masses of the poor encourage ethnically based political mobilization and the direction of hostilities against 'market dominant minorities' who become easy targets because of their ethnic distinctiveness and economic power. She refers to Sri Lanka as a case in point.[31] Benjamin Barber among other theorists has conceptualized political tensions and conflicts in the modern world as a dialectic between two forms of fundamentalism: economic fundamentalism of 'neoliberal' globalization and ethnoreligious fundamentalism of political extremism.[32] Although contemporary ethno-religious movements invoke 'imagined communities' and a return to a glorious past of ethnic or religious purity, they are highly sophisticated modern ventures led by sophisticated 'ethnic entrepreneurs' who use cultural difference to advance their own interests. Diasporas have emerged as a powerful ethnoclass category in the era of globalization and large scale immigration. As Yossi Shain and others have shown, ethnic diasporas, adept at using communications media, fund raising, lobbying tactics and purchase of the latest weaponry play evermore increasing roles in perpetuating so-called 'primordial' conflicts and support for secessionist movements in their distant lands of origin.[33]

These political-economic formulations need to be further explored and applied to the task of achieving a broader and deeper understanding of the Sri Lankan conflict. Only within a framework that transcends a narrow bipolar, ethnically based view will there be a possibility of achieving a genuine resolution of the conflict. This book seeks to contribute to that goal.

The Sri Lankan case

Like many of the world's political conflicts, the Sri Lankan conflict too is portrayed overwhelmingly as either a terrorist problem and/or an ethnic conflict. Those who identify the conflict as a terrorist problem call for military defeat of the LTTE. Those who see the conflict as an ethnic conflict between the Sinhala majority and the Tamil minority call for the creation of an autonomous Tamil ethno-national region as the solution. Devolution within a federal structure is presented as a moderate compromise between the Tamil nationalist demand for a separate sovereign Tamil state and the Sinhala nationalist demand for continuation of the centralized unitary state.

A terrorist problem?

According to Dingiri Banda Wijetunga, former President of Sri Lanka (May 1993–November 1994), 'There is no ethnic problem in Sri Lanka; there is only a terrorist problem'.[34] Sinhala nationalists are not the only ones concerned about LTTE terrorism. Leading global security analysts, such as, Rohan Gunaratna, Peter Chalk, Peter Leitner, Cecile Van de Voorde, have warned of the dangers posed by the LTTE to global peace and security.[35]

Since its inception in the early 1970s, the LTTE has carried out extensive attacks against strategic installations throughout Sri Lanka including its World Trade Center, national airport and its carriers, the central telecommunication building, army headquarters, sacred heritage sites, and innumerable homes, villages, buses, trains and airplanes carrying civilians. It has systematically eliminated political leaders and journalists and most Tamil dissidents. It has acquired tremendous military, financial and media capability with support from the Sri Lankan Tamil diaspora, the World Tamil Movement and alleged links to the global narcotic trade, human smuggling and other illegal activities. It is said to have links to other terrorist networks, such as, Al Qaeda and holds the dubious honor of popularizing suicide bombing in the modern world.[36]

Oxford economist Paul Collier, among others, has argued that the greed of rebel leaders, not popular grievance, is the motivating force for many contemporary civil conflicts.[37] This thinking is echoed by Paul Harris, the veteran British war correspondent in his observations of the Sri Lankan conflict. Harris was forced to leave Sri Lanka in 2002 for giving a public talk characterizing the 2002 Norwegian facilitated CFA which legitimized LTTE control of large areas of Sri Lankan territory as 'The Greatest Give Away in History'. He predicted that the peace process was 'doomed to failure and has continued to express his doubts of LTTE's sincerity and the strategy of 'appeasing terrorism' in the name of peace:

> Of course, the LTTE wants peace, that is to say, peace on its own terms: the terminal division of the sovereign state of Sri Lanka with two thirds of the coast and half of the landmass ceded to the LTTE authority in perpetuity … I regard [this] as not just a Sri Lankan issue but a universal moral issue.[38]

Ordinary Sri Lankans, especially the majority Sinhala community and many members of the Muslim minority believe that there is no reason for ethnic strife in their country and that the conflict is largely a terrorist problem. Their feeling, which is also corroborated by researchers, is that cooperation and co-existence have been the predominant experience in inter-ethnic relations and that the conflict itself is the cause of increasing division and animosity between the communities.[39] As a group of Sinhala farmers interviewed for an agrarian survey in the Eastern Province during the time of escalating violence in the mid-1980s put it 'There are no Sinhalese farmers and no Tamil farmers, only farmers'.[40] Similarly most Sri Lankans believe that there are no exclusive 'Sinhala', 'Tamil' or 'Muslim' lands: the entire island belongs to all its communities.[41] In other words, ethnicity is not the basis of primordial animosity. Accordingly, it is Tamil terrorism that has created ethnic hatred in order to separate the communities and legitimize its unjustifiable claim for a separate Tamil state.[42]

Unlike the Tamil separatist position, the Sinhala nationalist position is not widely represented in the international English language discourse on the Sri Lankan conflict. This has begun to change with the expansion of the Internet and increasing activism by the Sinhala diaspora. S.L. Gunasekara, a leading Sri Lankan lawyer and politician, states categorically that an 'ethnic problem' requiring a justifiable 'political solution' comparable to apartheid in South Africa does not exist in Sri Lanka.

> [T]he continuation of a war against rebels fighting for justice or for the recovery of rights or property which was rightfully theirs would be unjustifiable by any standards, for it would amount to waging war to achieve the ignoble end of continuing to perpetrate injustice. Thus, the conflict in South Africa between the 'White Supremacists' and the 'Black Rebels' was one which was manifestly amenable to a political solution…. But does a comparable situation amenable to a 'political solution' exist in Sri Lanka?'[43]

According to this perspective, the Tamil minority has not experienced particular grievances, such as violation of rights or loss of territory peculiar to them as a group.[44]

A few international analysts have also seen the Sri Lankan problem as a law and order issue rather than an ethnic one. Observing that by the mid-1980s, the Tamil separatist groups were responsible for the deaths of more Tamils than Sinhalese and that by 1990, 'the LTTE had killed more Eelam militants than had the Sri Lankan army'. Cornell political scientist Norman Uphoff, who did many years of extensive field research in conflict areas in Sri Lanka, pointed out that

> Sinhalese politicians were blinded by their own ethnic prejudices and perceptions, themselves seeing the conflict much as LTTE had defined it, as an ethnic struggle rather than as a blatant attempt by a minority to seize political power and territory.[45]

Sinhala nationalists who see the conflict as a terrorist problem did not repudiate peace talks and political negotiations with the LTTE at the early stages. S.L. Gunasekara participated in the 1985 Thimpu talks sponsored by the Indian government, which brought the Sri Lankan government and the armed Tamil groups to the table for the first time in 1985. Except for Eelam War I (1983–1987), the rest – Eelam War II (1990–1994), Eelam War III (1995–2002) and Eelam War IV (2006–) – were each preceded by a peace process and each time it was the LTTE that sabotaged the peace process.[46] LTTE's repeated walk outs from negotiations in 1985, 1987, 1989–1990, 1995, 2002 and 2006 and its use of ceasefires to build up military strength have hardened the feeling among many that there can be no negotiation with terrorists. The LTTE leader, Velupillai Prabhakaran's uncompromising position on Eelam and the policy of the United States and global powers against negotiation with terrorists have added weight to the growing sentiment. Based on extensive research on the LTTE and the separatist demand, geographer G.H. Pieris poses the poignant questions: when, Eelam is the core, unflinching demand, what is the government negotiating? What do the international community want the government to negotiate? As Pieris explained

> [N]either the LTTE nor the majority of Tamil political groups of Sri Lanka including those that are considered 'moderates' given the fundamental determinants of their interests and objectives, could have a genuine desire for a peaceful resolution of the country's ethnic conflict through a negotiated settlement that would conform to the paradigms of a sovereign nation state of Sri Lanka. This, it should be emphasized should not be understood as implying that the Tamil people including *some* of their political spokesmen do not have a genuine desire for peace within the existing geographical delineations of Sri Lanka's state structure. What should, however, be understood is that, at present, there is no means by which this desire could be heard above the din of separatism for it to have discernible impact upon the prospects for a negotiated settlement of the conflict.
>
> (emphasis in original)[47]

Of course the problem is not only the Tamil Tiger's unflinching demand for Eelam, but also their total disrespect for democracy, human rights and international humanitarian law.

Terrorism and human rights

The human rights group, University Teachers for Human Rights, Jaffna (UTHR), who authored the seminal work, *The Broken Palmyra*, dared point out that the LTTE is an oppressor rather than a liberator of Sri Lankan Tamils. They explained that Tamils have been forced to look up to the LTTE, the self-proclaimed 'sole representative' of Sri Lankan Tamils, only because it has eliminated all other Tamil groups. It blamed Tamil moderates, especially elite leaders of the TULF who first called Tamil youth to take up the struggle for Eelam for failing to challenge the rationale of terror from the beginning. They showed that this failure reinforced terrorism and the LTTE's uncompromising stance blocking a negotiated political settlement to the conflict. Rajani Thiranagama, Professor of Anatomy at the University of Jaffna, co-founder of UTHR and co-author of *The Broken Palmyra* was assassinated in 1989, allegedly by the LTTE.[48]

Tamil Tiger supporters and their sympathizers overlook LTTE terrorism, such as, the assassination of countless Tamil dissidents and moderates in the name of their ultimate goal of Eelam. Sinhala nationalists who focus on LTTE atrocities also downplay state violations as the inevitable outcome of a democratically elected government's efforts to combat terrorism. The Sri Lankan state is not immune from charges of 'state terrorism' against the Tamil minority and against the Sinhala majority although violations of Sinhala rights have received relatively little attention given the dominant ethnic characterization of the island's conflicts. Sri Lankan armed forces have been charged with indiscipline, disappearance, torture and indiscriminate killings of Tamil and Sinhala youth suspected to be members of the Tamil LTTE and the Sinhala JVP insurgent group in the early 1970s and late 1980s to early 1990s. Amnesty International, Human Rights Watch and other international bodies have issued innumerable reports documenting the disappearances, torture and other human rights violations. There is also evidence of widespread use of terror tactics and human rights violations including rape and torture on the part of the Indian Peace Keeping Force sent in by the government of India to maintain peace in the north and the east of the island between 1987 and 1991.[49]

Terrorism and international Human Rights Law

The difference between international Human Rights Laws which pertain to obligations of governments to their citizens and international Humanitarian Laws, such as Article 3 of the Geneva Convention of 1949 and the Additional Protocol 11 of 1977, which pertain to situations of armed conflict which require both states and non-state actors to abide by 'defined rules of engagement' is pertinent here. As Sri Lankan political analyst, Neville Ladduwahetty points out,

'Since Humanitarian Law deals specifically with armed conflict, no derogation from its provision is permitted. Although Human Rights Laws are supposed to apply both in times of peace as well as during armed conflict, a degree of derogation in regard to Human Rights Laws is inevitable as occurs in member states of the IC that are under threats of terrorism'[50]

Accordingly, by failing to recognize what is happening in Sri Lanka as an armed conflict, the 'international community' has failed to hold the LTTE accountable to international humanitarian law, for example the requirement to distinguish between combatants and non-combatants.[51] As a result, Human Rights activism has focused almost entirely on the Sri Lankan government. Ladduwahetty argues that this situation 'reflects a deliberate bias with hints of an underlying agenda'.[52] The failure to clearly distinguish between Tamil grievances and the LTTE has created an ironic situation where international human rights activism appears to side with LTTE terrorism. As Rajan Hoole, a Tamil nationalist and a staunch critic of the LTTE who had to operate underground for many years, has explained,

The task of human rights activism is to rise above the logic of terror and challenge it rather than become part of it. Paradoxically, the notion of 'political correctness' advanced by left-liberal sections in the West has frequently the effect of fortifying terror rather than challenging it. In a case like Sri Lanka, they could easily identify the evil of state repression and the resulting alienation. This leads them to [a] lenient view of a group like the LTTE. They refuse to see that such groups, while using this sympathy to challenge the State, do in fact stand for an order that is exceedingly more inhumane and archaic than what [is] obtained. Although very vocal in their anti-racism, the arrogance of some of these left-liberal sections is more insidious than racism paraded openly.

(emphasis in original)[53]

Though they hold both the Sri Lankan government and the LTTE accountable to charges of terror, Tamil dissidents like Hoole do not see terrorism as the cause, but, as the outcome of the ethnic problem between the Sinhala majority and the Tamil minority. The ethnic explanation is the dominant one in the English language discourse on the Sri Lankan separatist conflict.

An ethnic problem?

Domestic perspective

Many Sinhala and Tamil nationalists portray the conflict as a primordial conflict based on mutual distrust and violence spanning over more than two millennia. According to the Sinhala nationalist position, pre-colonial Sri Lanka prior to the advent of European invaders was a mono-ethnic and mono-religious Sinhala Buddhist state where the Tamils were migrant aliens.[54] This position emphasizes that even today, Tamil Nadu is the 'country of the Tamils' or the 'land of Tamil', not Sri Lanka. Invoking these historical and contemporary claims, the 2003 Report of the National Joint Committee of Sinhala organizations (NJC) argued against a federal constitution that would lead to devolution of power to the Tamils,

> The 'Tamil Ethnic Problem' ... is a fiction ... crafted by relatively recent migrants whose historical homelands lie in South India.... A migrant population never qualifies for national status in the host country ... the 5% Turks who live in Germany do not make a 'nation' – their nation is Turkey. Similarly the nation of the Tamil speaking Dravidian groups exists in South India. So the 'nation' thus defined is inconsistent with international norms of nation making, nationalism and aspiration to national self-determination.... Tamil nationalism ... make[s] a logical application in South India and not in Sri Lanka.[55]

In contrast, to this position which identifies Sri Lanka as a Sinhala Buddhist nation, some Tamil nationalists argue that Tamils were the earliest occupants of the island and that the 'entire island' of Sri Lanka was ruled by Tamil kings 'even before the Christian era'.[56] The more commonly asserted contemporary Tamil separatist position is that throughout history the Tamils occupied the northern and eastern 'districts' of the island while the Sinhalese inhabited the interior parts. The demand for an independent Tamil state of Eelam is justified on charges that the Sinhalese have historically oppressed the Tamils who make up a separate nation with right of self-determination and that the Northern and Eastern Provinces belong to 'the traditional Tamil homeland' (Map I.2).[57] In 1976 the Tamil United Liberation Front (TULF), led by the Tamil elites, put forward the Vaddukoddai resolution calling for the establishment of a Tamil separate state:

> Whereas throughout the centuries from the dawn of history, the Sinhalese and Tamil nations have divided between them the possession of Ceylon, the Sinhalese inhabiting the interior parts of the country in its southern and western parts from the river Walave to that of Chilaw and the Tamils possessing the northern and eastern districts ... the State of Tamil Eelam shall consist of the people of the Northern and Eastern Provinces ... And this Convention calls upon the Tamil Nation in general and the Tamil youth in particular to come forward to throw themselves fully in the sacred fight for freedom and to flinch not till the goal of a sovereign state of TAMIL EELAM is reached.[58]

Following the call of their elite leaders, young militants committed themselves to armed struggle to establish Tamil Eelam bringing the LTTE into leadership. As the armed struggle emerged as the youth wing of the moderate TULF, the elite soon lost control over the militant youth becoming victims of their terrorism. While the LTTE wants to establish Eelam militarily and immediately, the moderate elites continue to pursue a legalist and non-violent approach with external support. But they have not given up the final goal of a separate state.

Eminent lawyer, S.J.V. Chelvanayakam, the 'father of Sri Lankan Tamil separatism' the founder of the ITAK (Illankai Thamil Arasu Kadchi) Sri Lanka Tamil State Party in 1949 explained his moderate gradualist approach to a separate state as 'a little now, more later' influencing a similar approach among his moderate progeny.[59] The close inter-connection between the elite moderates and youth militant wings of Tamil separatism in Sri Lanka is paralleled by a deep connection between Tamil separatism in South India and Sri Lanka. Although the dominant domestically based approach has failed to consider it, the Sri Lankan separatist conflict cannot be adequately comprehended apart from the regional and global contexts of South India and the world Tamil movement.

Regional perspective

Widespread English-language Christian missionary education had given Tamil Nadu state the largest access – nearly 25 percent of all entrants to the Indian Administrative Services. The fear of north Indian Hindi linguistic dominance in an independent India, led to the call in 1938 for a separate Dravidian state – Dravidasthan – in South India encompassing Madras, Mysore, Kerala and Andhra where Dravidian cognate languages are spoken. In 1944, the Dravida Kazhagam (DK – Dravidian Federation), a 'highly militant mass organization' was established with the objective of achieving a sovereign independent Dravidian Republic.[60] During the early 1960s the Dravidasthan movement became 'one of the most fissiparous tendencies' and a major threat to the Indian Union.[61] After India adopted the draconian anti-secessionist amendment to its constitution in 1963, the South Indian secessionist movement was halted, but, South Indian support for a 'surrogate' Tamil state in the north and east of Sri Lanka expanded.[62] All Sri Lankan moderate and militant separatist groups, including the LTTE, were nurtured and protected by Tamil Nadu political parties. The LTTE's assassination of former Indian Prime Minister Rajiv Gandhi in Tamil Nadu in 1991 alone shows that the 'Sri Lankan' separatist conflict is a regional one. Even today, the manifesto of the MDMK (Marumalarchi Dravida Munnetra Kazhagam) in Tamil Nadu calls for autonomy for regional states in India and establishment of Tamil Eelam in Sri Lanka.[63] Indian political scientist K.P. Mukerji noted in 1962, 'the Tamil problem in Ceylon would [not have arisen] had not the Indian Tamil-Nad been geographically contiguous to Ceylon's Jaffna'[64] (Map I.2).

International perspective

The Eelam movement which has been a regional South Indian phenomenon from the beginning, is becoming an international movement as well. Tamils constitute a linguistic group with a rich and proud cultural heritage and a relatively large, western educated, wealthy diaspora. But, as the World Confederation of Tamils puts it, 'There is no state without a Tamil – but there is no state for the Tamils'.[65] Tamil Nadu, though it is the 'country of Tamils' is a regional state in India and not a nation state. There is understandable resentment that while

Table 1.1a Sri Lankan Tamil diaspora, 2008

Country	Sri Lankan Tamils
India	150,000
Canada	400,000
Germany	60,000
United Kingdom	300,000
France	100,000
Switzerland	40,000
United States	35,000
Italy	24,000
Malaysia	20,000
Australia	53,000
Norway	13,000
Netherlands	7,000
Sweden	6,000
New Zealand	4,000
Finland	600

Source: Peter Chalk, 'The Tigers Abroad: How the LTTE Diaspora Supports the Conflict in Sri Lanka', *Georgetown Journal of International Affairs*, 9:2, Summer/Fall 2008, p. 98; www.tamilnation.org/diaspora/060209sriskandarajah.pdf; http://en.wikipedia.org/wiki/Sri_Lankan_Tamil_diaspora (accessed 15 September 2008).

smaller ethnic groups, like the Sinhalese, seem to have states, Tamils are a 'nation without a state' or a 'trans state nation'.[66] This pan-ethnic sense of relative deprivation has played a significant role in regional and international Tamil support for the separatist struggle in Sri Lanka (Table 1:1a). Recent statements by the LTTE leader Prabhakaran, also reveals that his vision goes beyond Sri Lanka to encompass a 'Greater Eelam'. His 2007 Hero's Day speech stated that 'although 80 million Tamils live all around the globe, the Tamils do not have a country of their own.... I ask the entire Tamil speaking world to rise up for the liberation of Tamil Eelam'.[67] He also urged the Tamil diaspora to seek support in their host countries to establish a separate state for Tamils in Sri Lanka.[68] The growing Tamil nationalist movement in Malaysia, where there is a wealthy Sri Lankan Tamil community, seems to respond to this call despite the ban of the LTTE in that country. In a recent article in *TamilCanadian*, Ramasamy Palanisamy, former professor of Politics of the University of Malaysia, who serves on the LTTE Constitutional Affairs Committee (along with Siva Pasupathy, former Attorney General of Sri Lanka), praised Prabhakaran's call for global Tamil support for Eelam.[69]

Long distance Tamil nationalism is certainly a crucial factor behind the struggle ... being waged by the LTTE ... the eventual creation of Eelam would be testimony to the spirit and imagination of Tamil Diaspora. This powerful statement by the LTTE has given the struggle for Eelam an international basis ... it has provided for both material and intellectual support for the emancipation of Tamils long accustomed to Sinhala-state oppression. Among the Tamil Diaspora, Malaysian Tamils figure prominently in sustaining the quest for Eelam.[70]

Such sentiments fuel Sinhala fears that Eelam would become the homeland for the international Tamil community. Their resistance to federalism stems from this fear that international pressure would eventually establish a separate Tamil state displacing the Sinhalese, a relatively small global minority of about 15 million people, from their only island homeland.[71] The so-called 'minority complex' of the Sinhala majority and the 'majority complex' of the Tamil minority in Sri Lanka can be understood only by taking into account the regional and international demographic and political dimensions.

The liberal perspective

Ethno-nationalist approaches tend to see difference as essentialist, conflict as inevitable, and militarism as the solution. In contrast, liberalism as a philosophy tends to see inter-group conflict as historically produced and amenable to political solution. On the surface at least, the so-called 'left-liberals' involved in the Sri Lankan issue, most of them working for international and domestic NGOs, appear to present a middle-ground between extremist Sinhala and Tamil nationalisms. However, closer investigation shows that like most nationalists, many left-liberals – Sinhala, Tamil and international – also subscribe to an ethnically based separatist solution to the Sri Lankan conflict.

The liberal English language literature which dominates the analysis has approached the Sri Lankan separatist conflict overwhelmingly as a 'question of mindsets and attitudes' – 'perceptions, sentiments, fears, claims and counter-claims'.[72] *Ethnicity and Social Change in Sri Lanka* published by the Social Scientists Association of Sri Lanka in the immediate aftermath of the July 1983 anti-Tamil violence was influential in laying down the ethnic and psychologically based framework for analyzing the Sri Lankan conflict. It promoted an ideologically based analysis identifying majority Sinhala Buddhist consciousness as the root cause, and the transformation of that consciousness as the solution to the problem.

> [T]he concept of a Sinhala-Buddhist hegemony to be protected from the inroads of a South-Indian derived Tamil group has been pervasive from around 4th century AD and forms even today, the basis of Sinhala-Buddhist chauvinism and of ethnic conflict. That this concept arises from a distorted view of the island's history needs to be impressed on the minds of the Sinhala people, even though loosening the hold of such a powerful myth over their minds will be a difficult task.[73]

Academic, media and policy analyses published since 1983 overwhelmingly take Sinhala Buddhist nationalism as the starting point for examining the Sri

Lankan conflict. They attribute the alleged Aryan superiority of the Sinhalese and historical claims to Sri Lanka as Sihadvipa (the island of the Sinhala) and Dhammadvipa (the island of the Buddhist teachings – the Dhamma), the so-called 'Mahavamsa [Sinhala chronicle] ideology' as the root of present problems.[74] This 'fundamentalist' and 'hegemonic' consciousness of the Sinhala majority, particularly the Buddhist monks, it is argued, has resulted in a historical treatment of the Tamil minority as the cultural other.[75] Attempts to restore the historical relationship between Buddhism, the state and the society by the Sinhala Buddhist dominated post-independence state, it is argued led to the enactment of language, employment, land settlement and other policies which were discriminatory towards the Tamil minority. These policies, it is pointed out, gave rise to minority Tamil nationalism with its own claims to a 'traditional Tamil homeland', the demand for a separate state in the north and east of the island, the rise of militancy, the LTTE and the armed conflict. Upholding this perspective, Hoole categorically states, 'The focus on minorities as the agents of secession is ... misplaced. The principal threat to the unity of a nation is the chauvinism of the majority'.[76] In other words, as the movement for Inter-Racial Justice and Equality puts it, terrorism 'grew out of unresolved political questions, and the former cannot be stopped without resolving the latter'.[77]

There is validity to the critique of Sinhala Buddhist nationalism and post-independence state legislation. Post-independence educational and language policies aimed at increasing Sinhala access to the university and state employment threatened the Tamils as well as Christianized and westernized classes of all ethnic groups. It is necessary, however, to recognize that the political questions that have aggravated Sinhala–Tamil relations have been addressed by the Sri Lankan state over the last few decades. Sri Lankan citizenship has been extended to all Tamils of recent Indian origin. Policies that had limited Tamil as well urban Sinhala entry into the university science faculties have long been abandoned. Tamil is a national language in Sri Lanka, a status it does not enjoy in any other country including India which has over 60 million Tamil speaking people. The Constitution gives Buddhism a special place, but, it also upholds freedom of conscience allowing individuals to practice any religion or change their faith. Such religious tolerance is not necessarily available even in some western democratic countries like Norway which requires allegiance to its official religion Lutheranism.

Sri Lankan Tamils are not so such a regionally based community as claimed by the separatists: they, like the Muslims and the Sinhalese, are an island-wide community. The majority of Tamils live outside the Northern and Eastern Provinces demanded as the Tamil state. Tamils are not a majority in the Eastern Province (Table 1.2). Although Sri Lankan governments are commonly described as Sinhala dominated, due partly to the system of proportional representation introduced in 1978, minority Muslim, Indian Tamil and also non-LTTE Sri Lankan Tamil parties have played increasingly powerful roles in establishing and breaking coalition governments. Successive Sri Lankan governments have also put forward proposals for district and provincial level political

Table 1.2 Provincial population by ethnicity, 1946, 1971, 1981 (percentages)

Province	1946				1971				1981			
	Sinhala	SL* Tamil	In** Tamil	SL* Moor	Sinhala	SL Tamil	In Tamil	SL Moor	Sinhala	SL Tamil	In Tamil	SL Moor
Northern	7.2	72.6	5.5	14.7	7.3	69.2	11.3	11.1	7.7	69.7	12.4	9.8
Eastern	10.0	47.1	1.6	39.3	21.2	42.1	1.7	34.0	24.9	41.7	1.2	31.6
North-West	77.9	6.6	2.4	13.2	87.5	3.9	1.5	7.7	87.8	3.9	0.6	7.5
North-Central	85.9	7.2	2.4	4.6	90.0	2.5	0.4	6.8	91.3	1.7	0.1	6.8
UVA	58.0	4.2	34.6	3.2	74.4	2.4	20.0	2.7	80.9	4.0	11.7	3.1
Sabaragamuva	79.4	1.0	16.9	2.7	82.0	1.6	13.3	2.8	85.5	2.3	8.6	3.4
Western	86.2	2.6	5.5	5.6	84.8	3.7	3.8	6.2	85.6	4.9	1.9	6.1
Central	55.1	3.1	36.4	5.2	59.2	4.1	30.4	5.4	65.5	7.8	16.7	6.5
Southern	95.7	0.6	1.3	2.4	95.1	0.4	1.8	2.3	95.4	0.8	1.2	2.3

Source: Sri Lanka, Department of Census and Statistics 1946, 1971, 1981.

Notes
*Sri Lankan
**Indian

decentralization to address the territorial issue, and the Provincial Council administration introduced through Indian intervention has been in place in all but the Northern and Eastern provinces since 1987. The LTTE refused to join and improve upon the Provincial Council administration and has remained steadfast in its demand for a separate state. Thus, the territorial control of the north and the east remains the only major unresolved and intractable problem.

The liberal solution: regional autonomy

Unlike classical liberalism, which focuses on individual rights, much of contemporary liberal analysis takes a group-based approach to ethnic conflict. Like the Tamil separatists, the leftist liberals have approached the Sri Lankan conflict as a 'national question pertaining to group rights'.[78] Thus, 'Tamil desire for self-determination and Sinhalese fear of disintegration' interpreted along primordial lines has become the starting point for much of liberal conflict analysis and resolution.[79] Accordingly, NGOs in Sri Lanka, aided by INGO sponsors, have sought to undermine 'hegemonic' Sinhala nationalism, shape international opinion and influence successive Sri Lankan governments to accept Tamil aspirations for self-determination.[80] *Devolution and Development in Sri Lanka*, published in 1994 by the International Center for Ethnic Studies (ICES-Colombo) which has spearheaded the call for federalism asserted that 'the concept of autonomy has come to stay in Sri Lankan politics as an answer to the ethnic conflict'.[81] ICES-Colombo was founded by TULF parliamentarian Neelan Tiruchelvam, who was also the chief architect of the 1994 Devolution proposals. Promoting those proposals, the NGO, MIRJE (Movement for Inter-Racial Justice and Equality) called on the Sri Lankan government not only to accept 'justice of their [Tamil] demand for regional autonomy and implement measures for their realization' but also to acknowledge that the 'war against the LTTE is actually a war against the political aspirations of the Tamil people'.[82] *Unitarianism, Devolution and Majoritarian Elitism*, published by the Social Scientists Association in 1998 equated the 'outmoded unitary state' with Sinhala Buddhist hegemony and 'majoritarian democracy' and advocated regional autonomy for Tamils 'in areas where they are "predominantly inhabitant"' asserting a federal political structure as the only path to peace.[83]

Given the lack of any historical evidence that the Northern and Eastern provinces were exclusively Tamil areas, some Tamil moderates have acknowledged that the 'Tamil homelands' concept is a political myth rather than a historically or geographically accurate fact. While acknowledging that the 'Tamil homeland' concept is 'historically unsustainable and that colonisation of Sinhalese in the East is necessitated by reasons of social and economic justice', the Tamil human rights group, UTHR still maintains the fictitious homelands claim as 'less one of sound scholarship than one born through the experience of violence and insecurity'.[84] Radhika Coomaraswamy of the ICES has given legitimacy to the use of 'traditional homelands' thesis denying that it is a 'geographical concept'. She has claimed that it is only a 'political concept' that is 'a part of the arsenal of liberal, democratic discourse ... that attempts to find a solution to the ethnic conflict within the framework of a nation state'.[85] Although such arguments cannot hide the realities of the bloody territorial struggle to establish Eelam, they have influenced the creation of a massive national and international effort to provide regional autonomy for Sri Lankan Tamils.

At this time, the international community is not advocating for an independent Tamil state which is unacceptable to the powerful neighbor India and the Sinhala majority, as well as the Muslim minority. Although powerful countries like the US and UK refuse to negotiate with terrorists and although the LTTE has broken negotiations and ceasefires with the Sri Lankan government again and again, the international community continues to demand that the Sri Lankan government negotiate with the LTTE. The international formula for peace in Sri Lanka has called for the Sri Lankan government to address 'grievances' and 'aspirations' of Tamils; accept the Northern and Eastern provinces as the 'Tamil homeland'; merge the two provinces; adopt a federal system with the North and the East as a single unit with powers devolved along the Indian model'.[86] In other words, the international community is demanding that the Sri Lankan government and the people recognize the Tamil separatist claim based on assumptions of primordial Sinhala–Tamil enmity and the fictitious 'Tamil homelands' and accept devolution of power. This formula upholds Sri Lanka's sovereignty and territorial integrity. But, the LTTE refuses to give up the struggle for Eelam and the Sinhala nationalists resist federalism as unjust and as a stepping stone to a separatist state. Thus, the achievement of the supposed liberal middle-ground – Tamil regional autonomy – is fraught with difficulties. To understand the complexity of this issue and widespread opposition to federalism, the limitations of the liberal analysis itself must be considered.

Limitations of the liberal analysis

Like its global counterparts, the liberal analysis of the Sri Lankan conflict remains tied to a dualistic ethnic framework focusing on majority and minority relations and ethnically based solutions. Acceptance of the fictitious traditional homelands concept as the basis for political negotiation creates intractable problems. While it negates exclusive Sinhala Buddhist claim to the island, it upholds exclusive territorial rights and an 'apartheid' system which goes against the island's historical pluralist tradition which has allowed individuals to make one's home anywhere in Sri Lanka regardless of ethnicity or religion.[87] The framing of the conflict as one between 'a majority dominated expansionary state and a resistant regional minority' by South Indian political scientist, Amita Shastri among others legitimizes the 'homelands' myth neglecting contemporary demographic realities and socio-economic complexities.[88] The advocacy of regional autonomy to Tamil people 'in the areas in which they are predominantly inhabitant' overlooks the fact that the majority of Tamils now reside amidst the Sinhalese and other communities outside the territories being claimed as the 'traditional homelands'. It also overlooks the increasing multiethnic composition and non-Tamil majority – Muslim and Sinhala – of the contentious Eastern Province (Table 1.2 and Map 4.2). In this context, capitulation to the 'homelands' position amounts to a failure to distinguish between genuine grievances of Tamils and an appeasement of Tamil terrorism.

The singular focus on Sinhala Buddhist consciousness as the root cause of problems has created a highly imbalanced and narrow perspective depicting the Sinhalese (mostly Buddhists) as a monolithic aggressor and the Tamils (mostly Hindus) as a monolithic victim.[89] The horrific July 1983 anti-Tamil violence has been interpreted as an example of spontaneous outburst of primordial Sinhala hatred toward the Tamils rather than a state sponsored pogrom. The resulting worldwide sympathy for Tamil grievances has led to a relative neglect of the long standing grievances and suffering of other ethnic and religious groups. The absence of organized violence against Tamils in the south after July 1983, brutal LTTE killings of Tamil, Sinhala and Muslim civilians, state violence against Sinhala youth during the JVP insurrections in 1971 and the late 1980s and a host of other important political issues have received little attention given the dominance of the narrow Sinhala versus Tamil dualism. The official language policy of 1956, university standardization and other policies after the mid-1950s have been interpreted as pro-Sinhala and anti-Tamil ignoring the fact that those policies mostly backfired on the masses of the Sinhalese giving rise to Sinhala youth insurgencies against the state and the Sinhala elite several years before the emergence of the Tamil youth insurgency based on similar social class grievances.

The focus on Sinhala Buddhist nationalism has also contributed to a relative silence on the chauvinism and fundamentalism of minority ethnic and religious groups in Sri Lanka and their contributions to the creation and perpetuation of conflict. The concentration of peace education initiatives of the NGOs almost exclusively within the Sinhala Buddhist community in the south reflects this stance. In contrast to the long standing traditions of pluralism and accommodation in the south, the areas that came under the control of the LTTE in the north and the east have experienced forced cultural and political homogenization through ethnic cleansing, killing of dissidents, shut down of alternative media outlets, forcible recruitment of child soldiers and suicide bombers. As the UTHR has pointed out, left-liberal analysts and the local and international human rights networks have failed to grasp the mono-ethnic, totalitarian nature of the system that hoisted itself in the north in the name of Tamil rights and freedom.[90] Even after the banning of the LTTE as an international terrorist organization, many international NGOs have failed to distinguish between legitimate Tamil grievances and the LTTE's separatism and violence, thus contributing to ethnic polarization over reconciliation. The permeation of this biased perspective into international policymaking has solidified Sinhala nationalist opinion against the 'international community'.

A democratic approach to conflict resolution requires a framework in which the claims and concerns of all groups can be heard. Indeed, as Indian political scientist, Partha Ghosh has pointed out, there is no 'moral superiority to be attached to any particular ethic group'.[91] The narrow focus on identity has led to a failure to see the common oppression of Sinhalese, Tamils and Muslims. The vast majority of people belonging to all ethnic communities and toiling as peasants, fishermen, laborers and so on have remained 'outside the competition for securing opportunities for social mobility'.[92] To grasp the complexity of the separatist conflict in Sri Lanka it is necessary to move beyond psychologically based interpretations confined to ideology and consciousness and narrow views which see it as either a terrorist or an ethnic problem. It is necessary to examine the complex intersection of cultural and political-economic forces, such as the local and regional ethnoclass segments and international hegemonic interests which have aided terrorism and the ethnic and separatist conflict in Sri Lanka. Subsequent chapters of this book provide a historically based analysis of those interwined political–economic and cultural forces. The task of broadening the analysis is not an abstract academic or theoretical exercise. It is an essential component in finding a just, democratic and sustainable peace.

2 Prelude

The British colonial period and early years of independence

After three centuries of colonization, first under the Portuguese and then the Dutch, the coastal lowlands of Sri Lanka came under the control of Great Britain in 1796 when the Dutch territory was relinquished. In 1815, with the capture of the Kandyan kingdom, the entire island was consolidated under British rule, and would remain so until independence in 1948. The fault lines between the Sinhala and Tamil communities that show up in the modern Sri Lankan conflict were drawn during the period of British colonization from 1815 to 1948.

Colonialism integrated the previously separated regions of the island within a highly centralized colonial state. But by the inherently uneven and unequal manner of integration into the polity, British colonial policies contributed to new forms of ethno-religious competition and stratification.[1] Undermining the fluidity and inter-mixture that had prevailed in ancient Sri Lanka, colonial rulers promoted an essentialist approach which saw ethnic groups as inherently separate. Divide and conquer was a key to conquest, consolidation and maintenance of colonial regimes. In that sense, contemporary global policies of ethno-regional separatism and political fragmentation represent a continuation of the strategies of classical colonialism.

The major political consideration of the British was to avert the resurgence of Kandyan nationalism (following the harshly suppressed 1818 rebellion) and the major economic consideration was to open up the Kandyan highlands for capitalist development. The Colebrooke–Cameron Reforms of 1832–1833 laid the framework for dividing the island into five administrative provinces – North, South, East, West, and Central. In violation of the terms of the Kandyan Convention of 1815 which required the British to uphold Kandyan institutions, the separate administration of the Kandyan Provinces was abolished. The Kandyan kingdom was dismembered and its different parts attached to the artificially created new provinces. The locus of political control was firmly based in the capital city of Colombo on the southwest coast, and no legislative or executive powers were devolved to the provinces.[2]

The 'traditional Tamil "homeland" being demanded today constitutes the Northern and Eastern Provinces carved out by the British largely from the Kandyan kingdom rather than a unified Tamil political entity claimed to have existed from the 'beginning of history'.[3] The present Northern and Eastern

Provinces, were created for the administrative convenience of the British on the basis of 'lines drawn across the map of Sri Lanka ... than on the basis of any historical political divisions'.[4] As historian K.M. de Silva has pointed out, the entire Tamil separatist claim to the north and the east which was first put forward in the 1950s, was 'structured on a single erroneous minute' written by an early, controversial British official, Hugh Cleghorn in 1799:[5]

> Two different nations, from a very ancient period, have divided between them the possession of the island. First the Cingalese [sic] inhabiting the interior of the country, in its southern and western parts, from the river Wallouve [Walawe] to that of Chilow[sic], and secondly the Malabars [Tamils], who possess the northern and eastern districts. These two nations differ entirely in their religion, language and manners. The former, who are allowed to be the earlier settlers, derive their origin from Siam, professing the ancient religion of that country.[6]

Ironically, and without other historical grounds, Tamil separatists have repeatedly used Cleghorn's minute to claim the existence of two separate ethno-regional nations in Sri Lanka, the Tamils in the north and the Sinhalese in the south. But, as de Silva has pointed out, Tamil separatists have 'conveniently' dropped from their propaganda materials Cleghorn's reference (and references of all other British colonial writers) to the Sinhalese as the 'earlier settlers' of the island.[7]

Ethnicity and economic development

Failing to turn the Sinhalese peasantry into permanent wage laborers on their coffee and, later, tea plantations, the British imported low caste Tamils from South India through a state aided indenture system. According to some estimates, nearly 1 million South Indian migrants were brought in the 1840s and 1850s alone.[8] The Marxist analyst Fred Halliday has observed that the 'fortunes of British imperialism' founded on the 'super exploitation of this class' allowed 'the colonial state to manipulate and exacerbate ethnic antagonisms between Tamils and Sinhalese in a classic strategy of divide and rule'.[9] Unlike earlier waves of immigrants, the South Indian immigrants imported by the British were not absorbed into the Sinhala caste system and culture. As historian Eric Meyer has observed, the British planters 'were inclined to rely on apartheid as a means of social control and prevented to the extent possible "their" coolies from interacting with the neighbouring Kandyan villagers'.[10] The Kandyan peasantry lost much of their land to the Europeans and other social groups that came with plantation expansion.[11] By mid-twentieth century, agrarian pressure had become so acute that in Nuwara Eliya and Badulla districts, the landless Sinhala peasantry were respectively 42 percent and 38 percent of the population.[12] Alienation of village common lands (through instruments such as the Crown Lands Encroachment Ordinance of 1840) and plantation development had much to do with the plight of the Kandyan peasantry in the twentieth century.[13] The plight of the peasantry became the source of the JVP insurrection later in the post-independence period.

The Sri Lankan/Ceylon Tamils in the north were not particularly advantaged in the acquisition and ownership of plantation land located in the island's southern areas and the Kandyan Highlands.[14] But they held a decisive advantage in the realm of English language education. The colonial state's grants-in-aid provided the greater proportion of Christian missionary schools to the Northern Province. The American Ceylon Mission established exclusively in the Jaffna peninsula in 1816 provided elite English education comparable to university education in its schools.[15] This education, however, was not available to all Jaffna Tamils, but, mostly to a group who came to be known as the aristocratic 'first class vellalas'.[16]

The ready availability of English secondary schools in the north created a 'structural imbalance' giving the Sri Lankan Tamils, especially the vellala caste an 'intrinsic advantage' over the Sinhala majority and other minorities and Tamil groups with regard to higher education, colonial employment and the modern professions.[17] Next to the Burghers, the Ceylon Tamils were 'over-represented' in the administrative services relative to their proportions in the island's population. In 1925, the Sinhalese constituted 42.5 percent of the government medical service and 43.6 percent of the civil service, whereas, the Sri Lankan Tamils made up 30.8 percent of the medical services and 20.5 percent of the Civil Service although their respective proportions in the island's population were 67 percent and 11 percent.[18] These occupations brought many Tamils from the north to the south placing them in positions of social and economic superiority over the Sinhalese majority. The Jaffna vellala Tamils were treated as a loyal community with privileged access to employment not only in Sri Lanka, but, also in other British colonies, specifically Malaya and Singapore. Thus, the Jaffna vellala Tamils evolved a distinct ethnoclass and caste identity as a transnational elite, their descendants constituting a large part of the educated, professional diaspora today (Table 1.1a). As Sri Lankan Tamil scholars themselves have observed, privilege arising out of loyalty to the colonial master was 'the essential psyche of the educated Tamil'.[19]

Ethnicity and political representation

As historians Nissan and Stirrat have pointed out, there was a 'major paradox' in the center of Sri Lanka's colonial polity which was: '[S]ubject to one set of rules and one set of governors; in terms of citizenship, all should be equal. Yet,... British rule substantiated heterogeneity, formalizing cultural difference and making it the basis for social organization and political representation'.[20] The British, like the Dutch colonizers before them, advanced separate legal codes for ethnic groups, such as Islamic personal law for the Muslims and Thesawalami customary law for Jaffna Tamils which restricts the sale of land to residents outside the Northern Province contributing to the solidification of differences among local groups.[21]

From the beginning, the Sinhalese as a group were disadvantaged in the colonial system of political 'representation': although the overwhelming majority of the population, they were given only one slot out of a total of six of nongovernmental members in the Legislative Council created in 1832 to function in an advisory capacity. The rebellious Kandyans who attempted to regain their independence were deliberately marginalized. Sinhala representation was almost always given to a member of the favored Christian Sinhala govi caste rather than a representative from the disparaged Buddhist majority.[22] There was no separate representation for Muslims in the Legislative Council until the reforms of 1902. Given that most Muslims in Sri Lanka were Tamil speakers, the Tamil member was considered to be their representative as well.

In 1908, James Pieris, a Sinhala leader presented a scheme for legislative reform calling for the abolition of the 'present system of racial representation and the introduction of the elective principle in the place of nomination'.[23] But, refusing to introduce a system of political representation that could unify its diverse subjects, Governor McCallum justified primordial divisions arguing that:

> [N]eeds of the various provinces and of their heterogeneous populations differ widely according to race and to locality ... any attempt ... made to represent the people of Ceylon as forming a single entity welded together by common interests to an extent to nullify these differences is to the last degree misleading.[24]

As Tamil social anthropologist Thangarajah has pointed out, the definition of the 'status of the subjects as majority and minority predicated, not on numerical strength, but on the proximity to the rulers.[25] Thus, British policy bifurcated the Sinhala identity into two, but, created a single Tamil identity. Sri Lankan Tamils who constituted 12.9 percent of the population, and the recently arrived Indian Tamils who were also 12.9 percent (in 1911) were included as one Tamil group, whereas the Kandyans who were 24 percent and the low-country Sinhalese who were 43 percent of the total population were represented as two separate ethnic groups. As historian Ariyaratne has pointed out, 'This arrangement placed the [Tamils] on a par with each section of the Sinhalese in terms of the number of representatives. Hence their refusal to regard themselves as a minority, a term connoting "helplessness"'.[26] As other analysts have also observed, the 'psychological legacy of this colonial bias was that the Tamils came to see themselves as a "dominant community"'.[27] This dominance was achieved 'through their close cooperation with the British'.[28]

The Tamil political advantage became conspicuous when the elective principle was conceded in 1911 to the 'educated Ceylonese', that is, English literate males. The majority of the population educated in the local languages and the entire female population did not count. Less than 4 percent of the island's total population were literate in English. The Sinhalese adult males were 75.1 percent and the Tamils 14.5 percent of the total Ceylonese adult male population. But, Sinhalese were only 56.4 percent of the voters while Tamils were 36.4 percent.

Burghers were also over-represented while the Muslims were not represented at all in the educated Ceylonese electorate.[29] As K.M. de Silva has observed, none of the Sinhala representatives could match the political dynamism and maturity of the Tamil elite of the time.[30] They were the local leaders. The govi–karava caste rivalry among the Sinhala elite was a factor in the choice of Ponnambalam Ramanathan who belonged to the Tamil vellala caste, the equivalent of the Sinhala govi caste, over Marcus Fernando who was a Sinhala karava.[31] Ramanathan was re-elected to the same seat in 1917 which demonstrated that caste, not ethnicity was still the dominant political factor.[32]

The unity between the Sinhala and the Tamil elite during the first two decades of the twentieth century had much to do with the assumed parity between the '*two* majority communities [emphasis in original]', the Sinhalese and the Tamils, and minorities were the smaller 'racial' groups' like the Burghers and the Muslims at the time.[33] As political historian Nira Wickramasinghe has observed, the Tamil leadership insisted on upholding this parity in subsequent efforts at constitutional reform:

> The result of the 1912 election was seized upon as confirmation of their [Tamil] permanent right to be represented on an equal footing with the Sinhalese, despite their numerical inferiority. The Tamil leadership felt that a droit acquis should not be diminished and their new stand for communal ratios on the terms established in 1912 vindicated their self-esteem as a majority community.[34]

The outbreak of the Sinhala-Muslim riots in 1915, considered the worst communal riots of the colonial period, revealed the weak political position of the Sinhala majority. The riots were prompted by a British Ordinance – 'Police Ordinance' of 1865 – which prevented Buddhist traditional practices.[35] But, interpreting the riots as an attempt to overthrow British rule, the colonial state proclaimed martial law and 'promptly and vigorously' punished the rioters, confirming their stereotypes of Sinhala Buddhists as militant, 'excitable' and 'undisciplined' troublemakers.[36] The heavy handed treatment by the colonial authorities weakened the Buddhist temperance movement and contributed to the reemergence of its constituent units as the more ethnically defined Sinhala Mahajana Sabhai (People's Committees) in the 1920s.[37] The findings of the Commission of Inquiry on the 1915 riots revealed that the British incited communal conflict to flare into violent proportions.[38] A few of the British officers 'who had shot natives in cold blood at a time when disorder had ceased' were subsequently dismissed. However, the Colonial Office in London refused to appoint a Royal Commission to investigate the riots, arguing that such an appointment would revive religious antagonism. But, by their dismissal of the case, British colonial state revealed its inherent authoritarianism, disregard for human rights, deepened grievances of the Sinhala Buddhists and distrust between religious groups.[39]

The 1915 riots provided an opportunity for the spokesman for the educated Ceylonese in the legislative council, Ponnambalam Ramanathan to emerge as a national leader. A Tamil and a Hindu, he took great efforts to convince the British of the innocence of the Sinhala leaders accused of sedition.[40] Ramanathan's services to the Sinhala Buddhist community in general won him their respect and tribute.[41] Being the national leaders at the time, the Tamil elite led the movement for constitutional reform and the formation of the Ceylon National Congress (CNC). The CNC was founded in 1919 upon 'the twin principles of communal harmony and national unity' with the objective of agitating for constitutional reform. The first president of the CNC was the Tamil leader, Ponnambalam Arunachalam, brother of Ponnambalam Ramanathan who was chosen as the most suitable Ceylonese for the presidency of the CNC.[42] Unfortunately, however, the hope for national unity anticipated by the formation of the Congress did not last long.

Democratization and ethnic conflict

Introduction of territorially based representation signified the beginning of the island's movement toward political democracy. But, this shift aggravated the hitherto prevailing disjunction between numerical strength and political power and set the stage for the rise of the island's 'ethnic problem'. The first elections to the reformed Legislative Council based on territorial representation in 1921 changed the balance in favor of the majority community bringing 13 Sinhalese as against three Tamils. The Tamil members began immediately to campaign to restore the pre-existing ratio between Sinhalese and Tamil representation.[43] The issue which gave rise to the conflict in 1921 was the Tamil demand for a special communal seat in the Western Province specifically for the educated Jaffna elite who worked and lived in the metropolitan area – the idea that the north and the east were 'traditional homelands' was not yet manufactured. This created a major rift between the Sinhala and Tamil elites precipitating in the departure of Arunachalam and most of the Tamil members from the CNC in 1921.[44]

As Thangarajah has pointed out, 'The bone of contention ... was not representation of Tamils but a representation of "elite Tamils"'.[45] 'Tamil consciousness' put forward was really 'vellala consciousness' aimed at maintaining colonial privileges and traditional caste and regional domination.[46] The conflict in 1921, however, cannot be blamed entirely on the local Tamil and Sinhala elites. Manning, the Colonial Governor, achieved his objective through deliberate manipulation of communal differences and tensions. Manning's handling of constitutional reform was a classic example of *divide et impera*.[47]

Manning reinforced the ethnic framework of modern Sri Lankan politics by supporting the Tamil elites' demand for a special seat in the Western Province against the Sinhala leaders of the CNC.[48] The Tamil elite did not get the special communal seat, but the 1924 Constitution introduced by Manning, which gave them other additional seats, was considered 'a bequest to the Tamils'.[49] Exploiting the marginalization of the Kandyans and their fears of low-country Sinhala dominance, Manning had also offered the Kandyans separate communal electorates under the 1920 Constitution (this concession was taken away in 1923).[50]

With the demise of the CNC, the principles of communal harmony and national unity were undermined irrevocably. A series of communally minded mahajana sabhai (people's organizations) were organized during this period. The Sinhala Mahajana Sabhai established in 1919 and its emphasis on the Sinhala language and the Buddhist religion gave it a distinctly religious nationalist identity.[51] Soon after the break-up of the CNC, a Tamil Mahajana Sabhai was established in August 1921, and the Ceylon Tamil League was founded by Arunachalam in 1923 to give vigorous expression to the demands of the Tamils, who now came to see themselves as a minority community needing to resist Sinhala majoritarian dominance.[52] Embittered by the loss of pre-existing Tamil majority status and the concept of a united Sri Lanka, Arunachalam, turned to the concept of a pan-Tamilian state. At the inaugural meeting of the Ceylon Tamil League, he stated as its objective: 'to keep alive and propagate … throughout Ceylon, Southern India and the Tamil colonies … the union and solidarity of "Tamil akam" the Tamil Land'.[53] Arunachalam was the first Sri Lankan Tamil leader to articulate the sense of Tamils as an oppressed group and seek refuge in a vision of Tamil Eelam[54] (Map I.2). He was influenced by growing Tamil nationalism and the 'Dravidian uplift movement' in South India at the time.[55] The interpretation of the Aryan–Dravidian linguistic divide as a racial dualism advanced by European Orientalists gained prominence during this period influencing nationalist movements in both countries. Acceptance of this historically invalid thesis contributed to the perception of the highly inter-mixed Sinhalese and the Tamils in Sri Lanka as Aryans and Dravidians.[56]

The first community to call for a federal state in Sri Lanka were not the Tamils but the Kandyans, who had lost the most – their sovereignty, their land, their culture – under British colonialism. In 1925, a Kandyan communal organization, the Kandyan National Assembly, was formed in opposition to the CNC, which was dominated by low-country Sinhalese. The Assembly demanded the creation of a federal state in Ceylon with regional autonomy for the Kandyans on the basis that 'most of the grievances under which [the Kandyans] labour at the present day are directly due to the amalgamation of Government in 1833'.[57] The Kandyan demand for federal political structure was encouraged and supported by Hugh Clifford, who followed Manning as the Colonial Governor. Except for S.W.R.D. Bandaranaike, a young Sinhala Congressman, none of the influential politicians of the day, Sinhala or Tamil, found federalism appealing.[58]

Electoral democracy

In 1931 the Donoughmore Commission, which had been appointed in 1929 to undertake constitutional reform, introduced universal franchise based on territorial representation, making Ceylon one of the earliest colonies in the British Empire to receive the vote for both men and women and the working classes. The elites of both the Sinhala and Tamil communities opposed the reform. Sinhala elites in the CNC who represented the conservative interests of Sinhala landowners and the western educated opposed the extension of the vote to the masses. Sinhala politicians in the Legislative Council expressed fears that the enfranchisement of the large Indian Tamil population from neighboring India would 'swamp' the permanent population changing the distinct cultural make-up of the small island[59] (Table I.1). Tamil leaders like Ramanathan were even more strongly against universal franchise which they feared would guarantee permanent Sinhala political dominance and empower Tamil low castes against vellala privilege.[60] Afraid of losing Tamil elite privilege, Ramanathan traveled to England to argue against the Donoughmore proposals for electoral democracy and self-government for Sri Lanka.[61] Despite class, caste and ethnically based fears of the Sinhala and Tamil elites, the franchise was extended to all sections of the local population and a large section of the Indian Tamil plantation workers (with five years residence and intention to settle on the island).

The elections of 1931 on the basis of the Donoughmore reforms brought a drastic change in the composition of the new legislature.[62] Of the councilors elected in 1931, 38 were Sinhalese, five Tamil, two European and one Moor (four Tamils from the Jaffna constituencies were added in 1934). By religion, they were 27 Buddhists, 15 Christians, three Hindus and one Muslim. A further eight members were nominated including two Burghers, one Indian Tamil and one Malay. In percentage terms, Sinhalese increased from 28 percent to 56 percent and Buddhists from 20 percent to 41 percent. This extension of parliamentary democracy signified the beginning of what came to be seen as a 'reconquest' of power by the Sinhala Buddhist majority who had been marginalized during 400 years of colonial domination and a diminution of the power of minorities, especially the Sri Lankan Tamils who had 'benefitted' from colonial rule.[63]

Sri Lanka's social welfare state which emerged after 1931 was a product of electoral democracy. The free healthcare, 'free education' – that is, access to non-fee levying government schools to poorer segments of the population – and provision of a universal rice subsidy contributed to a relatively high physical quality of life (high life expectancy, literacy, low infant mortality).[64] The resettlement of landless Sinhala peasantry in the Dry Zone was also a direct by-product of political democratization and the 'electoral strength' of the rural sector.[65] However, when reform of the Donoughmore Constitution came up, the 'vexed question of minority representation' re-emerged as the dominant political issue over economic development and social welfare.[66]

In 1937, G.G. Ponnambalam, the spokesman for the All Ceylon Tamil Congress put forward a proposal for 'balanced representation' which came to be known as 'fifty-fifty'. It called for the restriction of Sinhala majority's representation to 50 percent of the seats and the allocation of the other 50 percent to the minorities in any future reformed legislature. An extreme demand couched in moderate language, it sought to make the Sinhala majority (70 percent of the island's population at the time) a minority, in denial of democratic principle.[67] As political scientist, Jane Russell remarked, the 'pharisaic consciousness', a 'recurring characteristic of Tamil communalism betrayed a superiority complex which was the obverse of their minority position'.[68]

'Ethnic entrepreneurs' from both the minority and majority groups contributed to the communalization of politics.[69] The Sinhala Maha Sabha (SMS) which was formed within the CNC under the leadership of S.W.R.D. Bandaranaike in 1937, sought to foster unity within the Sinhala community by transcending caste and regional differences such as govi–karava and the Kandyan and low country divisions. It was 'the first island-wide association giving expression specifically to Sinhalese ethnic interests',[70] Although they tapped into their respective ethnic identities as the basis for political mobilization, the aristocratic Bandaraniake and the vellala G.G. Ponnambalam shared a common anglophile cultural and class background. Still, there was a difference between their platforms in that the SMS appealed to the Sinhala electorate envisioning a social and cultural transformation whereas Ponnambalam's 'fifty-fifty' agenda put forward as a means to benefit all Tamils and all minorities, was only concerned with the preservation of the privileges of the Jaffna Tamil elite. Ponnambalam put it succinctly when he said, 'Government service and brains are the chief assets of our community and let us try to safeguard them'.[71]

Constitutional reform and ethnic competition

In 1944 a commission headed by Lord Soulbury was appointed to consider a draft constitution for Sri Lanka with the objective of granting independence. The impending arrival of the Soulbury Commission on the island intensified communal rivalries and the consolidation of ethnic identities. It led to the formation of the All Ceylon Tamil Congress (ACTC) in 1944 (the year when the DK emerged in Madras) by Ponnambalam and the revival of his 'fifty-fifty' scheme. In justifying his anti-democratic measure, Ponnambalam claimed that a parliamentary democracy of the English type could not exist in a colony such as Ceylon. But, the Soulbury Commission objected to the 'fifty-fifty' stating that 'any attempt by artificial mean to convert a majority into a minority is not only inequitable but doomed to failure'.[72] Ponnambalam made frequent trips to England to lobby both Conservative and Labour Party members against the grant of further constitutional rights to Ceylon, arguing that Sinhala leaders were conspiring to abuse their authority to the detriment of the minorities. Presenting himself as the representative of the island's minorities, he influenced leading British newspapers to carry articles projecting Ceylon as a country unsuited for self-government due to the acute minority problem. Ironically, the colonial Governor, Caldecott, had to use his influence to defuse Ponnambalam's international campaign to sabotage the island's progress towards political independence.[73] Bandaranaike was especially severe in his denouncement of Ponnambalam and his associates as 'local reactionaries' seeking the 'entrenchment of imperialism and exploitation, and the protection of vested interest'.[74]

The Soulbury Constitution, which was based on the Commission's recommendations, was accepted almost unanimously in the State Council and provided the basis for the grant of political independence in 1948. The Tamil Congress called it a 'charter of slavery' without 'any safeguards for the minorities'.[75] Indeed, an earlier proposed Bill of Rights which would have offered greater protection of minority rights was not included. In 1946, D.S. Senanayake established the United National Party (UNP) which was joined by the Muslims, some Sri Lankan Tamils and Bandaranaike's SMS, but not the Indian Tamils, Ponnambalam's Tamil Congress or the left parties. In the wake of Indian political independence and the spread of nationalism across the world following the Second World War, independence was granted to Sri Lanka on 4 February 1948 under D.S. Senanayake as the island's first Prime Minister.

Independence and the emergence of Tamil separatism

One of the first acts of the independent government was to pass citizenship legislation in 1948 and 1949 restricting Sri Lankan citizenship to those who could claim it by descent on 'stringent conditions' of registration – seven years of residence. This would hardly be considered a stringent requirement in most western countries today. Nevertheless, by simply re-defining the criteria for citizenship more tightly than under the Donoughmore Constitution, the vast majority of the Indian workers on the island were denied Sri Lankan citizenship and removed from electoral rolls.[76] There was no unanimity at the time on the Indian citizenship question. Given their unionization and increasingly militant struggles, the European planters and the local capitalists did not want to empower the plantation labor force which they feared as a 'powerful prop' of the leftist parties.[77] Most legislators from the minority communities, including Ceylon Tamils and Muslims, as well as those appointed from the European and Burgher communities, voted in favor of the legislation. Many Tamils voted for disenfranchisement while many Sinhalese opposed it.[78] In other words, the 'voting was very much on class lines which cut across ethnicity'.[79]

But, the Ceylon Tamil Congress split over the question of citizenship for Indian Tamils. Ponnambalam and most of the Tamil Congress parliamentarians voted in favor of the bills while a section broke away under its deputy, S.J.V. Chelvanayakam forming the Sri Lanka Tamil State Party ITAK (Illankai Thamil Arasu Kadchi) in 1949, just one year after independence. With its call for a federal political structure and regional autonomy for the Tamils, the demand for Tamil separatism in Sri Lanka was begun.[80] At the time, the ITAK's radical confrontational politics seemed futile and extremist,[81] while underneath the surface, the tides of Tamil separatism and Sinhala extremism were rising and were to flare into violence in the mid-1950s.

Tamil separatist sentiments had first become evident when the majority status that the Ceylon Tamils enjoyed in the Legislative Council was threatened in 1920. Two Ceylon Tamil leaders had sent petitions to Britain in 1936, with the assistance of Chelvanayakam, asking for a separate state for the Ceylon Tamils.[82] The break-up of India and creation of a separate Muslim state of Pakistan made an impression on the Ceylon Tamil elite. Chelvanayakam questioned why independence was being offered to Ceylon and also entertained the idea of a federation of Ceylon with India as a way to avoid Sinhala majority dominance.[83] On

4 November G.G. Ponnambalam had also cabled the British government on 20 November 1947 asking for self-determination for the Tamils.[84] On 26 November 1947 in his Address of Thanks to the 'Throne Speech' in the first House of Representatives, Chelvanayakam asked, 'If Ceylon is fighting to secede from the British Empire why should not the Tamil people if they feel like it, secede from the rest of the country?'[85] Although members of the Tamil middle class advised patience allowing time to assess the collaboration with the Sinhalese begun in 1948, Chelvanayakam declared that 'They could not wait one moment without fighting for the creation of the Tamil state ... If we wait, it may be too late'.[86]

Enthralled by the Islamic separatist movement in India, Chelvanayakam and his allies envisioned linguistic separatism for themselves in Sri Lanka.[87] Although they had not expressed sympathy or support for the Indian Tamils in Sri Lanka earlier, and the call for Tamil regional autonomy on the island was wholly inapplicable to the Indian Tamils, those looking for an opportunity seized upon the citizenship legislation to assert their own secessionist agenda. It is significant that the formation of the ITAK in Sri Lanka paralleled the break-up of the DK (Dravida Kazhagam) in Tamil Nadu and the birth of the 'Tamil chauvinist' DMK (Dravida Munnetra Kazhagam), the 'self-proclaimed vanguard of Tamil nationalism' in 1949. From the beginning, the Sri Lankan ITAK maintained close links with the DMK which dominated Tamil Nadu politics in the 1950s.[88]

Evolution of Sri Lankan Tamil separatism

Samuel James Velupillai Chelvanayakam was born in Malaysia, educated at the elite St. Thomas's College, a Christian and an eminent lawyer in Colombo.[89] Growing up in the very north of Sri Lanka in close proximity to Tamil Nadu, the anti-Hindi agitation and the Dravidasthan movement there made a lasting impression on Chelvanayakam. Unlike other leaders of the All Ceylon Tamil Congress, Chelvanayakam spurned cooperation and 'the loaves of office' in a Sinhala led government from the beginning. He refused to recognize the national flag (with the lion symbolizing the Sinhalese and saffron and green stripes representing Tamil and Muslim minorities respectively devised in a compromise with Ponnambalam).[90] Chelvanayakam was convinced 'that the Tamils would never be safe from the threat of domination and assimilation by the Sinhalese majority while the two communities existed together in a unitary state subject to control by the majority'.[91] He believed that political autonomy was necessary to maintain the cultural distinctiveness and integrity of the Tamils.[92]

While in English, Chelvanayakam's party gave itself the moderate sounding name The Federal Party (FP), a party wanting only federation, its official name in Tamil, 'Illankai Thamil Arasu Kadchi' (ITAK) which translates as 'Lanka Tamil State Party' carried a distinctly separatist connotation in Tamil. Ponnambalam accused Chelvanayakam that he was

[A]ttempting to foist on the Tamil people a party whose very name shows that it was formed to deceive and mislead the people and that the terms

'Tamil Arasu' ... connote an entity clothed with the absolute attributes of sovereignty.[93]

Chelvanayakam replied that 'Tamil Arasu' meant a Tamil state, whether 'sovereign or autonomous' and added that the term Federal Party was only an 'explanatory note' and was not the party's name.[94] Supporters of the ITAK, notably A.J. Wilson, Chelvanayakam's son-in-law, have claimed that 'till 1974 the FP did not demand self-determination, let alone separate statehood'.[95] However, the principal resolution adopted upon the establishment of ITAK in 1949 reads as follows:

> We believe that the only means of ensuring that the Tamils are guaranteed their freedom and self-respect by law, and of solving their problems in a just and democratic manner is to permit them to have their own autonomous state guaranteeing self-government and self-determination for the Tamil nation in the country and to work indefatigably to the attainment of this objective.[96]

Like communal parties elsewhere, the ITAK's justification for existence was founded upon the supposed primacy of communal identification and solidarity in politics and the primordial belief that 'common political interests of all members of the community, by virtue of their ethnic bond, outweigh political interests which internally divide the community'.[97] The ITAK focused singularly on its own ethnic issues, exaggerated charges against the ethnic 'other' and fanned communal fears against the enemy claiming moral and spiritual justification for its agenda.[98] Chelvanayakam proclaimed in 1949, 'Ours is a campaign meant as much to raise our standard of national honour as it is to build up a state. It is a sacred task'.[99]

Given that an island-wide Tamil ethnic identity did not exist at this time, the ITAK worked zealously to 'manufacture' such an identity exaggerating primordial Sinhala versus Tamil antagonism. Chelvanayakam sought to persuade the Indian Tamils that they were 'part and parcel of the island's Tamil population', just as he tried to convince the Ceylon Tamils that 'it was in their interests to swell their own ranks with their hill country brethren'.[100] Like the Sinhala nationalists, the Tamil nationalists looked upon the Indian Tamils opportunistically from the vantage point of numerical aggrandizement. Chelvanayakam also recognized the importance of the Eastern Province for a future Tamil state and the problems posed by differences between Tamils in the north and the east. As Wilson has pointed out, from the outset, Chelvanayakam focused his efforts on 'indoctrinating' the Tamil speaking people in the Eastern Province whom he claimed 'constituted the frontline' of a future Tamil state.[101]

At its annual convention in Trincomalee in 1951, the ITAK adopted several new resolutions clearly rejecting the existence of a multi-ethnic Sri Lankan nation. Instead, it asserted the existence of two separate nations with irreconcilable differences. One resolution condemned the government 'colonization' of territories 'traditionally' occupied by 'Tamil-speaking people' with 'purely Sinhalese people' as an 'infringement' and 'a calculated blow' aimed at the 'very existence of the Tamil-speaking nation in Ceylon'.[102] The Tamil homeland concept, then, was not born 'through the experience of violence and insecurity'[103] as argued by Tamil nationalists. It predated the introduction of Sinhala-oriented state policies and eruption of communal violence in the mid-1950s.

Tamil separatist claims overlooked the irony and injustice in simultaneously demanding integration and separation, i.e. Sri Lankan citizenship for Indian Tamils on the one hand and an exclusive territory for Sri Lankan Tamils on the other hand within the small, densely populated, multi-ethnic Sri Lanka. Yet, the repeated enunciation of the territorial claim by the ITAK established the myth of 'traditional homeland of the Tamils' and has guided the separatist discourse since then.[104] It is also interesting to note that the reference to the 'Tamil Nation' in the ITAK's 1949 resolution was changed to 'Tamil-Speaking People' in 1951 in an attempt to incorporate the Tamil speaking Muslims who have always resisted such an incorporation.[105]

Ponnambalam and the moderate Tamil leadership of the time warned against the demand for an exclusive Tamil state and the dangers of partitioning the pluralistic Sri Lankan society.[106] But, Chelvanayakam's attitude was deeply ingrained in the psyche of many Sri Lankan Tamil elites who were not willing to yield the status and identity as a dominant and a 'majority' community enjoyed during much of the British colonial period. 'Smaller minorities' like the Muslims and the Indian Tamils chose to advance themselves politically by working within the parliamentary democratic system. But, the Jaffna elite were too proud of their Tamil heritage and modern achievements to be dominated by the regionally insignificant Sinhalese. They wanted to establish themselves as a majority and this could only be done by partition and the establishment of a brand new nation state.[107] But, in the 1952 parliamentary elections the ITAK won only two parliamentary seats and Chelvanayakam even lost his seat to a UNP candidate. In many ways, the 1952 elections represented a verdict against federalism and Tamil separatism.[108] The growth and popularity of the ITAK came only after the introduction of the official language legislation which in turn was influenced by the rising tide of Sinhala Buddhist nationalism.

Competing ethno-nationalisms

The Westminster model of parliamentary democracy, which is built on the principle of competition, deepened Sinhala–Tamil embitterment in the post-independence period. It allowed the majority Sinhala parties to form governments without the need to win minority constituencies. Disenfranchisement of the Indian Tamils in 1948 and the delimitation of constituencies in subsequent years made the Sinhalese rural voter 'the arbiter of the country's politics'.[109] To respond to that constituency, in 1951 Bandaranaike left the UNP to form the Sri Lanka Freedom Party (SLFP), offering to change the colonial social order and bring social justice, dignity, and self-respect for the Sinhala Buddhist masses. However, the SLFP was able to win only a few seats in 1952.

In 1956, however, while discontent with the UNP grew, Bandaranaike was able to tap into Buddhist religious fervor as the country celebrated the two thousand five hundredth year since the Buddha's death to restore the island's historical legacy as the Sihaladipa (island of the Sinhalese) and Dhammadipa (island of the Buddha's teachings).[110] This new populist movement was able to speak to the growing social and economic crisis in the countryside.[111] Yet the exclusive emphasis on the 'unique ethnic patrimony' of the Sinhala Buddhists came to have a 'fundamentally divisive ... impact' on the multi-ethnic and multi-religious society of Sri Lanka.[112] The opportunistic identification with the politicized Sinhala Buddhism enabled Bandaranaike and a coalition of Sinhala parties – the Mahajana Eksath Peramuna (MEP, The People's United Front) – to win a massive electoral victory. Buddhist monks, indigenous ayurvedic doctors, Sinhala teachers, peasants and workers – segments of the population that had been marginalized under colonial domination – constituted its base of support.[113]

Bandaranaike promised to nationalize tea estates and mercantile firms, to evict the British from the Trincomalee harbor and the Negombo air field, and to replace the Soulbury Constitution imposed by the British prior to independence.[114] Despite their broad vision of democratic socialism, Bandaranaike and the MEP were politically beholden to introduce policies partial to the Sinhala Buddhist majority. The first issue to tap into this Sinhala sentiment was language.

Language recognition

Over the course of the electoral campaign, establishing Sinhala as the sole official language became the main objective of the MEP platform. In the frenzy leading up to the election, the MEP avowed to make Sinhala the national language in '24 hours' if voted into office.[115] Language would become a contentious issue between the Sinhala communities and a sparking point for violence.

The objective of the swabhasha bilingual movement was to advance the interests of the 90–95 percent or so of the Sri Lankan population who were not proficient in English. Despite the introduction of 'free education' or compulsory secondary education in the vernacular languages in the 1940s, only those with English education could still aspire to the limited number of white-collar positions available.[116] The call to make both Sinhala and Tamil official languages shifted to make Sinhala the sole official language, as the reality of replacing English began to dawn in the early 1950s. It was feared that Sinhala students would face grave disadvantages because of a lack of educational materials in Sinhala as opposed to Tamil students who had access to materials from South India where there were some 30 million Tamil speakers then. Prime Minister Bandaranaike, who had originally supported the dual language policy, began to give expression to the growing sentiment that parity between the regionally dominant Tamil language and the local Sinhala language could inevitably lead to the annihilation of the latter.[117]

Ceylon Tamil leaders, on the other hand, feared that the acceptance of Sinhala as the sole official language would lead to forced assimilation and loss of distinctiveness of the Tamil culture on the island. They viewed the recognition of their language as a symbol of respect for Tamil people and their full inclusion in the society. They criticized the 'Sinhala Only' policy as the means to subordinate the Tamils. Chelvanayakam sought to justify the Tamil demand by claiming to speak for the disparate Tamil-speaking groups in the island. Utilizing the language issue to mobilize support for separatism, Chelvanayakam pronounced in 1954: 'It is better to have our own territory, our own culture and self-respect than be a minority in the island living on the good fortune of the majority community'.[118]

Proponents of 'Sinhala Only' justified their demand on the ground that Sinhalese was the language of 70 percent of the island's population, and since Tamil government employees do not only serve Tamils but mostly the Sinhalese, it was only reasonable and moral that they have a working knowledge of the majority language.[119] As political scientist Robert Kearney observed,

> Tamil insistence on parity throughout the island was taken as a sign of Tamil arrogance ... reminiscent of the earlier 'fifty-fifty' demand ... and that the rightful position of the majority, denied under colonial rule, should be restored by declaring Sinhalese the sole official language.[120]

Although couched in cultural terms, the linguistic competition was largely an economic struggle to broaden access to employment opportunities for those educated in the vernacular. Thus it was directed against privileged elites of all ethnic and religious groups.[121] The island's rapidly rising population and the establishment of Central Schools providing English language education after the Donoughmore reforms, broadened the basis for recruitment into white collar employment, making the competition acute. Following independence, there was an efflux of Britons and capital from the island, but, no concerted program of industrial and agricultural development to increase wealth and employment. The ensuing 'ethnic' conflict was rooted in this lack of economic expansion. As had happened in the past and would again in the future, it was an economic issue framed and expressed as a cultural issue, making it all the more volatile.

As more and more Sinhalese sought government jobs, they felt that their opportunities were thwarted by prior entrenchment of Tamils in the public service.[122] Although Sinhalese were about six times more numerous than the Ceylon Tamils, the select Ceylon Service employed nearly half as many Tamils as Sinhalese, and the Judicial Service had two-thirds as many Tamils as Sinhalese in 1946.[123] In 1962, over 40 percent of the Medical Service, i.e. mostly doctors, were Tamil (Table 2.1). Making Sinhala the official language, then, was seized upon as a means to improve Sinhala competition and to lessen Tamil (as well as Burgher) entrenchment in the public service. With the switch of the language movement from swabhasha to Sinhala Only, the terms of the political conflict shifted from a struggle against English to a struggle against Tamil privilege.

Table 2.1 Ethnic distribution in higher state services, 1946–1975 (percentages)

	Medical				Judicial					Civil Service*			
	1946	1956	1962		1946	1956	1962	1973		1946	1956	1962	1975
Sinhalese	59.4	54.1	53.4		49.1	57.6	60.3	77.6		59.5	57.1	73.7	81.3
Tamil	33.3	38.1	41.1		26.4	30.3	26.9	18.8		26.7	29.4	17.9	15.9
Muslim	–	1.5	2.1		–	6.1	10.2	3.3		–	1.7	2.3	2.0
Burgher	7.3	6.3	3.5		26.5	6.1	2.6	–		13.8	11.8	6.0	0.8

Source: Charles Abeysekara, 'Ethnic Representation in the Higher State Services', in *Ethnicity and Social Change in Sri Lanka*, Colombo: Social Scientists Association, 1984, pp. 181, 184–186.

Note
* Ceylon Administrative Service replaced the Civil Service in the 1960s. Includes class I, II, III.

With the rise of Sinhala linguistic nationalism, the Tamil separatist position of the ITAK, which had once seemed to be extremist, gained popularity. The 'tide of Tamil fear of Sinhalese domination' helped the ITAK gain 52 percent and 42 percent of the popular vote respectively in the Northern and Eastern provinces in the 1956 elections. In 1956, for the first time since independence, the ITAK, a Tamil political party without organizational links to Sinhala parties, came into prominence.[124]

Under pressure from extremist Sinhala Only enthusiasts who opposed any concessions to Tamil, the MEP government passed its first legislative enactment, the Official Language Act, no. 33 of 1956, which made Sinhala 'the one official language of Ceylon'.[125] The lack of a bill of fundamental rights in the country's constitution resulted in the Sri Lankan Parliament passing the Official Language Act without qualifications to protect minority interests.[126] The actual effect of the new law was, however, unclear. The day after the Language Bill passed in the Senate on 6 July 1956, Government Gazette notification no. 10,949 was issued to accommodate the Tamil and English languages. It stated that 'where any language or languages has or have hitherto been used for any official purpose such language or languages may be continued to be so used until the necessary change is effected'.[127]

Despite this lack of specificity regarding the change, English-educated elites, including the Sinhalese who did not have a working knowledge of Sinhala, resented the new policy on language.[128] Muslims, who were mostly Tamil speaking, accommodated themselves to the new order by going along with the government's language policy.[129] The greatest condemnation and organized resistance to the Official Language Act and the Sinhala populism that it represented came from the Tamil elite. As K.M. de Silva put it,

> For the Tamils ... It meant that they would be at a great disadvantage in future employment, in the administration of the country, and eventually in the professions as well ... language became the focal point of a new ethnic consciousness, of two rival nationalisms.[130]

Tamil leaders claimed that the Sinhala language legislation would bring in an era of 'apartheid' with Sinhalese as the 'masters and rulers' and Tamils would be forced to 'accept subject status under them'. Chelvanayakam argued that in the absence of linguistic parity, Tamils had no alternative but seek 'Federalism or Separatism'. Even Ponnambalam who was opposed to federalism began to say that the Tamils might need to launch a movement for self-determination.[131]

Such sensationalist reactions obscured the fact that Tamil continued to be used as a medium of education and for official purposes. As Tamil scholars and activists themselves have argued, 'discrimination' pertained only to the elite.[132] Some of the most ardent champions of Sri Lankan Tamil separatism were caste fanatics who fought off Tamil untouchables (Dalits) from entering Hindu temples in Jaffna in the same period.[133] Hoole has pointed out that Tamil nationalism 'stemmed from the ... narrow interests of the educated middle class and was very much geared towards preserving the influence it had acquired chiefly in the professions and in the public sector.... It was literally conducted out of lawyers' chambers'.[134] What started out as a 'revolt of the privileged', to use veteran journalist H.L.D. Mahindapala's term, was in turn presented as a 'revolt of the oppressed',[135] even though the lives of the down-trodden, illiterate social classes and castes were to be relatively untouched by change of official language policy. However, it was not hard to mobilize the deep seated anger and frustration of the oppressed along ethnic lines against the Sinhalese, the majority of whom were themselves socially and economically oppressed and available for ethnically based mobilization by their own elites.

Sinhala–Tamil violence

Tamil resistance to the Official Language Act was unprecedented and widespread,[136] and marked a turning point in Sinhala–Tamil relations and a descent into violence. While the bill was being debated, the ITAK led a sit down protest in front of the Parliament with all the Tamil Members of Parliament participating. Sinhala mobs assaulted the pacific demonstrators and the police had to be brought in to maintain law and order.[137] Ethnic violence flared up in other parts of the country, especially in recent peasant settlements in the Eastern Province with a death toll of about 150 in total.[138]

The first communal riots took place in Ampara, in the Gal Oya settlement where a large number of innocent Tamils were killed.[139] The colonization schemes had 'large contingents of volatile urban elements, thugs and hooligans, henchmen of politicians'.[140] The 'race riots' that took place in the colonization schemes – and in the capital and smaller towns, for that matter – were not spontaneous outbreaks of primordial ethnic hatred. They were incited by external forces who had their own agendas.[141] Tamil resistance to the Official Language Act seemed to have been carefully planned from the beginning in anticipation of violent confrontation. A document submitted to Prime Minister Bandaranaike by security personnel in 1956 claimed that a group of Tamils had an extensive policy of opposition in motion. The document is prescient, if true, in describing the Tamil resistance:

> [T]hrough strikes, attempts at driving Sinhalese out of Tamil-majority areas, boycotting Sinhalese shops, refusing to pay revenue to the government, getting Tamil officers in all government departments to indulge in acts of sabotage, training volunteers to use arms, cutting telephone wires between Colombo and 'Tamil Provinces', derailing trains, representing matters to the Queen, the UNO and the Indian Prime Minister Jawaharlal Nehru and indeed to be ready for acts of violence. Funds were to be collected for this purpose: Members of Parliament were expected to donate a month's salary while Tamil government servants were expected to provide a week's salary and one day's pay in the case of daily paid labourers; Tamil professionals were asked to donate a month's earnings while business magnates were

expected to contribute Rs. 5000.00 each; there were expectations of liberal subscriptions from Ceylon and Indian Tamil Associations in Singapore and Malaya; money was also to be collected through the sale of tickets for raffles and the like.[142]

The authenticity of this document aside, it is a virtual blueprint of Tamil Tiger tactics in the future. Practically all of the acts of coercion and violence mentioned in it have come to pass since 1956 in the well-organized movement to establish a separate Tamil state in Sri Lanka.

As Thangarajah has pointed out, the construction of a 'discriminated and victimised Tamil entity' gave the Tamil leadership 'a politically necessary bargaining position' and the 'anti-national Tamil as constituted by the Tamils themselves' allowed 'later developments such as the opening up of the dry zone for increasing food production' 'to acquire the character of a contest for territory'.[143] Communal violence following the passage of the language bill provided the ITAK the anticipated opportunity to demand Tamil regional autonomy. From then on, political devolution, namely control over the territories of the Northern and the Eastern Provinces, became the primary objective of the Tamil struggle rather than linguistic parity.

From language to territory

During the 1950s, Tamil nationalists began to criticize peasant settlements in the Dry Zone, especially in the Eastern Province, as a form of state-sponsored encroachment of 'Tamil areas' by the Sinhalese. They alleged that since the benefits of settlement went largely to the Sinhalese, it constituted a form of state-sponsored 'discrimination' against the Tamils.[144] In January 1956, before the general elections and the passing of the language bill, Chelvanayakam was arguing that the Sinhalese were 'colonising the rich agricultural districts in Tamil provinces like Gal Oya and Kantalai'.[145]

Indeed, significant changes were occurring in the ethnic composition of the Dry Zone population, especially in the Ampara and Trincomalee districts in the Eastern Province due largely to the Gal Oya scheme in the former and the Kantale and Morawewa peasant settlement schemes in the latter. In the Ampara and Batticoloa Districts, the Sinhala population increased from 5.9 percent to 17.7 percent while the Tamil population declined from 50.3 percent to 46.4 percent and the Muslim population declined from 42.2 percent to 35.1 percent between 1946 and 1971. During the same period, the Sinhala population in Trincomalee district increased from 20.6 percent to 28.8 percent and the Tamil population declined from 44.5 percent to 38.2 percent and the Muslim population increased from 30.5 percent to 32 percent.[146]

For several centuries after the destruction of the ancient Raja Rata irrigation systems after about 12 AD, the only people remaining in those areas were the inhabitants of 'Purana' (ancient) Sinhala villages dependent on slash and burn agriculture. In other words, the areas of state-enforced settlements were not 'traditional Tamil homelands' 'from the dawn of history', as claimed by the Tamil separatists. As C.W. Nichols has shown, for the most part, the Gal Oya scheme, which settled 150,000 Sinhala peasants, was established on the important and ancient Sinhala territorial division known as Dighavapi-Mandala or Dighavapi-Rata.[147]

Ethnic bias and 'Sinhala hegemony' cannot be entirely ruled out as a factor in peasant settlement. Indeed, D.S. Senanayake was keen to reclaim the Sinhala Buddhist civilization of the Raja Rata. As the first Prime Minister, he felt obliged to preserve the territorial integrity and sovereignty of the country in the face of rising Tamil separatism. He wanted to settle Sinhalese in Trincomalee and the hinterland in Padaviya in the north, and in Seruwila and Amapara in the north and the east to block a contiguous and homogenous Tamil speaking area in the north and the east.[148] But destabilization of the ethnic composition of the east was not the predominant factor in the settlement of poverty-stricken Sinhala peasants in the Eastern Province and other parts of the Dry Zone.[149] The real issues were poverty and population growth.

Rapid population growth and lack of agricultural reform worsened the plight of the Sinhala peasantry. Between 1946 and 1953, Sri Lanka's population increased by the highest-ever annual average rate of 2.8 percent.[150] Landless families had increased from 26 percent of all agricultural families to 53 percent by 1962.[151] By the time of independence in 1948, the export sector, namely the plantations, had exploited the agricultural potential of the densely populated Wet Zone almost fully. In contrast, only about 16 percent of the total land area of the Dry Zone had been brought into agricultural use. The Dry Zone, which encompassed the Northern, North Central, and Eastern provinces, constituted less than one-third of the population, but it covered more than two-thirds of the island's land area[152] (Table 2.2). These economic and demographic realities influenced the Six Year Plan adopted in 1948 and subsequent economic strategies that gave priority to opening up land and agricultural development in the Dry Zone and resettlement of landless peasants who happened to be largely Sinhalese. Sinhala opposition to the Tamil demand for a large and exclusive territory was based on the reality of increasing multiculturalism in the rest of the country. The Sinhala Christian prelate Father Tissa Balasuriya voiced this sentiment:

> [O]ver the past two centuries, even prior to 1505, it is the Sinhala areas that have received new comers. Thus the Moors, Malays, Tamils of Indian origin and Ceylon Tamils have all settled down in the Southern half of the country. It is this area that was occupied by the plantations also. Nearly 1.1 million Indian Tamils, 500,000 Moors and Malays and about 400,000–500,000 Ceylon Tamils have made these areas their home. It would seem the Sinhala people have been quite hospitable.[153]

Not heeding these facts, at a party convention held in Trincomalee in August 1956 the ITAK made four explicit demands: 1) adoption of a federal constitution and the creation of 'one or more Tamil linguistic states', 2) absolute parity of status between Sinhala and Tamil languages throughout the country, 3) amendment of citizenship laws to provide Ceylon citizenship to Indian Tamils, 4) 'immediate cessation of colonizing the traditionally Tamil-speaking areas with Sinhalese people'.[154] The ITAK gave an ultimatum to the government and threatened to launch a campaign of non-violent civil disobedience if its demands were not met by 20 August 1957. Clearly, the passage of the Official Language legislation in July 1956 was being used to advance the separatist demand for an exclusive Tamil region.

Eleven months later, pressured by the ultimatum and fearing renewed ethnic violence, Prime Minister Bandaranaike made a pact with the ITAK leader, Chelvanayakam, which came to be known as the 'Bandaranaike–Chelvanayakam Pact'. It offered to establish Tamil speaking Regional Councils and give them power to select allottees and employees in land resettlement schemes. It also agreed to recognize Tamil as a 'national minority language' and the language of administration in the Northern and Eastern Provinces.[155] By agreeing to limit the number of Sinhalese in state settlement sponsored schemes in the Northern and Eastern Provinces, it agreed to maintain Tamil majority status in those regions. It conceded to the 'traditional Tamil homelands' demand by giving extensive authority to the regional councils over land development, 'colonization' agriculture, education and other matters. Moreover, it allowed the Regional Councils in the North and the East, to expand areas under their control by amalgamating with each other, thereby creating the basis for a separate Tamil administrative unit.[156]

Given mounting pressures from Sinhala nationalists against the Pact, Bandaranaike abrogated it in April 1958. That led to a mass civil disobedience movement by the ITAK focusing on the use of the Sinhala letter 'sri' on vehicle license plates in the north. Sri means resplendent in both Sinhala and Tamil, but the commonality between the languages and the people were forgotten in

Table 2.2 Population density by province (per square km), 1946–2001

Province	% Area*	1946	1953	1963	1971	1981	2001
Northern	13.4	54.0	64.2	83.5	98.4	128	126
Eastern	14.9	28.1	35.6	65.1	85.4	101	151
North-West	12.0	85.5	109.5	147.9	179.8	220	287
North-Central	16.3	13.4	22.1	36.7	51.5	81	114
Uva	13.0	43.9	55.0	65.2	80.5	109	141
Sabaragamuwa	7.6	152.1	182.2	229.4	268.5	302	363
Western	5.7	506.1	601.9	765.4	917.2	1,072	1,492
Central	3.6	191.4	230.4	303.6	349.4	360	433
South	8.5	172.9	203.2	257.4	289.9	341	423
Sri Lanka	100.0	101.5	123.4	161.3	193.5	230	299

Sources: Indra Gajanayake, 'Ethnic Conflict in Sri Lanka: A Demographic Perspective', UNV/WIDER Project on Social Change in Sri Lanka, 20 March 1989, table 3; Sri Lanka Department of Census and Statistics 1946, 1971, 1981 and provisional estimates for 2001.

Note
* Percentage Area as given for 1981.

manipulating a power struggle over sovereignty and political authority. Appapillai Amirthalingam, an ITAK parliamentary member, argued that the Sinhala 'sri' symbolized 'a slavery which every self-respecting Tamil is not prepared to tolerate in his territory'. Professor Suntherlingam threatened that 'if the Sinhalese will not agree to federation, the Tamils will have a fully autonomous Tamil linguistic State by whatever means they can get it, by all methods of history – rebellion, guerilla warfare or anything else you please'.[157]

These incendiary remarks and the 'anti-sri' campaign in the north led to a counter response against Tamil lettering on street signs and name boards in the predominantly Sinhala areas, especially, Colombo.[158] The result was renewed communal violence and the horrific 'race riots' of 1958 which led to a death toll of between 500–600.[159] Again, the rioting began in the colonization settlements, but this time spread more widely. Sinhalese and Tamils were both aggressors and victims. Extremist politicians from both groups fanned the seeds of ethnic hatred and lack of responsible leadership on both sides allowed the violence to spread. Sinhalese burnt down Tamil homes and businesses in the Colombo area while Tamils destroyed Sinhala homes and Buddhist temples in the Jaffna region, including the sacred Nagadipa temple. Ethnic cleansing ensued with thousands of Tamils being forced out of the predominantly Sinhala areas and thousands of Sinhalese expelled from the predominantly Tamil areas.[160]

Like previous and subsequent riots in Sri Lanka, the 1958 riots were not spontaneous outbursts of primordial hatred. As reporter Tarzie Vittachi observed, most of the Sinhalese rioters in the new settlements colonies were not the established settlers. They were mostly imported government laborers and newly arrived squatters without roots in those locales.[161] Likewise, Tamil rioting in the north including the desecration of the Nagadipa Buddhist temple was not the result of a spontaneous outburst. It is believed to have been the result of 'premeditated and planned' action by 'powerful behind-the-scenes-interests'.[162] As the rioting spread, both the Sinhalese and the Tamils became more and more frustrated with the leaders. They lost faith in the Bandaranaike government's ability to maintain law and order. Many Tamil refugees blamed their plight on the ambitions and provocations of the Tamil politicians. During the latter days of the 1958 riots, the attacks were directed noticeably against government officials and the middle class. Finally, an emergency was declared.[163]

After normality returned, Prime Minister Bandaranaike took efforts to quell the tide of communal violence unleashed by his own government's hastily enacted policies. He introduced a Bill for the 'Reasonable Use of Tamil' – Tamil Language (Special Provisions) Act No. 28 of 1958 – to allay Tamil linguistic grievances. This bill, approved by a vote of 46 to 3, contained safeguards for the use of Tamil which had been part of the original draft of the Official Language Bill of 1956. The safeguards did not include any new rights, but simply sought to give legality to existing rights even under the Official Language Bill of 1956.[164] Although the regulations necessary for implementation of the bill were prepared, they were not put in place due to the political instability following the assassination of Bandaranaike in September 1959 by one Somarama, who had recently entered the Buddhist order.[165] The shocking event made many Buddhists ambivalent about political monks, and allowed those opposed to Sinhala Buddhist nationalism to cast it as a dangerous and retrograde political force.

Failure of the Tamil satyagraha led some disillusioned ITAK activists to give up Gandhian tactics and seek militant struggle to establish a separate Tamil state. Indian journalist, Narayan Swamy has traced the origin of the armed Sri Lankan Tamil struggle to the formation of the Pulip Padai (The Army of Tigers) in August 1961 and its association with the ITAK from inception.

> Some 20 men associated with the Federal [ITAK] Party ... decided after long deliberations to form an underground group to fight for a separate state. Most of them were civil servants ... At a meeting in Colombo they christened their group Pulip Padai (Army of Tigers). A springing tiger was chosen as its insignia.... Some members ... succeeded ... in influencing the decisions of the Federal Party. One section floated a trawler company in Colombo to facilitate smuggling of arms should the need arise.[166]

When the ITAK decided to join the UNP in the 1965 elections, the Pulip Padai was broken up and eventually withered away. However, as Swamy notes, many of its activists remained strong advocates of a separate nation state.[167] The abandonment of both the anti-Hindi linguistic and secessionist struggles in Tamil Nadu during this period strengthened the resolve of Tamil nationalists to fight for Tamil as an official language and a homeland for Tamils on the Sri Lankan island instead. In a sense, after the adoption of the 16th Amendment to the Indian Constitution strongly banning secession from the Indian Union, India's South Indian/Tamil 'problem' was transferred to Sri Lanka.[168]

In January 1966 the UNP introduced the Tamil Language (Special Provisions) Regulations, encompassing all the safeguards spelled out in the Act No. 28 of 1958, which had been put forward previously by the SLFP. The safeguards allowed Tamils to use their language in correspondence with government departments and local government bodies and for all administrative purposes in the Northern and Eastern Provinces; to use Tamil in schools, in the universities and during public examinations throughout the island with the provision that Tamil entrants into the public service would gain proficiency in Sinhala without 'undue hardship'.[169] While the UNP made headway on the Indian Tamil citizenship and Tamil language issues, it was not able to do so on the more controversial devolution question.

Prior to the 1965 elections, the UNP leader, Dudley Senanayake, had come to an agreement with the ITAK leader, Chelvanayakam, regarding devolution, which later came to be known as the 'Dudley–Chelvanayakam Pact'. Given its explosive ethno-political implications, the Pact had been kept secret during the 1965 elections. Senanayake had agreed to make Tamil the language of administration in the Northern and Eastern Provinces and to devolve power to District Councils. Furthermore, he had agreed that in the state-aided colonization schemes in the Northern and Eastern Provinces, land would first be granted to landless persons in those districts; secondly, to Tamil speakers in the Northern and Eastern Provinces and thirdly, to other citizens of Ceylon with preference given to Tamil citizens in the rest of the island.[170] This pact too had conceded to the 'traditional Tamil homelands' concept like the earlier Bandaranaike–Chelvanayakam Pact. However, given formidable Sinhala as well as Muslim opposition, even the watered down District Council Bill of 1968 to devolve power to district units was abrogated before a draft bill could be issued.[171]

Unmet economic needs of the masses rather than concessions made to the Tamil minority on the language and citizenship issues were the foremost reasons for increasing unpopularity of the right wing UNP government with the Sinhala majority. By the end of the UNP's term in the late 1960s, there was 'unprecedented nation-wide dissatisfaction and militancy'.[172] The United Front (UF) coalition of the SLFP and the Marxist LSSP and the CP (Moscow) came into power in 1970 promising to combat unemployment through socialist policies.[173] The UF government was the first since independence to win a two-thirds majority in the parliament without the support of Tamil political parties.[174] This weakened the position of the Tamil political leadership and in a further setback, prominent ITAK members who raised the separatist cry – including Amirthalingam – lost their seats and Chelvanayakam returned only through a plurality of votes.[175] However, the popularity of the new government was short-lived. Unable to satisfy the rising expectations of their youthful supporters, or even to meet the basic food needs of the country, the UF coalition was soon confronting massive discontent, which fuelled armed insurgencies, first by Sinhala and then by Tamil youth. The country entered a new phase of armed violence and the militant separatist struggle.

3   From class struggle to ethnic separatism, 1971–1977

The preoccupation with Tamil elite concerns drew attention away from the massive social and economic problems facing the young in all of the Sri Lankan communities. To rise above the bipolar Sinhala versus Tamil analysis, it is necessary to look at the economic grievances that the youth from both the Sinhala Buddhist majority and the Sri Lankan Tamil minority had in common. Rather than joining in a common cause, however, their grievances gave rise to divergent movements given differential responses by elites of the two communities.

From 1960 to 1977, Sri Lanka spent nearly 10 percent of GNP annually on its welfare programs including the expansion of education. Though these programs enabled the country to surpass many other Asian countries in measurements of human development, Sri Lanka lagged behind in economic growth.[1] The sluggish economy could not meet the rising expectations of educated rural youth seeking urban administrative positions, jobs which provided higher salaries and an elite life style. The combination of the demographic and the educational 'explosions' resulted in a dramatic rise in the island's educated – but unemployed – population.

Educated but unemployed

As a result of free education, by the late 1960s Sri Lanka had achieved near-universal literacy, a remarkable achievement for an ex-colony in the South Asian region.[2] In order to widen opportunities for higher education and prestigious careers, university education was made available in the Sinhala and Tamil languages starting in 1959, resulting in a tripling of university enrollments. The change in instructional languages and the expansion of the university system benefited the rural Sinhala Buddhist in quantitative, but not qualitative, terms.[3] The Sinhala Buddhist students were overwhelmingly concentrated in social studies and humanities departments, not in the science programs that could lead to lucrative careers. A working knowledge of English continued to be necessary to enter the more prestigious scientific fields in the university, the private sector, and the higher echelons of the state sector. Until the late 1960s the overwhelming majority of students admitted to the science faculties were examined in

English. Given their superior access to English, Tamils were able to claim a disproportionate number of places in those faculties, nearly 50 percent in Medicine and Engineering in 1969–1970 (Table 3.1).

Charges of Tamil favoritism led the government to introduce language-based affirmative action that came to be called 'standardization', a policy to admit 'a politically-acceptable ratio of Tamil to Sinhalese students' in the engineering, medicine and other science faculties of the University of Ceylon in 1970 – that is, before the JVP insurrection.[4] The standardization policy abandoned the merit principle in favor of a preferential system that required higher marks for Tamil-language students than for Sinhala-language students to qualify to enter the university science faculties.[5] For example, for the medical faculty, a score of 250 was required for Tamil-language candidates, and 229 for Sinhala-language candidates.[6] In practice, the actual impact of differential qualifying marks for Tamil and Sinhala students was 'relatively small', causing only a slight drop in the percentage of Tamils in the science faculties from 1971 to 1972 but an absolute increase in their numbers in the same period.

The standardization policy stipulated that the number of students qualifying in each language be proportionate to the number sitting for examination in that medium.[7] As C.R. de Silva has explained, 'The Sri Lankan Tamils, though they constituted just 11.1 percent of the population, provided about 30 percent of the science students and the scheme of standardization ensured that this proportion of places in the University accrued to them'.[8] Despite this continued advantage, the Tamil political leadership vehemently opposed the standardization scheme, which in principle was designed to whittle down the advantages previously enjoyed by Ceylon Tamils. However, Sinhala nationalists and a group of Sinhala officials in the Ministry of Education firmly believed that an adjusting mechanism was necessary for disadvantaged Sinhala students to compete for coveted places in the science faculties.[9] In 1974 the controversial language-wise standardization was modified when a district-based affirmative action policy was introduced. Ethnically based animosities generated by affirmative action persist to the present day, even though language-based standardization was completely discarded in 1977.

The sense of deprivation and disillusionment with the state and the ruling class was 'much greater among the Sinhalese youths than among youths belonging to the ethnic minorities because their expectations had been much greater'.[10] The best jobs still went to the well-connected, English-speaking elite, and this contributed to a hardening of social class boundaries within the Sinhala community.[11] Government policies that were meant to benefit the Sinhala majority in fact backfired, resulting in massive discontent and ultimately a violent insurrection. The 1971 JVP insurrection is considered unique in the history of modern revolutions, representing the first occasion when 'an organized youth movement in a country, with no outside assistance, sought to seize state power by violence'.[12]

Table 3.1 University science faculty admissions, 1969–1977: by ethnicity (percentages)

Course of study	1969–1970			1970–1971			1975			1976			1977		
	Sinhala	Tamil	Muslim	Sinhala	Tamil	Muslim	Sinhala	Tamil	Muslim	Sinhala	Tamil	Muslim	Sinhala	Tamil	Muslim
*Phys, Sc., Bio-Sc. and Architecture	69.7	27.6	2.1	68.0	28.6	1.8	77.3	19.5	3.2	72.9	24.6	2.2	73.0	23.1	3.4
Engineering	51.7	48.3	–	55.9	40.8	2.0	83.4	14.2	2.4	76.1	22.4	1.1	79.5	19.1	1.4
Medicine	48.9	48.9	0.9	53.5	40.9	2.4	78.9	17.4	3.2	65.8	30.4	2.9	68.0	27.8	3.7
Dental Surgery	52.4	38.1	9.5	41.5	56.1	2.4	66.0	32.0	2.0	56.0	40.0	4.0	76.0	24.0	–
Agriculture	44.7	47.4	5.3	53.5	39.5	4.7	73.5	23.5	2.9	74.0	21.9	3.1	74.5	23.5	2.0
**Vet. Science	27.7	66.7	–	71.4	23.8	4.8	71.0	29.0	–	46.7	46.7	–	55.7	44.8	–
Total Science	57.7	39.8	1.6	60.6	35.3	2.2	78.0	19.0	2.9	71.3	25.9	2.7	73.3	23.6	2.8

Source: C.R. de Silva, 'The Politics of University Admissions: A Review of Some Aspects of the Admission Policy in Sri Lanka 1971–1978', *Sri Lanka Journal of Social Sciences*, 1978, I (2), pp. 85–123, Table 1.

Notes
* Physical Science and Biological Science.
** Veterinary Science.

JVP insurrection

Notwithstanding ideological differences, the leadership of the major Sinhala political parties on the right and left and the Sri Lankan Tamil parties all came from 'elite ranks, almost without exception'.[13] In this class context, the Janatha Vimukthi Peramuna (JVP), or People's Liberation Front – led by Rohana Wijeweera, who is considered to be the first Sri Lankan politician to come from a non-elitist 'village background' – was able to penetrate the rural areas and reach the new class of Sinhala educated, unemployed youth.[14]

The JVP's Marxist ideology was directed primarily against the Sri Lankan state and the Sinhala ruling class, not at the ethnic Other, and an explicitly Buddhist nationalism was absent from JVP doctrine.[15] The party did not bring charges against the indigenous Sri Lankan Tamil population, nor did the Tamil ethnic issue and separatist claims in the north and east play a role either in JVP ideology or the insurrection of 1971.[16] Still, as British journalist Fred Halliday and other leftist commentators have noted, the JVP's attacks on Indian expansionism, including Indian estate workers and foreign mercantilist control of sectors of the economy, roused anti-Tamil feelings among 'less politically formed followers', preventing class solidarity across the Sinhala–Tamil ethnic divide.[17]

By early 1971 the JVP had over 100,000 members, many of them operating in small cells around the country.[18] Criticizing the UF coalition and the evils of the capitalist system, Wijeweera publicly ordered JVP members to arm themselves against possible state repression.[19] Given the unprecedented threats to order and democracy posed by the JVP, the government declared an emergency and a curfew, giving the police and the army 'full powers of arbitrary arrest and disposal of bodies without having to carryout inquests or inform the relatives of those killed'.[20] As later became evident, the carte blanche given to the armed forces led to widespread intra-ethnic killing among Sinhala Buddhists.

JVP attacks on police and other government installations started on 5 April 1971, and spread over the next few days. But 'the uprising was ruthlessly crushed in a relatively short time'.[21] The Sri Lankan government received crucial military and financial assistance from a curious mix of foreign powers: Britain, India, Pakistan, Egypt, Australia, the US, the Soviet Union, Yugoslavia, and China. In addition to weapons and equipment sent by these countries, India sent 100 Indian Peace Keeping (IPK) Gurkha soldiers to guard the Katunayaka airport. Later Sri Lankan governments have not received such open and immediate international military support to crush the Tamil insurgencies because of the international sympathy for minority grievances and the powerful international Tamil separatist lobby.[22]

Despite strict censorship, news of the ill treatment of political detainees and horrific killings by both the JVP and the security forces came to light. It is believed that extra-judicial executions were carried out regularly in the Dadalla cemetery in the Galle area, where police shot prisoners after ordering them to dig their own graves. In one instance 16 youths who were suspected JVP insurgents, many of whom had merely attended JVP lectures, were shot down this way.[23] French reporter Rene Dumont reported seeing corpses float down rivers and that 'the police who had killed them let bodies float downstream to terrorize the population'.[24] Estimates of security personnel, JVP insurgents, and civilians killed in the 1971 insurgency have varied widely from as low as 1,200 to as high as 50,000.[25]

Of the 10,192 persons detained after the April 1971 JVP insurrection, the overwhelming majority were young Sinhala Buddhist males from relatively low socio-economic backgrounds in the 16–32 age range. Caste was also a factor in the JVP insurrection as it would be in the subsequent Tamil youth insurrection. Of 41 alleged insurgent leaders put on trial before the Criminal Justice Commission after the suppression of the insurgency, 14 were karava, four were vahumpura, and one was batgam, while only 11 were from the leading govi caste, which is assumed to include about half the Sinhalese population. The most intense and prolonged fighting during the insurrection and police and military brutality occurred in large scale against insurgents of lower caste, generating much fear in their villages in the southwestern coastal region.[26]

Declining to pursue criminal proceedings within the existing judicial system, the government passed the Criminal Justice Commission Act on 6 April 1972, by a two-thirds majority in parliament.[27] The CJC Act, was described by its critics as a 'retroactive ... sadistic and oppressive piece of legislation' because among other things it allowed the admissibility of confessions made to police (often under duress), acceptance of accomplice evidence without corroboration and the acceptance of hearsay evidence.[28] A total of 390 activists were sentenced to varying numbers of years of rigorous imprisonment. Many sentences were later commuted and all the JVP activists including Wijeweera, were released and the CJC Act repealed in 1977 after the UNP government came to power.[29] Many of the economic grievances and state repression facing the Tamil youth in the late 1970s were similar to those of their Sinhala counterparts, but the Tamil struggle, which was spearheaded by the Tamil elite, took on a distinctly ethnic and secessionist character as opposed to a class struggle.

Socialist response: employment and education

Shaken by the JVP insurrection, the UF government sought to both tighten its political control and to speed reform to move the country in a socialist direction by addressing the vexing problems in education and employment. These concerns were incorporated in a new constitution intended to provide the foundation for a new, more egalitarian and progressive society.[30] With the introduction of the Constitution of May 1972, using the UF's two-thirds majority in parliament, Ceylon became the Socialist Republic of Sri Lanka.[31]

Employment

Extending its term of office by two years through the new constitution, the UF government introduced a Five Year Plan with the objective to 'provide employment to rural youth'.[32] The constitution pledged to establish a socialist democracy providing full employment, distribute social product equally among citizens through adoption of a mixed economic framework, national control of key sectors of the economy, collective forms of ownership, ceilings on land ownership, income and the like. State control was extended to every sector of the economy, including trade, industry, and the local and foreign-owned plantations which brought in two-thirds of the island's foreign exchange. The Land Reform Act introduced in 1972 placed restrictions on land-holdings and house ownership.[33] Believed to have nationalized nearly one-fourth of the agricultural land on the island, the UF had plans to extend collective agriculture as an alternative to peasant colonization in the Dry Zone. In reality, the government made little headway on these controversial plans.[34]

The democratic socialist policies did not bring the expected benefits for the masses or the educated unemployed, the peasantry, or the urban or estate workers. There were serious problems in the operation of the redistribution programs. Restrictions on private initiative curbed economic growth and the creation of new employment. Nationalization of tea plantations and political interference led to a decline in international competitiveness and a loss of the market share of Ceylon tea.[35] Instead of achieving greater freedom from international capital and financial institutions, the country accumulated more international debt. To deal with the foreign exchange crisis, restrictions were placed on the import of basic necessities such as rice, other food stuffs, and cloth, and these were rationed by the state, creating a situation of endemic scarcity. A top-heavy system dependent on the state and political patronage became entrenched. The Sri Lankan economy became 'a highly restricted and regulated or closed economy': the growth rate fell below 3 percent, and unemployment rose to almost one quarter of the labor force in 1976.[36]

All ethnic groups were affected by the overall lack of growth and unemployment, and competition between groups increased for scarce resources and opportunities. Instead of addressing these problems, the government tried to meet the needs of disaffected Sinhala rural youth after the aborted JVP insurrection by introducing a new affirmative action policy – a district quota system for entry into the university science faculties. A consideration of this system reveals the limitations of the bipolar Sinhala south versus Tamil north model in understanding complex social class, intra-ethnic issues in a pluralistic society.

Education: the district quota system

The language-based standardization policy in education having failed, the socialist government turned to a geographically based policy for university admission – the district quota system. Places in coveted university science faculties had been going largely to students from the more 'advanced' Western and Northern provinces, which had facilities for science and English medium education. Even after the 'language-wise standardization' policy, the five provinces where the Kandyan Sinhalese were concentrated (Central, Uva, Sabaragamuwa,

North Central, South Western provinces), which accounted for 47 percent of the island's total population, gained only 19 percent of places in science courses in 1973.[37] Like the Kandyans, the Moor/Malay group also lagged behind in education.

The Kandyans and the Muslims, however, were influential in the UF government. Mrs Bandaranaike, the prime minister, was herself a Kandyan, and the Minister of Education, Badi-ud-din Mahmud, was the leader of the Islamic Socialist Front. As a result, the long-neglected Kandyan and Muslim concerns guided the socialist government's introduction of the new district quota system in 1973 for advancing regional equality, which allocated university places in proportion to the total population resident in each district and was aimed at increasing the representation of the Kandyan areas, the Batticoloa area where the Moors were concentrated, and the populous unrepresented rural areas in general. The Sinhalese as a group benefited substantially from the district quota system. Their proportion in the university science, engineering, and medicine faculties increased to the highest ever by 1975 (Table 3.1). As the Sinhalese were also 85 percent of the students in the Arts faculties, they 'now gained a predominant position in the University comparable to the position of their political leaders in the legislature', provoking Tamil charges of Sinhala hegemony.[38]

Under the Muslim Minister of Education, a specific refinement of the district quota system was introduced to favor the Muslim community by considering district of birth rather than residence allowing a greater number of university places for Muslims from 'backward' areas like the east.[39] These complexities are overlooked when university admissions policies are viewed within the dominant framework of Sinhala versus Tamil dualism. Sinhala politicians who saw Tamil demands as 'imperious' were more amenable to allowing concessions to Muslims, who were seen as a more accommodating and 'less threatening' minority.[40] Muslim students benefited greatly from the district quota system, their number in science faculties doubling between 1970 and 1975 (Tables 3.1 and 3.2). Due to the new educational opportunities, a large number of Muslims from families traditionally engaged in trade, business, cultivation and fishing were able to become doctors, engineers, accountants and lawyers, raising the economic status of the Muslim community.[41]

The improved economic competitiveness of Muslims threatened the traditional advantages of the Sri Lankan Tamil minority, as well as separatist claims to the north and east, where Muslims are a significant population. As political scientist Mansoor Fazil has observed, the divergence in the experiences of the two minorities lies in two contrasting approaches to success: advancement within the Sri Lankan political system on the part of the Muslims and secession on the part of the Sri Lankan Tamils.[42]

Though the district quota system helped students in certain rural areas, it did not benefit students from the most backward areas that lacked facilities for science education. For example, predominantly Sinhala districts, such as Hambantota, Polonnaruwa, and Moneragala, could not take most of the places reserved for them in the science faculties due to lack of educational facilities.[43]

Table 3.2 University admissions: candidates obtaining minimum requirement not selected, by district and ethnicity,* 1975 and 1976

District	Biological science 1975			Biological science 1976			Physical science 1975			Physical science 1976		
	Sinhala	Tamil	Muslim	Sinhala	Tamil	Muslim	Sinhala	Tamil	Muslim	Sinhala	Tamil	Muslim
Kegalle	17	–	–	51	–	–	25	–	–	25	–	1
Ratnapura	5	2	–	5	–	–	10	2	–	4	–	–
Anuradhapura	2	–	–	1	–	–	5	1	–	–	–	–
Polonnaruwa	4	–	–	–	–	–	2	–	–	–	–	–
Galle	69	–	–	124	–	–	56	–	–	118	–	1
Matara	26	–	–	73	–	–	22	–	2	39	–	3
Hambantota	7	1	–	4	–	1	7	–	–	–	–	–
Badulla	2	–	–	2	–	–	7	–	–	2	–	–
Moneragala	1	–	–	1	–	–	2	1	–	–	–	–
Kurunegala	23	–	1	57	–	–	8	–	–	27	–	3
Puttalam	7	4	1	16	–	–	18	1	1	22	1	–
Matale	15	3	–	24	1	3	11	–	3	36	–	–
Kandy	63	9	8	–	–	–	46	4	–	–	–	–
Nuwara Eliya	3	2	–	74	19	7	4	1	–	36	19	9
Jaffna	–	329	–	8	359	11	–	192	–	4	374	4
Vavuniya	2	8	–	2	–	–	1	2	–	–	–	–
Mannar	–	2	–	–	2	–	–	–	–	–	–	–
Batticaloa	–	5	–	1	15	1	–	12	1	1	20	–
Trincomalee	–	7	–	1	2	–	1	5	–	–	–	–
Ampara	1	–	–	–	1	–	1	2	1	–	–	–
Kalutara	26	1	2	68	–	1	49	–	3	62	1	–
Colombo	380	74	9	452	95	9	216	34	4	198	30	12
Total	653	447	21	964	494	33	491	257	15	574	445	33
Percentage	57.94%	39.66%	1.86%	64.35%	32.98%	2.20%	64.10%	33.55%	1.96%	54.15%	41.96%	3.11%

Source: C.R. de Silva, 'The Politics of University Admissions: A Review of Some Aspects of the Admission Policy in Sri Lanka 1971–1978', *Sri Lanka Journal of Social Sciences*, 1978, I (2), pp. 85–123, Tables 4 and 7.

Note
* Less than 1% belonging to other ethnic groups not included.

In the meantime, well-qualified students from the 'advanced' areas were shut out due to the restricted quotas imposed upon them (Table 3.2).[44]

For the Tamils from the Jaffna and Colombo districts, the district quota system was a major blow. In 1974, the absolute numbers of Tamils entering the science faculties dropped for the first time,[45] and in 1975 the percentage of Tamils in all the science faculties fell to an all-time low (Table 3.1). Although these percentages were still higher than their proportion in the population, such declining opportunities were understandably of grave concern to the Tamils, specifically the educated Jaffna vellala caste. The feeling that they were being openly discriminated against was a major factor in the alienation and increasing radicalization of Tamil youth.[46] The Sri Lankan Tamil leadership, which interpreted all developments through a narrow Sinhala versus Tamil lens, agitated against the district quota system as a policy of Sinhala state discrimination against Tamils replacing open competition.

Class divides

The gains and losses from the district quota policy were experienced differently *within* the Sinhala and Tamil communities as well as *between* the communities revealing class divides within them. For example, the policy had a negative impact on students from the educationally advanced Jaffna district and its dominant vellala caste, and a beneficial effect on Tamil students from relatively backward districts such as Batticoloa and Trincomalee. In the long run, the district quota system helped improved access to Tamil students from the Eastern Province and from the hill country plantation areas. In fact, more Sinhalese students from Colombo meeting minimum marks to enter the science faculties were kept out of the universities because of the district quota system than Tamil students from Jaffna and Colombo put together. In 1975, island-wide, of all students who obtained the minimum marks to enter the university, but lost the chance to enter the biological science and physical science faculties 58 percent and 64 percent were Sinhala students as opposed 40 percent and 34 percent Tamil students. In 1976, the comparable figures were 64 percent and 54 percent for the Sinhalese and 33 percent and 42 percent for the Tamils (Table 3.2).

In effect, district wise standardization was not directed explicitly at Tamils, but at urban elite privilege.[47] Interpreting standardization exclusively as anti-Tamil discrimination, however, the Tamil elite mobilized Tamil youth discontent along the Sinhala versus Tamil divide rather than seeking solidarity with their Sinhala elite counterparts. Sinhalese elites had not opposed language-based standardization which favored them, but now, losing out to their rural counterparts, educated, influential Sinhalese from Colombo and other urban areas strongly opposed the district quota system as iniquitous. Their pressure led to reviews of the policies and the adoption of a new, complicated policy for university admissions in 1976. According to the new policy, 70 percent of admissions were to be based on 'raw marks' gained by the students. The remaining 30 percent were to be selected according to district although 15 percent of that were to be reserved for ten backwards districts (Ampara, Anuradhapura, Badulla, Hambantota, Mannar, Moneragala, Nuwara Eliya, Polonnaruwa, Trincomalee and Vauniya).[48]

In 1977, the last year of the UF government's term in office, Tamil numbers and percentages in university science faculties improved significantly from the all-time low of 1975, although they did not reach the exceedingly high levels that had prevailed prior to 1970. Even without government intervention via the language-based standardization policy and the district quota system, Tamil percentages in the science faculties would have come down gradually over time, given demographic changes and increased competition between groups. Instead of taking greater initiatives to provide well-equipped schools and English language facilities needed for science education to the backward rural areas, the UF government took the seemingly easier route of reverse discrimination against privileged Tamils and urban Sinhalese.

The government's purported effort to speed up the democratization of science education backfired, creating a highly volatile and emotional ethnic issue. The sense of grievance and educational discrimination felt by the Tamils persisted providing the Tamil separatist leaders ammunition for ethnically based youth mobilization against the Sri Lankan state. And the decreased access to the university in the 1970s was compounded by Tamil loss of privileged access to state employment since the introduction of the Sinhala language policy in 1956.

Jobs: state employment

The relatively strong position of the Tamils in the professional occupations, such as medicine, engineering and accountancy was maintained up to the 1960s, if not later. However, a confluence of factors – Sinhala language policy, increased competition from rural Sinhalese, political patronage favoring the Sinhalese, and demographic change – caused the overall percentages of Tamils in the administrative services to drop (Table 2.2). Due to seniority held by those recruited in earlier years, there were still 'proportionally more Tamils ... in the higher occupational categories' in the early 1980s.[49]

Loss of their disproportionate access to state services represented more than a change in economic and political circumstances for the Ceylon Tamils, and Jaffna vellalas in particular. It signified a major psychological shift. English-educated Tamil professionals could not accommodate themselves to transformation in the post-colonial era and being replaced by the vernacular-educated Sinhalese: 'The subsequent sense of betrayal was strong and deep'.[50] The Sinhalese saw the changes 'as reversing the discrimination they had been subjected to in the past', while the Tamils felt that they were being deliberately discriminated against.[51] As educational opportunities became restricted to the vernacular-educated Tamil youth population, it was possible to mobilize them into a strong anti-Sinhalese Tamil nationalist movement.[52] As A.J. Wilson put it, 'the option for the Tamils of working within the framework of "Sinhalese first" and reconciling themselves to second-class status was never seriously considered; they found it objectionable and overwhelmingly rejected it'.[53]

Unlike the Sri Lankan Tamil politicians, Muslim leaders collaborated with the post-independence Sinhala governments to advance Muslim education at every opportunity, emerging ahead of the Sri Lankan Tamils.[54] The common focus on the Sinhala–Tamil conflict has overlooked the increasing competition and conflict between the Sri Lankan Tamils and Muslims and its role in the separatist struggle over the Northern and Eastern Provinces.

Thwarted aspirations

In the face of a severe economic crisis and the shortage of basic consumer goods, rising aspirations for employment and mobility of all groups were thwarted. Like the rural Sinhala youth of the JVP, Tamil youth in the North were increasingly frustrated with, and alienated from, successive governments in Colombo. Both groups wanted greater opportunities for education, employment, and political participation.[55]

The mobilization of discontent on explicitly ethnic lines mitigated against the emergence of a unified movement – a coalition that spanned ethnic boundaries – for social change. In the case of the Tamils, cultural marginalization and declining access to political patronage heightened the problem.[56] What began as an elite movement of the westernized Tamil elite based mostly in Colombo was transformed into a mass movement due to the increasing influence of a broader Tamil culture. Jayasekara and Amerasinghe point out that

> [F]rom the early 1950s several factors helped the emergence of a Tamil consciousness deeper than represented by this [ITAK] elite ... inspired by South Indian culture. This development in addition to increasing economic difficulties and unemployment, particularly among those educated in Tamil, broadened the base of the movement. The non-cooperation movement of the 1960s and the harsh government reactions it roused contributed to mobilization of the broader Tamil masses.[57]

When criminal youth gangs in the north came together with the disaffected Tamil students and the ideologically based separatist movement led by the TUF in the early 1970s, the violent secessionist struggle was born. Unlike the Sinhala elite who ruthlessly crushed the revolt of the lower class and caste Sinhala JVP youth, the Tamil elite, who did not have the reins of state power, encouraged and supported the insurrection of Tamil lower class and caste youth against the Sri Lankan state.[58] Maintenance of their own political legitimacy compelled identification with the growing youth rebellion. However, as in secessionist movements elsewhere, the elite envisioned the creation of a separate state where they would rule, while the poor youth were expected to make most of the sacrifice. It was the introduction of the new constitution in 1972 that the Tamil political elite used to launch the struggle for a separate state.

1972 constitution

The new constitution abrogated the preceding colonial Soulbury Constitution which derived authority from the British Crown and parliament.[59] The country's colonial name, Ceylon, was replaced with Lanka, a term used in ancient Indian epics over Sihale, the pre-colonial name which claimed the island as the land of the Sinhala people.[60] This choice of name reflected the need to incorporate ethnic and linguistic minorities. Notwithstanding the choice of an inclusive name, the nationalism espoused in the new constitution was distinctly Sinhala Buddhist. The constitution stated: 'The Republic of Sri Lanka shall give to Buddhism the foremost place and accordingly it shall be the duty of the State to protect and foster Buddhism' while assuring that every citizen shall have the right to freedom of thought.[61] This clause was meant to uphold state patronage of Buddhism which had prevailed since the arrival of Buddhism in the island in 3 BC, and the Kandyan Convention of 1815 whereby the British agreed to govern maintaining and protecting the institutions of Buddhism.[62] Given that western democratic states such as the US and Britain give allegiance to a Christian God, Sri Lanka's stated allegiance to both democracy and Buddhism is not entirely unique.[63] Sri Lanka did not become a Buddhist state along the lines of other Theravada Buddhist countries such as Burma or Thailand.[64] The constitution explicitly upheld freedom of thought, conscience and religion, including the freedom to practice, teach and adopt a religion or belief of choice. Thus, it allowed room for religious proselytization, a freedom not available in many Islamic and other states.[65]

However, the clause in the Soulbury Constitution relating to minority rights was left out of the new constitution. In its place the 1972 Constitution incorporated the Chapter on Fundamental Rights and Freedoms granting equality for all persons before the law, prohibiting discrimination in employment on the basis of religion, race, caste and gender, protecting life and personal liberty, allowing freedom of speech and peaceful assembly and association, freedom of movement and residence, etc. However, the constitution subjected fundamental rights and freedoms to wide ranging restrictions 'in the interest of national unity and integrity, national security, national economy, public safety, public order'.[66] These restrictions reflected the government's determination to tighten control following the suppression of the JVP insurrection. The 1972 Constitution also asserted that 'The Republic of Sri Lanka is a Unitary State'.[67] Such an assertion is not unique to the island; the constitutions of other countries such as India and Norway too contain clauses against secession and divisibility.

The strongest opposition to the new Constitution came from the ITAK.[68] It criticized the special status given to Buddhism and reaffirmations of the Official Language Act of 1956 as deliberate attempts to reduce Tamil culture and language to a subordinate status. The Tamil leadership was understandably incensed by the UF government's refusal to incorporate the Provisions of the 1966 Tamil Language Regulations passed by the previous UNP administration in the 1972 Constitution. The assertion of a unitary state in the new Sri Lankan

Constitution thwarted the federalist, if not, separatist aspirations of the Sri Lankan Tamil leadership.[69] When an amendment to the 1972 Constitution proposed by the ITAK to make both Sinhala and Tamil the official languages was defeated, the ITAK members walked out of the Constituent Assembly on 28 June 1971. Of the 19 elected Tamil representatives 15 boycotted the Assembly when the constitution was adopted on 22 May 1972.[70]

Tamil fears of being reduced to a subordinate status intensified, and the ITAK led the cry for separation. Opposition to the new constitution brought together the two main Tamil political parties, the ITAK and the Tamil Congress, for the first time since 1948. Together with the Ceylon Workers' Congress of Indian Tamil plantation workers, they formed the Tamil United Front (TUF, later to become TULF) on 4 May 1972, and openly advocated a separate state for the Tamil-speaking areas of the Northern and Eastern provinces.[71] The separatist cause also became inspired by regional and global changes. The creation of the new secessionist state of Bangladesh in 1971 also strengthened the resolve of Chelvanayakam and Tamil nationalists to fight for a Tamil state on the island.[72] The ITAK 'held a rousing commemoration of the birth of Bangladesh in the Jaffna Town Hall. People began to dream of India carving out a new Tamil nation in Ceylon'.[73] Like regionalization, the internationalization of the Sri Lankan Sinhala–Tamil conflict began in the early to mid-1970s. A systematic campaign started in Britain by Tamil expatriates was extended to western Europe and Scandinavia to bring attention to the concerns of the Sri Lankan Tamils and to put international pressure on the UF government.[74]

As K.M. de Silva put it,

> Once a separatist movement emerged among the Tamils of Sri Lanka it was fostered, nurtured and protected in Tamilnadu, as a surrogate for the Tamil state which the Tamils of Tamilnadu had been compelled ... to abjure in their own country.[75]

From the early 1970s, South Indian politicians looked upon increasingly volatile politics in the Jaffna Peninsula in Sri Lanka 'as an integral part of the internal politics of Tamil Nadu'.[76] As A.J. Wilson has reported, the Tamil Nadu political parties, the DMK, and its split away group ADMK, 'were highly committed to championing the rights of Tamils in South Asia [and] supported Chelvanayakam and his FP and TULF and later the LTTE'.[77] In 1972 Chelvanayakam was received with 'respect and affection' in Madras by leaders of both the DMK and Indian Congress Parties. There he declared that 'only separation' would save the Tamil people in Sri Lanka from the oppression of the Sinhalese.[78]

A call to satyagraha in Sri Lanka was raised and the analogy with Bangladesh was also drawn. Chelvanayakam and his deputy Amirthalingam urged Tamil Nadu leaders to pressure the Indian Prime Minister Indira Gandhi to intervene on behalf of the Tamil population in Sri Lanka.[79] Despite the need for electoral support in Tamil Nadu, Mrs Gandhi did not intervene at this stage. Indeed, without the support of politicians in neighboring Tamil Nadu and the policies of the Indian central government, the Tamil separatist movement in Sri Lanka could not have emerged, let alone prospered.

In 1973, at the twelfth annual convention of the ITAK, the TUF's new position – namely, separate statehood – was confirmed.[80] University admissions policies and growing unemployment intensified the grievances of Tamil youth, encouraging them to support the TUF campaign for separate statehood.[81] With the incorporation of criminal gangs, the Tamil separatism became a militant armed struggle.

Separatist violence

Criminal gangs were active in the north when Chelvanayakam and the TUF called for secession in 1972. VVT (Valvettithurai) in the tip of the northern Jaffna peninsula had become the virtual smuggling capital of Ceylon well before the emergence of the Tamil separatist struggle. The demise of their trade in rice transport, the difficulty in investing in land in the Jaffna Peninsula given land scarcity and vellala monopoly had led the kariyar kadalodiekal of VVT to turn to large-scale smuggling between India and Ceylon.[82] The easy access to, and refuge in, Tamil Nadu was a major factor in the coming together of smugglers and terrorists and the birth of the armed Sri Lankan Tamil separatist struggle (Map I.2).

Frustrated with the ITAK's nonviolent tactics, Tamil organizations with a more violent bent began to form. Kuttimani, a smuggler in VVT, formed an informal group, the Tamil Liberation Organization (TLO, which later became TELO, the Tamil Eelam Liberation Organization), during 1967–1969 to carry out violent struggle.[83] Prabhakaran, the leader of the LTTE, his one-time deputy Mahathaya and their relatives were all members of the kariyar kadalodiekal elite.[84] Some members of Pulip Padai (Tamil Army) formed in 1961, remained committed to armed struggle for a separate state though the group had withered away.[85] Like the Sinhala youth armed struggle, the origin of the contemporary armed Tamil struggle is attributed to student activism, specifically the Tamil Youth League (TSL) begun in 1970. It later became the Tamil New Tigers (TNT) under Chetti Tanabalasingham, 'a common criminal' from VVT. Velupillai Prabhakaran developed the military wing of the TNT which became the LTTE in May of 1976.[86]

The educated unemployed were a substantial element in the Tamil society in the north by the early 1970s. Like the educated unemployed Sinhalese youth, they were frustrated by blocked educational and employment opportunities. Standardization, district quotas, the Constitution of 1972, unemployment and rising cost of living contributed to growing unrest among them. The JVP insurrection, no doubt, influenced them to seek violent alternatives: some of them had met insurgent Sinhala youth in jail.[87] Sathyaseelan, who was involved in a series of politically motivated conspiracies and crimes in the early 1970s, for instance, had campaigned against standardization as an undergraduate. Later, as an unemployed science graduate, he led the Manavar Peravai, the Tamil Student League

(TSL).[88] Instead of a JVP-style revolution, however, Tamil students joined the TUF elites to further the campaign for a separate state as the solution to their problems.[89] Unlike the JVP which had a Marxist analysis and a socialist vision, the Tamil militancy's ideology and vision never went beyond condemnation of 'Sinhala chauvinism' and Eelam.

The rigid caste system and vellala domination of the Tamil community was also a significant factor in the rise of youth violence in the north. For the most part, Tamil terrorists came from the oppressed low castes, and the Tamils they murdered were mostly vellala. Had the enterprising kariyars who had converted to Catholicism and received missionary school education in large numbers in colonial times been allowed more room for political and social advancement by the vellalas, individuals such as Prabhakaran, and organizations such as the Tamil Tigers, may have had less reason to emerge. Instead of addressing the deeply entrenched caste and class oppression among Tamils, the vellala-dominated TUF succeeded in directing the anger of lower-caste Tamil youth entirely towards the Sinhala ethnic other, instead of at Tamil elites.[90] Although ethnically based mobilization could not entirely transcend the entrenched class and regional hierarchies among Sri Lankan Tamils, in the long term Tamil militancy came to undermine the vellalas and the entire Tamil caste system. Many of the leaders of the LTTE, including Prabhakaran are Catholics, not Hindus. The Catholic identity became a significant source of support to the LTTE from the Tamil Catholic clergymen and silencing of many Sinhala Catholic clergymen on LTTE terrorism over the course of the secessionist struggle.[91]

In the early years, the TUF played a significant role in leading the Tamil youth into the struggle for Eelam, justifying it as a holy war (punitha yutham) against the oppressive and alien Sinhala state.[92] A hartal and day of mourning was called for by the TUF two days after the adoption of the constitution on 24 May 1972. Black flags were flown, schools were boycotted by students and buses were stoned. Amirthalingam, who spoke at the protest meeting in Jaffna on 24 May, seemingly endorsed the use of arms by a future generation of Tamils.[93] Kasi Ananadan (a leader of the TULF Youth Wing), a militant speaker at that meeting, openly threatened Tamil members of Parliament who voted for the new constitution: 'the six Tamils who voted for the new Constitution would not die by illness, by accident or by natural Causes, but would meet their death by some other ways'.[94] Although Chelvanayakam remained committed to non-violence until his death, he tolerated the threats and the 'new mood of totalitarianism' growing within the militant youth movement. He was reportedly on the platform at the meeting where Kasi Ananadan made his threats and his speech was 'editorially quoted in *Suthanthiran*, a newspaper that Chelvanayakam owned'.[95] As a veteran journalist who was at that meeting remarked, 'such a speech which had the blessings of Tamil leadership was a foretaste of things to come'.[96] Assassination squads were already active trying to eliminate pro-government Tamil leaders and Sinhala politicians.[97] These events marked a turning point: from the 1970s on, the Tamil-separatist movement in Sri Lanka was characterized by violence. Intimidation and the killing of Tamils considered as traitors has been its hallmark.[98]

The security situation in the north rapidly deteriorated from 1972 on. Criminal gangs engaged in the thefts of cars, robberies of banks, government establishments and cooperative stores to obtain funds to carry out political killings. The first of many successful robberies of the Tamil militants, from the Cooperative Society of Tellipalli in 1974 is attributed to Chetti and his associates from VVT. Subsequently Chetti is believed to have escaped to Tamil Nadu and joined a group from VVT camping there. Prabhakaran, also from VVT is blamed for the first successful bank robbery in Jaffna, from the state-run People's Bank in Puttur on 5 March 1976 (exactly two months prior to the formation of the LTTE). The VVT smuggler, Kuttimani, leader of the TELO, was also involved in a robbery of a People's Bank in the Jaffna Peninsula when Rs.7.5 million was stolen.[99] TELA (Tamil Eelam Liberation Army) which is suspected to be the military wing of TELO is believed to have been formed by T. Maheswaran a graduate of the University of London.[100] According to Indian journalist, Narayan Swamy, training of Tamil terrorists in Lebanon began as early as 1976.[101]

The relationship between the moderate TUF and Tamil terrorist youth gangs defined the secessionist movement from the beginning. The formation of the TUF was followed by the establishment of the Tamil Elaingyar (TYL Tamil Youth League) in 1973. Though not officially a TUF affiliate, the TYL acted as one, bringing many disaffected youth to the forefront of the separatist movement. Radical ITAK parliamentarians like Amirthalingam and Kathiravelupillai deviated from the Gandhian vision of Chelvanayakam aiding Tamil youth militancy.[102] As the Tamil authors of *The Broken Palmyra* noted, 'having directly or indirectly aided the growth of the militant movement, the TULF had to ride it'.[103] They also noted that Amirthalingam kept saying that they had a 'secret plan' to bring about Eelam, thus aggravating Sinhala fears of an Indian invasion.[104] As Swamy has reported in *Tigers of Lanka*, the relationship between the Tamil militants and the so-called moderates was extremely close from the beginning:

> The TYL organized processions and hunger strikes and whatever else the TUF exhorted it to do. 'Amirthalingam gave support to our activities' said Annamali Vardaraja Perumal, an activist. 'He gave us a political cover, a political justification for all that we did. He was the mass leader although Chelvanayakam was the figurehead.... We did whatever the TUF asked us to do.[105]

Retired Chief Justice M.C. Sansoni, a Burgher Christian who headed the Presidential Commission of Inquiry into the disturbances of 1977, later noted that the TUF carried on a 'prolonged and almost continuous campaign of civil disobedience' with the support of the youth movements in the north since 1972.[106] During hartals and days of mourning, the TUF flag was raised and the Sri Lankan lion flag lowered; schools and shops were closed. Moving beyond the civil disobedience campaign of the TUF, youth militants attacked and burnt buses, railway carriages and Buddhist temples and murdered police officers.[107] There were attempts on the life of the Tamil Mayor of Jaffna, Alfred Duraiappa in February and March 1971. Prabhakaran, who was 18 years old at the time, threw bombs at a carnival organized by the mayor in a Jaffna stadium in August 1971. Bombs were again lobbed at the stadium in September 1971, and at the mayor's residence in December 1972.[108] Frequently the police could not find any witnesses, even when bombings and murder of police officers, many of them Tamils, had taken place in broad daylight in markets, road junctions and other congested places. Innocent Tamils who dared to come forward and give evidence were targeted as informants and eventually killed by the militants.[109] This, too, was a characteristic of the separatist movement from the beginning.

As violence began to dominate the political atmosphere in the north, the police found it difficult to distinguish between routine maintenance of law and order and legal political activity, and the activities of common criminals and terrorists.[110] So they took severe action against all. Mass arrests of youth militants crippled the TYL and the older TSL. TSL leader Sathyaseelan was arrested in February 1973 (he had escaped to Canada by the late 1970s). Yet, the arrests could not deter the spread of violence and growing conflicts between the government security forces and Tamil youth in the north.[111] High-handed action by the police at the fourth International Conference of Tamil Research in Jaffna in 1974 left nine people dead. The incident further embittered the youth, inflaming violence and helping mobilize more Tamil militants.[112] The police in turn kept arresting hundreds of youths, many of whom were left in jail for long periods of time without being charged or convicted. Some were inhumanly tortured in custody creating a reign of police terror in the north.[113]

Both the Sri Lankan state and the Tamil political leadership bear responsibility for failing to curb the violence that was spreading in the mid-1970s. Tamil officers became the easy targets of Tamil youth militants, and as a result, the police force in the north came to be filled entirely by Sinhalese. This sharpened the ethnic cleavage and the perception of the police as an alien occupying force. Many new officers had been hastily recruited into the Sri Lankan police after the JVP insurrection and many of those sent to Jaffna were relatively ill-trained.[114] The government's failure to enforce discipline and deter brutality in the treatment of detainees increased Tamil resentment and the justification of separatist violence against what was seen as an army of occupation.

The leftist UF government, which had denounced the previous UNP regime for ruling through emergency powers, ended up doing the same. From March 1971 when it imposed emergency rule to crush the JVP until February 1977 – practically its entire term in office – the UF operated under repressive emergency regulations.[115] Police excess and the abuse of detainees became routine. The government allowed, if not, encouraged police excess in crushing the JVP rebellion of the Sinhala youth in 1971. The kind of summary executions that took place in the south have not been reported from the north in the 1970s and most Tamil militants taken into custody were released due to lack of evidence.[116]

The failure of the government between 1970 and 1977 went beyond its inability to control police excesses in the north. Having exhausted its political capital in confronting the JVP insurgency, the government failed to respond to the increasing grievances of the Tamils.[117] Initiatives were not taken to address the language, decentralization, and other Tamil concerns. Sinhala–Tamil relations worsened pushing Tamils towards separatism and violence.

Moderate and militant separatists

Moderate Tamil leaders were complicit in supporting the militant separatists and causing a worsening of the situation. Unlike the Sinhala youth of the JVP, the Tamil youth militants in the north were supported by the Tamil political leadership in their exploits against the Sri Lankan government. Many middle-class Tamils referred to their militants adoringly as 'the boys', while their Sinhala counterparts dreaded the very name of the JVP. Many of the educational and economic grievances of the lower classes in the two communities were the same, although the Sinhala youth revolt was interpreted as an intra-ethnic and intra-religious Sinhala Buddhist class struggle, while the Tamil revolt was seen entirely as an ethnic one. By tacitly supporting youth terrorism, the TUF contributed to the spread of political violence. Even the cult of suicide, popularized globally by the LTTE's invention of the suicide jacket, can be traced to practices endorsed by the moderate Tamil politicians.[118]

When Sivakumaran, a public servant and a leader of TSF who had attempted political murders, including that of a Sinhala Minister in 1970 and the Mayor of Jaffna in 1971, killed himself by swallowing a cyanide capsule to avoid capture by the police in 1974, the TUF helped establish the cult of martyrdom associated with the cyanide pill. Instead of condemning the suicide, the leaders of the TUF helped organize a martyr's funeral for Sivakumaran where hundreds of youths cut their fingers and placed pottus of blood on the dead body pledging not to retreat or rest from the struggle until Tamil independence was won. A bronze statue of Sivakumaran, 'a defiant youth, his clenched fist outstretched and dangling a broken chain' (symbolizing the cyanide capsule worn around the neck) was erected by the TYL and his death commemorated annually on 5 June by the TUF. Sivakumaran's mother was also given an honored place in the Women's Wing of the TUF.[119]

After several failed attempts on his life, Alfred Duraiappa, the Tamil Mayor of Jaffna and supporter of the UF government, was finally killed by Prabhakaran and two associates on 27 July 1975. This assassination is considered by some to be the first 'heroic' act of Prabhakaran, the son of a minor government official who later emerged as the supreme leader of the LTTE and introduced many of the strategies of modern terrorism to the world. Many cheered the news of Mayor Duraiappa's death, but hundreds also attended his funeral despite the threats and fears. The murder led to yet another wave of arrests of Tamil youth by state forces. Seven persons were charged, but, they were all acquitted.[120] Duraiappa's killing was the first political murder in the north of Sri Lanka, yet neither Chelvanayakam, who was a Ghandian, nor his party, condemned the murder of the fellow Tamil politician.[121] As Swamy has noted, the Tamil leaders 'could not afford to criticize the murder'.[122] At the time there were no more than 50 hard core Tamil militants in Jaffna, but their value was great for the Tamil moderates who could use them as a pressure tactic on the Sinhala government. Many Tamils believed that the young guerillas were acting under the orders of the TUF and that they could be controlled as need be.[123] This instrumental attitude emboldened terrorism, eventually bringing down the Tamil politicians, the Tamil community and the Sri Lankan society at large.

The interest of the moderate Tamil political leadership was in the achievement of the separate state rather than curbing the growing violence. In fact, political instability in the north helped strengthen charges against the government and justify the demand for secession. In February 1975 Chelvanayakam won the by-election for the Kankesanthurai parliamentary seat with an overwhelming majority. Interpreting the victory as a mandate for secession, he argued that the 'Tamil Nation should exercise the sovereignty already vested in the Tamil people and become free'.[124] The addition of the word 'liberation' and change of the organizational name from TUF to TULF (Tamil United Liberation Front) in 1975 signified a shift away from the unitary state.[125]

The Vaddukoddai resolution

The Tamil separatist aspirations were included in a resolution adopted at a convention of the TULF held in May 1976. This resolution, which came to be called the Vaddukoddai Resolution, brought together the hitherto disparate separatist aspirations in one statement calling for the establishment of a separate state. The Vaddukkodai Resolution was taken almost verbatim from the erroneous Cleghorn Minute, but the militant Tamil youth interpreted the claim made by the TULF as an accurate depiction of history and its call for unflinching dedication to a separate state as a justification of armed struggle. Most maps that began to appear of the projected Eelam encompassed the North Western Province and parts of other provinces (Map I.2), although the Vaddukoddai resolution only calls for the Northern and Eastern Provinces. It sought to embrace all Tamil speakers by offering Eelam citizenship to Tamil-speaking people living in any part of the island and to Tamils of 'Eelam origin' living in any part of the world.[126]

The response to the Vaddukoddai Resolution differed across and within the ethnic communities. Sinhala resistance to regional devolution stemmed from the fear that separatists would eventually seek to expand beyond the north and the east and annex Sri Lanka within a broader South Indian Dravidasthan. The Ceylon Workers Congress, representing the Indian plantation Tamils, had serious reservations regarding the call for separatism from the beginning. Given the social differences between the two communities and its interest in extending Sri Lankan citizenship and improving the status of the Indian Tamils within the Sri Lankan polity, the CWC left the TULF soon after the adoption of the

Vaddukoddai Resolution.[127] While the Muslims were perturbed by increased Sinhala presence in the east and a few Muslim politicians such as H.M.H. Ashroff had supported the separatist demand in the early 1970s, the Muslims in the east and in Sri Lanka at large also rejected the call to separatism.[128]

The TULF continued to advance the separatist cause at every opportunity, notwithstanding its fundamental erroneous premises. When Amirthalingam, along with another TULF member and a former MP, faced trial for sedition for distributing pamphlets calling for a separate state, the lawyers who appeared (apparently some 69 in number) in defense of Amirthalingam used it as an occasion to challenge the validity of the Emergency Regulations (in place since the JVP insurrection) and the 1972 Republican Constitution and to 'sharpen the juridical and historical underpinning of the new corporate identity of the Tamil people'.[129] The conference of the non-aligned nations held in Colombo in August 1976 allowed the TULF to draw international attention to the escalating violence, government repression and plight of Tamils in the north. The government sources, on the other hand, charged that the TULF itself was the instigator behind the attacks against government property as well as an attempted murder by Tamil youth in the north, during the time of that conference.[130] Thus both the TULF and the government were responsible for the escalation of violence in the north and communal polarization across the island by the time of the 1977 parliamentary elections.

The 1977 elections

The 1977 parliamentary elections took place during escalating violence in the north and growing polarization across the island. It is considered by some to be the last legitimate election in the north and east. Although the election did not give the TULF a resounding victory even in the north and east, it drew a hard line between moderates and advocates of violence and separation.

The separatist claim to the Northern and Eastern Provinces was advanced by the concept of 'traditional Tamil homelands' incorporated in the TULF manifesto for the 1977 general elections. Issued in July 1977, after Chelvanayakam's death four months earlier, it stated that 'Even before the Christian era the entire island [of Sri Lanka] was ruled by Tamil kings' and that since 'the beginning of the thirteenth century', the Northern and Eastern Regions were 'firmly established as the exclusive homeland of the Tamils'.[131] This claim was a falsification of history given widespread evidence of the Sinhala Buddhist and Muslim cultures of the North and East.[132] However, enumerating Tamil charges against Sinhala 'domination' and 'imperialism', the TULF election manifesto called upon Tamils to vote for the TULF in order to establish the state of Eelam by peaceful or other methods:

> The Tamil Nation must take the decision to establish its sovereignty in its homeland on the basis of the right to self-determination. The only way to announce this decision to the Sinhalese government and to the world is to vote for the Tamil United Liberation Front. The Tamil speaking representa-

tives who get elected through these votes, while being members of the National State Assembly of Ceylon, will also form themselves into the 'NATIONAL ASSEMBLY OF TAMIL EELAM' which will draft a constitution for the State of Tamil Eelam and to establish the independence of the Tamil Eelam by bringing that constitution into operation by peaceful means or by direct action or struggle'.

(emphasis in original)[133]

Responding to the TULF charges and claims, the opposition UNP put forward a conciliatory response. Stating that 'the lack of a solution to their problems has made the Tamil speaking people support even a movement for the creation of a separate state'.[134] The UNP election manifesto pledged to call for an all party conference to undertake constitutional reform with reference to minority rights, if elected into office. It also promised to decentralize the administration through district development councils and to take explicit actions regarding Tamil grievances with regard to education, colonization, language and employment in the public sector. In other words, the UNP promised to reverse the policies of the SLFP/UF government repudiating the Sinhala Buddhist agenda of both previous SLFP and UNP governments and to initiate a new beginning in Sinhala-Tamil relations.[135]

The Sinhalese electorate, for whom the economic issues of employment and access to consumer goods were uppermost, had lost faith in the UF government. The UNP won a massive electoral victory over the SLFP in much of the country, while the TULF won massively in the north. Having gained over 50 percent of the national vote, the UNP was able to count on over a five-sixth majority in the legislature. For the first time, the left-wing parties failed to win a single parliamentary seat. Due to distortions in the electoral system that had been in place since 1960, the TULF which got only one-fifth of the island-wide popular vote won by the SLFP, secured 18 parliamentary seats against eight by the SLFP. As a result, Amirthalingam the TULF leader became the Leader of the Opposition, making him the first Tamil to hold that position since independence in 1948,[136] representing greater integration and power for Tamils within the Sri Lankan parliamentary system and an opportunity for non-violent conflict resolution. But the opportunity would be lost.

Support for the TULF in the north and east, the proposed area for Eelam, was mixed. A majority in the overwhelmingly Tamil Northern Province voted for the TULF, but a larger majority of the electorate in the ethnically mixed Eastern Province, opposed the separatist mandate[137] (Table 3.3). Notwithstanding the rejection of Eelam in the Eastern Province and the UNP government's election pledges to introduce a new constitution and policies favorable to the Tamils, the Tamil leadership did not make positive use of the new opportunities presented. As Father Balasuriya pointed out in 1979:

While the majority community and its leaders are not without blame in communal relations, we may also ask whether the Tamil leadership has not been deficient in not concerning itself with the overall problems of the

Table 3.3 1977 general election results: TULF results

Province/districts	Number of candidates	Number of seats won by TULF	TULF % of valid votes
Northern Province			
Jaffna	11	11	72.1
Mannar	1	1	51.6
Vauniya	2	2	56.0
Total	14	14	68.7
Eastern Province			
Trincomalee	3	1	27.3
Batticoloa	4	2	36.2
Ampara	5	1	20.3
Total	12	4	27.1

Sources: Robert N. Kearney, 'Territorial Elements of Tamil Separatism in Sri Lanka', *Pacific Affairs*, vol. 60, no. 4, Winter 1987–1988, p. 570; Vijaya Samaraweera, 'Sri Lanka's General Election', *Asian Survey*, vol. 17, no. 12, December 1977, pp. 1195–1206.

country specially of the oppressed Sinhalas, Moors, Malays and Plantation Tamils? Today the Tamil leaders have an opportunity to return to the political scene as national leaders. They form the main opposition group in Parliament. They can safeguard the human rights of all in this country.[138]

The TULF was a parliamentary party of mostly career lawyers representing a privileged elite from the colonial period. With the introduction of majoritarian parliamentary democracy, they began to see themselves as a group without power over their destiny, let alone power over the rest of the society. They employed Tamil nationalism for political mobilization and as a strategy for regaining their own lost status and privilege. Though high in rhetoric, the TULF provided no direction and structures for Tamil people's participation and determination of their future beside the panacea of Eelam. Unable to launch a non-violent struggle, the TULF members rode 'the incipient militant movement in order to retain their influence'.[139]

As Thangarajah has noted, spurred by the TULF victory on the separatist platform, the militant Tamil youth 'felt there was no further need to negotiate for political rights and began their campaign in earnest to dislodge the "Sinhala state" from the north and the east'.[140] As the separatist struggle intensified, Sinhala fears and animosities were roused by the unusual situation which made the secessionist TULF the main opposition party in 1977 and its controversial leader, Amirthalingam, the leader of the parliamentary opposition. As K.M. de Silva has noted

There was no precedent in the history of parliamentary democracies of the Commonwealth for the position of the Leader of the Opposition being held by the head of a party committed to a separatist program, and thus to the dismemberment of the polity.[141]

The rhetoric in Tamil separatist publications and media heightened Sinhala sense of injustice, fears and insecurity. It was felt that while Tamils had the right to settle anywhere in Sri Lanka, the TULF's separatist agenda denied that same right to the Sinhala people and overlooked the fact that the majority of Tamils in Sri Lanka were living outside the Northern and Eastern provinces.[142] Sinhala opposition to the creation of an exclusive Tamil state within the island needs to be placed within the prevailing socio-economic and demographic context. Father Balasuriya voiced the Sinhala concerns:

Eelam will create an explosive socio-economic situation in the island. One third of the island would … be carved out for less than 1/6 the of the population The remaining 85% of the population will be cramped into the North-Central, South, Western and Central parts of the country. They would have less of the sea as an outlet. There is already acute landlessness in these areas. A good portion of the under populated area that could be developed would be in 'Eelam'. This is bound to cause much social tension inside the reduced Sri Lanka and the proposed Eelam … how fair is the Tamil leaders' demand to reserve the colonization of the Northern and Eastern Provinces exclusively for the Tamils.[143]

Post-election riots

Post-election violence had become an endemic feature in Sri Lanka by this time, as the divisions created by the party system had deepened. The mob violence that erupted after the 1977 elections did not begin as primordial communal violence, but as political party violence. After the 1977 elections 'UNP thugs were let loose' on the defeated supporters of the SLFP. But the violence turned communal when 'powerful persons' re-directed it against the Tamils.[144] The ensuing riots, the worst since 1958, erupted after a clash between the police and a Tamil crowd at a school carnival in Jaffna and then spread to many parts of the south in the wake of rumors, many of them false, that Buddhist temples had been burned and Sinhalese people murdered in the North.[145] Latent Sinhala hostility, aggravated by the TULF demand for secession, was vented against innocent Tamils. The result was looting and arson of Tamil shops in the south and 'inevitable repercussions in the North'.[146] With the lapse of the emergency in May 1977, all the Tamil militant suspects who had languished in jail without court charges had been released, and many had returned to their clandestine trade and violent political activities.[147]

A presidential commission, headed by M.C. Sansoni, a highly-respected Burgher judicial commissioner, was created to investigate the communal violence of August and September 1977. The commission's report gives details of the extensive destruction of businesses and religious sites and killings by both the Sinhalese and the Tamils. Individuals who had worked together and lived in harmony for years were turned into enemies overnight. Practically all the Sinhalese were ethnically cleansed from the Jaffna peninsula, and thousands of Tamils, including hundreds of Indian Tamils from the plantation districts, were driven out of the south. Plantation Tamils who were not party to the secessionist conflict between the Sinhalese and Sri Lankan Tamils suffered greatly.[148] Those who never demanded Eelam became easy targets of Sinhala attacks because they were Tamils and were living close to the Sinhalese. Frightened to return to the estates, they became refugees and later many of them settled in the north and the east.[149]

Although the conflagration in 1977 came to be identified entirely along Sinhala versus Tamil lines, there was an intra-ethnic Sinhala political party dimension to it. The governing UNP Party blamed the SLFP for instigating the riots, while the SLFP leader held the government responsible for the killing of 30 of her supporters and the loss of property of hundreds of other SLFP supporters during post-election rioting.[150] Moreover, as the Presidential Commission Report showed, the criminal behavior of ordinary Sinhalese and Tamils was instigated by politicians of both communities.[151] The Sansoni Commission concluded that the inflammatory speeches and demand for Eelam by the Tamil leaders and the wide media coverage they received contributed to the spread of violence against Tamils in many areas of the country.[152] While marauding gangs and mobs from the two communities rampaged across the land, the police failed to quell the spread of violence. An emergency was not declared and the state failed to discipline the police and protect innocent victims. A curfew was imposed on 18 August as thousands of displaced Tamil refugees in affected areas in the south were airlifted to the north because rail and road travel had become dangerous.[153] Even official estimates vary in the total number of victims and their ethnic identities. According to one official estimate, by 22 August, when the curfew was lifted, 125 individuals – 97 Tamils, 24 Sinhalese, one Muslim and three unidentified, had been killed in the riots.[154] Other estimates claim over 300 deaths and the estimates of displaced have varied between 25,000 and 50,000.[155]

The 1977 violence deepened the ethnic polarization and strengthened the separatists' cry for Eelam. For the TULF leader Amirthalingam, the demand for Eelam was 'vindicated to the hilt' by the ethnic violence of 1977. He pointed out that 'if we do not have some place of safety, we shall have to live eternally in refugee camps'.[156] The DMK in Tamil Nadu organized a strike in support of their Sri Lankan brethren. An international propaganda campaign against the Sri Lankan government was begun during this time by expatriate Tamils living in the western countries.[157]

The dropping of the Sinhala nationalist agenda hitherto promoted by both the SLFP and the UNP and conciliatory policies introduced by the new UNP government after 1977, such as the enactment of a new constitution in 1978 and changes in language and university admissions policies, did not change the Tamil separatist resolve to establish Eelam. Their uncompromising stance, along with staunch Sinhala opposition to secession, the failures of local politicians, the contradictions of regional politics, and the forces of economic and cultural globalization, would ultimately combine to provoke a civil war.

4 Liberalization, authoritarianism, and communal violence, 1977–1983

The United National Party (UNP) came to power promising economic development and improved employment opportunities. It attributed mass discontent to
the socialist policies of the previous left-wing regime and under the rubric of the
Open Economy opened the country to greater foreign investment and imports
and tried to spur economic growth by dismantling the welfare state. These policies transformed the political, economic, and cultural character of the island and
realigned class as well ethnic relations. The complex forces that came into play
between the 1977 parliamentary elections and the explosion of violence in July
1983 illustrate that the conflict in the country was multipolar, not simply a
bipolar clash between two ethnic groups.

Post-1977 economic liberalization and the policy mix popularly known as
structural adjustment under terms set down by the IMF and the World Bank promoted export-oriented production, devaluation of the local currency, liberalization of imports, privatization of state-owned sectors, social service cutbacks, and
removal of food subsidies and price controls on consumer goods. Incentives for
foreign investment were introduced, and restrictions on movement of capital,
goods and services between the country and the outside world were removed.

The Open Economy was built upon a huge influx of foreign loans, outright
grants and investments. The country's dependence on this 'explosion of aid'
made satisfaction of foreign interests one of the biggest priorities of the state.[1]
Following deliberations between local and foreign policymakers, the Sri Lankan
government cut back social welfare provisions and eliminated the rice subsidy
replacing it with a limited food stamp program.[2] Capitulating to World Bank and
the IMF conditionalities, per capita spending for education was reduced from
US$12 in 1972 to US$8 in 1978, and health expenditures from $6 to $5 in the
same period. Total government expenditures for food, education, and health
declined from 42 percent to 26 percent of the budget between 1971 and the
1978–1980 period.[3] Under the new policies, the confluence of inflation, internationally imposed structural adjustment policies, and the dismantling of the
welfare state worsened the growing income inequality and poverty that cut
across ethnic, regional and class divides.

Widening inequalities

The process of economic liberalization begun in 1977 gave rise to a newly rich element in Sri Lanka of 'speculators, contractors, bookies, gem merchants, and Middle East job recruitment' agents and the like who were tied to external interests.[4] At the same time, due to the indiscriminate liberalization of imports, many local entrepreneurs were unable to compete with cheap foreign goods and were forced to close down their small-scale manufacturing, dairy, agricultural, hand loom industry, and other ventures, depriving thousands of their employment.[5]

Since the era of colonial capitalist development, economic growth had been centered in the Western Province and the Colombo metropolitan region.[6] The new liberalization policies intensified this unequal and uneven pattern of regional development. Economic resources were drained from the rural backward regions, aggravating poverty and social and political discontent in much of the country.[7] With only a few exceptions, the average income of all other agro-climatic zones on the island consistently declined from 1973 to 1986/87 in comparison to the Colombo Municipality. The Dry Zone Districts in the Southern, North Central, and Eastern and Northern Provinces were all adversely affected by the early 1980s. 'In the north and the east (which has provided most support for the LTTE), mean incomes were almost in par with those of Colombo in the early 1970s, but had almost halved by the early 1980s'.[8]

The main development projects under the Open Economy – the FTZ (Free Trade Zone), Greater Colombo Development, promotion of tourism, and housing development – did not benefit the Northern Province. Yet, no alternative development policies were introduced there or in the Southern and other distant provinces, causing ordinary people in the distant provinces to feel marginalized. The continued economic neglect of the Northern and the Southern Provinces and other outlying areas, as well as continued unemployment among educated youth, were major factors in the intensification of both Tamil militancy in the late 1970s and the re-emergence of the JVP's Sinhala nationalism in the mid-1980s.[9]

Cut backs in the state sector and public employment worked against the rural areas and the 'swabahasha-[local language] educated mono-lingual youth, in both the south and the north'.[10] The expanded private sector under the Open Economy favored the English-educated graduates from the prestigious Colombo schools and the recently established international schools preparing students for college education abroad and new employment opportunities in the internationally driven corporate NGO sector. In 1979 unemployment rates were 19 percent among Low Country Sinhalese; 14 percent among Kandyan Sinhalese; 11 percent among Sri Lankan Tamils and 6 percent among Indian Tamils.[11] Unemployment was still highest among the educated youth. With access to state employment even more difficult for them, 41 percent of young Tamil males with GCE Advanced Level qualifications were unemployed at the time.[12] This youth constituency became potential recruits for the strong anti-Sinhalese Tamil nationalist movement.[13]

Meanwhile, a new class was emerging within the growing NGO sector. The substantial influx of bilateral and multilateral aid since 1977 opened up new employment in the sector, which provided higher salaries than those available for government positions of comparable or higher rank. More than two-thirds of the development NGOs working in Sri Lanka in 2001 were established after 1977.[14] As sociologist Siri Hettige has put it, these processes of economic and cultural globalization helped the emergence of a new urban middle class (NUMC) 'with strong external links and ... almost totally dependent on such links for their sustenance'.[15] The NUMC of all ethnic groups – Sinhala, Tamil, and Muslim – benefited from private-sector and NGO expansion. However, the majority of the country's rural youth, who looked to the state sector as their avenue for upward social mobility, saw the return of a new form of colonialism and re-enthronement of a ' "neo-colonial," English-educated middle class as freezing their own chances for upward mobility'.[16]

Between 1973 and 1982, the share of the highest quintile income earners rose from 46 percent to 57 percent of the total income in Sri Lanka. The cost of living of an average middle class family more than doubled during the same period. Lower middle class pauperization added to the percentage living below the poverty line and nearly half the population was pushed below the official poverty line. The 'ultra poor' increased from less than 20 percent of the total to 25 percent in 1981–1982.[17] Polarization within the urban areas sharpened in the aftermath of liberalization: the income of the highest quintile consisting of the business and new urban middle classes rose while those of all others declined throughout the island. This was especially evident in the Colombo Municipality where the Gini coefficient (a measure of income inequality) rose from 0.39 in 1978 to 0.59 in 1981–1982 and in the Northern Province and the Trincomalee and Batticoloa Districts from 0.33 to 0.48[18] (Table 4.1).

Unemployment was worse in the urban sector than the rural and estate sectors, the rates being 19.5 percent, 13.2 percent, and 7.8 percent, respectively, in 1985–1986.[19] The urban poor, made up of rural migrants and slum dwellers, were 'most vulnerable to increased insecurity from cuts in safety nets urged by external development agencies [and] ... markedly incapable of exercising autonomous political power through other means'.[20] The urban poor were also easily amenable to ethnically based political manipulation and mobilization.[21] Like the newly developed Mahaweli areas, the city of Colombo attracted a disproportionate number of males from the densely populated rural areas.[22] Indeed, the 1983 anti-Tamil riots in Colombo have been attributed largely to mobs recruited from among Sinhala males from the marginalized urban class. The insecurity associated with poverty and social dislocation and the self-interested agendas of local and external elites provided the ground for ethno-religious mobilization within all local communities.

Deepening ethno-religious identities

While the Open Economy offered new economic opportunities for some, at the same time it increased competition between groups by deepening social class inequalities and ethnic rivalries. Under the new economic liberalization, Sinhala

Table 4.1 Income distribution: five survey zones, 1978, 1978–1979, 1981–1982 (percentages)

Ranked income receivers	Zone 1	Zone 2	Zone 3	Zone 4	Zone 5
1978					
Lowest 20%	4.47	5.96	7.03	5.67	5.03
Second 20%	9.84	12.35	12.59	11.09	11.09
Third 20%	15.45	17.31	17.68	16.15	16.15
Fourth 20%	22.72	22.95	22.29	23.49	23.69
Highest 20%	47.52	41.43	40.41	45.19	44.04
Gini coefficient	0.43	0.35	0.33	0.39	0.39
1978–1979					
Lowest 20%	3.95	2.92	4.07	4.17	3.19
Second 20%	9.2	7.75	8.21	8.76	6.49
Third 20%	14.62	12.51	13.01	13.67	10.34
Fourth 20%	21.25	18.63	18.78	21.02	16.84
Highest 20%	50.99	58.18	55.74	52.38	63.14
Gini coefficient	0.46	0.54	0.51	0.48	0.59
1981–1982					
Lowest 20%	3.95	3.65	4.5	3.69	3.31
Second 20%	9.1	8.54	9.26	7.45	6.48
Third 20%	13.96	12.81	13.29	11.59	9.75
Fourth 20%	21.07	19.23	19.02	18.3	16.34
Highest 20%	51.92	55.77	53.93	58.97	64.12
Gini coefficient	0.47	0.51	0.48	0.54	0.59

Source: W.D. Lakshman, 'Income Distribution and Poverty', in W.D. Lakshman, *Dilemmas of Development: Fifty Years of Economic Change in Sri Lanka*, Colombo: Sri Lanka Association of Economists, 1997, p. 195.

Notes
Agro-climate zones:
• Zone 1 Districts of Colombo (excluding the Colombo Municipality) Gampaha, Kalutara, Galle, and Matara.
• Zone 2 Districts of Hambantota, Monaragaia, Ampara, Polonnaeuruwa, Anuradhapura, and Puttalam.
• Zone 3 Districts of Jaffna, Mannar, Vavuniya, Mullativu, Trincomalee, and Batticaloa.
• Zone 4 Districts of Kandy, Matale, Nuwara-Eliya, Badulla, Ratnapura, Kegalle, and Kurnwgala.
• Zone 5 Colombo Municipality.

entrepreneurs lost many of the special concessions and political patronage they had enjoyed under the previous government, weakening their competitiveness and enabling the Tamil and Muslim entrepreneurs who had historically dominated local and regional trade to re-assert their position.[23] Many of the local industries that had to be closed down in the face of cheap foreign imports belonged to Sinhala entrepreneurs, and those closures led to large-scale retrenchment of Sinhalese workers. There is some evidence that the Tamil businessmen in the south benefited disproportionately from deregulation and the weakening of state control of the economy. Although overrepresentation of Tamils at the top levels of the private sector has been reported, due to interlocking directorates and foreign ownership patterns, it is difficult to determine the exact ethnic breakdown in the control and ownership of the newly expanding private sector under the Open Economy.[24]

Most commercial activity continued to be centered in the capital city of Colombo, which also continued to have the highest median personal income of any spatial zone in the country. In the early 1980s, the population of Colombo was mixed: 50 percent Sinhalese (24 percent points below the national average), 22 percent Sri Lankan Tamils (10 percent points above the national average), and 21 percent Muslim (14 percent points above the national average).[25] Metropolitan Colombo has poor ethnic areas, but, a large proportion from among the Sri Lankan Tamil and Muslim minority groups also benefitted from the expanding commercial sector.[26] In the atmosphere of increased competition, this created ground for resentment and room to mobilize the Sinhala urban working class along ethnic lines. Their real grievances were economic, but the rallying cry for mobilization would become ethnic.

Both popular and academic attention has been focused on the competition between Sinhala and Tamil entrepreneurs after 1977 and the sense of deprivation experienced by the former as an underlying cause of the 1983 riots which was the major turning point in the Tamil separatist struggle.[27] Although the new Open Economy abolished advantages the Sinhalese had previously enjoyed under the state dominated economy, it was not designed to level the differential impact of regional and global forces on local economic and cultural competition. Compared to the Muslim and Tamil communities, the Sinhalese were at a disadvantage in the increasingly globalized economy. Under the leadership of Muslim leaders in the UNP government, especially the Minister for Transport, M.H. Mohamed, who was also the Chairman of the Muslim World League, and A.C.S. Hameed who was Sri Lanka's Foreign Minister (1978–1989), Muslims sought 'donations from the Middle Eastern nations' to further Sri Lankan middle-class Muslim interests.[28] Foreign policy analyst, Meghan O'Sullivan, observed that 'this option of externally funded development was not open to the Sinhalese and to a much lesser extent to the Tamils'.[29]

The sense of separate Islamic identity and consciousness of Sri Lankan Muslims deepened through extensive external economic and ideological inputs obtained by the Department of Muslim Religious and Cultural Affairs, established under the UNP. These included aid to large numbers of mosques and Arabic Colleges from Saudi Arabia, donations to Islamic centers, texts of the Quran and numerous scholarships and funds from other oil-rich Islamic countries in the Middle East.[30] The growth of Islamic social welfare and educational activities in Sri Lanka, as in many other parts of the world, was partly a response to the dismantling of the welfare state and the excessive westernization accompanying the Open Economy. When structural adjustment policies and privatization diminished the role of the state after 1977, as in many other countries, hundreds of international and foreign-funded private nongovernmental organizations (NGOs) stepped in to fill the vacuum created by the loss of state support in Sri Lanka. Some of these powerful organizations, such as the Christian evangelical groups, have come with their own sectarian, if not fundamentalist ethnic or religious agendas, which threaten the liberal norms of pluralism and universalism supposedly promoted by the Open Economy.[31]

The political, economic, and cultural ascendancy the Sinhala Buddhists enjoyed after political independence was halted by a confluence of local and external forces after 1977. The Open Economy and the culture of consumerism, the decline of economic competitiveness, and the loss of electoral strength intensified the Sinhala Buddhist sense of being a threatened and beleaguered minority in the world.

Materialist culture advanced by economic liberalization undermined both the socialist-populist values prevailing since the introduction of democratic politics and the welfare state in the 1930s and the values of moderation and simplicity guiding the behavior of ordinary people since pre-colonial times. The nationalist-socialist values and the Sinhala Buddhist values which were integrated into a relatively coherent populist world view during the Sinhala Buddhist revival in the late colonial period was translated into state policies since the mid-1950s with the ascendancy of the Bandaranaikes.[32] Both the socialist and Buddhist values and life styles represented by this world view were threatened by the forces of economic and cultural globalization. As Sri Lankan governments shifted away 'from Sinhala Buddhists towards the various minorities' after 1977, Sinhala resistance came to be identified with the preservation of Sinhala Buddhist culture against western imperialist dominance as well as against re-emerging local minority political-economic and cultural dominance.[33] In a context where globalization seemed an all powerful and inexorable force, it became easier to direct latent hostility and resentment against the ethnic Other rather than the transnational corporations or the local authoritarian state.

The English-educated minority representing the transnational elite tended to uphold ostensibly multicultural internationalist norms associated with liberal economics. But the marginalized and alienated masses of youth shut out of the new economic order veered more and more towards 'particularistic' tendencies upholding ethno-religious cultural identities: Sinhala Buddhist and socialist world view on the part of the majority community, and Tamil separatism on the part of the Sri Lankan Tamil minority. These competing particularistic tendencies reinforced each other while at the same time deflecting attention from the common problems facing underprivileged youth from both, if not all, communities.[34]

The distortion of socio-economic realities was evident in the case of the Mahaweli River diversion scheme, the lead development project of the government. Although the project has often been criticized as favoring the Sinhalese, closer examination shows that social and economic results were not favorable for the majority of Sinhala peasants settled, and the project was an economic and ecological disaster for the country as a whole.[35]

Mahaweli program

Plan to divert the Mahaweli, the major river of the island, had begun long before the UNP came to power in 1977. But under the UNP government it was sped up, telescoping the project for completion in six years, and renamed the Accelerated

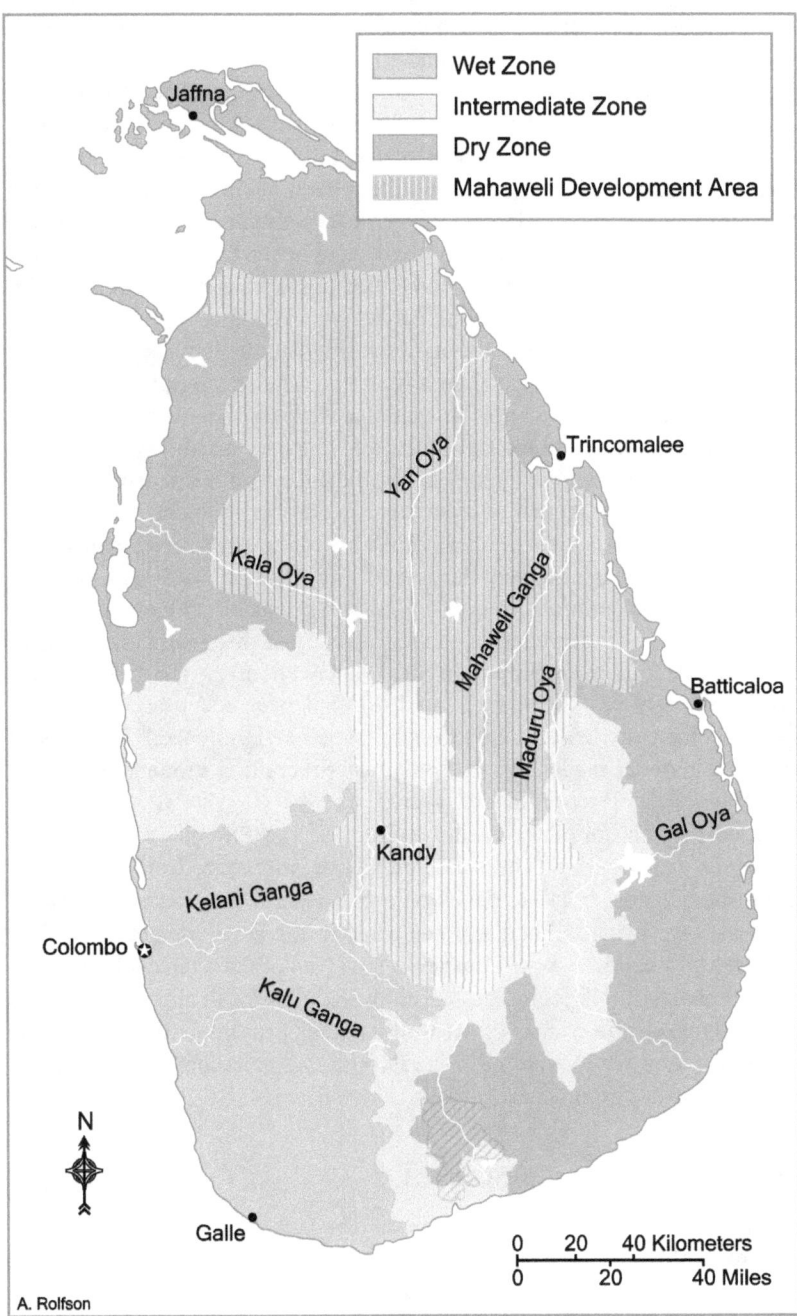

Map 4.1 Sri Lanka: climatic zones (source: Mahaweli Authority of Sri Lanka: www.adb.org/Water/
narbo/2006/mahaweli/MASL_Overview_Wellappilli.pdf (accessed 15 February 2008)).

Mahaweli Development Program (AMDP). The new plan was to build 15 reservoirs on the Mahaweli River and its tributaries to generate hydro-electric energy, irrigate 360,000 hectares of barren land, and settle 750,000 landless on small farms in the island's Dry Zone. When completed, this project, costing more than US$1.5 billion and funded by the World Bank and western governments, was expected to cover almost 39 percent of the island and 55 percent of the Dry Zone.[36]

Relieving population pressure in the overcrowded southwest Wet Zone and alleviating poverty among the landless Sinhalese peasantry were goals of the project (Table 2.2). But those ambitious goals were never fully realized. Indeed, the AMDP became itself the source of contention among the ethnic communities of the country over land and population distribution.

The massive influx of foreign aid and state involvement in the AMDP left much room for political patronage and corruption.[37] The leasing of thousands of newly irrigated Mahaweli lands to transnational corporations to cultivate cash crops using peasants as contract labor made a mockery of the government's alleged commitment to national food self-sufficiency and perpetuation of the small holder peasantry.[38] A new entrepreneur class that included non-settlers, mostly traders and government officials, were able to acquire operational control over land allotted to the peasants by the state.[39] The AMDP, which was intended to improve the living conditions of landless peasantry, ended up increasing class differentiation, peasant indebtedness, pauperization, and discontent. The disproportionate presence of young men in the Mahaweli areas (with sex ratios between 112 and 129 per 100 females in 1981) has been identified as a major factor fuelling ethnically based political mobilization and violence.[40] The lack of alternative employment made the new settlements recruiting grounds for armed forces and anti-state JVP rebels in later years.[41]

The state's support for the Buddhist culture of the Sinhala settlers in the Mahaweli areas was seen by Tamils as a deliberate attempt to Sinhalize 'traditional Tamil homelands'.[42] These developments added to the charge that Tamil majority areas were being deliberately neglected in the development in the Dry Zone.[43] There is no doubt that the ethno-religious bias of the Mahaweli Program aggravated Sinhala–Tamil relations, which were already deteriorating.[44] The central issue, however, in Mahaweli as well as other peasant settlements in the contested areas, was not competing Sinhala and Tamil ethnic myths but the future control over land and water.

Peasant settlement and ethnic conflict

Instead of helping to resolve existing problems, the Mahaweli program became a source for 'exacerbating communal strife'.[45] The majority of settlements were in the under-populated predominantly Sinhala districts of Anuradhapura and Polonnaruwa in the North Central Province (Map 4.1).[46] But, from the very inception of the AMDP, the ethnic composition of settlers in the Eastern Province considered by Tamil separatists to be part of a future 'Eelam' became the main focus of contention.

National quotas versus district quotas

The Sri Lankan government was committed to a 'national ethnic quota' for Mahaweli settlement that reflected the ethnic balance in the country. The Tamil separatists favored district ethnic ratios, whereby Mahaweli resettlement was to proceed on the basis of already existing ethnic proportions in any given district. The national quota would provide for a composition of settlers that was 74 percent Sinhalese; 12 percent Sri Lankan Tamils, 6 percent Indian 'Plantation' Tamils; 6 percent Muslim and 2 percent other. This 'seemingly fair provision' advanced by the government, however, quickly became 'politically explosive'.[47] Because a number of the irrigation projects were located in the Tamil majority districts, the national resettlement quota threatened to weaken the Tamil majority position of those areas. The Northern Province was overwhelmingly Tamil, but in the Eastern Province the population was mixed: 42 percent Sri Lankan Tamils; 25 percent Sinhalese and 32 percent Muslims in 1981. The Sinhala nationalists and the Tamil separatists were both interested in preserving, if not in improving, the numbers of their own communities in the Province to strengthen their respective positions for or against separatism. A major conflict emerged, for example, over the proposed resettlement of a large number of Sinhalese on the right bank of the Maduru Oya in the Batticoloa District, where Tamils were two-thirds of the population (discussed in chapter 5). As Canadian analyst, David Gilles later pointed out, 'Following the national formula [at Maduru Oya] would have altered the existing demographic balance and undermined the precarious Tamil claim on the eastern province as a whole'[48] (Map 4.2 and Table 4.2).

The Sri Lankan government insisted that the benefits of Mahaweli settlement should be available to all ethnic groups. It rejected the concept of an exclusive Tamil 'traditional homeland' and denied that it had attempted to deliberately change the ethnic balance.[49] The government, like most Sinhalese, took the position that given the increasing ethnic mix and Sri Lankan Tamil presence in the so-called Sinhala areas, including the national capital, Colombo, state-sponsored Sinhalese settlements in the so-called Tamil areas were justified.[50] However, the Tamil separatists who were singularly committed to safeguarding the Tamil majority position in the politically sensitive areas charged that the main objective of the government was not alleviation of population pressure or peasant poverty but, rather, weakening of the Tamil numerical position and therefore one of the arguments for a Tamil separate state in the Eastern Province. Thus the realities of electoral politics and the multiplicity of historical and socio-economic developments that necessitated Sinhala settlements in the Dry Zone were reduced to a single ethnic motivation. In a widely cited study, the Tamil geographer Manogaran asserted that

[F]rom the very beginning, colonization schemes in the Eastern Province were not designed to alleviate the overcrowding and unemployment problems in the Tamil districts but were intended to change the ethnic composition of the province, since the allottees were largely Sinhalese rather than Tamils.[51]

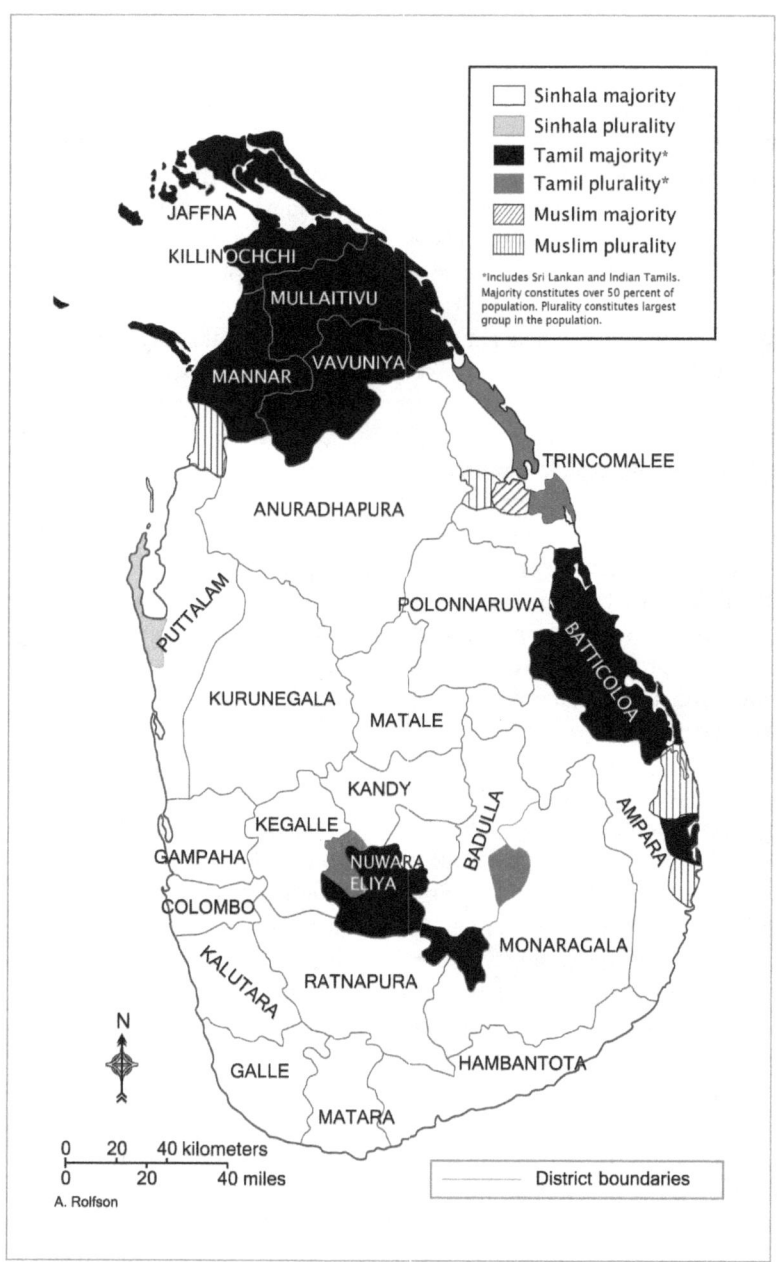

Legend:
- ☐ Sinhala majority
- ▨ Sinhala plurality
- ■ Tamil majority*
- ▨ Tamil plurality*
- ▨ Muslim majority
- ▨ Muslim plurality

*Includes Sri Lankan and Indian Tamils. Majority constitutes over 50 percent of population. Plurality constitutes largest group in the population.

JAFFNA
KILLINOCHCHI
MULLAITIVU
MANNAR
VAVUNIYA
TRINCOMALEE
ANURADHAPURA
POLONNARUWA
BATTICOLOA
PUTTALAM
KURUNEGALA
MATALE
KANDY
BADULLA
AMPARA
KEGALLE
GAMPAHA
NUWARA ELIYA
COLOMBO
MONARAGALA
KALUTARA
RATNAPURA
N
GALLE
HAMBANTOTA
MATARA

0 20 40 kilometers
0 20 40 miles
A. Rolfson

——— District boundaries

Map 4.2 Geographical distribution of ethnic groups (sources: Sri Lanka Population Census, 1981, Robert Stoddard 'Regionalization and Regionalism in Sri Lanka', Paper Presented at Session on South Asian Geography: Changing Trends and Patterns, Annual Conference on South Asia, Madison, Wisconsin, 7 November 1986, Map 6 (based on Assistant Government Agents' Divisions)).

Table 4.2 Ethnic composition of district populations, 1981 and 2001* (percentages)

Districts	Sinhalese		Sri Lankan Tamils		Indian Tamils		Sri Lankan Moor	
	1981	2001	1981	2001	1981	2001	1981	2001
Jaffna	0.6		95.3		2.4		1.7	
Mannar	8.1		50.6		13.2		26.6	1.2
Vavuniya	16.7	4.8	56.9	93.7	19.4	0.3	6.9	
Mullaitvu	5.1		76.0		13.9		4.9	
Trincomalee	35.8	23.4	32.0	48.0	2.5	0.1	28.8	28.2
Batticaloa	3.2	1.3	70.8	74.5	1.2	0.1	24.0	23.5
Ampara	37.6	39.9	20.1	18.4	0.4	0.1	41.5	41.3
Colombo	77.9	76.6	9.8	11.0	1.3	1.1	8.3	9.0
Gampaha	92.2	91.0	3.3	3.2	0.4	0.4	2.8	3.8
Kalutara	87.3	87.1	1.0	1.2	4.1	2.7	7.5	8.7
Galle	94.4	94.4	0.7	1.1	1.4	0.9	3.2	3.5
Matara	94.6	94.2	0.6	0.7	2.2	2.2	2.6	2.9
Hambantota	97.4	97.1	0.4	0.4	0.1	0.1	1.1	1.1
Kandy	74.3	74.1	4.9	4.1	9.3	8.1	10.7	13.1
Matale	79.9	80.1	5.9	5.5	6.7	6.3	7.2	8.7
Nuwara Eliya	42.2	40.2	12.5	6.5	42.4	50.6	2.5	2.4
Badulla	68.5	72.4	5.7	3.8	21.1	18.4	4.2	5.0
Moneragala	92.9	94.5	1.8	1.4	3.3	1.9	1.9	2.0
Ratnapura	84.7	86.8	2.3	2.8	11.1	8.1	1.7	2.0
Kegalle	86.3	85.9	2.1	1.9	6.4	5.6	5.1	6.4
Kurunegala	93.1	91.9	1.1	1.2	0.5	0.2	5.1	6.5
Puttalam	82.6	73.7	6.7	6.8	0.6	0.3	5.1	18.8
Anuradhapura	92.1	90.7	1.0	0.7	0.1	0.1	6.5	8.3
Polonnaruwa	90.9	90.4	2.2	2.0	0.1	0.1	6.5	7.5

Sources: Sri Lanka government census on population and housing 1981 and 2001.

Notes
* 2001 census not conducted in Northern and Eastern Districts except Ampara.
Estimates given for Trincomalee, Batticola and Northern Province in total.

Eastern Province

The argument by Tamil separatists that settlement should occur according to district ethnic ratios meant, for example, that the right bank of the Maduru Oya would be settled predominantly by Tamils instead of Sinhalese or Muslims.[52] Muslims, who were the largest community in the Eastern Province, did not want the Sinhalese to surpass their numerical position in the Province, but they also opposed Tamil separatism, which threatened to make them a much smaller minority in a combined Northern and Eastern Province.[53] In the 1977 general elections, the vast majority of people in the Eastern Province opposed Tamil separatism. The TULF, which contested under the separatist mandate, received only 27.4 percent of the total votes polled in the Province.[54] Nevertheless, for the Tamil separatists who claimed the Northern and Eastern Provinces as the exclusive traditional Tamil homelands, the very presence of non-Tamils in the Eastern Province became more and more of an 'affront'.[55] The international community also increasingly subscribed to the 'Tamil homeland' thesis, dismissing the broader demographic and economic issues and the landlessness and poverty of the Sinhala peasantry and their settlement in localities that were uninhabited or inhabited largely by Sinhalese prior to the establishment of settlements, especially in the Eastern Province.[56]

Changing ethnic distribution

Sri Lanka's historical tradition of island-wide pluralism upholds the right of islanders to migrate and live anywhere on the land irrespective of ethnicity or religion.[57] This tradition further expanded during the colonial period with the influx of Indian Tamils and Jaffna Tamils into the south during the process of colonial capitalist development. It is necessary to understand the changing regional ethnic distribution from an island-wide, multipolar perspective. What is often forgotten in the debate over Sinhala settlements in the north and the east, is the process of Indian Tamil settlements that has taken place over the decades and its implications for ethno-territorial claims. Individual migration and planned settlement of Indian Tamils from the plantation areas in the Northern Province increased their proportion of the population in the Northern Province between 1946 and 1981. This furthered the Tamilization of the Northern Province decreasing the proportion of the Muslims who had been the second largest group next to the Sri Lankan Tamils (Tables 1.2 and 4.2).

The separatist Tamil position, which portrays Sri Lankan Tamils as a region-ally based minority also overlooks their increasing 'locational diversity' and increasing island-wide minority status.[58] This separatist argument is undermined by an island-wide perspective on migration and shifting ethnic composition which shows, among other changes, increases in the Sri Lankan Tamil and Muslim populations in the Western and Central Provinces. With the extension of citizenship to Indian Tamils originally brought in by the colonial state, Nuwara Eliya in the Central Province emerged as a Tamil plurality electoral district. In 1971 more than half the Ceylon/Sri Lankan and Indian Tamils in Sri Lanka were already living outside the North and the East. Colombo, with 103,000 Sri Lanka Tamils, was the biggest city of Sri Lankan Tamils in the island.[59]

Meanwhile, as the arguments over state colonization went back and forth, the contest over ethnic quotas in Mahaweli settlement remained unresolved. The Sri Lankan government was unable to carry out much of the planned settlements due to ethnic conflict and the mounting security problems. In this atmosphere, politically motivated land encroachments in the Northern and Eastern Provinces became even more explosive than the state-sponsored Mahaweli settlements.

Encroachment

Encroachment – the illegal occupation of state-owned land – had been a problem in Sri Lanka since colonial times, when peasants who were barred from the so-called 'crown lands' asserted their traditional rights to common lands in defiance of colonial laws.[60] With increasing population pressure and decreasing land size and poverty, squatting became even a bigger problem in the post-independence era. Encroachers from previously established state settlements like Gal Oya colonies and other parts of the island outnumbered officially sponsored settlers in the Mahaweli region up to about 1982.[61] Encroachment accounted for a total of 585,477 people as opposed to 89,578 persons settled in state aided settlements including the Mahaweli and 470,695 persons given land through official Village Expansion schemes throughout the island circa 1980.[62] In the Eastern Province, encroachers, desperate landless and poverty stricken individuals seeking a means of livelihood, Sinhalese and Tamil, mostly Indian Tamils, far outnumbered those settled on state sponsored colonies at that time.[63] In the 1970s, after the declaration of the Tamil separatist objective, ethnically competitive encroachment became a major issue in the territorial conflict over the Northern and Eastern Provinces.

Many Indian Tamils from the island's plantation districts were attracted to the under-populated northern and eastern districts, where land was readily available. Among them were those displaced by the nationalization of the plantations under the United Left government during the 1970–1977 period and stateless persons seeking to avoid repatriation to India. After the growth of Sri Lankan Tamil separatism, however, many of the Tamils of Indian origin arriving in the north and the east were political refugees, many of them victims of Sinhala attacks during the riots of 1977 and 1981. Many of these low-caste Tamils squatted on state lands, with a large number settling in the Vanni region in the Northern Province, where the caste system was not as rigid as in the adjacent Jaffna Peninsula. The Indian Tamil population in the Vauniya district increased from less than 1,000 to nearly 30,000 between 1946 and 1981.[64]

After the 1977 riots, radical youth groups encouraged the ousting of Sinhalese from the north and settlement of Indian Tamils there because it helped to consolidate the Tamil ethnic identity of the north and the east and to create a 'buffer zone, against prospective Sinhalese settlers moving in'.[65] Arguing that the south was no longer safe for the Tamils and that the Tamils needed a separate state to live in safety, Amirthalingam and other TULF leaders opposed the return of Sinhalese ousted from the north after the 1977 riots.[66] The Sinhalese did not return, and the north became almost an exclusive Tamil region, as desired by the secessionists, while the Sri Lankan Tamil population in the rest of the country steadily increased.[67] Securing borders of Tamil Eelam had been a 'burning Tamil concern from the 1950s' and in the late 1970s it provided the passion and cutting edge to the Tamil militancy.[68]

Sinhala nationalists complained that large numbers of Tamil settlers were being brought to the north with support of Tamil politicians and that a 'well-organized movement was paying substantial allowances' to Tamil plantation families to encroach in the north and the east.[69] They also claimed that ancient Sinhala 'villages were being given Tamil names. District boundaries were being altered'.[70] The first organizations to help settle Indian Tamils in a systematic manner were TRRO (Tamil Refugees Rehabilitation Organization, later TRO) and SEDEC (Social and Economic Development Centre) of the Catholic Church. Other foreign-funded local and international NGOs, such as, the Sarvodaya Shramadana Movement and the Norwegian NGO, Redd Barna, also helped in the settlement of stateless Indian Tamils in the area.[71] In the early 1980s an organization called Gandhiyam 'with the help of the church agencies from West European countries' settled some 85,000 Tamil plantation workers in the Yan Oya basin, which surrounds the Trincomalee district in the Eastern Province, in the Mullativu and Vauniya districts in the Northern Province, and in the Anuradhapura district in the North Central Province making it the most strategic area in the territorial battle between the Sinhala government and the Tamil separatists[72] (Map 4.1). These areas were needed by the Sri Lankan government to maintain the island's territorial and political unity, and by the secessionists to carve out a future Eelam. The government had been seeking to break up the contiguity of Tamil majority areas in the north and the east and to destroy the demographic basis for Tamil separatism by settling Sinhalese in the contested areas.[73] The government suspected that Gandhiyam was a front organization for Tamil separatism and that the intention of its leader, Dr S. Rajasunderam, and some of his Catholic priest colleagues was to link up the Northern and Eastern Provinces through a corridor of exclusively Tamil settlements. Thus when terrorist activities increased in the early 1980s, the government removed settlers by force, fearing that they would help the separatist cause.[74] Sadly, many Indian Tamils who had sought refuge from ethnically motivated attacks in the plantation areas were once again subjected to harassment and abuse, this time by security forces seeking to wipe out terrorism.[75] However, many of the Tamil and Muslim refugees who fled from the conflict in the north and east managed to take refuge among Sinhala populations in the south and southwest.[76]

State action to remove illegal Tamil settlements in the north and the east in the late 1970s and early 1980s led to Tamil charges that the Sinhala government was lenient toward Sinhalese squatting on state land but not towards Indian Tamils who did the same.[77] Following the introduction of a government program to 'regularize', or legalize, encroachments in the mid-1980s (a practice that had begun in British times), Indian Tamils received legal rights to lands they had encroached upon. In fact, the majority of those receiving land under encroachment regularization in the Northern and Eastern Provinces in 1979 were non-Sinhalese.[78] Given their linguistic and cultural similarities, Indian Tamils were absorbed relatively easily into the Sri Lankan Tamil population in the north. By the mid-1980s the Vauniya district had the largest number of people of plantation Tamil background outside the Central Highlands (Table 4.2). Tamil nationalists have lauded the consolidation of the 'Tamilian character' resulting from these settlements. As the Tamil scholar K. Sivathamby has written,

> The pressure of Indian Tamil population – the over flow from the estates – is very important for it is at this level that one sees a tendency towards an Indian–Sri Lankan Tamil merger through marriages. Being the border area, 'communal consciousness' is markedly obvious.[79]

In 2003, Tamilchelvam, leader of the LTTE political wing, stated that '35% of our fighters are Tamils of Indian origin'[80] meaning that they are descendants of relatively recent arrivals in Sri Lanka brought to work on British plantations rather than descendants of the so-called 'traditional Tamil homeland' in the north and the east of Sri Lanka.

Ethnic integration and the 1978 constitution

Notwithstanding the intensifying territorial battle, the UNP, which made an electoral pledge to address the problems of the Sri Lankan Tamils, sought a new beginning in ethnic relations by reversing policies put in place to redress the grievances of the Sinhala Buddhist majority since 1956, first by addressing issues of higher education and then by enacting a new constitution.

Higher education

To satisfy minority, specifically Christian, concerns, in 1978 the government reintroduced state assistance to all non-fee-levying and, to a lesser extent, fee-levying private schools.[81] The UNP also removed language-based ethnic quotas or media wise standardization immediately after coming into office in 1977.

Despite the reverse discrimination it represented, the district quota system for admission to university science faculties was maintained, with modifications, into the late 1980s and beyond, reserving 15 percent of all university places for students from 12 educationally backward rural and plantation districts. The policy had great support from rural Sinhalese, the Muslim and Indian Tamil communities, and Sri Lankan Tamils outside the Jaffna district.[82] The percentage of Sri Lankan Tamils in the state universities dropped after 1978, but it remained 'consistently higher' than their proportion to the island's population. In the engineering and medicine faculties they held at least 35 percent of the positions for more than a decade following 1978 and around 25 percent for all the science faculties.[83] Following economic liberalization in 1977, private university education became widely available to the privileged social classes of all ethnic groups, who shifted their interest to securing places in elite international universities. Globalization of university education contributed to the deterioration of the standards of local higher education. While governmental efforts to bring about Sinhala–Tamil reconciliation were useful steps, however, the 1978 Constitution was more important than university admissions policies.

The 1978 Constitution

Using its five-sixth majority in parliament, the UNP government introduced a new constitution replacing the 1972 Constitution which had incited the formation of the TUF and the declaration of separatism. Ethnic integration was one of the major objectives of the new Constitution.

Chapter III of the new 1978 Constitution incorporated more substantial fundamental rights than the previous Republican Constitution of 1972 by extending those rights to noncitizens of Indian Tamil origin. Religious and language recognition were contentious issues. Sinhala nationalist pressures to elevate Buddhism to the status of the state religion and to legally restrict the presidency to a Sinhalese Buddhist did not succeed. Likewise, the TULF demand for equality of all religions was also not incorporated in the new constitution. Foremost position was given to Buddhism while also assuring the rights of all religions, including freedom of religion and individual right of choice in religion.[84] Sinhala was maintained as the official language, but significant modifications were made of the Official Language Act of 1956. Chapter IV of the constitution recognized Tamil as a national language. The rights of Tamils to receive education in Tamil, to be examined in Tamil for entry into public service, to receive government communications in Tamil and in other matters throughout the country were spelled out. Moreover, the position of Tamil as the language of administration and of the courts in the Northern and Eastern Provinces was asserted.[85] Thus the Tamil language was essentially given the same position as Sinhala and elevated to a position that it did not have in any other country where Tamil populations lived, including India, where it still remains a regional language.

Abandoning the Westminster-style parliamentary system, Chapter VII of the new constitution established a presidential system under which an executive president was to be elected directly by popular vote. A complicated system of proportional representation was introduced whereby the number of representatives to the parliament was determined by the proportion of votes gained by the contesting political parties, replacing the plurality system (first-past-the post voting), which promoted majoritarianism. The effect was to start a trend towards coalition politics requiring consensus building.[86] The new system of proportional representation and changes made in the area-basis of allocation of seats in the legislature in the constitution purposefully reduced the previous advantage enjoyed by Sinhala voters. At the same time, it increased the number of seats for the Northern and Eastern Provinces and the plantation districts with large Indian Tamil populations.[87] Thus the proportional representation system allowed the island's minorities to play a decisive role in the outcome of the competition between the two major Sinhala parties, the UNP and the SLFP, and to advance their own agendas. While this enabled other minorities to assert themselves within the Sri Lankan polity, the Sri Lankan Tamil politicians could not be reconciled by the new constitution which asserted The Republic of Sri Lanka as a Unitary State.

Minority assertiveness

The increased electoral strength of the minorities restrained the influence of Sinhala Buddhist nationalism and ethnic outbidding between the Sinhala parties. Over time, it led to the dropping of the Sinhala nationalist agenda by both the UNP and the SLFP to a large extent and a strengthening of communal politics among the minorities, especially the Muslims and the Indian Tamils.[88] Taking advantage of proportional representation and educational and other policies, the leaders of the Muslim and the Indian (plantation) Tamil communities integrated themselves more firmly into the electoral system and the island's democratic and pluralistic political structure. The CWC under the able leadership of S. Thondaman, who had come to agreements with the UNP prior to the 1977 elections, was able to extract several key concessions in the new constitution. As K.M. de Silva has noted, these and an administrative decision rescinding a hitherto restriction against voting in local government elections 'conferred on the Indian Tamils in Sri Lanka, in the main plantation workers, a distinct improvement in legal status, and underlined their equality with Sri Lankan citizens by descent'.[89] The improved political status of this community was further consolidated when Thondaman joined the government as a cabinet minister in 1978.[90]

The Muslims too used their increased electoral strength and educational advances, along with their improved economic competitiveness following economic liberalization in 1977, to improve their overall political-economic and cultural status.[91] The consistent appointment of Muslims as cabinet ministers in important areas such as Ports and Transportation helped solidify Muslim middle-class advancement. The 1978 Constitution is considered a watershed in Muslim politics. The complicated system of proportional representation subordinated individual politicians to political parties 'if they wanted to attain priority ranking on that party's nomination list'.[92] Considering the Muslim's best option was to form their own party under this system, M.H.M. Ashroff, a lawyer from the Eastern Province, formed the first Muslim political party, the Sri Lanka Muslim Congress (SLMC) in 1981 to champion Muslim interests.[93] Muslim economic expansion and the electoral gains from the new proportional representation system translated into a 'new aggressiveness' on the part of the Muslim leadership and a shift of political emphasis from 'concessions' from the Sinhala majority to the assertion of 'Muslim rights' within the Sri Lankan political system.[94]

While the pragmatic Indian Tamil and Muslim leaders took advantage of these new opportunities to integrate themselves more fully into the political system, the Tamil secessionists basically rejected the offers for accommodation provided by the government's educational policy and the 1978 Constitution. Sri Lankan Tamil leaders remained steadfast in their commitment to a separate Tamil state. Growing state authoritarianism and repression in turn encouraged the spread of separatist violence and the emergence of a civil war.

Separatist rejection

The Tamil secessionists' interest did not lie in integrating themselves into the Sri Lankan polity but in separating from it. The language recognition, university admissions, fundamental rights, and equality they had sought were now available to them, but they were not satisfied. A. Jeyaratnam Wilson has explained that the TULF's refusal to be responsive stemmed from its rigid and outmoded thinking as a 'dominant' community and the pressure put on it by the Tamil militants:

> [T]he Ceylon Tamil minority still continues to look on itself as one of the two major communities in the island,... as one of the two founding races. The Ceylon Tamil political leadership cannot therefore be easily satisfied or even 'purchased' because of increasing militancy and political violence among underground movements of Ceylon Tamil youth.[95]

Although legislation was passed giving equal status to Tamil with Sinhala, implementation was weak due to notorious government inefficiency and lack of sensitivity towards Tamil grievances. Outside of the Northern and Eastern Provinces, it was difficult to transact business in Tamil. This has made Tamils feel inferior and hold a sense of grievance and disillusionment with the Sinhala government.[96] Most importantly from the point of view of the TULF, the 1978 Constitution made 'no concession to federalism ... nor ... provision for the decentralization of power'.[97] Perhaps a compromise on political decentralization could still have been worked out if the TULF had been engaged in the parliamentary Select Committee proceedings that preceded the enactment of the new constitution. But Amirthlingam refused to participate in the Select Committee on the ground that it did not amount to an all-party conference as promised prior to the election by the UNP.[98] Because the Select Committee did not constitute an all-party conference; it did not allow political parties without representation in the National Assembly to participate in constitutional drafting.[99] But the TULF's reasoning was disingenuous. The fundamental reason for the TULF's refusal to participate was its deepening ideological commitment to separatism. Amirthalingam justified this unequivocal position:

> [T]he sovereignty of the Tamil nation,... [is] ethnically, geographically and linguistically separate, identifiable and distinct ... The United National Party had a clear, unequivocal mandate to assert the sovereignty of the Sinhala nation and enact a new constitution. The mandate of the majority of the Tamil nation pointed to a different duty.[100]

Supporters of the constitution viewed it as 'the most notable and resolute initiative in ethnic reconciliation taken in the recent political history of the island'.[101] Critics, on the other hand, charged that it was a 'betrayal' of the UNP's election pledges to the Tamils, providing 'too little and too late'. The assumption was that what may have satisfied the Tamils 20 years earlier was no longer sufficient.[102] By this time the TULF was under strong pressure by the youth terrorist groups not to give into the compromise measures put forward by the government.[103] To worsen matters, while seeking accommodation with the TULF, the government was at the same time pursuing a repressive policy to wipe out Tamil terrorism in the north, a policy that alienated the TULF from the government.

In this atmosphere of increasing distrust, the government's new initiative for decentralization of the administration – the District Development Councils (DDCs), which fulfilled a pledge made in the UNP election platform – could not succeed. Although the TULF entered the elections for the DDCs, from its separatist point of view the DDCs did not devolve sufficient power to the districts or confer authority to embark on development projects on their own[104] Elections for the new DDCs held in June 1981 proceeded peacefully in all the districts throughout the island except Jaffna, where the elections were marred by terrorist attacks and excesses by government's security forces responding to them. With rising separatist violence and government's determination to wipe out terrorism and the ensuing Presidential elections and the Referendum of 1982, discussed below, the DDCs and the crucial matter of political decentralization took a backseat. Even the limited authority of the DDCs was not implemented sufficiently to devolve authority to regions.[105] On the contrary, the centralization of political power in the hands of the new executive president and increasing state authoritarianism further convinced the Tamils that the government was not serious about devolution of power to the north and the east. The next section examines how since 1977 both economic liberalization and the TULF separatist platform contributed to the growth of state authoritarianism, weakening the parliamentary democratic traditions that Sri Lanka had enjoyed since 1931.

State authoritarianism

The heavy dependence on foreign funding made political stability a prerequisite of the Open Economy.[106] The expansion of large public-sector projects, especially the AMDP, which had a long gestation period, required centralized control over major economic decisions and a stable and strong government.[107] Economist Mick Moore has argued that the dependence on external funding and the growing sense of economic prosperity freed the UNP government from the populist and democratic style of politics that had prevailed in the country since independence.[108]

The newly imposed policies of economic liberalization and the austerity measures imposed by the IMF and the World Bank negatively affected workers. The UNP leader Jayawardena believed that the government was elected to govern effectively and must not be hampered with too much opposition. Thus the UNP government set out to make its position secure by eliminating challenges from all opposition forces.[109]

This objective led to the introduction of the new presidential system of government in September 1977 and the quick enactment of the new constitution in 1978, using the UNP parliamentary majority limiting public debate. The powers of government were concentrated in the new office of President which was not dependent on or constrained by the parliament. The new 'Gaullist' constitution, created principally to 'attract foreign investment and to convince international aid-givers that Sri Lanka is a safe bet', elevated Jayawardena to the position of 'Executive President'.[110] He also became the head of the cabinet,

Commander in Chief of the Armed Forces, leader of the UNP and Minister in charge of several ministries. The continuity of presidential power and the five-sixth majority of the UNP were ensured by imposing strong controls: UNP members of parliament, for instance, were required to submit signed undated letters of resignation to the President, which he could then use to dismiss MPs as he needed.[111] The weakening of the parliament as an institution contributed in turn to the devaluing and control of the mass media, especially the state-owned media. As a result, there were no worthwhile debates in parliament to be reported even under the many periods of emergency under the UNP between 1978 and 1989.[112]

Tamil militants who represented the biggest threat to the state and the society were not the only ones to experience the effects of political authoritarianism and increasing state repression. The list of measures taken to repress the legal and democratic Sinhala political opposition was already a long one by the time the severe ethnic conflict erupted in 1983. Moore observed two aspects to this repression: 'the simple use of physical violence against opponents, and … the manipulation of law and the constitution'.[113] The Sinhala and Tamil democratic opposition, the media, students, the working class, union movements, and any sector or institution that posed a threat to the new political and economic order were targeted since the UNP came to power in 1977. Thugs were used routinely against groups that sought to redress grievances through public protests and peaceful demonstrations – 'students, women workers on strike, nurses, 700 blind weavers, Buddhist monks, joint clergy gatherings, the Sinhala Balavegaya, Prof. Ediriweera Sarathchandra and others'.[114] Legislation restricting individual rights and emergency powers were widely used. The UNP weakened political opposition by depriving the civil rights of Sirimavo Bandaranaike, the leader of the SLFP, the main opposition party, who had been Prime Minister for 12 years. These restrictions were achieved through the courts and by the enactment of new laws.[115] Restriction of her civil rights prevented Bandaranaike from contesting the presidential elections in October 1982.[116]

Attacks were made against student opposition on the Vidyalankara campus in March 1978, the Katubedda campus in April 1978, the Polgolla campus in February 1979, the Vidyodaya campus in March 1979, the Colombo campus in March 1980, and the Kelaniya campus of the University of Sri Lanka in June 1980.[117] The subversion of democratic processes and popular participation was also directed at the powerful and vibrant trade union movement that had been active since the 1930s. The labor unions that were anchored in the public sector were closely allied with Marxist political parties but had remained autonomous from the state and had challenged every government since independence.[118] State authoritarianism vis-à-vis the unions was largely the product of the Open Economy, which called for state protection of private investment and foreign interests. Requirements for the registration of unions were tightened, and the unions decreased in number. Unions were banned altogether from the Free Trade Zone in the southwestern region, a common requirement of export-processing zones globally. After 1977, the left-wing unions were undermined by the UNP government-backed union, the Jathika Sevaka Sanghamaya (JSS), which in the late 1970s and 1980s wielded unprecedented power through its own intelligence network and goons paid for by the state. The JSS is known to have used 'brute force against anti-government unions during strikes'.[119]

The harsh repression of a general strike in July 1980 virtually destroyed the trade union movement. More than 40,000 workers were dismissed from their jobs, mostly in the government sector and many of them were never reinstated.[120] Due to this severe treatment of organized labor and other factors, such as the vast exodus of workers to the Middle East, the unions were unable to mount significant resistance. As elsewhere in the world, the processes of economic globalization increased worker resignation to social class and transnational corporate exploitation, and that exploitation intensified culturally-based ethno-religious conflicts.[121] As is discussed below, the JSS, which was controlled by Cyril Mathew, Minister of Science and Industries and the most chauvinistic Sinhala Buddhist in the Cabinet, was involved in the anti-Tamil attacks in July 1983.

The new political authoritarianism and the imperious style of J.R. Jayawardena played a significant role in both the deterioration of public trust in the government and the worsening of Sinhala–Tamil relations. More than any other individual, Jayawardena has been held responsible for the institutionalization of political violence after 1977 and the repression that would transform the ethnic conflict into a civil war.[122] But not all of Jayawardena's policies towards the Tamils were repressive. The government pursued a two-pronged approach towards the Sri Lankan Tamils: a moderate conciliatory approach towards the TULF and harsh repression towards youth terrorists in the north. The government soon realized, however, that it was not possible to keep the strategies separate because the two Tamil groups were closely intertwined. On the horizon was a heightening of violence and armed conflict, provoked by both the government and Tamil separatists.

Armed separatist struggle

A large number of Tamil resistance groups, many of them small armed gangs mixing Tamil political aspirations and criminal activity, had emerged by the early to mid-1970s with the support of the moderate TULF. At first the different militant youth organizations were united by overlapping memberships. Although there were over 40 such groups at one stage, by the end of the 1970s only five of them remained durable and actively committed to creating a separate Tamil state:[123] TELO (Tamil Eelam Liberation Organization); EROS (Eelam Revolutionary Organization of Students); LTTE (Liberation Tigers of Tamil Eelam); PLOTE (People's Liberation Organization of Tamil Eelam); and EPRLF (Eelam People's Revolutionary Liberation Front). These Tamil resistance groups were involved in assassinations, attempted assassinations, bank robberies, and other criminal activities, as well as fratricidal violence among themselves. According to an LTTE spokesmen, since their inception in 1972 and July 1978, their score was '20 policemen killed, together with five politicians and five informers',[124] and by 1983 the LTTE emerged as the leader among the groups.

The mounting acts of terrorism led the government to tighten security and increase the military presence in the north. On 22 May 1978, Parliament approved a bill to proscribe the LTTE and similar organizations for one year.[125] Yet terrorist activities increased and extended to the south. In a daring attack on 7 September 1978, an Avro aircraft of Air Ceylon, the national airline, was blown up on the runway of the Ratmalana airport in a suburb of Colombo during celebrations to mark the introduction of the new Constitution.[126] The resulting heavy military presence, road blocks, searches, and arrests, which were part of military excesses and harassment of suspected Tamil terrorists, were vehemently condemned by the TULF leader Amirthalingam.[127] As de Silva has noted, as 'militant groups continued their program of terrorist activities…, the ambiguity of the TULF position within the country's political system was emphasized with every violent incident'.[128] This ambiguity was further revealed in the Tamil moderates' role in the regionalization and internationalization of the armed separatist struggle. The leaders of the Tamil Catholic Church, a significant group in the Sri Lankan Tamil elite also played a controversial role moving from a moderate Tamil nationalist position towards supporting separatism after the 1977 ethnic violence.[129]

Internationalization of the conflict

The TULF had been clandestinely supporting the LTTE since the mid-1970s. After the 1977 elections, Amirthlingam was said to be using his position as the leader of the parliamentary opposition to write letters of reference on government stationery to raise funds for the LTTE and other Tamil insurgent groups.[130] Breaching the neutrality expected from his position as the leader of the opposition, Amirthalingam actively supported the internationalization of the Tamil separatist cause.[131] On 5 October 1978 Krishna Vaikunthvasan, a Sri Lankan Tamil, slipped into the UN General Assembly, seized the microphone and called for Eelam before the Sri Lankan Foreign Minister Hameed could make his address at the rostrum. On 10 November 1978 Amirthalingam attended the inaugural meeting of the Tamil Coordinating Committee (TCC), an LTTE front, established by Vaikunthavasan.[132] The prosperous Tamil expatriate lobby in Boston succeeded in having the lower house of the Massachusetts state legislature adopt a resolution on 9 May 1979 in support of Tamil Eelam. The then-governor of Massachusetts, Michael Dukakis, declared on 22 May 1979 (the anniversary of the proscription of the LTTE in Sri Lanka) as 'Eelam Tamils' Day'.[133] In July 1981, the Sri Lankan Parliament brought a no-confidence motion against Amirthlingam, based on allegations that he had sought to negotiate direct aid to Jaffna from the IMF and the IBRD during a visit to the US. The allegations were unfounded, but the motion was passed by an overwhelming vote, souring relations between the government and the Tamil parliamentary opposition.[134]

The separatist cause has been advanced by World Eelam Conferences held every year since 1982, the first three in the United States. The Sri Lankan government's ineffectiveness in countering the Tamil separatist charges and the lack of a balanced perspective outside Sri Lanka on the Sri Lankan conflict helped legitimize the Tamil separatist struggle internationally. The result was a general lack of condemnation of Sri Lankan Tamil terrorism. Without the regional and international bases of ideological and military support that the LTTE was able to build up, the Sri Lankan conflict could not have turned into a civil war. While Tamil moderates were championing the separatist cause and raising funds abroad, terrorists were receiving clandestine training outside the country. Edgar O'Ballance, the author of *The Cyanide War*, has reported that according to documents captured by the Israelis from the Palestinians in Lebanon in 1982, 'over 300 Tamils had been trained in the terrorist camps'.[135] But the biggest support for the Tamil insurgency came not from distant lands but from neighboring India, even prior to the escalation of the conflict in July 1983. After the violence of July 1983 the Indian involvement would grow dramatically and become a key force in the conflict for the next eight years.

India and the separatist struggle

India's direct entry into the Sri Lankan conflict and its controversial role as the protector and patron of Sri Lankan Tamil terrorists would complicate the island's crisis.[136] From the early 1970s, the politics in the restive Jaffna Peninsula were viewed in India as part of internal Tamil Nadu politics. As de Silva has remarked, 'seldom has a constituent unit (a province or state) of one country influenced the relationship between it and a neighboring country with the same intensity and to the same extent that Tamil Nadu did'.[137] The large base of supportive co-ethnics enabled the LTTE to link up with a number of small political groups in Tamil Nadu, and enable Prabhakaran and other Sri Lankan Tamil militants and criminals seeking to evade arrest in Sri Lanka to find refuge there. The first contact between the Sri Lankan Tamil activists and the state government in Tamil Nadu was established in 1972 when a delegation from the Tamil Manavi Peravi, a Sri Lankan Tamil youth group committed to armed struggle, met with the then-leader of Tamil Nadu, E.V.R. Periya.[138] Chelvanayakam and Amirthlingam also traveled to Tamil Nadu in 1972 and were warmly received and given the support of the DMK and ADMK as well as the Indian Congress Party. From then on, the Indian central government's policy on the Sri Lankan separatist issue has been driven by South India and its ethnocentric political leaders.

Indian prime minister Indira Gandhi did not intervene in the Sri Lankan conflict in the early 1970s. However, as her political position changed after 1977, India came to play a critical role in the legitimizing and strengthening of the Sri Lankan separatist movement.[139] Prior to 1977, when Sirimavo Bandaranaike was the Prime Minister, Sri Lanka, like India, had pursued policies of nonalignment and democratic socialism, and the two women prime ministers, Gandhi and Bandaranaike, enjoyed a close personal relationship. The Sri Lankan President Jayawardena, elected in 1977, however, did not have good personal relations with Gandhi and mismanaged relations with India. After the introduction of economic liberalization in 1977, the Jayawardena government was beholden to the World Bank, IMF, that supplied the foreign aid for economic development and indirectly for the subsequent war effort. The new economic policy led to the realignment of Sri Lanka's foreign policy, leading it closer to the West. This in turn affected the ethnic conflict.[140] Not only were Israeli and British foreign intelligence and counter-insurgency operatives believed to be present in Sri Lanka, but there were rumors that the US was planning to establish a military presence in the strategic port of Trincomalee. China and Pakistan were increasing military assistance to Sri Lanka.

After Indira Gandhi returned to power in 1980 (she had lost the Indian elections in 1977), she encouraged M.G. Ramachandran, the Sri Lankan-born ('Plantation Tamil') movie idol and Chief Minister of Tamil Nadu, to give covert support to the Sri Lankan Tamil insurgents. As a result, the number of camps in Tamil Nadu training Sri Lankan insurgents were increased, as were arms and other assistance to the insurgents. For years the Indian government continued to deny their presence in India, insisting that they were just refugees 'fleeing from a repressive regime, who were simply being given humanitarian aid'.[141] Indira Gandhi's decision to destabilize the Sri Lankan government is believed to have stemmed from two motivations: concern with Indian security in the region[142] and the Congress Party's need for the electoral support of Tamil Nadu.

It is unlikely that the Sri Lankan Tamil militants would have been able to emerge as a strong threat to the government of Sri Lanka had it not been for the military support given by India, starting well before the riots of July 1983.[143] Military camps to train Sri Lankan Tamil militants existed in various parts of India. While most of these camps were opened after July 1983, security analyst Rohan Gunaratna has reported the existence of camps prior to that. Training camps were provided for the LTTE, TELO, PLOT(E), and TELA in Tamil Nadu. A military camp in Parangimal, where 'Indian recruiters were channeled through RAW (Research and Analysis Wing of the Indian government) to train TELO recruits' was reportedly in 'complete operation' by October 1982.[144] Gunaratna also reports that members of the Indian military hired by RAW trained PLOT(E) recruits in various camps in South India from March 1983 on, and that PLOT(E) and TELO members were also trained in an Indian Army camp close to the Delhi International Airport prior to May 1983.[145] Clearly, Indian military support for Tamil separatism estranged relations between the governments of Sri Lanka and India: 'Sri Lanka accused India of interfering in her internal affairs. India on the other hand accused Sri Lanka of violating the human rights of Tamils'.[146]

The government campaign

The Eelam campaign gained sympathy abroad while LTTE's terrorist activities in the island, such as the killing of police officers, steadily increased. The proscription against the Tigers was extended on 1 July 1979. After incidents like the killing of Police Inspector Guruswamy at his residence in Jaffna, the government imposed emergency rule in Jaffna on 12 July 1979. On the same day, President Jayawardena issued a harsh directive to Army Brigadier Weeratunga 'to eliminate the menace of terrorism in all its forms from the island and more specially from the Jaffna District' within six months.[147] As the Movement for Inter Racial Justice and Equality (MIRJE) pointed out, the emergency rule increased repression and human rights violations in the north. The imposition of censorship only contributed to arbitrary arrest and abuses of Tamils, especially suspected youth terrorists in the north.[148] After complaints by Amirthlingam, some of the harshest of emergency regulations were withdrawn.[149] But as the violence continued, in July 1979 the government enacted the draconian Prevention of Terrorism Act (PTA).[150] The PTA, which was modeled after the Prevention of Terrorism Act in Britain to deal with the terrorist Irish Republican Army (IRA), incorporated rigorous regulations into the legal framework of the country. Like the earlier Criminal Justice Commission Act imposed by the SLFP to deal with the JVP in 1971 and which the UNP at the time had denounced, under the PTA suspects could be detained without trial for up to 18 months and brought to trial on charges based on confessions inadmissible under the normal laws of the land.[151] The emergency in Jaffna, which worsened ethnic relations, was lifted at the end of 1979 although President Jayawardena's goal of eliminating terrorism within six months was not achieved. Instead, both Tamil separatist terror and state terror intensified.

The DDC elections in 1981 led to an escalation of violence in the north. Militants bent on establishing Eelam set out to disrupt the elections for the DDCs, which represented the government's response to the demand for devolution of power. On 10 June 1981, just ten days prior to the scheduled DDC elections, Dr Thiagarajah, the UNP's top candidate for Jaffna, was murdered. It was the second major killing of a leading Tamil politician, following the assassination of Alfred Duraiappa in July 1975. In response to the incident, the government sent police officers from other areas of the country to maintain law and order during the elections in the already tense and volatile Jaffna peninsula. On the eve of the elections on 4 June 1981, terrorists killed four Sinhala policemen who were on election duty. For the next week, enraged Sinhala policemen retaliated in a rampage of destruction in Jaffna, targeting property, not people. Among the most barbaric acts of police terrorism was the burning of the Jaffna Public Library and its collection of 95,000 volumes. The destruction of the original library and its priceless volumes wounded the psyche of the people in the north, deepening their distrust and animosity of the Sri Lankan government and the Sinhala people.[152]

The violence in July 1981 was contained within Jaffna by the state's declaration of an emergency there. The overwhelming TULF victory of the postponed DDC elections in Jaffna helped to improve relations between the TULF and the government and to resume amity talks between them. However, the resurgence of communally based violence dampened the reconciliation efforts.[153] In August 1981, the communal violence erupted in the Ampara district of the Eastern Province, in areas of the southwest, and in the hill country where, once again, helpless Indian Tamils became the targets of Sinhala attacks. The government of India expressed concern, and mass demonstrations were held in Madras to protest attacks against the plantation Tamils in Sri Lanka.[154] The cycle of violence and counter violence deepened, making 1981 a year of 'racial violence'.[155] There were further killings of security personnel, attacks on the Colombo–Jaffna mail train by the Tamil terrorists, and retaliation and excesses by army personnel in Jaffna. The government passed an amendment (Act no. 48 of 1979) to the PTA in March 1982 to make the PTA a permanent piece of legislation.[156]

Placed among a population that was culturally and linguistically distinct from them, the Sri Lankan armed forces found it difficult to suppress the Tamil militants. Like their counterparts in other countries facing an insurgency, they too found conventional fighting methods inadequate to fight an escalating guerilla war.[157] The government's attempt to increase the number of Tamils in the police to 40 percent in 1982 did not succeed; instead, the Tamil numbers declined. In August 1982 a new paramilitary police commando, the STF (Special Task Force), opened a training camp and interrogation center in Elephant Pass in the north. Serious lapses of discipline. on the part of the security forces increased Tamil resentment of the Sri Lankan state.[158] In addition to the cycle of violence, the acceleration of the Sri Lankan conflict and its eventual transformation into a civil war can also be traced to two elections in 1982: the first-ever presidential elections and a referendum to extend the life of parliament.[159]

Presidential elections and the referendum

J.R. Jayawardena won the presidential elections held in October 1982, with Hector Kobbekaduwa of the SLFP coming in second and Rohana Wijeweera of the JVP third. The JVP, which entered electoral politics for the first time, had already become the third largest party outside the North and the East. Wijeweera gained more votes than either of the candidates from the two traditional left parties (the Trotskyite LSSP and its break away NLSSP). Support for the JVP and its Sinhala nationalism was strongest in the remote and poverty stricken Hambantota, Moneragala and Polonnaruwa districts in the south.[160] After the presidential elections, the JVP organized rallies throughout the island in anticipation of parliamentary elections, which were due any time up to the last quarter of 1983.[161] It is interesting to note that in the presidential elections the Sri Lankan Tamils in the north voted for the SLFP candidate, as opposed to Jayawardena or the Tamil candidate, Kumar Ponnambalam.[162]

President Jayawardena surprised the country by calling for a referendum in December 1982, asking the electorate to extend his government's term of office for another six years instead of going to the polls in 1983. Possible outbreaks of election violence, a 'Naxalite threat' from radical elements in the SLFP, and the need to deal with Tamil terrorism were the reasons given for this controversial and authoritarian move by Jayawardena to maintain himself in power.[163] All the other political parties were opposed to referendum, with the TULF and the JVP leading the opposition.

A public statement issued by the Civil Rights Movement documented extensive 'improprieties, irregularities and illegalities' in the conduct of the referendum. It pointed out, that the banning of opposition newspapers enabled the government-controlled media 'to imply that a "NO" vote at the referendum would be tantamount to a vote of no confidence in its development policies, and thus blur the actual issue [the extension of parliament for six years without holding a general election]'.[164] Moreover, the actions of the government represented a 'tragic setback' after 50 years of universal franchise, during which the electoral process had functioned smoothly and fairly in Sri Lanka: the use of emergency regulations to hold opposition SLFP organizers in detention; intimidation of voters and prevention of access to polling stations; harassment of polling observers and officers; impersonation of voters; and threatening behavior by the police.[165]

Although the government claimed an electoral mandate to extend its term in office, others have questioned the validity of the referendum's outcome: 5.8 million votes were cast out of a total of 8.1 million registered voters, of which 3.1 million, or 38 percent of registered voters, were recorded to have voted 'yes'. A Civil Rights Movement statement pointed out that even if the 3.1 million figure is correct (notwithstanding impersonations and other polling irregularities), some 2.6 million voters, that is 62 percent of registered voters 'voted for a general election or had nothing to say, due either to indifference or to being prevented for one reason or another from coming to the polls to express their wish'.[166] Significantly, in the Northern and the Eastern Provinces every electorate except the predominantly Sinhala electorate of Seruvila voted against the extension of the life of the parliament. In the volatile Jaffna district, 265,000 voters were against the referendum to extend the government's term in office and only 25,000 in favor of it.[167] This meant that despite all the violence that had transpired in 1977, 1979, and 1981, the north still wanted general elections and was willing to remain within a united Sri Lanka with a new parliament.[168] As such, the Sri Lankan Tamils were greatly affected by the vitiation of the system of parliamentary democracy and representation. Their loss of confidence in Sri Lanka's parliamentary system was complete when the Tamil MPs resigned their seats on 22 July 1983 when their six year term in parliament was completed.[169]

With the fraudulent referendum, the UNP government lost its legitimacy and moral claim to rule. The loss of faith and alienation from the government contributed to increased violence on the part of disaffected youth in both the Tamil and Sinhala communities. Even Jayawardena, in one of the last interviews he gave in retirement in October 1989, admitted that 'holding a referendum was a mistake I made'.[170] Had parliamentary elections been conducted in 1983, perhaps, the fateful July 1983 ethnic disturbances that turned the ethnic conflict into a civil war could have been avoided. As Father Balasuriya has reflected,

> If ... general elections had been held, Parliament would have been dissolved by 23rd July, 1983 and the entire mood of the country would have been different. From early 1983 general elections would have gripped the people's

attention. In the North and the East too the youth would have had an interest in contesting general elections. If general elections had not been given up in 1983, they would have had a year of the renewal and the revival of the democratic process. The Government and the opposition parties too would have wooed the Tamil votes, as the Government did in 1977 ... The Government would have to render an account to the people of its steward-ship and also respond to the Tamil people.[171]

By holding the referendum and by fixing the electoral map for 12 years, a gener-ation was denied its right to elect its leaders. The SLFP opposition party was moribund, and both Sinhala and Tamil opposition was driven outside the parlia-ment.[172] After the presidential elections and the referendum, the JVP still remained committed to participating in mainstream politics and entered by-elections in May 1983. But Jayawardena and his government were threatened by the growing popularity of the JVP after the controversial referendum, a massive military-style JVP rally on 1 May 1983, and the alleged JVP claims to double their numbers in the rural areas and come to power by the end of that year. Moreover, despite four years of intense efforts since Jayawardena's order in July 1979 to wipe out terrorism in six months, the Tamil insurgency in the north was intensifying.[173]

During the referendum in December 1982 there were serious clashes at Per-adeniya University between UNP and anti-UNP groups. The UNP's extension of its term of office through the referendum emboldened right wing elements in the university to believe 'they could act with impunity with the forces of the State backing them'.[174] Whereas previous clashes on the university campuses had not been along communal lines, the attacks which took place in May 1983 in Per-adeniya were attacks by Sinhala students against fellow Tamil students. The attacks were externally motivated and not spontaneous outbursts arising out of anger against the Tamil insurgency and the worsening conflict. The leader of the attacks was known to be a UNP agent whereas the JVP, commonly regarded as a Sinhala chauvinist party, is reported to have come to the aid of the Tamil victims.[175] There was a sense that the government was planning some kind of 'showdown'. While alternative accounts of those incidents are needed, Rajan Hoole's argument that the May 1983 incidents at Peradeniya were a premonition of what took place in July 1983 needs to be considered. He writes:

> The ideas that surfaced at Peradeniya in May were those which emerged from the mouths of attackers at the end of July ... It suggests that at least by May 1983, an influential section of the UNP was planning for the big show while also laying down the line for those who still had some sanity left.[176]

Black July

The ongoing cycles of conflict would culminate in the worst outbreak to date – the violence of July 1983. Black July, as it came to known, would cause the conflict to spiral into civil war. Indeed, the country as a whole has yet to recover from that terrible tragedy and its political reverberations.[177]

The news of the killing of 13 Sri Lankan soldiers by Tamil militants in Jaffna on 23 July 1983, then the arrival of their dead bodies in Colombo, is usually viewed as the incident that sparked the horrific Sinhala violence against Tamils. The government controlled media played its role in ethnic polarization by blacking out the news that on the following morning, 24 July, the armed forces had gone on a rampage and killed 14 Tamils in the north as a revenge for the killing of the 13 Sinhala soldiers. According to Balasuriya, 'The sense of anger of the Sinhala mob might have been tempered if this information was also given equal publicity by the media, which were then controlled by the Government'.[178] In the meantime, rumors had been circulating prior to 25 July of 'something about to happen ... something nasty, of a lesson to be taught'.[179]

The mood of the large crowd that had gathered at the funeral of the dead soldiers at the Kanatte cemetery in Colombo on the evening of 24 July had at first been anti-government. There was growing frustration over the inequities generated by the Open Economy and the government's authoritarian policies. The crowd was already moving towards the heavily guarded house of the president in the neighborhood, but after pro-government gangs were brought in to incite anti-Tamil feelings, the anti-government cry apparently turned into an anti-Tamil cry and an outbreak of arson and murder of Tamils. The attacks on Tamils in Colombo that started on the night of 24 July continued through the next day, and for several more days. Hundreds of Tamil and Indian shops and property in the business areas of Colombo were attacked and burned down. Homes of Tamils in residential areas in the city and its suburbs were identified by electoral lists carried by the mobs, attacked, and many occupants killed. Estimates of the number of Tamils killed in the July 1983 violence have varied widely from about 200 to about 2,000 (the latter figure was given by Amirthalingam).[180] Some 100,000 Sri Lankan Tamils were forced to enter refugee camps when several thousands of their homes, shops, factories, vehicles, and other belongings were destroyed. About 30,000 became unemployed due to the destruction of work sites, and the country experienced incalculable damage economically, politically, and morally. The Tamils were traumatized by the experience of utter helplessness and victimization in the face of Sinhala mob attacks. Many Sinhala individuals did come forward to help Tamil victims, but the Tamils' sense of insecurity, anger, and distrust of the Sinhalese generated by the terrible events of 1983 still remain.

While the entire Sinhala community has been blamed for the shameful events of July 1983, there is 'substantial evidence' that they were not 'a sudden and spontaneous outbreak of the Sinhala population against the Tamils', but a 'concerted attempt ... made by means of a carefully laid out plan over a long period of time to destroy the houses and belongings of Tamils in the professions and the trade'.[181] Even Thondaman, leader of the hill country Tamils and an admirer of the LTTE, acknowledged this in his remarks on the July 1983 violence:

There are many people who claim that these disturbances are a further manifestation of the Sinhala uprising against the Tamil. But I do not share the
view. The vast majority of the Sinhala people condemn these atrocities on
these innocent Tamil people and have shown sympathy and understanding,
Many have given shelter in their own homes in spite of intimidations and
threats. In those circumstances, to say that this is a Sinhala uprising against
the Tamils is absurd.[182]

Who is responsible for provoking the events of Black July? Sinhalese from
among the urban poor spontaneously joined in the carnage, but there is strong
evidence that the organized violence was carried out by thugs and agents of
government ministers and prominent UNP members. Members of JSS, the
government-backed union that had developed its own intelligence function, are
reported to have drawn up dossiers on Tamils 'including where they lived and
the houses and businesses they owned'.[183] According to some accounts, the
'goon squads' that attacked Tamils in July 1983 were the same individuals and
groups which were trained and paid to crush political dissent, smash strikes, terrorize, and even kill when needed.[184] An account of the 1983 riots published
under the pseudonym L. Piyadasa claims that

[I]n Kelaniya, Industries Minister Cyril Mathew's gangs were identified as
the ones at work. The General Secretary of the government 'union', the
Jathika Sevaka Samithiya (JSS) was identified as the leader of gangs which
wrought destruction and death all over Colombo and especially in
Wellawatte, where as many as ten houses a street were destroyed. A particular UNP municipal councilor of the Dehiwela-Mount Lavinia municipality
led gangs in Mount Lavinia. In the Pettah (the bazaar area where 442 shops
were destroyed and murders committed) the commander was the son of
Aloysius Mudalai, the Prime Minister's right-hand man ... The thugs who
worked regularly for the leaders of the UNP, both ministers of state and
Party Headquarters, and in some cases uniformed military personnel and
police, were seen leading the attack. They used vehicles of the Sri Lanka
Transport Board (Minister in charge, M.H. Mohamed) and other government departments and state corporations. Trucks of the Ceylon Petroleum
Cooperation's Oil Refinery came from many miles away bringing the men
who destroyed so much of Wellawatte [main Sri Lankan Tamil residential
area in Colombo] ... in the neighborhoods, after the initial shock, Sinhalese
and Burghers organized themselves and kept off gangs who had been sent to
burn and kill.[185]

Black July, then, was not a sudden and spontaneous riot or outbreak of passion,
not an inevitable eruption of primordial resentment and hatred between two
ethnic groups. It was a pogrom, 'an organized and officially encouraged massacre or persecution of a minority group'.[186] And it provoked a predictable
result. After July 1983, Tamil insurgent attacks on government security forces

and Sinhala civilians in the north and the south increased dramatically. Yet that Tamil backlash did not instigate Sinhala backlashes against Tamil civilians in the south, which necessitates questioning the common assumption that the Sinhalese are inherently violent towards Tamils. The government's inaction in the face of the 1983 violence gives further credence to the charge that Black July was government-supported. The police and the army failed to take action against the mobs, and in some cases they were in league with the attackers who were cheering 'Victory to the Sinhalese Army'. President Jayawardena did not declare curfew in Colombo until 2 pm on Monday 25 July, when the worst was over. Similarly, in other areas like Kandy, Badulla, and Nuwara Eliya curfew was declared only after mobs had already rampaged against the hill country Tamils.[187] The President finally addressed the country on television on 28 July, but he justified the violence as the righteous anger of the Sinhalese against Tamil terrorism. Jayawardena did not take a firm stance against the violence and did not offer sympathy to Tamil victims. Instead he announced that he would soon introduce legislation making the demand for Eelam illegal.[188]

When placed in the context of government apathy, if not collusion, it is doubtful that the killing of Tamil terrorist suspects being held under the PTA in the government's Welikada prison in Colombo on 25 July and 27 July was due, as officially described, to a single spontaneous event – 'an attempted mass jail break out'. Thirty-five Tamil prisoners, including Dr. Rajasunderam, head of the suspected separatist outfit Gandhiyam, were killed on 25 July, and 18 more on 27 July. Given how the Sri Lankan state had dealt with JVP suspects and detainees in the past and given increasing repression under the state authoritarianism in the 1980s, there is reason to suspect that the killings of Tamil terrorist suspects in Welikada was also 'well planned' and backed by state complicity.[189]

A number of political, economic, and ideological factors converged in the culmination of the 1983 riots. Unable to deter the spread of Tamil separatist militancy in the north, and in the face of the JVP's rising popularity in the south after the controversial 1982 referendum, the Sri Lankan state was increasingly insecure. Targeting of Tamils in the south, then, could have been a multi-pronged strategy adopted by a 'dominant faction' within the UNP to marginalize Tamil influence in the political life of the country, to teach the Tamil terrorists a lesson, and to deflect Sinhala discontent.[190] But as Newton Gunasinghe, among others, has noted, there was also an economic motivation behind the Black July violence.[191] Many Sinhala middle- and small-scale entrepreneurs who lost their import quotas and other advantages after 1977 resented the successes the Tamil businesses enjoyed after the introduction of the Open Economy. There was a widespread impression that Tamil control of the economy and the financial sector had increased after economic liberalization and that 60 percent of the wholesale trade and 80 percent of the retail trade in Colombo were in the control of Tamils.[192] Some Sinhala businessmen who wanted to destroy their Tamil competition may have instigated the urban poor to direct their hostility against the Tamil business and professional class rather than the Sri Lankan state. The

Tamil businesses attacked included those belonging to leading Tamil industrialists, such as Gunaratnam, Gnanam, and Maharaja.[193] The account of Anita Pratap, an Indian journalist who witnessed and reported on the 1983 Sri Lankan violence, provides insight into the class conflict underlying the attacks:

> [T]he attacks on the Tamils were systematic, pre-planned and well organized. The Sinhalese mobs seemed to be targeting the economic base of the Tamil community – textile and other factories owned by the Tamils were all completely gutted. Armed with voters' lists, the gangs came in empty trucks in which they carried away the goods looted from Tamil homes – television sets, radios, refrigerators, music systems, jewelry, clocks, clothes. They not only knew where the Tamils lived but seemed to have a list of their belongings as well.[194]

The attacks were directed not only at Tamil interests but also at Indian enterprises, since they too were perceived to be alien and exploitative of Sinhala natives. For instance, the premises of the Hidramanis and Jaferjees, prosperous Indian business families, the former Hindu and the latter Muslim, who had been based in Sri Lanka for decades, were destroyed. As *India Today* later reported, 'the most dangerous of all misconceptions abroad that frenzied week was that every Indian is a Tamil, and that every Tamil is a terrorist'.[195] There is no evidence of local Muslims being either victims or aggressors in the 1983 riots. On the one hand, there were rumors that the Sinhalese were planning to go after Muslim businesses after they finished with the Tamils. On the other hand, there were allegations that Muslim businesses who wanted to see the downfall of their Tamil competitors had played a role in instigating the mobs. Some Muslim gang members supporting Prime Minister Premadasa and Transportation Minister Mohammed may have been active in the riots, although there is no evidence of instigation by Muslim business people.[196]

There were complex political and economic factors at work in the emergence of the 1983 mob violence. The marauding gangs may not have been all Sinhalese or Buddhists. Yet the belief that Sinhala Buddhist ideology was the driving force behind the riots is widely held. The active roles said to have been played by two Sinhala Buddhist nationalists – Cyril Mathew, the Minister of Industries and Scientific Affairs and the Buddhist monk, Elle Gunawansa, the head of the Sinhala Peramuna (Front) – has much to do with this impression. Mathew was the government's leading campaigner against the traditional Tamil homelands myth and spent a great deal of time identifying the neglected Buddhist sacred sites in the Northern and Eastern Provinces. Mathew also tried to apply the 'Bhumiputra' (sons of the soil) thesis, popular in Malaysia, to the Sri Lankan situation. Arguing that 'to be truly indigenous one must belong to no other race but that truly identified with a given country', he asserted that the Sinhalese Buddhists are the only indigenous people in Sri Lanka because the Tamils, Muslims and Christians all have their cultural origins beyond the shores of the island.[197] The aboriginal Vedas aside, this argument has validity just as the protection of Buddhist sites in the North and the East, which Mathew championed, has an archaeological value of global significance.[198] What is illegal and abhorrent, however, is Mathew's alleged use of violence and the deployment of gangs to destroy Tamil businesses and property during the 1983 riots. Likewise, the allegation that the monk Elle Gunawansa led mobs with hit lists in hand, if true, is not only reprehensible but criminal.[199] The highlighting of the roles of Mathew and Elle Gunawansa helped attribute the 1983 riots to Sinhala Buddhist fundamentalism, thereby diminishing the roles of the state, class antagonism and the forces of economic liberalization and political authoritarianism.[200]

5   Internationalization of the secessionist struggle, 1983–1987

The Sri Lankan government's mishandling of the political situation following Black July turned the island's crisis into a regional and international conflict. Its first misstep was to push the more extreme elements of both the Sinhala and Tamil communities out of the political process, leaving a vacuum that would be filled by the armed militants within both communities.

The government blamed the riots on a 'Naxalite conspiracy', (a term given to radical, violent revolutionary communist movements in the Indian subcontinent) and immediately banned the JVP and the smaller Communist and NLSSP (New Lanka Equal Society Party) parties. There was no evidence that the leftist parties had played any role in the 1983 violence, and the government's action was widely seen as an effort to cover up its own role. The JVP also had no record of being anti-Tamil: the violence it perpetrated in 1971 and subsequently was directed at the Sinhalese. After JVP leaders had been released from prison in 1978 and entered electoral politics, the party sought to attract Tamil voters by advocating equal status for the Sinhala, Tamil, and English languages and Sri Lankan citizenship for Indian Tamils.[1] But by banning the JVP in 1983, the UNP forced it back into underground activity and laid the conditions for its re-emergence as a violent anti-state force.[2] JVP defense lawyer Prins Gunasekara also blamed the 'human rights' lobby for this situation, asserting that the human rights groups that 'jumped into the fashionable "ethnic" bandwagon – camouflaging the armed violence of the Eelam rebels ... remained discreetly silent about the suppression of the elementary democratic rights of the majority community..., among whom the JVP had the strongest following'.[3]

On 8 August, the government also effectively banned the TULF from the parliament and the democratic process by passing the 6th Amendment to the constitution, which outlawed support for a separate state within Sri Lanka.[4] The TULF was committed to separatism, but, it was also the main opposition party in parliament and the only democratic political voice of the Tamils. The delegitimization of the TULF and the lack of state sympathy and support, heightened the fears and anxieties of Tamils. Apparently, even Indira Gandhi was not able to persuade President Jayawardena to say 'a few reassuring words to restore the confidence of the Tamils' after the violence in July 1983.[5] Refusing to take an oath abjuring advocacy of separatism, the TULF leadership left for Tamil Nadu. As the TULF gave up working within the Sri Lankan polity, the armed Tamil groups began to fill the power vacuum and to monopolize the Tamil political agenda.[6]

The isolation of moderate forces and the sense of exclusion from the benefits of the Open Economy pushed more and more Tamil and Sinhala youth into political extremism and armed struggle. As a consequence of the 1983 riots, large numbers of Tamils living in the predominantly Sinhala areas in the south left for the north thus solidifying ethno-regional bifurcation and the Tamil demand for separatism.[7] As Rohan Gunaratna observed, within three months of July 1983, 'the insurgents had increased their cadre strength by several fold', becoming the 'de facto leaders of the ... Tamil people'.[8] But local elites were not the only ones responsible for the escalation of the conflict and its trans-formation into a full-fledged civil war. If the Sri Lankan conflict had been a domestic phenomenon up to then, the 1983 riots externalized it, hastening Indian intervention and the involvement of other interests groups from the 'inter-national community'.

Indian mediation and military support

Black July caused an immediate reaction in the South Indian state of Tamil Nadu. Tamil Nadu Chief Minister, M.G. Ramachandran, went to New Delhi to urge Prime Minister Indira Gandhi to intervene in Sri Lanka to protect the Tamil minority. He argued that Indian intervention in the secession of Bangladesh in 1971 was a precedent for such action.[9] Following a report that the Sri Lankan government had requested assistance from the US, UK, Pakistan, and Bangladesh, on 2 August 1983, India's Minister of External Affairs cautioned all foreign powers to 'keep out of the current turmoil in Sri Lanka'.[10] India was particularly keen to exclude its enemy Pakistan, which was allegedly supplying relief assistance as well as military support.[11] Indira Gandhi also took an emphatic position that India could not 'remain a silent spectator to any injustice done to the Tamil community'.[12] Indian defense expert S.D. Muni later pointed out 'In every official statement and public speech made by leaders up to the highest level, sympathies for Tamil sufferings were expressed in a strong and unqualified manner'.[13]

Apart from its professed sympathy for the Sri Lankan Tamils, India was keen to preserve its own 'perceived interests'.[14] The *Telegraph* from Calcutta called July 1983 'the worst case of anti-Indian violence ever known in a foreign country'.[15] The Indian government was concerned about Indian business and Tamil interests in Sri Lanka. Indira Gandhi was also keen to placate Tamil Nadu, which had a population of over 50 million Tamils, and consolidate the Congress Party's electoral base there. Because there were 'no Sinhala votes in India', Sinhala grievances did not seem to be of concern to the Indian govern-ment.[16] Gandhi reportedly telephoned Jayawardena, pressuring him to control the violence during Black July. On 29 July the Sri Lankan government was com-pelled to receive Indian Foreign Minister Narasimha Rao, sent to assess the situation.[17] Soon, relief supplies of medicine and food were brought for the Tamil refugees in chartered civilian planes from India, and chartered Indian civilian ships also transported refugees from Colombo to Jaffna.[18] Tamils in Sri Lanka welcomed Indian intervention and looked to India as their protector, but the Sinhalese feared an Indian invasion and loss of the island's sovereignty and territorial integrity.[19]

Mediation

From the aftermath of the 1983 violence until the signing of the Indo-Sri Lanka Treaty in July 1987, the Indian government tried to mediate between the Tamil secessionists and the Sri Lankan government to work out a political settlement.[20] India was concerned about the spillover effects of the Sri Lankan violence in India. By the end of 1987 there were over 150,000 Sri Lankan Tamil refugees in the state of Tamil Nadu, and the activities of some Sri Lankan Tamil militants and the underworld were contributing to increased internal disorder there.[21] As J.N. Dixit, India's Ambassador to Sri Lanka during the 1987 Indian intervention has clearly stated, Indian involvement in Sri Lanka was motivated primarily by the desire to safeguard India's political unity and territorial integrity from the threat of a potential expansive, regionally based Tamil secessionist state (Map I.2).

> [T]he first reason why we went to Sri Lanka was the interest to preserve our own unity ... what the Tamils in Sri Lanka were being compelled to follow in terms of their life,... would have affected our polity. Let us not forget that the first voice of secessionism in the Indian Republic was raised in Tamil Nadu in the mid-sixties. This was exactly the same principle of Tamil ethnicity. Tamil language. So, in a manner, our interests in the Tamil issue in Sri Lanka, Tamil aspirations in Sri Lanka, was based on maintaining our own unity, our own integrity, our own identity in the manner we have been trying to build our society.[22]

A rare confession such as Dixit's notwithstanding, Indian mediators in general tended to depict the Sri Lankan crisis as a domestic ethnic conflict between a hegemonic Sinhala majority and a victimized Tamil minority although in many ways, Sri Lanka was really fighting a proxy war, namely, India's Tamil secessionism. The simplistic Sinhala versus Tamil dualism informing Indian mediation contributed to its long-term failure. India's choice of mediators also did not help confirm its presumed role as 'honest broker'.[23] The Indian Prime Minister's principal policy advisors on Sri Lanka, Gopalaswami Parthasarathy and his successor, P. Chidambaram, were South Indian Tamils partial to the Sri Lankan Tamil cause. A top diplomat, Parthasarathy was a close confidante of Professor A.J. Wilson, Chelvanyakam's son-in-law and supporter of Eelam.[24] Before he was sent to Sri Lanka, Chidambaram, a minister of state in India, was known to have participated in pro-Tamil demonstrations in Tamil Nadu against the Sri

Lankan government.[25] The 'double-track strategy', mediation on the one hand and military pressure on the other hand, had much to do with India's failure to find a peaceful settlement to the Sri Lanka conflict.

During the last quarter of 1983, the Indian government helped to conduct talks between the TULF and the Sri Lankan government. When the bilateral talks failed, an all-party conference was held in January 1984 (the SLFP did not participate), where a set of proposals, which came to be known as Annexure C for the All Party Conference, were put forward.[26] India backed the TULF demand for a comprehensive devolution of power with an over-arching regional council linking the Northern and Eastern Provincial Councils. The objective was to create a large regional unit in which the Tamils would be the overwhelming majority. Among other things, Annexure C proposed that in land colonization, 'All settlement schemes should be based on ethnic proportions so as not to alter the demographic balance subject to agreement being reached on major projects'.[27] Thus, began an externally imposed process to accept the fictitious Tamil 'homelands' thesis and to ethnically bifurcate the island. But, it was not a proposal to create a separate sovereign state. The proposals failed. The Sri Lankan government was unwilling to concede to Indian and TULF demands for devolution, and the TULF in turn rejected any plan that fell short of its 'acceptable minimum for regional autonomy as an alternative to Eelam'.[28]

Military support

While Parthasarathy was engaged in the search for peaceful resolution to the conflict, the RAW Research and Analysis Wing, the agency of the India government that dealt with external intelligence, was entrusted with the task of advancing a secret Indian foreign policy.[29] RAW apparently knew that foreign militant groups, such as the PLO in Lebanon (since 1978) and the PFLP in Syria (since 1983), had provided training to the Tamil separatist groups EROS, LTTE, and PLOTE. When Indira Gandhi took the policy decision in August 1983 to support the Tamil insurgency in Sri Lanka, RAW received the go-ahead to provide military training, money and arms to all the Sri Lankan Tamil insurgent groups.[30] The objective of this secret strategy was not only to pressure the Sri Lankan government against a military solution to the Sri Lankan ethnic crisis but also to address India's concerns about regional security arising out of Sri Lanka's cooperation with the West, China, and Pakistan. But, as Muni has explained, 'this gave RAW considerable leeway for operating with the militants, which eventually became a slippery zone for India's policy on the issue'.[31] India's duplicitous policy sent a confusing message to the Sri Lankan Tamil militants. They openly spoke on platforms about their 'Movement' providing an opening for India into Sri Lanka and that a future Tamil Eelam separate state would ensure India's control over Sri Lanka. Given this perception, the Sri Lankan militants could not understand India's continuous reiteration of its respect for the territorial integrity and unity of Sri Lanka.[32]

India's involvement was not only shaped by its national government but by the state government of Tamil Nadu as well. The 'generous patronage' offered by the government of Tamil Nadu to Sri Lankan Tamil separatists compounded the problems. After the 1983 riots, the plight of Sri Lankan Tamils became a major political concern of both Chief Minister Ramachandran and his political opponent Karunanidhi.[33] As British military analyst Edgar O'Ballance has reported, the state government of Tamil Nadu 'provided residences, offices, telephones, and other facilities to enable them [Sri Lankan Tamil insurgents] to plot, recruit and prepare for their armed struggle'.[34] In addition to freedom of movement and publicity, all Sri Lankan Tamil militants were given sanctuary, training, and bases in South India. From late 1983 to mid-1987, the leading Sri Lankan Tamil militant groups TELO, PLOTE, LTTE, EPRLF, EROS, TELA, and ENDLF were all headquartered in Tamil Nadu, and had covert military establishments outside Tamil Nadu in Andhra Pradesh, New Delhi, and Uttar Pradesh as well.[35] History, culture, and geography made Tamil Nadu the inevitable 'external sanctuary of the Eelam Movement'. But, as political analyst, Dayan Jayatilleka has observed, of all the states in India, Tamil Nadu has the weakest presence of the Indian Left and possibly 'the most right-wing reactionary political culture in India' which in turn undermined the development of a leftist orientation by Sri Lankan Tamil militant groups.[36] Each Sri Lankan separatist militant group developed strong links with different Tamil Nadu nationalist groups and political parties. The LTTE developed close links with Veeramani's DK (Dravida Khazagham) and the Tamil Nadu government 'lionized' the LTTE due to its vision of a Greater Eelam that the South Indian groups themselves had to give up after an anti-secession amendment was imposed by the Indian Constitution in 1963[37] (Map 4.1).

Within a year of Indira Gandhi's policy decision, the number of Sri Lankan Tamil training camps in Tamil Nadu had increased to 32. There were only about 300 terrorists belonging to the five principal groups when Black July occurred. But, according to Gunaratna's estimates, by July 1987, when the Indo-Sri Lanka Accord was signed, as many as 20,000 had been given sanctuary, finance, training, and weapons by the central government of India, the state government of Tamil Nadu, or the insurgent groups themselves.[38] By the mid-1980s, terrorist activities were escalating, posing serious threats to peace and security both on the island as well as the South Indian mainland. On 2 August 1984, 30 civilians were killed at the airport in Madras in Tamil Nadu when time bombs placed in two Air Lanka flights by insurgents belonging to a group called the TEA (Tamil Eelam Army) exploded. On 22 October 1984, Tamil insurgents carried out their first bombing attempt in Colombo opposite the Fort Police station, injuring 11 civilians.[39] This act of terrorism was to be followed by hundreds of other acts against Sinhala civilians in Colombo and the southern areas since then.

Until the end of 1985, the Tamil guerilla groups were better equipped and perhaps also better trained than the small Sri Lankan security services in the north of the island.[40] RAW is believed to have trained the LTTE and other Tamil terrorist groups in both anti-aircraft tactics and underwater sabotage.[41] These and other RAW training tactics helped the Tamil militant groups 'to effectively checkmate the Sri Lankan security forces'.[42] Indeed, without support of both the Tamil Nadu government and the central government of India, the Sri Lankan Tamil insurgency could not have prospered or even emerged in the first place. As K.M. de Silva wrote in 1986, India's controversial role had much to do with the political destabilization and worsening of the Sri Lankan conflict.

> This double standard on separatism and terrorism – to crush separatism ruthlessly when it is seen to pose a palpable threat to the Indian polity ... and yet to feign ignorance of the existence of training camps and 'bases' for Tamil guerillas and terrorist groups on Indian soil ... continues to be one of the great stumbling blocks to cordial relations between India and Sri Lanka.[43]

Indian Prime Minister Rajiv Gandhi, who succeeded his mother, Indira, after her assassination by her Sikh bodyguards in October 1984, accused Sri Lankan security forces of 'indiscriminate killings', 'heavy loss of human life', and the 'rapidly deteriorating situation' in a speech in the Indian Parliament on 11 December 1985.[44] But the irony was that most of the major attacks by Tamil militant groups in this period, 1984 and 1985, which also involved indiscriminate killings and destruction, 'are believed to have been orchestrated by the Indian agency RAW'.[45] At the same time, the leaders of the five Sri Lankan Tamil terrorist groups 'remained comfortably ensconced in Madras living openly, courting the international media and radioing orders to their commanders in the field in Sri Lanka'.[46] As the Indian correspondent to *The Hindu*, Thomas Abraham noted, not only did India's arming of the militant groups violate 'the norms of civilized international relations' but it also did not work as an effective 'lever to place pressure on the Sri Lankan Government'. The result was an increased level of conflict in the north and the east of Sri Lanka and the victimization of the civilian population – Tamil, Muslim, and Sinhalese – that was caught in the violence between the militants and the Sri Lankan military.[47] People of all ethnic groups were also continuously victimized by suicide bombings and other attacks in Colombo and the multi-ethnic south.

While continuing to arm and train the Sri Lankan Tamil insurgents, the Indian government also espoused the Sri Lankan Tamil cause internationally through its diplomatic missions in western countries and support for the United Nations and its sub-committee initiatives.[48] This overt Indian bias towards the Tamil cause aggravated historical Sinhala fears. These fears were reflected in President Jayawardena's reaction to increasing Indian pressure on Sri Lanka: 'India is a powerful country and we cannot fight India, but if India intends to invade us we will not give in'.[49] Although India was heavily involved in secret support of the Sri Lankan separatist war, the Sri Lankan government's own international endeavors antagonized India. Unable to secure government assistance from the West to fight the insurgency, in 1984 the Sri Lankan government hired, with US help, a private British security service and several Israeli intelligence experts from Mossad for the purpose of crushing the armed Tamil separatists.[50] India was concerned about these developments, as she was with agreements made by the Sri Lankan government in December 1983 to allow a Voice of America transmission facility on the island and to lease the oil tank farm in the northeast port of Trincomalee to a US firm.[51] The geopolitical concerns raised by these moves, not just electoral votes in Tamil Nadu, hardened India's support for the Sri Lankan Tamil cause.[52]

Until India's intervention, there was only limited international financial and ideological support for the Eelam separatist struggle. The birth of a Tamil diaspora-insurgent network and support from a host of INGOs and other external institutions also damaged Sri Lanka's image and further internationalized the Sri Lankan conflict.

Tamil diaspora-insurgency network

By the end of 1983, there were over 100,000 Sri Lankan Tamil refugees in Tamil Nadu and a growing number in the West. While the poorer classes fled to Tamil Nadu, the educated professional elite with access to English education and other resources were able to emigrate to the West. Many western countries revised their immigration policies and quotas for Sri Lanka to allow easy entry to Tamils seeking political asylum. Claims made by international human rights organizations, such as Amnesty International's argument that 'if returned against their will, all members of the Tamil community have reasonable grounds to fear' arrest by the Sri Lankan government, helped Tamil immigration.[53] Because there was a perception that all Sri Lankan Tamils were political victims, those who simply desired economic advancement were able to immigrate to the West as political refugees. Canadian journalist Stewart Bell has pointed out that around 1992, after the Canadian government fast-tracked claims made by young Tamil males and females from the north and east of Sri Lanka, 'Basically, with the right coaching, anyone could become a Canadian. Migrant smuggling rings brought thousands of Sri Lankan Tamils to Canada, and pretty soon Toronto was the largest Tamil city outside of Asia'.[54] By the mid-1990s the total number of the Sri Lankan Tamil diaspora was over 450,000, and the total in the West in 2008 according to high estimates is over one million[55] (Table 1.1).

The vast majority of Tamil emigrants are, of course, law-abiding citizens. But as Bell has observed with reference to Canada, some have abused 'their new found wealth and freedom' to fund the war in Sri Lanka and bring the Eelam war to the host societies.[56] From the beginning, many wealthy Tamils, especially doctors in the US, were galvanized to support separatism in Sri Lanka. Although they themselves had benefitted from the free university education system in Sri Lanka, the restrictions placed on entrance into the science faculties in the 1970s and July 1983 violence had left a lasting negative impact upon the Tamil diaspora. As Tamil militant groups monopolized the political space, members of the diaspora who were disinterested in communal politics were persuaded, if not coerced into supporting separatism.[57] Though living in democratic societies, diaspora members found that they were not free to take independent positions on the Sri Lankan situation. Over the course of the Sri Lankan separatist struggle, a global class system reflecting divergent realities and interests emerged between the Tamil diaspora funding the separatist war and their poor brethren at home made to sacrifice their lives for Eelam. As Rajan Hoole has put it:

> It is for the LTTE supporters abroad to enjoy the vicarious glory accruing to them from the birth of the new state, where their role is to be rulers, investors, consultants and benefactors ... there is an intimate correspondence between ... a wealthy elite who are allowed to love life, and a proletarianised mass who are expected to die for them.[58]

Pressure from the growing 'resident Tamil lobbies' led host governments to develop an attitude of 'tolerance and leniency' towards political activities of the Tamil diaspora. The Sri Lankan government's laxity and ineffectiveness in challenging the separatist propaganda internationally allowed the LTTE to build up a massive global financing network for advancing the separatist cause.[59] In Norway, a country with an influential Tamil separatist lobby, the police have not intervened to stop threats and extortion of members of the Tamil diaspora or punish the LTTE for attacks on anti-LTTE political meetings.[60] Until very recently, specifically the 9/11 attacks in the United States, there has been little effort on the part of host governments in the West to assess the domestic and international implications of their contradictory policies. As Gunaratna points out,

> It is ironic that a bulk of the war budget of many of these actors [insurgents] is raised from the heartland of continental Europe and North America, the guardians of human rights and the proponents of democracy. It is also a paradox that a bulk of the weapons and explosives to kill and maim hundreds of thousands of men, women and children of this country [Sri Lanka] is being produced in the West.[61]

The internationalization of Tamil grievances – that is, the growing acceptance of their legitimacy – strengthened the Tamil separatist position and contributed to the marginalization of Sinhala concerns both locally and internationally. The Sri Lankan government tried to confront Tamil separatism and terrorism, but it was careful not to advocate a specifically Sinhala Buddhist agenda at the international level. Instead of reaching out to the external world and presenting their own grievances and claims, as did the Tamil separatists, Sinhala nationalists, many of whom lack access to the English language and western media and NGOs, sought refuge in an insular Sinhala Buddhist nationalism and a hardened anti-separatist position. The competing Tamil and Sinhala ethno-nationalist positions, supporting and opposing separatism, resuscitated the historical 'minority complex' of the Sinhalese and the 'majority complex' of the Tamils. Indeed, the Sinhala psyche as a beleaguered regional and international minority and the Tamil psyche as a regional majority and a 'trans nation' community hardened respective grievances of the two communities intensifying the territorial struggle over the Northern and Eastern provinces in Sri Lanka.

Intensified territorial struggle

As had been revealed in the earlier discussion of the Mahaweli irrigation and relocation project, much of the tension between the Tamil and Sinhala communities focused on land. After Black July, the Tamil secessionist struggle to make the north and the east an exclusively Tamil area and the Sinhala nationalist struggle to maintain, if not, increase the ethnic mix in those regions deepened.

Maduru Oya

A proposed state settlement of Sinhalese in the right bank of the Maduru Oya in the Batticoloa District of the Eastern Province came under increasing opposition from Tamils, the Indian government, and international aid donors (Map 4.1). In response, some influential Sinhala nationalists undertook an illegal Sinhala settlement there with the tacit support of Gamini Dissanayake, the Minister of Mahaweli Development, the chairman of the Mahaweli Board, and other Mahaweli officials.[62] The Buddhist monk Ven. Kithalagama Seelankara, popularly known as the Dimbulagala monk, led the movement to settle some 40,000 landless Sinhala peasants in the Maduru Oya, claiming the right to settle there because ancient records showed that the land belonged to his temple, the Dimbulagala Maha Vihara. The monk, who cared for and was liked by all ethnic and religious communities in the area, was explicit that his opposition was not to Tamil people but only to separatists.[63] The Dimbulagala monk, like a number of other Buddhist monks in the contested areas, was later assassinated, allegedly by the LTTE.

Coming as it did just a few weeks after July 1983, which drove large numbers of Tamils out of the Sinhala majority areas, the Sinhala encroachment in the Maduru Oya invoked massive opposition from Sri Lankan Tamil politicians, particularly Home Affairs Minister K.W. Devanayagam, as well as from South Indian Tamil politicians and western donor agencies. Under their growing pressure, Sri Lankan President Jayawardena ordered the forcible removal of all the Sinhala encroachers from Maduru Oya. The settlements were dismantled, and the Sinhala peasants who had come looking for land were evicted by government officials.[64]

India was not the only external force that opposed Sinhala settlements in the so-called 'Tamil homelands'. After economic liberalization in 1977 and increased dependence on international aid, the Sri Lankan government became more susceptible to donor pressure on internal political matters. With the rise of ethnic violence, donors began to threaten to suspend aid in order to force the government to stop its alleged human rights violations and discrimination against Tamils. In the early 1980s Norway was alone in voicing human rights charges and taking action against the Sri Lankan government. But after Black July, prodded by the growth of protests from the Tamil diaspora, other western countries and international institutions also came to focus on Sri Lankan Tamil grievances and aspirations at the expense of concerns of other communities.[65]

Canada, a major donor, eventually withdrew its support for the AMDP because the Sri Lankan government refused to comply with district ethnic quotas favored by the Tamils in Dry Zone peasant resettlement. Canada's overall bilateral aid to Sri Lanka also dropped from $46.02 million in 1982–1983 to $17.87 million in 1986–1987.[66] Subsequently, the Maduru Oya scheme and 20 other smaller projects were closed down, and the World Bank, the main architect of the original Mahaweli scheme, abandoned the AMDP in March 1990 due to lapsing funds and security concerns.[67] Canada, like other western donor countries 'wished to avoid any perception that it was taking sides in a conflict, or that it was associated with actions which discriminated against the Tamil community'.[68] But in their eagerness to appear impartial and sympathetic to minority grievances, international donors inadvertently supported Tamil separatism.

International opinion, as articulated by US political scientist Ronald Herring, was that the 'demographic dilution of Tamil-majority areas would render any devolution of power as a solution to the ethnic conflict less effective'.[69] This position was reflected in the Canadian stance on the Maduru Oya settlement, which accepted district ethnic quotas favored by the Tamils over the national ethnic quotas advocated by the government. While district quotas seemed a pragmatic move in the short term, in the long term it helped to strengthen the fictitious claim of a traditional 'Tamil homeland', thus potentially closing off vast areas of the island to its Sinhala majority population as well as the Muslim minority. Moreover, it overlooked the 'demographic dilution' of the Sinhala majority areas that was occurring during the course of the conflict. Yet Canadian government officials took satisfaction over the influence their 'principled intervention' on the Maduru Oya project had on the subsequent Indo-Sri Lanka 'peace' accord:

> One of the first breakthroughs in the discussions between Sri Lanka and India which led to the peace accord was an agreement that the right bank of the Maduru Oya would be mostly Tamil. As one senior official observed, 'I like to think our initiative had some influence. Had we agreed with the [national ethnic formula] this breakthrough may never have been possible'.[70]

As will be discussed later, the Indo-Sri Lanka Accord of 1987 went far beyond designating the Maduru Oya right bank as Tamil. Not only did it recognize the Northern and Eastern Provinces as Tamil areas, but it took the unprecedented action of merging the two. In building their 'principled' stance upon the false and unjustifiable claim for an exclusive 'Tamil homeland', the international organization, and the regional power India, attempted to solidify the Tamil hold on the north and the east. Gradually, internal and external policymakers began to pressure the Sri Lankan government to yield to the territorial ambition of the terrorists for the sake of conflict resolution and peace at any cost. The Sinhala Buddhist heritage and the historical and contemporary pluralism of the contested regions aside, such calls for territorial renunciation undermined the capacity of the legitimately elected Sri Lankan state to stop the 'blatant attempt by a [an extremist] minority to seize political power and territory'.[71]

Yan Oya Basin

After July 1983, Tamil separatist activity in the strategic Yan Oya area increased (Map 4.1). The LTTE destabilized the Padaviya settlement and drove away Sinhala villagers from the Gomarankadawala Divisional Secretariat. In response, the government established System L of the Mahaweli Program, which came to be known as Weli Oya, and resettled Sinhalese who were previously chased out of the Maduru Oya settlement. From the government's point of view, it had no option but to establish a strategic settlement corridor in Weli Oya in order to defend its territory and safeguard the unity and pluralism of the country. It was envisioned as a 'peaceful, economically and socially productive way to combat Eelam'.[72] But from the Tamil separatist point of view it was a military-led demographic transformation to forcibly Sinhalize the 'Tamil homelands', in this case to transform Tamil Manal Aaru into Sinhala Weli Oya.[73]. Thus even the planting of a bodhi tree and the placement of a Buddha statute by the Sinhala settlers in the 'Tamil areas' came to be seen as a 'stamp of territorial conquest' in sharp contrast to the 'Sinhala areas' in the south where non-Buddhist symbols flourish freely.[74]

Accepting the Tamil 'traditional homelands' thesis, international opinion increasingly accused the Sri Lankan government of invasion and military-backed colonization of 'Tamil territories'. Thayer Scudder, who wrote several reports on the Mahaweli Program for USAID in the mid-1980s, charged that the Mahaweli officials intended to use the AMDP as 'a mechanism for enhancing the control of the Sri Lankan majority ... over the Tamil speaking minority by creating a wedge of Sinhala-speaking Buddhist settlers between Tamil-speaking communities in the eastern and northern regions'.[75] Scudder pointed out that 'such recruitment also crassly placed at risk the poverty-stricken Sinhala-speakers who were settled in their midst'.[76] Indeed, Tamil terrorists continuously targeted settlers, and their systematic ethnic cleansing led to large-scale killings of Sinhalese in the Weli Oya and other 'border' settlements. On 30 November 1984, The LTTE massacred nearly 100 unarmed Sinhala settlers – men, women, and children – in Weli Oya, in the areas which at the time were known as Kent and Dollar farms. It was the first mass-scale killing of civilians by the LTTE in its preparation of the area for an exclusive Tamil Eelam.[77] Government troops avenged the deaths by killing 63 Tamils in a cycle of violence and counter-violence.[78] On 11 December, the LTTE killed 11 Sinhalese, people who had enjoyed close amicable relations with their Tamil neighbors for generations, in the long-established Catholic fishing community along the Kokkilai-Nayaru coast in the Mullaitivu District.[79]

In a paper published in a special issue on Sri Lanka in the *Journal of Asian Studies*, US historian Patrick Peebles argued that 'in the Dry Zone, the alternative to resolving the ethnic conflict is maintaining Buddhist colonies in spite of massacres of Tamil separatist guerillas – which at the time of this writing occur weekly'.[80] This could have been interpreted as another call from the 'international community' to the Sri Lankan government to accept the false claim of the 'Tamil homelands' and to capitulate to terrorism. Be that as it may, there is no denying the fact that the government's failure to provide adequate security made Sinhalese in the 'frontier' areas ever more vulnerable to gruesome terrorist attacks. Just as the LTTE came to recruit child soldiers and suicide bombers from among the most disadvantaged Tamil families, the Sri Lankan state and Sinhala elites recruited impoverished Sinhalese to hold the frontier without giving them adequate protection.[81] Subsistence farmers and fishermen were not capable of fighting trained guerillas, and the Sinhalese began to leave the areas of conflict in large numbers.[82]

Muslims and territory

Muslim civilians were also caught in the intensified territorial struggle in the north and the east after July 1983. Due to increasing Tamil separatist claims on Muslim-held lands, differences and hostilities between the Tamils and Muslims became a distinct aspect of the Sri Lankan separatist conflict.[83] As political scientist Manzoor Fazil described the situation:

> Tamils began to harass the Muslims, waylay and rob them when they traversed Tamil areas on their way to and from their paddy fields. Tamil government officials denied vehicle amenities to Muslim villages, extorting money, jewelry, motor vehicles and agricultural products from Muslims. Finally, they abducted Muslim youths and forced them to collaborate with the separatist movement.[84]

During Tamil–Muslim violence that broke out in April 1985, Tamils and Muslims fought each other as separate communities for the first time. The violence, which began in Akkaraipattu in the Ampara District on 14 April 1985, quickly spread to other areas of the Eastern Province, including Kalmunai, Eravur, Orttamadevi, Valaichenai, Muthur, and Kinniya. Armed Tamil separatists killed hundreds of Muslims and destroyed Muslim property worth billions of rupees. Muslims living in the Tamil majority areas in the Eastern Province were attacked and made to flee, as were Tamils in Muslim majority areas.[85] The Tamil–Muslim violence in the east, including the Yan Oya basin, has increased since then, aggravating Muslim fears of living in a future Tamil Eelam.

Human rights violations

The intensification of the armed conflict after July 1983 resulted in massive human rights violations on the part of both the Tamil terrorists and the government forces.[86] In situations of armed conflict and terrorism, it is difficult to uphold personal liberties and human rights laws. This fact is recognized in the distinction between international human rights laws, which pertain to obligations of states toward their citizens during times of peace and war, and international humanitarian laws, which pertain specifically to situations of armed conflict. In the latter case, both state and non-state actors are required to abide by rules of engagement as laid out in the Geneva Protocols (Article 3 of the Geneva Convention of 1949 and Additional Protocol 11 of 1977).[87] The post-independence Sri Lankan state was faced with the challenge of upholding human rights while fighting the JVP and Tamil separatist insurgencies since the early 1970s, long before the more powerful, democratic countries were faced with the problem after 9/11. In general, international human rights monitors have failed to hold non-state actors accountable to international humanitarian laws. The tendency of human rights organizations based in the West to use human rights to pressure weak 'Third World' states over selected, ethnically identified issues without exerting similar pressures on their own states have led to the charge of 'human rights imperialism' from some in the South.[88] While such charges should not be used to uphold repressive regimes and condone their human rights violations, the complexity and politicization of the human rights discourse needs to be acknowledged. In this context, Neville Ladduwahetty's observations of the current 2008 Sri Lankan situation also has validity for the earlier periods of the island's separatist conflict.

> [S]ince the IC has failed to recognize that what is taking place in Sri Lanka is an armed conflict, they have failed to hold the LTTE to the standards required by a non-state actor engaged in armed conflict, and have focused only on the GOSL ... Without holding the LTTE responsible for ... violations such as the deployment of children in war, the focus of Human Rights activists has been only on the GOSL.[89]

International human rights organizations, including the International Commission of Jurists (ICJ), Law Asia, Amnesty International (AI), and the British Parliamentary Human Rights Group, became involved in the Sri Lankan conflict after 1983. They sent their representatives to Sri Lanka periodically and condemned the excesses of the Sri Lankan armed forces.[90] The influential report by the ICJ to the United Nations Sub-Committee on Human Rights, issued on 19 August 1983, harshly criticized the Sri Lankan security forces for brutal retaliatory attacks on Tamils. It also criticized the Sri Lankan state for passing emergency legislation permitting the police to cremate bodies of those dying in custody without a formal inquiry, inquest, or post-mortem.[91] The Sri Lankan government lost international credibility after the July 1983 riots, and many

international human rights activists and organizations, as well as the international media, became sympathetic to the Tamil separatist cause as a response
to discrimination and violation of Tamil rights. The ICJ report written by Virginia Leary, for example, accepted and legitimized the fictitious 'traditional
Tamil homelands' concept.[92]

On the other hand, the large numbers of soldiers and civilians killed by insurgent attacks on Sri Lankan government positions did not receive much international publicity or sympathy. The land-mine attack in January 1985 on the Yal
Devi train carrying soldiers paralyzed the security forces in Jaffna. In addition,
when the Sri Lankan Navy blockaded Jaffna, the Tamil militants developed their
own naval capability, weakening the ability of the government to patrol the
coasts.[93] Terrorist attacks on the armed forces and civilians escalated after the
TELO, LTTE, EPRLF and EROS, at the instigation of RAW, formed the Eelam
National Liberation Front (ENLF) in April 1985 in order to provide a unified
force against the Sri Lankan government. The attacks on Muslims in the Eastern
Province on 14 April 1985 was an example. (ENLF dissolved in March 1987
due to internecine warfare and decimation of other groups by the LTTE).[94] As
government forces suffered increasing casualties from mines and ambushes by
the Tamil insurgents, they retaliated by going on rampages of their own, killing
and injuring Tamil civilians and destroying property.[95] Mark Tully, the BBC
correspondent who was based in New Delhi at the time, called the Sri Lankan
Army 'the most undisciplined army in the world'.[96] An Asia Watch Report published in December 1987 reviewing the post-1983 situation charged that:

> [E]specially after July 1983, the security forces of Sri Lanka engaged in
> large-scale arbitrary arrest and detention, torture of prisoners, and reprisals
> against civilians including killings and disappearances. The Army, Navy,
> and Air Force, as well as the Police Special Task Force (STF) all partici-
> pated in these violations to some extent; most of the abuses in the Northern
> Province were by the Army, and most of those in the Eastern Province were
> by the STF. A number of reports of incidents of extra-judicial executions
> and massacres also implicated the Home Guards, an armed auxiliary force
> of non-Tamil civilians.[97]

Asia Watch argued that repressive measures such as the Prevention of Terrorism
Act (PTA) and emergency regulations under which normal legal safeguards are
suspended facilitated abuses by its armed forces by allowing

> [L]engthy incommunicado detention without charge or meaningful judicial
> review, permit the use of confessions made to police officers in court and
> burden the defendant with proof of duress, and significantly ease restriction
> of dead bodies and requirement to hold inquests.[98]

It did note that Tamil guerilla groups, especially the LTTE, were also responsible for political assassinations, execution of prisoners and hostages, and

massacres of Sinhala civilians.[99] In a widely publicized report published on 10 September 1986, Amnesty International described the cases of 270 Tamil men who had 'disappeared' since late 1983, many suspected to be 'shot in custody or died under torture and … their bodies … disposed in secret'.[100] In particular, AI took up the case of the 'LTTE martyr', Father Mary Bastian, a Tamil Catholic priest doing 'relief work' who had 'disappeared' in January 1985 and was allegedly killed by security personnel.[101]

The Sri Lankan government dismissed the AI charges, arguing that AI has been 'misdirected' by 'the powerful Separatist Eelamist Terrorist Lobby the world over', that the evidence, namely affidavits and eye witness accounts of Tamils presented by AI were 'mere hearsay and invalid in any Court of Law', and that many of the 'disappeared' had actually left the country seeking 'economic asylum'. The government further implied that Father Mary Bastian had harbored insurgents in his church and that he did not 'disappear' but may have escaped to India. The government further claimed that it was difficult to investigate the charges, given that terrorists were operating under new names and identities not known even to their parents, and that AI should bring its evidence before a court of law in Sri Lanka for legal scrutiny and cross-examination.[102] AI received government clarification on only a small number of the 270 cases.[103] In February 1986, International Alert, an international human rights group established specifically to support the Sri Lankan Tamil cause, appealed to donor countries to withhold aid from Sri Lanka until the government agreed to more generous terms for resolving the conflict with the Tamil minority.[104] In June 1987 Norway stopped aid to Sri Lanka in protest against human rights violations.[105]

While the Tamil diaspora lobby mobilized international opinion against the Sri Lankan government on human rights charges, the Tamil militants continued their killing spree and abuses of both Sinhalese and Muslims. In alleged retaliation to the killing by the armed forces of 70 Tamils in Valvettithurai, the home of the LTTE leader, the LTTE carried out a gruesome reprisal attack on 14 May 1985, in the sacred city of Anuradhapura in the predominantly Sinhala North Central Province, killing over 150, including Buddhist pilgrims worshipping at the sacred Sri Maha Bodhi.[106] The attack took place a week before the Vesak celebration honoring the birth of the Buddha.[107] With the 'Anuradhapura massacre', attacks on Sinhala civilians and Buddhist cultural symbols became a matter of Tamil militant policy. According to later media reports, RAW was allegedly behind the Anuradhapura massacre. As Hoole, from University Teachers for Human Rights (Jaffna), has stated, 'all the [Tamil militant] groups were then very dependent on India and whether an attack of this nature would have been launched without Indian clearance needs to be questioned'.[108]

There were other attacks against civilians, such as the terrorist attack on 2 June 1987, when the LTTE shot 33 people, including 29 Buddhist monks, many of them novices, who were travelling in a bus in Arantalawa, in Ampara in the Eastern province.[109] These attacks on Sinhala civilians and Buddhist monks were aimed at provoking a Sinhala backlash against the Tamil community. Fortunately, however, there have not been backlashes by Sinhala civilians against

Tamils since July 1983, which, too, was not a spontaneous outburst of prim-ordial Sinhala hatred as much as a state-orchestrated pogrom. But the continued depiction of the conflict in ethnic terms fuelled enmity between the Sinhala and Tamil communities and obscured the terrorist threat facing the entire country and the common suffering of all communities. Sri Lankan government statistics estimated that 120,000 people from all communities spread over ten districts were internally displaced by November 1986. Among the 49,000 of them housed in government-run welfare centers, 70 percent were Tamil, 25 percent Sinhalese, and the rest mostly Muslims. Of the 71,000 of them living outside camps with relatives and friends, 62 percent were Tamil and 37 percent Sin-halese.[110] In other words, because a relatively larger number of displaced Sinhalese, mostly those driven out of the north and the east, were living outside the refugee camps, it contributed to the perception of the refugee problem as just a Tamil problem.

Toward a political solution

Among the peace proposals advanced under Indian leadership between July 1983 and direct Indian intervention in 1987 were Annexure C noted earlier, the 'Thimpu Principles', and the 'December 19 Proposals'.

The Indian government's acceptance of the simplistic dichotomy of Sinhala oppressor versus Tamil victim, its secret arming of the Tamil terrorists, and Tamil Nadu interference put it in a difficult position to negotiate a political set-tlement acceptable to the many different groups implicated in the Sri Lankan conflict. Still, India attempted to do so.

Thimpu 'principles'

India persuaded the Sri Lankan government and the Sri Lankan militants to observe a three month ceasefire starting on 18 June 1985, and to attend a confer-ence in Thimpu, the capital of the Himalayan mountain state of Bhutan, to bring a political settlement to the worsening crisis. The Tamil secessionist groups – that is, the five militant groups (LTTE, PLOTE, TELO, EPRLF and EROS) and the mod-erate TULF – demanded that the Sri Lankan government accept four non-negotiable 'basic principles', which came to be known as the Thimpu Principles: (1) recognition of the Tamils of Sri Lanka as a distinct 'Nation', (2) recognition of an identified Tamil 'Homeland' and the guarantee of its territorial integrity, (3) recognition of the inalienable right of self-determination of the Tamil nation, and (4) recognition of the right of full citizenship and the fundamental rights of all Tamils who look upon Sri Lanka as their country.[111] Since Thimpu, Tamil seces-sionists have held these 'principles' as non-negotiable – making attempts at polit-ical settlement, in the eyes of critics, a futile if not dangerous exercise.[112]

The Sri Lankan government was at the time engaged in negotiations to grant citizenship to the Indian Tamils. Hence, the fourth principle was not controver-sial. But the government delegation refused to accept the first three of the

Thimpu Principles, seeing their acceptance as amounting to a 'surrender by the government at the negotiating table everything they [Tamil secessionists] hoped to achieve by their Civil War'.[113] The demands made at Thimpu, however, were not new: they were a reiteration of demands made by Chelvanayakam and ITAK since the 1950s and rejected by successive Sri Lankan governments for decades. The Thimpu Principles differed from earlier demands, however, in that they referred to the 'Tamil Nation' instead of the 'Tamil-speaking people', thereby excluding Tamil-speaking Muslims living in the Northern and Eastern Provinces who did not identify themselves as Tamil.[114]

When the Sri Lankan government restricted all Sri Lankan forces to barracks for three months during the Thimpu talks, the LTTE took the opportunity to mine 'all roads leading out of these camps and to build up concrete bunkers to barricade them'.[115] On 22 August 1985 the Tamil representatives suddenly walked out of the second round of the Thimpu talks, accusing the Sri Lankan government of breaking the ceasefire and preparing for war.[116] Angered by this walk-out, New Delhi ordered the deportation of three Sri Lankan Tamil leaders (LTTE spokesman Anton Balasingham, TELO spokesman N. Satyendra, and S.C. Chandrahasan, son of S.J.V. Chelvanayakam) from Tamil Nadu. Within 48 hours of the orders, opposition political parties in Tamil Nadu organized massive street protests against the order. Invoking India's historical north–south antagonism, Veeramani, the leader of the DK warned, 'If the orders are not withdrawn, Gandhi will face agitations like Punjab and Assam [i.e. on-going secessionist struggles in those areas] and we will not allow any North Indian to set foot here'.[117] In the face of the mounting opposition in Tamil Nadu, Gandhi withdrew the deportation order. As Tamil writer, A. Sivarajah later noted, 'it is the Chief Minister [of Tamil Nadu], and not Rajiv Gandhi, who plays the most vital role in determining the Indian actions in relation to the search for a solution to Sri Lanka ethnic crisis'.[118] In reality, the ethnocentric Tamil Nadu government was itself a major part of the problem. By supporting Sri Lankan Tamil terrorism, it made it difficult to find a peaceful solution to the island's crisis.

The declaration of their demands at an international forum and their engagement with Sri Lankan government and Indian government representatives in open talks for the first time at Thimpu accorded legitimacy to the Tamil separatist struggle. In 1985 the international legitimacy of the Tamil separatist cause was at its peak.[119] Clearly, Indian government's cultivation of the terrorist groups to pressure the Sri Lankan government and its failure to force the militants to respect the ceasefire was inimical to the creation of stable conditions necessary for a negotiated political settlement. *The Hindu* correspondent Thomas Abraham noted: 'It was an open secret that India was backing the Tamil militants and this produced a backlash among the Sinhalese which ... made Jayawardena even more reluctant to agree to any Indian sponsored proposals.'[120]

19 December proposals

Despite worsening violence following the failed Thimpu talks, India continued many rounds of talks outside the Thimpu framework, putting forward proposals to find a political solution. The Sri Lankan government was willing to consider proposals for devolution, but it opposed a proposed merger of the Northern and Eastern Provinces, seeing it as a stepping stone for a separate Tamil state. After three rounds of talks between the Sri Lankan President Jayawardena and two Indian Ministers of State, Natwar Singh and Chidambaram, respectively, a set of proposals called the 19 December proposals emerged in 1986. These proposals, the product of the Colombo–Madras–Delhi shuttle diplomacy of Chidambaram, advanced the claims made in Annexure C at the All-Party conference in early 1984 and at Thimpu by trying to create a separate 'homeland' for the Tamils. They proposed to do so by 'slicing off' the Sinhala majority Ampara district from the Eastern Province and linking up the remaining parts of the Eastern Province, that is, the Trincomalee and Batticoloa Districts, with the Northern Province within a federal system. It also called for a referendum in the Eastern Province prior to such a set-up (Maps I.1 and 4.2).[121]

Prabhakaran was flown to Bangalore with the help of Tamil Nadu Chief Minister Ramachandran when the Sri Lankan government and the TULF met during the SAARC (South Asian Association for Regional Cooperation) summit of all South Asian nations in November 1986. His attendance granted implicit recognition of the LTTE as the dominant Tamil militant group.[122] The Tamil secessionists in the Eastern Province, especially those from the EPRLF, which was strong in the Province, were open to a settlement on the basis of the December 19 proposals. However, Prabhakaran (and also EROS) vacillated because the proposals fell short of a separate state.[123] The difference in positions provided a glimpse of the differences between northern and eastern Tamils that would contribute to the split of the LTTE years later:

> In Jaffna which was relatively secure, a more hawkish mood prevailed … there arose a widespread feeling amongst Eastern Tamils, that the Jaffna based Tamil leadership had failed them. The Eastern Province Tamils will in the years to come have to resolve the question of their dealings with Northern Tamils and their relations with Muslims and Sinhalese in the East.[124]

The Indian government put enormous pressure on the Sri Lankan government to accept the 19 December proposals despite massive opposition from Sinhala nationalists within and outside the Jayawardena administration. The JVP charged that the Sri Lankan government was 'obeying the orders of their imperialist masters in the face of Tamil Eelamists and deliberately retreating militarily'.[125] The SLFP, MEP, and the JVP came together against the Indian proposals for devolution. A Sinhala nationalist organization named Maubima Surakeeme Viyaparaya (MSV – the Movement to Protect the Motherland) was organized by several leading Buddhist monks. In November 1986, the MSV split into two –

the radical MSV, comprising many JVP members, and the less radical Mavu-bima Surakeeme Sangamaya (MSS) led by Mrs Bandaranaike, the head of the SLFP.[126] Muslims, who represented at least one-third of the population in the Eastern Province, also opposed the extrication of the Ampara District from the Eastern Province and the proposed merger of the Northern and Eastern Provinces.[127] Like subsequent peace proposals in 1995 and 2001, the Indian 19 December proposals which were founded upon the Sinhala versus Tamil dualism marginalized the Muslims.

While India was pressuring the Sri Lankan government to concede at the negotiating table, the LTTE – as it had done earlier during the ceasefire for the Thimpu talks – increased its own pressure on the government by bringing its guerilla war to the capital. On 3 May 1986, it destroyed an Air Lanka plane, killing 17 passengers, mostly foreigners. Four days later, a bombing by Tamil militants destroyed the government's central communication office in Colombo and killed 14 people.[128] The international human rights agencies had no mechanisms to bring charges against such atrocities or to curb the flow of money from western countries that was funding these heinous crimes on Sri Lankan soil. The violence perpetrated by Sri Lankan terrorists on Indian soil, however, had a detrimental effect on their position and hardened Indian and Tamil Nadu attitudes towards them. Unlike Indira Gandhi, who had encouraged the Tamil insurgency, her son, Prime Minister Rajiv Gandhi, began to take a harder line towards the Tamil militants and began to favor a federal solution to the Sri Lankan problem

The Sri Lankan government had advanced nine conditions in February 1986 as a basis for implementation of any agreement to end the conflict. The proposed terms included the abandonment of the demand for a separate state; cessation of hostilities; closing down of insurgent training camps; surrender of arms by the Tamil militants; lifting of the emergency in the predominantly Tamil areas; and general amnesty to militants. The Sri Lankan Tamil leadership rejected these conditions.[129]

Because the Indian government failed to take a tough stance against separatist violence, the Sri Lankan government gradually retracted from the December 1986 proposals. With all peace efforts having failed, it appeared that the only recourse was military action. Instead of conceding to India and the separatists, the government decided to a make a final and decisive military victory over the LTTE, which was then establishing a separate administration in the Jaffna Peninsula. Frustrated with both the Sri Lankan government and the LTTE, Rajiv Gandhi also suspended Indian mediation efforts in February 1987.[130]

Toward a military solution

Following the failure of the Thimpu meetings, the Sri Lankan conflict became more militarized and violent. The government increased its weapons procurement while the militants actively collected 'protection money' from Tamil people and increased its recruitment of cadres from among the most impoverished families, especially those who had suffered from government military operations.[131] Desperate to build up its military capability, in late 1986 the LTTE began to recruit women into its fighting units. It also began to recruit children into its Black Tiger suicide cadres, silencing any protest within the Tamil community against these oppressive measures.[132]

Confident that it alone could defeat the Sri Lankan armed forces, the LTTE engaged in a systematic campaign to wipe out all its rival Tamil terrorist groups. RAW's exploitation of differences among the militant groups has also been blamed for the internecine warfare that emerged after Thimpu.[133] LTTE killed 150 cadres of the TELO and 70–80 cadres of the EPRLF in 1986. It also killed the entire politbureau of the EPRLF (except for Suresh Premachandran) in Madras.[134] Having killed and also sent hundreds of its rivals underground, the LTTE began to claim that it was the 'sole representative of the Tamil people'.[135] Jayatilleka has argued that as the right-wing LTTE became dominant and the 'Tamil Eelam Left', represented by PLOTE and EPRLF, were wiped out, the potential for a 'progressive alliance' between Tamil and Sinhala leftists was lost.[136] Be that as it may, the dominant view of the Sri Lankan conflict as an 'ethnic conflict', the view also advanced by India, precluded the intra-ethnic conflicts from receiving much local or international attention. Hoole has written:

> To many influential outside observers, violations of Human Rights remained violations by the Sri Lankan forces against the Tamil people fighting for self-determination. What the Tamil people were doing to themselves [and the Sinhalese to themselves] was mostly lost sight of.[137]

Following Indian pressure and growing criticism that he had been living comfortably in exile in Madras (since 1983) rather than sharing the dangers of life in the battlefield, Prabhakaran and many of his cadres returned to the Jaffna Peninsula on 6 January 1987.[138] By this time the LTTE was in virtual control of the peninsula and its population. It was also in the process of replacing the Sri Lankan government administration with its own courts, transport, food distribution, and media, in violation of Sri Lankan sovereignty. In the first week of January 1987, when the LTTE announced that it would issue its own vehicle licenses and rationing measures, the Sri Lankan National Security Minister, Athulathmudali, placed an embargo on all fuel supplies. He also threatened to cut off electricity and food from the south.[139] During the first three months of 1987, the Sri Lankan security forces launched several small operations against the Tamil insurgents, 'often as reprisals, which provoked counter-reprisals … thus perpetuating a cycle of violence'.[140] As tensions heightened, the Indian government repeatedly warned the Sri Lankan government against a military solution to the conflict. A resolution adopted by The United Nations Human Rights Commission in March 1987 also called on all parties to respect human rights laws.[141]

In response to Indian pressure, the Sri Lankan government relaxed the fuel embargo on Jaffna in March and declared a unilateral ceasefire from 11 April to 20 April to observe Sinhala–Tamil New Year and Christian holidays. The LTTE did not respond in kind. Instead, on 17 April it attacked Sinhalese passengers travelling in a bus on the Trincomalee–Habarana Road, butchered 127 injuring more than 60, in what came to be known as the 'Good Friday Massacre'. The Sri Lankan President responded that his air force would bomb Tamil Tiger locations in the north 'until all terrorist camps are destroyed'.[142] On 21 April 1987, a car bomb exploded in the main market in Colombo, killing 113 and injuring over 200 people. The LTTE is reported to have collaborated in this explosion with EROS, which was receiving support from the Indian government. On 27 April 1987, Rajiv Gandhi again warned the Sri Lankan government to stop its offensive against the Tamil militants, while the Tamil Nadu Chief Minister, Ramachandran, gifted Rs.40 million to the LTTE and other Tamil militants.[143] Unlike the Tamils, the Sinhalese do not have an ethnic community or an influential diaspora in India or elsewhere. Thus there were no regional or international human rights or other lobbies to take up the grievances of Sinhala civilians victimized by the LTTE.

In the face of brutal terrorist attacks on civilians and continuing Indian support for the militants, the Sri Lankan government launched a major military offensive on 26 May 1987 – called Operation Liberation – to take back the LTTE-controlled Jaffna Peninsula. In response to Indian protests, Athulathmudali argued that it was the only way to get the terrorists to the negotiating table.[144] Given superior fire-power and numbers, the Sri Lankan security forces were able to capture Vadamarachchi, 'the cradle of the Tamil Eelam liberation struggle', and Velvettiturai, the home town of Prabhakaran on 29 May.[145] Capture of the Vadamarachchi strip severely curtailed insurgents' access to Tamil Nadu, paving the way for the Sri Lankan army to retake the rest of the Jaffna Peninsula. At that point, only Jaffna town and the nearby area remained, and they appeared about to fall. It looked like the LTTE would be defeated and the armed conflict would end. Operation Liberation is said to have come 'within a hair's breadth' of capturing Prabhakaran who was in Vadamarachchi.[146] The terrorist problem may have been stopped there. But Indian military intervention precluded that.[147]

India's show of force

Because the media were excluded and communications were cut off during Operation Liberation, there are no factual reports of events that took place in the Jaffna Peninsula. But there were allegations by the international Eelam lobby that the Sri Lankan security forces indulged in 'carpet bombing'.[148] O'Ballance claims that these allegations were 'probably not justified', although he says that there is confirmation that the air force used drums of petrol, 'poor man's napalm'.[149] Sri Lankan Tamil refugees fleeing across the Palk Straits brought stories of 'massacre, atrocity, deprivation and hunger', giving rise to anger and alarm in Tamil Nadu.[150] Ramachandran rushed to New Delhi and demanded that Rajiv Gandhi intervene in Sri Lanka 'to save the Tamils'.[151] In a speech made two years later, J.N. Dixit, who was the Indian High Commissioner in Sri Lanka at the time of the Indian intervention, claimed that the Sri Lankan National Security Council had defined 12,000 civilians as the 'acceptable casualty level' during Operation Liberation. He argued that the Indian intervention was therefore motivated by the need to prevent such high casualties among Tamil civilians.[152] Even if Dixit's alleged number is an exaggeration, there is no doubt that mounting civilian deaths was a major human rights concern. But there were also other political-economic motives behind India's so-called humanitarian intervention.

The Indian Foreign Minister, Natwar Singh, expressed concern that the Sri Lankan government's military action indicated 'increasing influence of external elements inimical to security and stability to peace in our region'. His comment was in reference to allegations by the Tamil Eelam Information Service that foreign mercenary pilots were serving with the Sri Lankan military. Both Singh and Rajiv Gandhi warned the Sri Lankan government of tragic consequences if it continued the military offensive.[153] Notwithstanding Sri Lankan Foreign Minister Hameed's message to the UN Secretary General that Sri Lanka was facing an imminent 'threat to its independence, sovereignty and territorial integrity', India sent in a flotilla of 20 boats with relief supplies for the beleaguered Jaffna Peninsula on 3 June 1987. The flotilla was intercepted and turned back by the Sri Lankan navy for entering the island's territorial waters. The Sri Lankan government insisted that relief supplies had been distributed in the north after the first phase of Operation Liberation. Both Pakistan and China had also offered humanitarian aid to Sri Lanka. Seeking to pre-empt these rivals, India hurried in with her own humanitarian gesture to 'ameliorate Indian Tamil discontent' over the plight of their brethren in Sri Lanka. The Indian government air-dropped 22 tons of relief supplies on the Jaffna Peninsula on 4 June, violating Sri Lanka's sovereignty and air space.[154]

The Sri Lankan government protested Indian action, charging that it was a 'naked violation' of Sri Lankan independence. 'We have no military or other means of preventing this outrage. It is an unwarranted assault on our sovereignty and territorial integrity. We shall hold India responsible for all consequences'.[155] Invoking historical Sinhala fears, President Jayawardena called India's violation of Sri Lanka's air space the seventeenth invasion of Sri Lanka from India in the island's 2,500 year history.[156] Although Pakistan, Bangladesh, Nepal, and the Maldives also protested the Indian action, they could not stem the worsening tide of events. Outside the region, the international reaction to India's move was muted, and Sri Lanka felt abandoned by the western powers.[157] In June 1987, Minister Athulathmudali traveled to many countries looking for support against a potential Indian military action, but he had little success. The 'international community' did not want to upset the regional status quo. The US administration would not increase its limited aid, while China and Pakistan continued their small amount of aid but did so covertly so as not to antagonize India.[158]

Had Sri Lanka possessed oil or other strategically valuable resources, it is likely that the western nations would have taken a different stance. The Sri Lankan government's wholehearted embrace of the neo-liberal development model since 1977 had not improved her economic standing in the world, and the country was faced with a financial crisis and severe foreign exchange problems. In 1987 foreign aid, mostly loans, accounted for about 40 percent of the national budget. At the meeting of donor countries in Paris in June 1987, the Sri Lankan Foreign Minister could only get a pledge of US$600 million and was warned that unless the 'ethnic conflict' was resolved, even this amount would be reduced.[159]

Indo-Sri Lanka Accord

Following its show of force over Sri Lanka, the Indian government sought to end the Sri Lankan conflict through a political settlement. Since India hinted at a military intervention, Jayawardena yielded to the Indian plan. Despite the fact that that Operation Liberation had been near victory and had only been thwarted by Indian intervention, Jayawardena was pressured by India into accepting the Indian claim that the Sri Lankan armed forces were not capable of beating the Tamil insurgents into surrender and that the war was 'unwinnable'. Thus Jayawardena agreed to the terms laid down by the Indians in the interest of what was considered 'sheer national survival'.[160] In an 'extraordinary meeting', the Indian High Commissioner, Dixit, met with 12 Sri Lankan cabinet ministers and argued that the merger of the Northern and Eastern Provinces should precede a referendum rather than follow it, as had been deemed under the previous December 19 proposals. In return for this compliance, India was to return all Tamil militants to Sri Lanka.[161]

India's intervention in Sri Lanka was motivated by mixed interests. As Muni has put it, 'In terms of the ideological challenge precipitated by the Sri Lankan crisis, it was clear that India could neither stand the victory of the Sinhala hegemonic state nor the establishment of a separate state'.[162] LTTE leader Prabhakaran, who was staunchly committed to the establishment of Eelam, was seen as the biggest stumbling block to the Indian plan. On 24 July Prabhakaran was taken in a Indian military transport to New Delhi and put up in a first-class hotel while Rajiv Gandhi tried to persuade him to accept the Indian plan instead of a separate state.[163] At this meeting, the LTTE was awarded Indian Rs.5 million (US$300,000) a month as part of the settlement.[164] Feeling entrapped, Prabhakaran 'prevaricated'. On 26 July in Colombo, Sri Lankan President Jayawardena and in Madras the leaders of EROS, EPRLF, TELO, and PLOTE also 'reluctantly' accepted the Indian plan.[165] On 29 July, India and Sri Lanka signed 'The Indo-Sri Lanka Agreement to Establish Peace and Normalcy in Sri Lanka'. The Annexure to the Agreement, namely the letters exchanged between Prime Minister Rajiv Gandhi and President Jayawardena, were also accepted therewith. The accord, which was hammered out in secrecy without the consultation of the Sri Lankan people or the democratically elected Sri Lankan Parliament, was signed during a 48-hour curfew when Rajiv Gandhi arrived in Sri Lanka. But instead of peace, the Indian intervention ushered in one of the most violent and anarchic periods in the island's modern history.

6   Indian intervention, Indo-Sri Lanka Accord, and intensification of violence, 1987–1994

The stated objectives of the Indo-Sri Lanka Peace Accord were 'nurturing' the 'traditional friendship' between India and Sri Lanka and 'resolving the ethnic problem of Sri Lanka'. These were to be achieved by preserving the 'unity, sovereignty and territorial integrity of Sri Lanka' and by recognizing that 'the Northern and Eastern provinces have been areas of historical habitation of the Sri Lankan Tamil speaking peoples, who have at all times hitherto lived together in this territory with other ethnic groups'. In accordance with the latter claim and in an attempt to create a Tamil majority area, the accord resolved to join the Northern and Eastern Provinces to form one administrative unit with one elected provincial council, one chief minister, and a board of ministers. It also called for a referendum to be held by 31 December 1988, to determine if the people of the Eastern Province wished for their Province to be joined to, or separated from, the Northern Province. The President's discretion to postpone such a referendum was also stipulated. It was agreed that the governments of India and Sri Lanka 'would cooperate in ensuring the physical security and safety of all communities inhabiting the Northern and the Eastern Provinces'. The accord also called for Tamil – which was already a national language under the 1978 constitution – to be an official language and re-imposed English as an official language along with Sinhala.[1] The 13th Amendment to the Sri Lankan Constitution, passed on 14 November 1987, introduced Provincial Councils and made Tamil an official language. Thus, Sri Lanka became the only sovereign state in the world where Tamil is an equal official language.[2]

Hostilities were to cease within 48 hours of the signing of the accord on 29 July 1987. Within 72 hours, the Tamil militant groups were to surrender their arms, and the Sri Lankan security forces were to be confined to barracks (as they had been before the 26 May offensive). The Sri Lankan President agreed to grant a general amnesty to 'political and other prisoners now held in custody under the Prevention of Terrorism Act and other emergency laws, and to combatants, as well as to those persons accused, charged and/or convicted under these laws'. The Sri Lankan government was to disband the Home Guards and withdraw paramilitary forces from the Eastern Province. GOSL also agreed to lift the state of emergency in the Northern and Eastern provinces by 15 August. India and Sri Lanka agreed to cooperate to prevent militant movement across the sea, and India agreed to 'afford military assistance' (an Indian peacekeeping contingent) to Sri Lanka, 'as and when requested'. India agreed to take 'all necessary steps to ensure that Indian territory is not used for activities prejudicial to the unity, integrity and security of Sri Lanka' and to 'underwrite and guarantee' the implementation of the proposals. The annexure to the accord, i.e. letters exchanged between Prime Minister Rajiv Gandhi and President Jayawardena, ensured that Sri Lanka would not engage in activities 'prejudicial' to the interests of India. It called for Sri Lanka to have an early understanding with India about the relevance and employment of foreign military and intelligence personnel in order to ensure that 'such employment will not prejudice Indo-Sri Lankan relations'. It also stated that any foreign broadcasting facilities based in Sri Lanka will not be used for 'any military or intelligence operations'. Further, it ensured that the Trincomalee harbor would not be made available for military use by any country 'in a manner prejudicial to India's interests' and that the restoration and operation of the Trincomalee oil tank farm would be 'undertaken as a joint venture between India and Sri Lanka'.[3]

A controversial accord

What made the accord controversial was not the grant of official status to the Tamil language, but the loss of Sri Lanka's sovereignty and the acceptance of the 'Tamil homelands' thesis. With one stroke of the pen, the Indo-Sri Lanka Accord brought Sri Lanka into the Indian security fold for the first time in her modern history by abrogating Sri Lanka's right to make independent decisions over the strategic Trincomalee harbor, the oil tank farm, foreign radio broadcasts, the hiring of intelligence and military personnel, and on other matters. India turned Sri Lanka into a satellite state akin to Bhutan and Sikkim, whose external relations are controlled by India.[4] In a speech that Rajiv Gandhi made in Uttar Pradesh, India, in November 1987, he justified the accord on grounds that it prevented Sri Lanka from 'coming into the orbit of some superpower trying to tighten their hold in Sri Lanka on the pretext of helping to find a solution to the four year old ethnic conflict'.[5] Electoral support in the south and the satisfaction of ethnic sentiments in Tamil Nadu were other major objectives behind the accord. Gandhi asserted at a public meeting in Madras on 2 August 1987 that '[t]his agreement secures everything that the Sri Lankan Tamils had demanded, short of breaking Sri Lanka's unity'.[6]

There was no Sinhala or other lobby outside the island to challenge the legal, moral, and historical basis of the Indo-Sri Lanka Accord and India's violation of international norms of state sovereignty and independence. India's role as arbiter in the Sri Lankan conflict was also compromised by its involvement in questions on devolution that were within the domestic jurisdiction and the Sri Lankan Parliament.[7] Despite fears of regional leaders and concerns raised by a few western media analysts who compared the Indian imposition of the agreement to the Munich Agreement and 'events ... which preceded the Sudetan–German crisis of the 1930s', the Indo-Sri Lanka accord was welcomed as a 'diplomatic breakthrough' by the international community.[8] Within Sri Lanka, the accord was highly controversial and divisive from the beginning. A pact that was meant to bring unity and peace instead convulsed the society, aggravating the violence and suffering of the Sri Lankan people in both the north and the south.

The depth of Sinhala antipathy to the accord was evidenced by the attack on Indian Prime Minister Rajiv Gandhi with a rifle butt by a young navy cadet during the guard of honor immediately following the signing of the accord. The Sri Lankan President did not have the full backing of his government for the accord. Agriculture Minister Gamini Jayasuriya resigned, and Prime Minister Premadasa and National Security Minister Athulathmudali did not participate in the signing ceremony.[9]

The widespread Sinhala opposition to the accord was expressed in massive street protests and anti-government demonstrations, starting in Colombo on 28 July. Despite the island-wide curfew imposed on 29 July, the protests spread throughout the south into Mt Lavinia, Nugegoda, Kalutara, Galle, Hambantota, Kandy, Ratnapura, and Polonnaruwa.[10] The agitation and violence were both spontaneous and organized in that the SLFP, JVP, MEP, MSV, and even a few prominent members of the UNP were involved in launching the campaign against the accord.[11] But as the opposition and violence spread, the JVP moved to strategic areas ensuring that anti-UNP and anti-accord groups caused maximum damage.[12] The three days of rioting is estimated to have cost the lives of 74–100 persons, including Buddhist monks. Property damage was estimated at Rs.4 billion.[13] More killings and destruction would occur in the soon-to-come JVP insurgency, which was sparked by resistance to the Indo-Sri Lanka Accord.

In order to combat the growing insurgency against the accord, President Jayawardena requested military assistance from India under the terms of the accord. And on 30 July 1987, 7000 soldiers of the Indian Peace Keeping Force (IPKF) were flown into the north to assist in the cessation of hostilities and surrender of arms while the Sri Lankan troops in the north were moved to control growing rioting in the south.[14] The IPKF troop size would eventually increase to 100,000 men at its peak in 1989.[15] The controversial accord and the IPKF presence to enforce it sent Sri Lanka into one of the bloodiest and anarchic periods of her post-Independence history.

The accord: support and opposition

From its inception, the accord received support of the small non-JVP Sinhala left-wing parties, which took the position that a resolution of the ethnic conflict required comprehensive devolution through a political settlement.[16] In 1948, in their heyday, some of the same leftist parties had fought against a defense agreement with Britain and the presence of British bases in Sri Lanka as violations of Sri Lanka's sovereignty and independence. But now the non-JVP left parties, 'think-tanks', and foreign-funded 'peace-oriented NGOs' associated with them welcomed the accord and the subsequent Indian military intervention.[17] While this group represents mostly the small Colombo-based westernized elite, their access to international funding, media, academia, and other global networks has made them a key opinion maker on the Sri Lankan crisis.[18]

Under the Open Economy and privatization policies, foreign-funded private institutes came to displace state-funded universities in conducting social science research that would define the Sri Lankan conflict in ways acceptable to their funders. The privatization of conflict resolution and expansion of aid led to the proliferation of national and international NGOs in the country. Marga Institute, the Social Science Association and the International Centre for Ethnic Studies, established in 1972, 1977, and 1982, respectively, came to play an influential role in conceptualizing the Sri Lankan conflict as an 'ethnic conflict'. After July 1983, a large number of organizations, including the National Peace Council, the Center for Policy Alternatives, and the Women's Media Collective, also became prominent actors in the Sri Lankan 'ethnic studies industry' (a term attributed to Susantha Goonatilake). They have furthered the bipolar Sinhala oppressor versus Tamil victim analysis and Tamil regional autonomy as the solution. The controversial International Alert (IA), funded by Norway, was founded in the early 1980s specifically to alert the world to 'the conflict within Sri Lanka between Sinhalese and Tamil'.[19]

The supporters of the accord justified the violation of Sri Lanka's sovereignty and independence and the 'consultative democratic processes' on the grounds of conflict resolution and 'geopolitical realities'. Their basic argument was that 'we are a small neighbour of a country of immense size ... Given that reality, our external relations and our foreign policy had always to be fully sensitive to the regional concerns and other external interests of India'.[20] Notwithstanding the questionable 'peace-at-any cost' position this signified, the supporters of the accord presented themselves as liberal, social democratic, and peacemakers as opposed to the extremist, right-wing warmongers who opposed the accord.[21] Since then, this self-proclaimed distinction – liberal peacemakers versus extremist warmongers – has been extended to subsequent peace initiatives, such as the 1995 Kumaratunga initiative and the 2002 Norwegian-facilitated initiative, which are discussed in later chapters.[22]

The accord, with its promises to end hostilities and to merge the north and the east, was, in general, welcomed with relief, if not jubilation, by the Sri Lankan Tamils and the TULF, the accord's principal local supporter. Fearful that the non-Tamil majority in the Eastern Province would oppose a merger with the Northern Province, TULF opposed the idea of holding a referendum in the Eastern Province. Similarly, the non-LTTE Tamil militant groups, which laid down arms under the terms of the accord, also opposed the referendum clause, seeing it as an obstacle to a future Eelam.[23] Indeed, the Eastern Province was the 'weak link' in the Indo-Sri Lanka Accord.[24] For the core Tamil militants and their external sympathizers, the accord did not go far enough.[25]

The gravest threat to the accord came from the militant LTTE leader Prabhakaran. He appeared to cave into Indian pressure when flown to India to meet with Gandhi, and upon his return to Jaffna declared on August 5, 1987 that he would give up arms. This statement was greeted with cheers by a crowd of some

50,000, clearly indicating the Jaffna people's abhorrence of violence and yearning for peace.[26] But, Prabahakran also emphasized:

> [T]he only certain solution to the Tamil question is the state of Eelam. I have a great conviction that we will achieve the state of Eelam. We will certainly continue to fight for our cause – the state of Eelam. The method of war has changed, but our determination for Eelam has not changed.[27]

This has been Prabhakaran's steadfast position from the beginning. He has made it very clear, and has demonstrated again and again, that his struggle will continue until the creation of Eelam – a position that does not allow for compromise or negotiation and leaves the Sri Lankan government with a choice: accept Eelam or militarily defeat Prabhakaran and the LTTE.

Accord: Muslim opposition

Although it had nurtured the LTTE and the other Sri Lankan Tamil separatist groups, India was unequivocally opposed to the Eelamist demand for a separate Tamil state. By proposing a referendum, the accord recognized the justifiable opposition of the Muslims and the Sinhalese in the Eastern Province to a merger with the Northern Province. Yet the accord's virtual acknowledgement of the fictitious Tamil 'homeland' and the imposition of a temporary merger of the Northern and Eastern Provinces without a prior referendum, violated the island's pluralist history and democratic political traditions. The assertion of the existence of a unified 'Tamil speaking people' overlooked the significant regional differences between the Northern Jaffna Tamils and the Eastern Batticoloa Tamils and marginalized the Muslims who did not identify themselves as Tamils.[28] (The differences between the Northern and Eastern Tamils would lead to a split in the LTTE in 2004 discussed in Chapter 8.) Indeed, a lasting settlement to the Sri Lankan dilemma would need to take into account the views of the moderates and the concerns of Sinhalese, Muslims, and Tamils in the contentious Eastern Province. Failing to recognize the fundamental differences between the North and the East would doom the accord to failure from the beginning.[29]

The accord did not recognize the Muslims as a distinct ethno-religious community. Whereas Muslims were 32 percent of the population in the Eastern Province and 10 percent in the Northern Province, in a merged North East, under the Indo-Sri Lanka Accord, they would constitute less than 20 percent of the total population (Table 1.2). In negotiations leading up to the accord, the SLMC along with Eastern Province Muslim organizations had made a demand for a separate administrative unit, 'a Muslim majority Provincial Council' covering predominantly Muslim areas in the Eastern as well as the Northern Province. But their demands were not incorporated in the accord.[30] The SLMC leader, Ashroff, who had once supported Tamil Eelam but was now championing Muslim separatism, opposed the accord, arguing that it 'will ensure and invite not only a Tamil Muslim conflict but also a Tamil Sinhala conflict in the region'.[31]

As predicted, after the accord the Tamil separatist violence and ethnic cleansing of Muslims and Sinhalese intensified, leading to increased calls for a separate Muslim administrative unit.[32] The concept of one Muslim community, like the concept of a single Tamil community, overlooks significant regional and cultural differences between Muslims in the east and the south, and between Moors and Malays. Nevertheless, Muslim opposition to the Indo-Sri Lanka accord, was a decisive factor in the emergence of a Muslim separatist position. As Fazil explains:

> [T]he Tamils were trying to pull the Muslims into their camp under the title of 'Tamil-speaking people' a banner covering both Tamils and Muslims. Muslims dreaded that they might next be referred to as 'Muslim Tamil' and therefore felt a greater need to separate themselves from the Tamil community.[33]

Post-accord violence

As the University Teachers for Human Rights (Jaffna) noted, the failure to provide mechanisms for 'reaching a democratic consensus' and for correcting human rights violations placed the accord on a 'weak footing' from the beginning: 'In time, the accord tended to look more and more like a strait-jacket imposed on the people of the island'.[34] Indeed, by promoting a dualistic approach to the Sri Lankan crisis as a conflict between the majority Sinhalese and the minority Tamils, the Indo-Sri Lanka Peace Accord ignored the complex multipolar nature of the conflict. This is evident in the rise of the JVP's opposition to the accord and the brutal intra-ethnic Sinhala violence.

JVP insurgency

Prompted by the regional and international support for TULF and the ineffectual nature of the Communist Party and the NLSSP, the Sri Lankan government quickly lifted the proscriptions that had been placed on those parties following July 1983 violence. The government could not produce evidence in support of its allegations that the JVP was behind the 1983 anti-Tamil violence or that it had established a link with a Tamil terrorist group in the north to launch a joint anti-state revolution.[35] The JVP, on the other hand, had little, if any, external backing. Although an Amnesty International report of 1985 defended the JVP against government charges that it was involved in violence, the proscription against the JVP was continued. Thus the JVP, which had been operating within the democratic system since 1977 and had a growing mass base, was forced out of the mainstream and into 'a clandestine mode of existence'.[36] The Sri Lankan political elite bears responsibility for the rise of the violent JVP insurgency in the late 1980s.[37]

The JVP repeatedly asked why 'the TULF has not been proscribed while the JVP which resolutely opposes the division of the country has been proscribed'.[38] A large number of JVP supporters and sympathizers, including Buddhist monks and students, did not advocate violence. But increasing police crackdowns on JVP activities, arrests, molestation of supporters, and lack of official attention to their suffering and grievances, forced many young men and women to make the JVP once more an armed militant organization. 'To ensure its continuity ... the JVP cadres ... began to arm themselves by late 1985'.[39] And by early 1987 the JVP military wing, the Patriotic People's Movement, Deshapremi Janatha Viyaparaya (DJV), began to mobilize forces to overthrow the government.[40] An effective women's wing was also developed. Like the Tamil militants in the north, the JVP engaged in robberies to accumulate funds and attacked government security forces to steal arms and ammunition.[41] The DJV membership included ex-Sri Lankan army soldiers who had been dismissed because of 'anti-Tamil excesses ... as well as those who left or deserted, humiliated by their removal from the North and the East front-lines when the Indian army landed in mid-1987'.[42] The total number of desertions had risen to 2,250 between 1984 and 1988.[43]

The signing of the Indo-Sri Lanka Accord and the arrival of the IPKF exacerbated Sinhala fears of Indian expansionism and Tamil Eelam. The accord provided the JVP with the opportunity to return to the public realm to campaign against the 'Indian invasion' and to call for a patriotic struggle to overthrow the Sri Lankan administration, allegedly the 'henchmen' of India.[44] It attacked President Jayawardena as one 'who betrayed the motherland to India' throughout his political career.[45] DJV attacks against security installations became justified as a means to arm the patriots to liberate the north and the east from the Indian troops. There was also widespread support for the JVP campaign among Buddhist monks, the traditional defenders of the unity and political integrity of the island, students in the schools and universities, trade unionists, and others in the south. They specifically rose up against the Indian army presence (which increased to some 100,000 troops by 1989 and the Indian-imposed merger of the Northern and Eastern Provinces.[46]

The JVP had followed a 'consistently anti-Indian line' since 1971, criticizing India's regional political and economic expansionism. As political scientist Shelton Kodikara noted, the JVP struggle was

[A] confrontation between the JVP and the government of Sri Lanka as much as it is a confrontation between the JVP and India.... As Rohana Wijeweera, the JVP leader, put it, 'Of the twenty-six joint ventures that India has entered into with foreign countries, eighteen are in Sri Lanka. Today can the Sri Lankan security forces buy equipment from any country of their choice ... India forces Sri Lanka to buy cheap substandard goods it produces ... recently, when the Air Force wanted to buy helicopters from another country, India opposed it'.[47]

While Sinhala opposition to the accord and fears of Indian expansionism were the immediate reasons, socio-economic grievance was the root cause for the rise of the JVP in the late 1980s. The caste factor was even more visible during the duration of the 1980s insurgency. As Chandraprema observed, 'Whenever Balakayas (forces) were formed the JVP leadership made it a point to arm the most oppressed castes. Thus the economic factor was linked to a powerful 'primordial loyalty' which served as a good mobilising factor'.[48] In 1990, 30.4 percent of all households and 34.7 percent of all households in the rural sector were below the poverty line.[49] Figures for 1989 showed an unemployment rate of 20 percent for youths between 15 and 20 years of age, constituting 70 percent of the unemployed. Unemployment was especially acute in the Southern, North Central and Uva provinces, which were JVP strongholds in 1971 and again in 1987. In the district of Hambantota in the Southern Province, 75 percent of the population was reportedly living on food stamps.[50] Of a total population of about 15.5 million in 1985–1986, 11 million, or 70.3 percent, of the population was under the age of 35.[51] In the 1980s, 80 percent of the JVP politbureau and the central committee were either university graduates, university drop-outs, or teachers. Educated unemployment was a major factor contributing to JVP mobilization, as it had been in 1971.[52]

Utilizing underlying mass frustration and anger and hiding behind the cloak of patriotism, the JVP began a brutal campaign of assassination, targeting select public figures, all Sinhalese, who were considered to be supporters of the accord. In early October 1987 the LTTE was waging attacks and driving out Sinhala peasants from Trincomalee under IPKF sponsorship.[53] During this time the DJV attacked the Sri Lankan army camp in Kantale and claimed that it would use the captured weapons 'for the freedom of the motherland ... to drive away the Indian monkey army and the Tigers who have been a curse on the motherland'.[54] But as Chandraprema's incisive account of the JVP terror in the years 1987–1989 points out, 'the JVP never did such a thing. They concentrated on killing their Sinhala opponents with the weapons they took from the army camps'.[55]

After Indian soldiers were flown to the island's north, Sri Lankan soldiers were flown in Indian Air Force planes from the north to the south to control the growing anti-accord insurgency.[56] Both the Sri Lankan army and the police were expanded, and a special task force known as Operation Combines was created to coordinate army, navy, air force, and police activities in the Colombo district.[57] STF (Special Task Force), considered the 'best fighting force in the country' to protect Sinhalese in the north, was now used against the Sinhala JVP in the south.[58] But the government found it difficult to maintain law and order because the JVP insurgency, in some ways like the Tamil insurgency, was an unconventional 'hit job war'. There was also widespread popular sympathy for the anti-Indian and anti-separatist cause. Moreover, the armed forces were demoralized by the way the government had stopped 'Operation Liberation' in its tracks in 1987 when the war against the Tamil terrorists was almost won.[59]

The JVP reign of terror

JVP attacks on the government became open and daring after the signing of the accord. A bomb attack on 18 August 1987, at the UNP parliamentary group meeting inside the parliamentary complex killed one MP, and a number of other ministers were injured.[60] The next day, the DJV justified the action, accusing the government of signing the accord and bringing in the IPKF, and warning that 'all those MPs and lackeys who like to live should resign their seats'.[61] Due to the threats of the DJV, large numbers of UNP members and government personnel began to leave their posts. The DJV explained that targeting was not on UNP/anti-UNP lines, but accord and anti-accord lines: '[T]hose who were in favour of the accord will receive the same treatment whatever their political affiliations were'.[62] The Indian High Commissioner, J.N. Dixit, referred to as the 'viceroy' himself, narrowly escaped a bomb attack.[63] A JVP publication issued in January 1988 identified as targets 'all those who support the Rajiv–Gandhi–JR Pact and the provincial councils system, all those who support the Jayawardena regime, all those who whitewash the destructive acts of the Indian Army and describe them as a "peace keeping force"'.[64]

The JVP's violent campaign disrupted the civil administration through strikes, demonstrations, and threats to any and all who did not conform to its orders. Attacks on Indian civilians and businesses and a boycott of Indian goods, triggered a demand for wage increases and crippled the transport system throughout the island.[65] People were warned to keep away from work. Shops were closed, and food shortage became acute. Bank, postal, and telecommunication facilities were virtually halted. University education was brought to a standstill: universities were closed for three years, from 1987 to 1990. Even hospitals were not functioning due to JVP threats and orders.[66] By November 1988 there was 'near anarchy', and an unseen parallel JVP government, referred to as the 'little anduwa' (small government), seemed to be running the south.[67]

The JVP killed hundreds, if not thousands, of armed service personnel, police officers, and their relatives as well as politicians, media people, and government officials. The most prominent politician assassinated by the JVP (in February 1988) was Vijaya Kumaratunge, the movie idol and popular leader of the SLMP who was an outspoken supporter of the accord.[68] Prominent Sinhalese were not the only ones killed. The JVP threatened members of the Sri Lankan security forces, most of whom came from the same rural social class as its own cadres. They were asked to join the JVP or die. The JVP killed people considered to be 'informers', including members of the Buddhist clergy, those who broke strikes called by the JVP, newsagents selling newspapers 'blacklisted' by the JVP, and sellers of Indian goods.[69] The bodies of many JVP victims were 'openly displayed as warnings to others'.[70]

There was increasing fear among the public that through sheer terror the JVP would come to power by the end of 1988. On 7 November President Jayawardena said India would come to help if the JVP tried to topple his government, but ten days later he invited the JVP to talks, which it ignored. In the midst of the violence and turmoil, presidential elections were held on 19 December 1988. The Jayawardena regime finally ended when Ranasinghe Premadasa, the Prime Minister and UNP stalwart who was opposed to the Indo-Sri Lanka Accord and was eager to send the IPKF back to India as soon as possible, was elected as the new president. But the JVP rejected the election as a 'false election' held 'on the 'instructions of Rajiv Gandhi', and ordered people not to vote.[71] Due to JVP intimidation and threats (and Tamil militant threats in the north), only 50–55 percent of registered voters cast their votes, the lowest poll recorded in Sri Lanka.[72] Soon after his election, President Premadasa sought to appease the JVP in January 1989 by releasing 1,800 detainees and lifting the emergency. Instead of returning to the democratic process, however, the JVP continued killing political opponents, security forces, and anyone considered to be a sympathizer of the hated accord.[73] The period leading to the parliamentary elections in February 1989 saw a heightening of the violence. The official election death toll was 433 people between 11 and 16 February including 70 on election day. Actual figures were probably much higher.[74]

Violence continued after the election, with the JVP killing defeated candidates as well as those in power. In March 1989 it enforced 'protest days' when people were ordered to boycott work, not to travel on roads, and to turn off lights and television in order to mark the killings in the north by the IPKF and the LTTE and killings in the south by state sponsored groups.[757] Unlike previous Sri Lankan heads of state, Premadasa was a 'common man' from a relatively underprivileged social class background. He expressed sympathy for both the JVP and the LTTE struggles as the outcomes of socio-economic and political injustices and made overtures to appease both groups. He offered to vacate some UNP seats in parliament and give them to the JVP if it were to lay down arms. Instead of complying, the JVP charged that 'On the Indian front, this government is no different to the previous government ... the struggle ... will continue'.[76] The government announced a six-day unilateral ceasefire with the JVP and the LTTE during the Sinhala–Tamil New Year in April 1989, and called for both to enter the political mainstream. The LTTE agreed to talks with the government, but the JVP refused.[77]

The JVP was a major force by April 1989. The Indian government was refusing to remove its troops from Sri Lanka, and the JVP was exhorting youth to 'join the JVP to drive the Indians away'[78] But gradually people had begun to see that the JVP was brutally killing fellow Sinhalese, not driving away Indians.[79] And the JVP's crippling of the economy was affecting the poor and lower middle classes the most harshly. People began to withdraw their sympathy from a group that was increasingly seen as engaged in self-destructive violence.

According to estimates by Rohan Gunaratna, every day 200 people died due to killings and counter killings in Sri Lanka in 1988; according to International Alert, in the 1988–1989 period Sri Lanka had the highest average death toll of any conflict in the world at the time.[80] The JVP killings were similar to the Tamil militant struggle, which targeted Tamils deemed traitors to its cause. But, unlike the Tamil militants, who routinely massacred Sinhala civilians, the JVP did not kill Tamils, although most Tamils, excepting the LTTE, which claimed to represent all Tamils, supported the accord. Chandraprema's comparison of the LTTE and the JVP help to question the dominant ethnic analysis of the Sri Lankan conflict:

> [T]he JVP killed in the space of two and a half years several times the number of innocent Sinhalese killed by the murderous attacks of the Tamil terrorists over the past decade. The LTTE was also accused of having killed more Tamil militants than the Sri Lankan Army. But while killing their own people, the LTTE also fought the Sri Lanka Army and the IPKF. Thus, they had some saving graces which left them a considerable amount of sympathy to bank on. The JVP never killed a single Tamil terrorist or an Indian solider. Thus, when public opinion turned against the JVP, there were no extenuating factors to mitigate the fury of the reaction.[81]

The JVP gave an ultimatum in August 1989 that it would kill the relatives of security personnel who did not resign their positions. This turned the tide against the JVP. Posters began to appear in prominent places throughout the south, threatening that for each of the army's relatives killed, 12 relatives of JVP supporters would be killed in return.[82] The retaliation often entailed a horrific cycle of murder and reprisal killings, a massive orgy of violence.[83] By the time the second JVP insurgency was crushed in November 1989, it had left some left some 40,000 dead in the interior of the island, although some estimates give a higher figure of 60,000 Sinhala deaths.[84]

Counter violence

The violence that the JVP had wreaked on the country for nearly two years since the signing of the Indo-Sri Lanka Accord was turned back on it by a vicious government reprisal. In a later interview, Minister of State for Defense, Ranjan Wijeratna, who was in charge of the counter-insurgency operation against the JVP, stated:

> I started this beginning August 1989 soon after my return from India, and after the first week of November the politbureau of the JVP was in the bag. Once the politbureau was smashed, it was only a mopping up operation that was necessary.[85]

After August 1989, reprisal killings against the JVP became a daily occurrence.[86] Most of the reprisals were carried out by paramilitary groups believed to be in collusion with the police and army. Some of the most 'spectacular killings' were in Kandy among low caste communities such as the Batgam.[87]

The first vigilante group to carry out reprisal killings against the JVP was the PRAA (People's Revolutionary Red Army), which first appeared in October 1988. This was followed by the 'Black Cats' in the North Central Province,

'Ukussa' in the Central Province, and the 'Green Tigers' and other faceless groups throughout the south, all of which 'killed and killed without even bothering claim to responsibility'.[88] There was a great deal of speculation at the time as to who was behind these paramilitary groups, yet to date there is no conclusive evidence. It is reported that 'almost every section of the left – NGOs, intellectuals and the opposition parties were involved in working with the State towards crushing the JVP'.[89] PRAA was believed to be the creation of left-wing activists seeking revenge against the JVP for killing hundreds of their own.[90] The creation of PRAA has also been associated with death squads operating under government ministers and with Tamil terrorist groups, such as TELO and PLOTE. According to the Batalanda Commission, appointed by the subsequent Sri Lankan government, Ranil Wickramasinghe, Minister for Science and Industries in the late 1980s and other government officials had connections to PRAA and the 'Black Cats'. They have been linked to 'unlawful detention and torture chambers' in certain houses in the Batalanda Housing Scheme.[91] However, because legal proceedings were not initiated on the basis of the Batalanda Commission Report, the allegations remain unproven.

Human rights violations

The Sri Lankan state, like all legitimate states, is obliged to maintain law and order and provide security to its citizens by taking appropriate actions, including arrest and trial of persons engaged in political and criminal violence regardless of ethnicity. But when terrorism is fought outside the constitution, violates internationally accepted international human rights norms, and is waged under news blackouts, as was done frequently in the late 1980s, widespread abuses occur.[92] An Asia Watch news report issued in September 1989 noted:

> Under the provisions of the state of Emergency, the Sri Lankan security forces were given 'almost unlimited powers to combat the JVP, including shooting suspects on sight and disposing of the bodies without inquest. Under the Indemnity Act of December 1988, [passed before the Presidential elections of the same month] security personnel have been granted immunity from prosecution for any such abuses committed.... In recent months, reports of particularly savage attacks have included the killing of JVP suspects by 'necklacing' – throwing gasoline-soaked tires over their heads and igniting them – have been attributed to vigilante death squads composed or acting under the orders of the security forces.[93]

As in Sri Lanka's north, in the south there was an age, class, and gender basis to the repression. Most of the 'disappeared' were young men from lower socio-economic backgrounds. An Amnesty International report issued in September 1990 noted that '[m]any of the 'disappeared' are from poor, rural communities which, for reasons of economic and social status, are believed by the authorities to be collectively sympathetic to the JVP'.[94] The report also observed that a

large number who 'disappeared' and were 'extrajudicially executed' had connections to student organizations with suspected links to the JVP. Many were
also young Buddhist monks. The report charged that thousands of people suspected to be JVP sympathizers simply 'disappeared' after arrest, tortured and
killed in custody without post-mortem investigations.[95] Lawyers engaged in
filing habeas corpus petitions on behalf of JVP prisoners and alleged sympathizers were themselves killed.[96]

Counter-terrorism involving sophisticated surveillance and intelligence
operations helped crush the JVP insurgency by the end of December 1989.
Rohana Wijeweera and his deputy Upatissa Gamanayake were arrested by the
armed forces and reportedly killed on 13 November. Their bodies were quickly
cremated without post-mortem or inquest, as officials were empowered to do
under emergency regulations. All other JVP politbureau members (except
Somawansa Amerasinghe, who escaped to Paris) were also captured and
killed.[97]

The public was relieved to see the JVP reign of terror end. Even after the decimation of its leadership, deaths, and surrender of thousands of JVP cadres and
alleged sympathizers, the 'mopping up' operation did not stop immediately.
There were 1,160 'disappearances' recorded in the south in 1990; as the subsequent Disappearance Commission noted, and most of the victims were very
young.[98] A number of disappearances and extrajudicial killings that had no connection to the JVP are recorded from this period. Well-known among these was
the case of 32 schoolboys from Embilipitiya who were taken to Sevana (shade)
army camp and later found killed. Charges of JVP links had been brought
against the boys by the school principal, who held a personal grudge against
them (the principal was later sentenced to prison).[99] The case that brought the
greatest attention to 'disappearances' in Sri Lanka at this time was that of the
prominent media personality Richard Zoysa, who was abducted on 18 February
1990, and killed, apparently because of a political satire he had produced.[100]
Subsequently, Zoysa's mother, Dr Manorani Sarvanamuttu, helped form an
organization called Mothers of the Disappeared to bring attention to the problem
in both the north and the south.[101]

Despite the tremendous destruction and human suffering, the violence in the
south has received relatively little attention because it did not fall within the
rubric of majority–minority ethnic conflict. JVP cadres, including its leaders,
were known to have been tortured and killed in custody without access to due
process of law. Yet there were hardly any groups to call for their fundamental
rights. As noted earlier, practically every section of the leftist NGOs, intellectuals, and opposition parties that had brought up human rights charges against the
government's handling of the northern Tamil insurgency were themselves under
threat from the JVP and had therefore worked with the state to destroy the
JVP.[102] The Sinhala elites, who were collectively threatened by the JVP, united
across political party lines to decimate it. Notwithstanding the Amnesty International, Asia Watch, and International Alert reports cited here, there was relative silence on the part of the international media and human rights and peace

activists on the way the JVP was suppressed. Journalist Subhash Wickramasinghe echoes a common view when he says that the government was able to crush the JVP insurgency because it was treated as a purely domestic conflict:

> [T]here had been no interference from anybody. It was purely a terrorist problem and the outside world correctly stood away ... the countries from where Lanka sought assistance, including India [and] Pakistan helped militarily to overcome the terrorist attacks. The matter ended there as an internal terrorist act which the then government crushed without negotiating with the terrorists as there is no room to negotiate with those who violate allegiance to State which is treason. Treason is punishable with death.[103]

The JVP had no nearby ethnic motherland to escape to or a diaspora-insurgency network to raise funds and lobby the international community and the media on its behalf. Had it been able to explain the rise and repression of the JVP along lines of ethnic discrimination, ethnic cleansing, and genocide, as did the LTTE, the JVP is likely to have found more sympathy among local and international human rights and peace networks. Additionally, its Marxist credentials were repellent to many liberal human rights and peace organizations.

Like LTTE terrorism, JVP terrorism had to be eliminated to protect Sri Lankan society. The JVP had legitimate grievances beyond poverty and unemployment. Its charges against Indian expansionism and its proscription on unproven charges for the July 1983 violence were legitimate. But, as Clifford Bob's work, *Marketing Rebellion* and other evidence from various parts of the world increasingly show, it is not the validity and justice or extent of grievances that determine a movement's success as much as its political savvy and sophistication in cultivating an international lobby.[104] The JVP 'terror monster' could be easily eliminated because it was purely local, whereas the LTTE 'terror monster' has its roots elsewhere. Its 'retractable legs and the hands were in Sri Lanka', but, 'its vital organs, the heart and the brain were in Madras and Delhi' and increasingly in the West and southeast Asia.[105] The so-called 'Sinhala hegemonic' state of Sri Lanka, under two different political parties, twice succeeded in crushing Sinhala insurgencies in the post-independence period. But it has found it nearly impossible to eliminate the LTTE, given the international breadth of the movement backing a separate state in the north and the east of Sri Lanka.

Violence in the north

Soon after the signing of the accord, the Sri Lankan government began to meet its obligations. It immediately withdrew its troops to barracks, released several thousand Tamil political prisoners, and granted them amnesty. It passed the 13th Amendment to the constitution, making Tamil an official language with English as a 'link language', (as in India to connect linguistic communities) with essentially the same official status. The 13th Amendment also instituted the provincial council system as the basis for political devolution and administrative decentralization.[106] In September 1988 the Sri Lankan government merged the Northern and Eastern provinces into the North Eastern Province, preparing the way for elections to the North East Provincial council in November 1988.[107] These steps were intended to meet Tamil grievances and the demand for the devolution of power and autonomy to the north and the east.

The accord, however, was seriously flawed because the LTTE was not a party to it. India signed the accord with the Sri Lankan government 'leaving the LTTE free to do what it wanted'.[108] All of the Tamil militant groups except the LTTE surrendered arms. The LTTE had promised to do so but quickly reneged, demonstrating that it was never serious about disarmament, peace, or the accord. As Dayan Jayatilleka put it, 'The LTTE, once on the [violent] path, never left it, never deviated from it and kept building upon it, adding momentum to its war, and evolving as an army'[109] The failure to disarm the Tigers, also a failure of all subsequent peace accords, brought the intra-ethnic and multi-ethnic dimensions of the conflict in the north and the east into the forefront. India's failure to bring about a cessation of hostilities and a surrender of arms by the Tigers strengthened the LTTE vis-à-vis all other groups.[110]

The LTTE went on a killing spree of the other Tamil militant groups, which had disarmed. Nearly 150 political rivals, belonging mostly to the EPRLF, PLOTE, and TELO (collectively known as 'Three Stars' and sponsored by RAW), were killed by the LTTE in the immediate aftermath of the accord.[111] In its unwavering commitment to separatism, the LTTE threatened all Tamils who supported the accord and any of its critics and dissidents (as the JVP did to the Sinhalese). TULF leaders who had fought long and hard for Eelam and who now supported the accord's devolutionary plans were not spared. Amirthalingam, who had been very close to Prabhakaran in the 1970s, was murdered in his home on 13 July 1989.[112] Instead of condemning the murders and taking a principled stance against the culture of violence and auto-genocide, the TULF continued to seek its survival by condemning the Sinhalese, 'telling the Tamil people that there is no hope under the Sri Lankan polity'.[113] TULF complicity with LTTE terrorism has been a major barrier to resolving the Sri Lankan conflict.[114]

Rajani Thiranagama, who was a staunch critic of the Sri Lankan government and the IPKF and had been a supporter of the LTTE, was gunned down on 21 September 1989, after she began to criticize the LTTE's genocidal policies towards Tamils. After that, members of the University Teachers for Human Rights that she helped form were forced to leave Jaffna and operate clandestinely in Colombo, and the Tamil community was gripped in fear.[117]

LTTE's inter-ethnic killings paralleled its intra-ethnic killings, especially in Trincomalee, which exploded in the aftermath of the Indo-Sri Lanka Accord. Citizens committees in the north and the east sought help from the IPKF to resettle Tamils who had been displaced earlier in the territorial struggle between the Sri Lankan army and Tamil militants. About 2,000 Tamil youths, suspected terrorists, freed under the Indo-Sri Lanka Accord had also been released in Trincomalee. The first Sinhala–Tamil communal violence erupted in Trincomalee on September 1987, followed by civilian massacres on 24 September.[116] Soon, the

LTTE began to use the volatile situation to carry out ethnic cleansing of Sinhalese from the east. As reported by Asia Watch, the massacres appeared to be 'an organized pogrom', and the victims were mostly Sinhala refugees who had been recently resettled in their original villages by the Sri Lankan government as a precondition for holding the referendum proposed in the Indo-Sri Lanka Accord.[117]

The IPKF had not allowed the Sri Lankan army to leave their barracks to help the Sinhalese. On the contrary, some soldiers of the IPKF reportedly instigated the anti-Sinhala violence.[118] In one incident on 4 October 1987, the IPKF itself murdered a Buddhist monk of the China Bay Buddhist Temple who was leading a demonstration against the IPKF.[119] A Tamil Madrasi Regiment of the IPKF had openly supported the Sri Lankan Tamils in the violence against the Sinhalese.[120] A November 1987 Asia Watch report gives details of brutal treatment of the Sinhalese by the IPKF and reports charges brought by the Sinhalese refugees against the IPKF: failure to protect Sinhalese civilians against attacks by Tamil militants; victimization of Sinhala civilians by individual undisciplined Indian soldiers; systematic assistance or participation in the assault of the Sinhalese through discriminatory enforcement of the curfew; expulsion of people from their homes; transporting armed militants in military vehicles; and burning homes and killing people.[121]

Even after the IPKF began its offensive against the LTTE, the ethnic cleansing of Sinhalese in the east continued apace. An Asia Watch news bulletin covering the period from January to April 1988 reported an incident where 'Tamil militants ... machine-gunned 9 children and 6 adults in their homes in the Trincomalee District' and went on to comment that 'Similar attacks are reported almost daily'.[122] The Indo-Sri Lanka Accord had asserted that the north and the east of Sri Lanka were historically inhabited by Tamil speakers. The IPKF in turn endorsed the false claim of 'traditional Tamil homelands' in their dealings with local people. Many of the Sinhalese murdered in Trincomalee were long-term residents in the area who had had close relations with their Tamil neighbors.[123] But the IPKF regarded the Sinhalese in the region as 'colonists' and, hence, dispensable.[124] The IPKF's indifference, if not collusion, in the LTTE's anti-Sinhala violence, along with the disarming of home guards stipulated by the accord and the departure of the STF, left the Sinhalese unprotected, fearful, and powerless. The victimization of Sinhalese in the east did not bring much international media attention, but it intensified anti-accord feelings and anger against the IPKF in the south, although, as noted earlier, the JVP campaign did not target Indians.

Lack of protection also contributed to LTTE killings of Muslims in the Eastern Province and the eruption of Tamil–Muslim communal violence in places such as Kalmunai and Ampara in March and April 1988.[125] Asia Watch reported an attack on a Muslim mosque and the burning of 200 Muslim homes by Tamil militants on 1 April 1988. Notwithstanding stipulations of the accord that India would protect all groups, the IPKF, which was a predominantly Hindu army, turned a blind eye to the attacks against the Muslims, as they did to attacks against the Sinhala Buddhists in the east. The victimization of Muslims by Tamil militants is alleged to have led to the funding of an armed Sri Lankan Muslim group, Al-Jihad, by Islamic fundamentalist countries during this time.[126] Though the IPKF overlooked, if not supported, LTTE violence against other Tamil political groups and non-Tamil communities in the north and the east, the Tigers began to charge that the IPKF was not giving protection to the LTTE. The Tigers used these charges to begin attacks to drive out the IPKF and continue the struggle for Eelam.

The LTTE–IPKF war

Thileepan, the 25-year old political head of the LTTE in Jaffna, died on 26 September 1987, following a death fast during which he demanded, among other things, that the LTTE be given the majority of seats in the proposed North East Provincial Council. The LTTE blamed his death on India. The LTTE could have asked Thileepan to call off the fast when Dixit, the Indian High Commissioner, agreed to give the LTTE seven out of 12 seats as well as the chairmanship of the interim administration. Instead the LTTE allowed Thileepan to die and cleverly used popular anger over his death to rouse anti-accord sentiments among Tamils.[127] This brought into sharp focus the differences in the Sri Lankan Tamil moderate and extremist approaches to separation – the gradualist non-violent approach of the former and the violent militarist approach of the LTTE. As Hoole later put it, 'the LTTE's strategy for separation is not through strengthening devolution ... but, is rather by discrediting what hard-won devolution that already exists'.[128]

A key incident in October 1987 provided an opportunity for the LTTE to build up charges to scuttle the accord's plans for devolution. On 2 October 1987, after an LTTE boat bringing illegal weapons was captured by the Sri Lankan navy, 17 LTTE cadres who were on board, including two senior LTTE members, swallowed cyanide capsules, and 12 of them died. This event triggered a violent rampage in Velvettiturai (VVT), the LTTE stronghold and the home of Prabhakaran and six of the cadres who had committed suicide. The brutal killings of Sri Lankan armed forces and civilians that started in VVT spread to other areas of the north and the east. Nine captured Sinhala soldiers were killed, and their blindfolded bodies displayed near the Jaffna university campus, and 25 civilians were murdered in a newly resettled Sinhala village near Trincomalee.[129]

Soon, the LTTE began to provoke military action against the IPKF. On 8 October it killed five Indian para-commandos and 'necklaced' them. Following India's joint declaration with Sri Lanka that the LTTE would no longer be accommodated, the IPKF began a counter-insurgency operation against the LTTE on 10 October. The result was an all-out war for control of the north and the east.[130] The LTTE, which had initially supported the Indian presence, now charged that the IPKF was a foreign invader waging a war against the Tamil people and must be driven out of the 'Tamil homeland'. Even when the IPKF was fighting the LTTE, the Tamil Nadu government funded the LTTE with Rs.50 million and Tamil Nadu provided training and hospital facilities to wounded LTTE cadres.[131] It is also noteworthy that the Tamil Madrasi Regiment of the IPKF was withdrawn from Sri Lanka in 11 October 1987 – not because of the partiality it had shown to local Tamils in the communal violence in Trinco-malee, but because some of its members refused to engage in the subsequent IPKF offensive against the LTTE in Jaffna.[132] Regional Tamil ethnic identity and support for a Tamil separate state seemed stronger than support for the Indian union.

'Operation Pawan', the first phase of the IPKF's 30-month-long counter-insurgency campaign that began in October 1987, led to the capture of Jaffna by the end of 1987. The cost, however, was huge: it is estimated that the operation drove out 75–100 percent of the population from the peninsula.[133] Asia Watch, Amnesty International, and other organizations reported that massive human rights violations were involved in the IPKF's house-to-house searches and other operations when looking for LTTE cadres. Rape of women, orders to shoot on sight, disappearances, torture, and extra-judicial killings were widely reported.[134] An Asia Watch news bulletin reported that in March 1988 the IPKF took into custody all the members of The Mothers Front, the Batticoloa Tamil organi-zation, which had been demanding that both the LTTE and the IPKF lay down their arms.[135] But reprisal killings by the LTTE and the IPKF intensified. On 2 August 1989, the 'Valvettiturai Massacre' occurred when the IPKF entered the town and killed 52 Tamil civilians, men, women, young and old.[136]

With several civil wars seemingly going on at the same time – in the south, the north, and the east – the social fabric of Sri Lanka was unraveling. *The Far Eastern Economic Review* described the situation as 'political cannibalism'.[137] A report submitted in February 1990 to the United Nations Commission on Human Rights by the Canada–Asia Working Group stated that in the north and the east, killings and disappearances were being carried out by the 'the full range of active military forces: the IPKF, the LTTE, the EPRLF, the Civilian Volunteer Force, and the Tamil National Army' and that a human rights organization based in Jaffna had recorded 676 killings between February and September 1989. The report also noted that torture and death of detainees at the hands of the IPKF was considered commonplace.[138] The IPKF, which had come as the protectors of the Tamil people in the north and the east, had become their enemies and was being referred to as the Innocent People Killing Force. In this situation, LTTE was able to emerge as the protector and the 'sole representative' of the Tamils. In a later account, Harikat Singh, GOC (Commander General) of the IPKF in Sri Lanka, explained the many challenges that faced the IPKF in its guerilla war against the LTTE. The terrain, the culture, the language were all foreign to the Indian soldiers, and the confusion in the IPKF chain of command made matters worse.[139] Perhaps the greatest difficulty was in the confusion of purpose. As Singh put it,

> The IPKF personnel did not know exactly what their mission was in Sri Lanka because at one stage, they were told to protect the LTTE ... to fulfill

the aspirations of Tamils. But, then, in a sudden turnaround, the IPKF was told that it was required to train its guns on the LTTE.[140]

Confusion was also evident in India's political strategy, namely the North East Provincial Council (NEPC), which was meant to bring political decentralization and autonomy for the north and the east. At first, the LTTE supported the idea of the North East Provincial Council and sought to assert its own dominance over the Council. Given its war with the IPKF, however, the Tigers began to oppose the NEPC altogether and the different political groups and individuals that supported it. India pressured the Sri Lankan government to introduce a merger of the Northern and Eastern Provinces and hold elections to the NEPC in November 1988, and the LTTE boycotted the elections. The 'elections' were 'rigged and controlled to bring about the desired outcome by IPKF troops who manned the polling booths'.[141] Civil servants were flown in from India to administer the elections, a first-time occurrence in modern Sri Lankan history.[142] The EPRLF, which was a creation of India, won the elections, and its leader, Vardhadaraja Perumal, who had served prison sentences (including once after the murder of Alfred Duraiappa) was appointed the Chief Minister of the new Northeast Provincial Council.[143] Perumal was not from the north or the east; he was a Tamil of recent Indian origin from the hill country.[144] The only Muslim representation in the NEPC was given to an individual who was an 'atheistic' member of the Central Committee of the Communist Party who was also not from the Eastern Province. After Dayan Jayatilleka, who also was not from the north or the east, resigned, the Sinhala representation in the NEPC was given to a Keralite, Karathara Thomas George.[145]

Obviously, the Indian-imposed NEPC was not representative of the Tamil, Muslim, or Sinhala people of the north and the east. Nor was it supported by the Sri Lankan government. Not wanting to settle for anything less than Eelam under its own hegemony, the LTTE vehemently opposed the NEPC despite the fact that the council laid the basis for provincial autonomy under Tamil dominance. The EPRLF was not able to establish the NEPC as an independent political entity, and from the council's inception India was saddled with the task of maintaining it as a puppet regime.[146] Instead of disarming paramilitary groups as India was expected to do under the accord, it armed its proxy, the EPRLF, against the LTTE by creating the TNA, the Tamil National Army – the combined forces of the EPRLF, ENDLF, and TELO.[147]

In the climate of growing warfare, the different Tamil militant groups began to abduct, disappear, and forcibly recruit young boys, including those as young as 13–15 years of age. It was widely reported that RAW originated forced conscription and that the IPKF was involved in the training of hundreds, if not thousands, of youths.[148] Formation of the TNA through forced conscription, forcing children without any political understanding to carry weapons, has been called India's 'most inexcusable decision'.[149] By August 1989, TNA had conscripted an estimated cadre of 10,000, both boys and girls, forcing large numbers of Tamil youth to flee to the south to avoid forced conscription.[150]

In the meantime, Rajiv Gandhi was defeated in the Indian elections in December 1989 and V.P. Singh, the new Indian Prime Minister, declared that the IPKF would be completely withdrawn from Sri Lanka by March 1990. Three weeks before the departure of the IPKF from Sri Lanka, Perumal, the Chief Minister of the NEPC, unilaterally declared independence for the north and the east. Although this was not taken seriously by the Indian and the Sri Lankan governments or the LTTE, it revealed the true motivation of the EPRLF: 'a de facto Eelam under the protection of mighty India'.[151] The LTTE, however, knew that India did not want a separate Tamil state in Sri Lanka, and the Tigers were determined to drive out the IPKF.

Premadasa–LTTE alliance

Despite the difficulties of fighting a guerilla war in alien territory, the IPKF drove the Tigers out of the Jaffna Peninsula and surrounded them in the Vanni. Just as the Sri Lankan army might have vanquished the LTTE in May 1987 if India had not intervened, had the IPKF been allowed to continue its operation in 1990, it could well have finished the LTTE, though again the civilian costs would have been very heavy.[152] Faced with the combined military challenge of the IPKF and the TNA and its possible annihilation, the LTTE was keen to find a political route out of the crisis, as it previously had in similar situations. It found a political strategy in a controversial alliance with the new Sri Lankan President Premadasa, who wanted to get the IPKF out of the country for his own political survival. Cultivating solidarity with the Sri Lankan government and inciting Sinhala fears, LTTE deputy, Mahattaya, cleverly stated,

> Sinhalese and we belong to this island ... who are the Indians to come and dictate terms...? They are aggressors. After they finish with the Tamils, they will turn against the Sinhalese ... public opinion,... (in) Tamil Nadu, will demand this.[153]

Premadasa wanted to send away the IPKF to neutralize the JVP in the south and the LTTE in the north, and he wanted to negotiate a political settlement with the LTTE to bring it into the political mainstream. In April 1989 the Premadasa government declared a ceasefire and offered the LTTE a peace package including amnesty and rehabilitation. Like previous and subsequent ceasefires with the LTTE, disarming of the LTTE was not required. In June 1989 the government and the LTTE formalized the ceasefire. India did not acknowledge it on the ground that it was not consulted. India also refused to comply with Premadasa's demand that the IPKF leave Sri Lanka by 29 July 1989.[154] What was most questionable in the alliance between the Premadasa government and the LTTE was the government's covert arming of the LTTE to strengthen it against the Indian-sponsored TNA – when, for example, it reportedly transferred a shipment of arms and equipment to the LTTE at a camp in Weli Oya in July 1989.[155] Another questionable action on the part of the government was the release of LTTE cadres held in custody as one of the first 'favors' requested by Prabhakaran. During the peace talks with the LTTE in October 1989, the Sri Lankan government released the woman suicide bomber imprisoned for seven years for the Maradana bombing on 9 November 1987, which killed 23 people and injured 106.[156] This was not first or the last time that the Sri Lankan government released convicted terrorists in the name of peace. Additionally, the government closed down strategic army camps in places such as Thondaimannar, Velvettiturai, and Point Pedro at the behest of the LTTE. While maintaining the 'charade' of negotiating a political settlement, the LTTE prepared for war.[157]

Increasing pressure from Sri Lankan and Indian critics led to the complete withdrawal of the IPKF from Sri Lanka by 24 March 1990. The Indian Army, the fourth largest in the world, departed in humiliation, leaving behind a trail of death and destruction. India had spent US$1.25 billion on its IPKF experiment in Sri Lanka. An estimated 1,555 IPKF soldiers died in Sri Lanka, including 49 officers. The IPKF had killed 2,592 LTTE cadres.[158] To these figures need to be added the thousands of civilian deaths in the hands of the IPKF and the LTTE in the north and the east and the approximately 60,000 deaths that took place in the JVP–Sri Lankan government war in the south during the Indian peacekeeping mission.

As the Indian army moved out of their camps, the LTTE moved in to prevent the Sri Lankan government forces from returning to their posts[159] The LTTE got hold of the weapons left by the IPKF, becoming stronger than ever. Using Premadasa's refusal to repeal the 6th Amendment to the Sri Lankan constitution (the anti-secession clause) and to dissolve the NEPC, the LTTE broke off talks with the government and resumed war – Eelam War II – in June 1990 (1983–1987 period being considered Eelam War I).[160] Immediately, the Tigers started attacking police stations and army camps, killing hundreds of troops. After taking over most of the police stations in Batticoloa and Ampara on 11 June 1990, the LTTE in a calculated provocation butchered in cold blood 600 policemen, both Sinhalese and Muslim, who had orders to surrender from Colombo based on false promises of safe passage from the LTTE.[161] Later, the bodies of some 300 of those soldiers were found in a mass grave at Rufus Kulam, off Thirukkovil.[162]

The LTTE continued its killing of Tamil dissidents and drove out and killed Sinhalese and Muslim civilians in the north and the east in its quest to create a mono-ethnic Tamil separate state. The innumerable killings in August 1990 included 30 Sinhalese in Ampara and 25 Sinhalese travelling from Morawewa to Horowpothana. On 3 August 1990, the LTTE killed 140 Muslims praying at a mosque in Kattankudy, and on 12 August 1990, it killed 122 Muslims, men, women, and children, in Eravur in the Eastern Province.[163] On 30 November 1990, 75,000–100,000 Muslims were driven out of Jaffna overnight by the LTTE and their jewelry and other possessions plundered. This was one of the worst incidents of ethnic cleansing in any country at any time. Most of those displaced have continued up to date to live as refugees in the 'Sinhala areas', unable to return to the north or to recover their economic assets. Thousands of acres of land belonging to the Muslims were also confiscated by the LTTE, especially paddy land in the east.[164]

The LTTE's intra-ethnic killings did not stop with the departure of the IPKF. Its campaign to eliminate the EPRLF extended into Madras, where the EPRLF leadership was living as refugees. In June 1990 the LTTE killed 14 EPRLF members, including its Secretary General and one of its MPs in the Sri Lankan Parliament.[165] But M. Karunanidhi, the pro-LTTE Chief Minister of the Tamil Nadu government, reportedly shielded the 'LTTE hit squad from arrest' in open support of Tamil separatist terrorism.[166] Using the same network and a suicide bomber, yet another dispensable young woman from a poor Tamil family, the LTTE assassinated Rajiv Gandhi on the eve of elections on 21 May 1991, fearing he would reintroduce Indian troops to Sri Lanka if reelected. Rajiv Gandhi paid with his life for India's arming of Tamil militants and collusion with terrorism. As K.M. de Silva explains, it was only after Gandhi's death that the full extent of the Indian and South Indian involvement in the Sri Lankan separatist conflict became apparent to India herself:

> At last India itself woke up to a realization of the full extent of the price she had been called upon to pay for the support extended to Tamil separatism in Sri Lanka. The LTTE had established a government within a government in parts of the Tamilnadu coast; its smuggling enterprises included narcotics; it had infiltrated the Tamilnadu administration and it had introduced the culture of violence into parts of India which had not known it before'.[167]

The Gandhi assassination turned the vast majority of the people in Tamil Nadu against the Tamil Tigers.[168] New Delhi proscribed the LTTE in 1992, followed by Malaysia. The loss of Tamil Nadu as an operational and logistical base did not stop LTTE militancy or violence. Rather, it expanded its international operations for arms import and export into southeast Asia, especially Burma and Thailand, and expanded the operations of its international secretariat, based in London. A highly sophisticated propaganda network was developed to influence the international community and to politicize the Tamil diaspora, 'the backbone of LTTE finance generation'. These funds, as well as monies raised from refugee trafficking, heroin smuggling, major credit card scams, and counterfeit passport rackets, were used to procure weapons, including deep-sea vessels, in its intensified war against the Sri Lankan government.[169] The LTTE also was linked to other regional and international terrorist organizations; the Sikh separatists, for example, reportedly raised money for the family of the Gandhi assassin.[170]

The LTTE carried out its war on multiple fronts in Sri Lanka, continuing to eliminate Tamil dissidents and ethnically cleansing Sinhalese and the Muslims from the north and the east. In the south, it targeted key political and security personnel and installations, and used bombings to terrorize the population. Sri Lankan Defense Minister Ranjan Wijeratna, who had finished the JVP and was expected to do the same to the LTTE, was killed by a suicide car bomb in

Colombo on 2 March 1991. On 22 June 1991, an LTTE car bomb destroyed the headquarters of the Sri Lankan government's Joint Operations Command in Colombo, killing 21 people and injuring 114, and in November 1992 an LTTE suicide bomber killed Sri Lanka's navy chief, also in Colombo.[171] As the Sri Lankan army prepared a massive offensive against the LTTE-held Jaffna Peninsula, some peace and human rights NGOs put pressure on the government to re-enter peace talks. Although the LTTE had tortured and killed thousands of Tamils, the LTTE managed to elicit support from some Tamil Christian churchmen, like Jaffna Bishop Ambalavanar (Church of South India), who were able to play on the guilt of Sinhala church leaders 'to esteem the LTTE as the spokesmen for the Tamil people'. This significantly neutralized a tendency in the World Council of Churches to look critically at the LTTE.[172] Anglican Bishop Kenneth Fernando, who met Prabhakaran in January 1993, declared that the LTTE leader was 'humane' and that the LTTE is ready for peace talks, leading many to charge that the 'Church was sanctioning terrorism'.[173]

The LTTE assassinated the former National Security Minister Athulathmudali at a rally in Colombo on 23 April 1993. On 1 May President Premadasa was assassinated, allegedly by an LTTE suicide bomber who had infiltrated the President's inner circle, also at an election rally in Colombo. Both Rajiv Gandhi and Premadasa had trusted the LTTE, believing that it could be brought around to the path of peace and political settlement. They paid for that trust with their own lives, whereas the LTTE leader went on to praise the LTTE suicide bombers, 'the Black Tigers': 'I have groomed my weak brethren into a strong weapon … the Black Tigers constitute the armor of self-defense of our ethnic group, and also serve to remove the barriers coming in the way of our struggle'.[174]

Taking advantage of security lapses on the part of the government, in November 1993 the LTTE overran the Pooneryn Sri Lankan military base in the north and killed over 600 Sri Lankan army personnel. One-third of the Sri Lankan navy was also destroyed by the LTTE in 1993.[175] Despite LTTE killings of the Sri Lankan President Premadasa, Ministers Wijeratne and Athulathmudali, and hundreds if not thousands of civilians, there were no backlashes against the Tamils in the south after 1983. This fact is generally unacknowledged in the literature, which blames the conflict on 'Sinhala Buddhist chauvinism'.[176] From 1989–1990 onwards, large numbers of Tamils fleeing LTTE oppression in the north and the east also found sanctuary among the Sinhala majority in the south. In the final analysis, the LTTE's image as the Tamil liberator fighting the oppressive Sinhalese was built not only on the powerlessness of ordinary Tamils, but also the silence and complicity of the Tamil diaspora, intelligentsia, churchmen and external supporters of Tamil separatism.[177]

7 A 'peace package', war, and the international community, 1994–2002

As Indian intervention in the Sri Lankan conflict ended after the failure of the IPKF operation and the assassination of Rajiv Gandhi, intervention of the international community increased. Chandrika Bandaranaike Kumaratunga, who headed the People's Alliance (PA) that came to power in the August 1994 parliamentary elections, was closely associated with the foreign-funded peace lobby. Her selection as prime minister over her mother, who was aligned with Sinhala nationalist interests, was itself considered a victory for the NGOs and the supporters of federalism.[1] Three months after being elected prime minister, Kumaratunga was elected president in November 1994.

Kumaratunga accepted the definition of the Sri Lankan struggle as an 'ethnic conflict' between Sinhalese and Tamils and all the major grievances of the Tamils, e.g. language, education, land settlement, law and order, administration, and the overarching demand for regional autonomy.[2] Tamil had already been made an official language akin to Sinhala. The Jaffna district, which was considered one of the most educationally advanced districts since colonial times, was added to the list of educationally backward districts and was granted increased quotas for entry into the university science faculties in 1996–1997. This decision was driven by pressure from Tamils, who had previously been the most vocal critics of the district quotas.[3]

Peace talks with the LTTE were begun in Jaffna on 13 October 1994, and on 5 January 1995, the 'Declaration of Cessation of Hostilities' was signed between the Sri Lankan government and the LTTE. Four peace-monitoring committees were set up in February 1995, two from Norway and one each from Canada and the Netherlands.[4] On 3 August 1995, the Kumaratunga government released plans, which came to be known as the 'devolution package', for substantive political autonomy for the Tamil majority areas in the north and in the contentious east.[5] It did not call for a separate, sovereign Tamil state unacceptable to the majority of the island's population.

The devolution package

While the Kumaratunga initiative was built on earlier plans, such as, the Bandaranaike–Chelvanayakam Pact and the Indo-Sri Lanka Accord, it called for a more extensive devolution and decentralization of power from the center to the regions than previously proposed. Neelan Tiruchelvam, a TULF parliamentarian, director of the International Centre for Ethnic Studies, and advisor to the President, was the chief architect of the package. He advanced the position that 'meaningful devolution was not possible within a unitary framework' and proposed changing the 'unitary character of the Sri Lankan state', a step not envisaged in the earlier Indo-Sri Lanka Accord.[6] Although the Kumaratunga proposals were not translated into actual policy changes, it generated a lively, but polarizing, ideological discourse that profoundly influenced the analysis of the Sri Lankan conflict and its resolution.

The devolution package proposed that the 'Republic of Sri Lanka shall be united and sovereign. It shall be a Union of Regions'. Each of the existing provinces was expected to become a region of the republic with a separate regional council and a governor exercising power over law and order, justice, education, public service, finances and the regulation of cultural activity. Each region was also to have its own regional police service, high court, education and higher education service, public service, and administrative bodies for taxation, foreign aid, and investment. The boundaries of the Northern and Eastern provinces were to be redrawn, and a single North East Province was to be created. It was explicitly stated that

> Land will be a devolved subject and State land within a region will be vested in the Regional Councils ... Priority in future land settlement schemes will be given to persons first of the district and then of the Region.[7]

The central government was expected to retain 'defense, national security, foreign affairs, immigration, currency, international economic relations, airports and harbors, inter-regional transport, ... national archives and museums'.[8]

Support for the package

There was great enthusiasm for the package on the part of the foreign-funded NGOs and the international community, who saw it as a major political breakthrough. Immediately upon the release of the devolution package, more than 100 'eminent persons' mostly from the English-speaking urban elite released a statement hailing it as an 'opportunity to work towards rebuilding a secular, democratic and multi-ethnic country on the basis of a genuine sharing of power between communities'.[9] Thirty NGOs also issued a statement endorsing the proposals for devolution.[10] Kumaratunga was internationally hailed for her 'courageous political package', with the Indian press and policymakers in the west leading the wave of accolades.[11] The Committee of Foreign Affairs of the US House of Representatives gave its stamp of approval by its unanimous adoption of a resolution supporting the Sri Lanka Peace Package.[12]

Opposition to the package

But support for the package within Sri Lanka was far from unanimous, and the foreign-funded peace NGOs stepped in to build local consensus. For example, the Campaign for Peace and Democracy, led by the leader of the NLSSP and NGO activists, held meetings and seminars in the south and organized a 'peace train' to Vauniya in the north.[13] The NGO peace lobby also collaborated with the PA government in the so-called Sudu Nelun Viyaparaya (the white lotus movement) and in setting up the National Integration and Planning Unit under the Ministry of Constitutional Affairs and Ethnic Integration with assistance from the Norwegian government.[14] The Movement for Inter-Racial Justice and Equality (MIRJE) and other groups travelled across the country to educate people, mostly Sinhalese, about the need for political reform.[15] But notwithstanding lavish foreign funding and media exposure, the NGOs could not create a strong 'platform for peace', especially in the north, where the totalitarian LTTE did not allow a peace movement to emerge.

The Christian leadership of the peace movement and general distrust of foreign NGOs were also barriers to reaching the masses of the local Buddhist, Hindu, and Muslim communities to advocate for the package. As a 1995 report of the United Church Board for World Ministries on behalf of the US NGO Forum on Sri Lanka observed, peace efforts were limited largely to Sinhala and Tamil activists within the Christian community.[16] The National Peace Council (NPC) was established in 1995 to correct some of these problems and to coordinate local peace advocacy, especially through the media and international networking.[17] The NPC too drew its secretariat largely from the activist Christian community, and despite generous foreign funding it has yet to reach its avowed objective of building a 'powerful and non-partisan people's movement'.[18] Joint statements by international NGOs in support of the 'Tamil Homeland' issued at sessions of the United Nations Commission for Human Rights in Geneva and signed by leading Christian organizations such as *Pax Romana*, Canadian Council of Churches, and World Alliance of Reformed Churches added fuel to the Sinhala nationalist charge that Christian organizations, which had been trying to destabilize Buddhist Sri Lanka for 500 years, were now trying to do so by supporting the Tamil separatist cause.[19]

There was massive opposition to the devolution package on the part of Sinhala nationalists, who saw it as a capitulation to Tamil separatism and a grave threat to the unity and sovereignty of Sri Lanka. A large group of Sinhala professionals and academics released a document pointing out that 'nearly 50% of the Tamil population (excluding the hill country Tamils) live harmoniously' with the Sinhalese and that the implementation of the government proposals would undermine this historical pluralism and co-existence, aggravating rather than easing the separatist conflict.[20] Economist Buddhadasa Hewavitharana raised concerns over the allocation of state land on the basis of 'ethno-political regionalism' for the country's future economic development.[21] The MEP and a number of Sinhala Buddhist organizations, including the YMBA (Young Men's

Buddhist Association) and the All Ceylon Buddhist Congress, called for a with-drawal of the package in order to safeguard Sri Lanka's unitary state.[22] A new organization, Sri Lanka Ekiya Sanvidhanaya (SLES – Sri Lanka Unitary Organi-zation) issued a statement by lawyer S.L. Gunasekara (himself a Christian by birth) and writer Gunadasa Amarasekara pointing out that the devolution pro-posals would disqualify Sinhalese from being allotted state land in the North and the East and

> [N]ullify the principle that that all parts of Sri Lanka are equally the home-land of all where they are all entitled to equal rights, and render the citizens resident in different regions akin to citizens of different countries.[23]

The SLES statement noted that given the extent of the 'envisaged abdication of power by the Government of Sri Lanka' under the package, the government will be unable to dissolve a regional council or assume any of its powers, even if faced by war or rebellion.[24] Article 2 of additional devolution proposals pre-sented on 16 January 1996, stated that regional administrations cannot promote initiatives towards separation or secession from the Union of Regions and the Republic of Sri Lanka, but it did not specify how the central government would prevent secession.[25] In *Tigers 'Moderates' and Pandora's Package*, S.L. Gunasekara elaborated his opposition to the package, observing that it gives 'all the institutions necessary for the creation of a separate state'. He predicted that its implementation would lead to 'the vivisection of our Country' pointing out that 'Sovereignty once ceded cannot be taken away except by consent or mili-tary might'.[26] He further noted that the package put forward as a means to restore peace would never be able to do so unless the LTTE was disarmed, accepted rule of law, respected the Judiciary, and allowed other groups to freely engage in political activity, including allowing them the right to criticize the LTTE. The LTTE never agreed to such pre-conditions, and it was feared that like previous peace efforts, the package too would fail to restore peace. When the LTTE broke the ceasefire in April 1995, Gunasekara called for a 'well planned and unremitting military endeavor to rid the Country of the dreadful incubus called the LTTE' instead of 'engaging in ill-advised "peace talks" '.[27]

The Muslims, as always, resented being lumped into the category of 'Tamil-speaking people', and feared having to live in a Tamil-dominated North Eastern Province created under the devolution package. As M.M. Zuhair, a SLMC member of parliament, put it, the LTTE 'should not insist on the Tamil home-land. If it did then why shouldn't the Sinhalas ask for the entire country as the Sinhala homeland where they formed 76 percent of the population'.[28] The SLMC, which won six seats (as opposed to the four won by the TULF) in the 1994 Parliamentary elections had emerged as the representative of the North East Muslims. In the course of the debate over the package, SLMC leader Rauf Hakeem negotiated a deal with the Tamil political parties, the TULF and CWC, for a potential division of the North-East Province and the creation of a separate South-Eastern Regional Council for the Muslims. This entailed excision of the predominantly Sinhalese Ampara district and establishment of a South East Council with the Potuvil, Samanthurai, and Kalmunai areas of the Eastern Province, where Muslims would be 57 percent of the population and Tamils and Sinhalese 28 percent and 15 percent, respectively[29] (Map 4.2). The SLMC also insisted that nothing should be done that would tamper with Muslim personal law, and called for the return of Muslims driven out of the Northern Province.[30] The contradictory position of the SLMC was evident in the call for Muslim self-determination on the one hand and criticism of the LTTE demand for self-determination and the 'right of secession' on the other hand.[31]

When views were expressed that were not consistent with the international community's peace tendency to support the Tamil position, they were frequently marginalized. After war had broken out, in December 1996, an alliance of 46 Sinhala NGOs, under the umbrella of the newly formed National Joint Committee (NJC), convened a 'Sinhala Commission' to inquire and report on injustices to the Sinhala people. Holding 76 sittings in different venues across the country, it collected 752 memoranda and evidence from 304 witnesses. Based on this evidence, it issued an interim report in 1997 and two subsequent reports, in 1998 and 2001, detailing historic language and religious discrimination under colonial rule and continued grievances in the current period.[32] The commission stated that the package would destroy the 'uniformity of policy throughout the country' and opposed the merger of the Northern and Eastern Provinces.[33] It also criticized foreign-funded NGOs, which had 'proliferated in the Colombo area and always talked in the language of the West without much of a grass-roots understanding of the Sri Lankan situation'.[34] It criticized the government's 'gigantic propaganda campaign' to make people accept the devolution as the only basis for peace, arguing that:

> Peace can be restored only by defeating those who have broken the peace, namely the LTTE. The LTTE has already rejected the 'Package'. The implementation of the so-called 'peace proposals' will therefore not bring peace. It is therefore the duty of all those who are concerned with safe-guarding the sovereignty, unity and territorial integrity of our country and wish to ensure that it is not broken up and who are aware of the dangers of the Government's' devolution proposals, to educate the people and see that they are not deceived by government propaganda, so that when they are called upon to vote on these proposals they will vote to reject it.[35]

By the time the Sinhala Commission Report was published in September 1997, Eelam War III had broken out and the peace was, indeed, broken. But the Sinhala Commission's interim report was strongly condemned by the liberal civil society elite, a section of the PA, and many Tamils.[36] The state-controlled media downplayed the Sinhala Commission Reports, and the Media Minister, Mangala Samaraweera, further alienated the Sinhala nationalists by declaring that the Sinhala Commission Report belongs in the 'dustbin of history'.[37] A response to the Sinhala Commission Report published by the Social Scientists

Association claimed that the assertion of the 'out-moded' unitary state is 'a thinly veiled argument for a state that could be dominated by the Sinhalese'. Claiming that a 'majoritarian democracy' does not leave room for tolerance and space for minorities, it endorsed devolution, self-governance, and autonomy for the Tamil minority in areas where they are 'predominantly inhabitant' as a necessary condition for their 'safety, security and empowerment'.[38] It dismissed the Sinhala Commission's concerns about future land scarcity for the Sinhalese as 'backward and archaic', arguing that future economic development will not be based primarily on land resources.[39] ICES publications (Colombo) also celebrated the magic formula – devolution.[40]

Failure of the peace process

Notwithstanding the lively debate, compromise measures, and international support generated by the package, the Kumaratunga peace process faltered. It did not receive the support of the opposition UNP despite the so-called Ranil–Chandrika Agreement signed on 4 April 1997 with mediation of British parliamentarian Liam Fox calling for refrain from undermining the peace process by government in office.[41] Just as the SLFP had opposed devolution proposals of the UNP when it was out of office, the UNP sided against the Kumaratunga devolution package. Such opposition has been interpreted as 'ethnic outbidding' and attributed to Sinhala chauvinism, though it needs also to be seen as a problem inherent in parliamentary democracy.[42] The PA government could not muster the two-thirds parliamentary majority and did not even table the draft bill of August 2000 to change the Sri Lankan Constitution to provide a new legal framework for devolution.[43]

While competition among Sinhala parties and the government's failure to put forward a strong team for political negotiations with the LTTE were significant factors, LTTE intransigence was the most serious factor in the failure of the Kumaratunga peace process. As Ghosh has explained:

> The main obstacles to peace ... seemed to be two. One, the government was interested in roping in all the Tamil parties in the overall peace process, but, the LTTE insisted upon the fact that it was the sole representative of the Tamil people.... Two, the LTTE position seemed to be inflexible on a 'federal' solution, where the federating units had complete autonomy.[44]

At the very time that the LTTE entered talks with the new PA government, it engaged, as it had so often before, in arms procurement, regrouping, and retraining of its cadres.[45] The fact that the LTTE was never serious about peace was borne out by its alleged assassination of presidential candidate Gamini Dissanayake and 51 others in a suicide bombing on 24 November 1994, in Colombo.[46] It was believed by the LTTE that Dissanayake, who was known for his pro-Indian position, would invite Indian peacekeeping forces back to Sri Lanka if elected into office and scuttle plans for Eelam. The LTTE leader

Prabhakaran never budged from his separatist goal. In an interview he gave to the BBC in September 1994, he asserted 'This is a historical fact. The areas that consist of North-East province had been the homeland of Tamil-speaking people. That includes the Muslims'.[47] Chiding the Sri Lankan government for engaging in talks with other Tamil political groups, he asserted that the LTTE is the sole representative of Tamils: 'Who are the authentic representatives of the Tamil people? Who are those who are shedding blood in waging a struggle for the Tamil people's rights?... we who truly represent the Tamil people's aspirations'.[48]

Such claims aside, LTTE fratricidal killings continued. LTTE deputy Mahattaya and fellow 'conspirators' were executed in December 1994 for alleged conspiracy against the LTTE leader. Mahattaya, a childhood friend of Prabhakaran, was considered 'the only man in the LTTE who had the courage to speak out against Prabhakaran'. His elimination solidified the intrinsically violent and undemocratic nature of the LTTE.[49] The continued support of the LTTE by influential sections of the Tamil community mitigated against the LTTE from making a genuine commitment to peace talks and the democratic process. Indeed, as UTHR has pointed out, Tamil elite, leading academics and prominent Christian church officials bear responsibility for LTTE intransigence and failure of the peace process. They discredited the government and justified the actions of the LTTE telling the world that the LTTE and the Tamil people were one. When war broke out in April 1995, a church journal, the *Morning Star* editorialized that 'when God is creating a new nation no one could stand against it'.[50]

From the beginning of the ceasefire in January 1995, there was discord between the LTTE and the government due to continued LTTE pressure on the government to accede to further preconditions for political negotiations. The Tigers demanded, for example, that the government remove the army camp at Pooneryn, allow LTTE cadres to carry weapons in the Eastern Province, and relax restrictions on fishing.[51] The government refused because those concessions would strengthen the LTTE militarily. The ceasefire agreement did not require the LTTE to dismantle any of its own camps or allow civilians or members of the Sri Lankan security forces, even those without arms, to enter any area of the North and the East under LTTE control without its permission.[52] The Sri Lankan government could not capitulate to all the demands of the LTTE, which had neither laid down arms nor entered the democratic process. During the peace talks, the LTTE built up its military strength, extending its ability to sink ships and acquiring the capacity to down aircraft.[53] The peace talks collapsed and the ceasefire broke when the LTTE sank two Israeli-built Devro gun boats of the Sri Lankan Navy, killing 22 sailors on 19 April 1995.[54] The country returned to one of the worst periods of war, Eelam War III.

Eelam War III, 1995–2001

The LTTE carried out 27 attacks in the north and the east, killing 264 security personnel and 57 civilians in just the first 39 days after abrogating the peace talks. Of those attacks, 17 were in the Eastern Province.[55] An attack on 25 May 1995, killed 42 Sinhala villagers in Kallarawa in the Trincomalee District, prompting Amnesty International to question LTTE's 'respect for human rights and basic principles of humanitarian law'.[56] The LTTE justified the killings by charging that the Sinhalese were recent government settlers in the 'war for land' in the East.[57] The government retaliated by launching a major military offensive in July 1995 to take back the Jaffna Peninsula. Many people fled Jaffna in fear of the impending offensive, mostly on the orders of the LTTE, which called on 'all civilians to quit the city', thus forcing people to move east to the Vanni region.[58] Not only was much of this exodus 'effected within 24 hours in panic and disarray amidst heavy downpours of rain', but, the suffering was made worse by the LTTE's alleged refusal to allow young people between the ages of 13 and 25, its potential recruits, to travel out of areas under its control.[59] With the resumption of war, there was massive displacement of the people of Jaffna, many of whom lost homes, possessions, and their entire way of life. By mid-December 1995, 120,000–140,000 people were living in 91 refugee camps in the Northern Province.[60]

International humanitarian relief operations meant to reduce the impact of war on the displaced contributed to new conflicts among the poor, such as competition between refugees and host populations over relief assistance.[61] The escalation of war also intensified ethnically based antipathy of Tamils towards the Sri Lankan government as an alien aggressor force, providing new opportunities for the LTTE to impose itself as 'liberators' and forcibly recruit Tamil school children. But ordinary Tamils who desired peace could not express their opposition. The differences between ordinary people in the north who had to sacrifice their offspring as child soldiers and the 'nationalist war-mongering' Tamil elites living elsewhere around the world sharpened. To quote, UTHR, the consistent advocate of the rights of ordinary Tamils in the north and the east, again:

> Once news of a son or daughter joining reached the home of the recruit, the atmosphere often changed to one of a funeral house. Women cried their hearts out.... There was nobody, no priest, no comfort from institutional religion.... A son or daughter ... had been taken away. It was not the honourable decision of a mature mind that they had to come to terms with. They knew in their heart, although they could not say it, that their son or daughter, sister or brother had been tricked. But, what a stark contrast it provides to the life of the people who live outside the North-East and especially abroad, who advocate the cause of the LTTE in various forms![62]

Eelam War III hastened militarization of the entire society and the destruction of the Tamil, as well as the Muslim and Sinhala, communities in the north and the east. But their inclination to depict the violence as Sinhala versus Tamil led international human rights groups to overlook the intra-ethnic and class dimensions of the war. Human Rights Watch charged both the government and the

LTTE with killings of hundreds of civilians in 1995. The government was blamed for indiscriminate aerial and artillery bombardment in its attempts to 'flush out LTTE cadres hiding in residential areas', including Christian churches.[63] Amnesty International expressed concern over reports of continued arbitrary arrests, torture, disappearances, and extra-judicial executions by government forces.[64] An Amnesty International report issued in December 1995 made 17 recommendations to the Sri Lankan government, among them the revision of the Emergency Regulations and Prevention of Terrorism Act in line with relevant international standards, particularly the ICCPR (International Covenant on Civil and Political Rights).[65]

LTTE massacres of civilians, mostly Sinhalese, bore 'the hallmarks of indiscriminate killings aimed at destabilising strategic areas of the north and the east provoking displacement, insecurity, ethnic tension and forced relocation'.[66] In October 1995 the LTTE carried out a spate of horrific attacks in so-called border areas of the Northern and Eastern provinces claimed as the 'Tamil homeland'. These attacks disrupted prevailing patterns of ethnic co-existence, including intermarriage between Sinhalese and Tamils in some villages, aggravating the suffering of local or regional minorities.[67] The attacks were intended to further ethnic polarization, ethnically cleanse the Sinhalese, and prepare the area for a future Eelam. As discussed earlier, those upholding the Tamil homelands thesis tended to view Sinhala villagers in the disputed areas as interlopers and to see their removal as a solution to the 'ethnic conflict'. Perhaps, this is a reason why there has been relatively little sympathy expressed by the NGO peace lobby toward Sinhala victims of LTTE atrocities.

The government forces took back Jaffna in December 1995 after '50 days of bitter fighting', forcing the LTTE to quit the Peninsula, the Tamil heartland.[68] But Eelam War III was not restricted to the north and the east; the LTTE brought the war to the south and the multi-ethnic capital of Colombo in a spate of suicide bombings and political assassinations. The fall of Jaffna in December 1995 was followed by a bomb blast on 31 January 1996, in Colombo, the biggest bomb attack up to that point, even as the PA government was preparing to push forward the peace package to end the war. A truck laden with explosives was rammed into the Central Bank, destroying the entire financial district of Colombo and killing some 86 people, injuring some 1,400 men and women, and severely hurting the island's tourist industry and economy.[69]

An LTTE attack on the Mullativu army base on 18 July 1996 killed 1,200 Sri Lankan soldiers (including some 300 who had surrendered). This, the 'heaviest single loss' up to that point revealed the extent of negligence and incompetence of the government security establishment. The LTTE escaped with US$70 million worth of military equipment after the attack in Mullativu, in which many young LTTE women cadres took part.[70] Following LTTE killing of the Sri Lankan Army's Commander in Jaffna and LTTE's overrunning of the Mullativu army base, army discipline loosened and there were increasing random reprisals against the Tamil population. Large number of disappearances were reported in Jaffna in 1996, although the situation did significantly improve in 1997.[71]

Many Tamils walking past Sri Lankan army check points in the north were taken for questioning for suspected connections with the LTTE, and some so taken died after being assaulted.[72] This became evident in the much publicized case of Krishanthy Kumaraswamy, an 18-year-old school girl who was gang raped and murdered on 7 September 1996. Three others, the girl's mother, brother, and neighbor who went looking for her, also disappeared and were found murdered. Due to massive pressure from human rights groups, including women's groups, President Kumaratunga ordered a judicial investigation in mid-October 1996. The rank-and-file soldiers directly involved in the rape and murder were sentenced to life imprisonment and death. The government received praise for bringing state actors to justice. Although evidence revealed that high-ranking officers may have ordered torture, murder, and disposal of bodies, they were not charged or convicted. The entire blame seems to have been placed on ordinary soldiers from poorer families who could not afford experienced lawyers for their defense. The suspected 'cover-up' raises questions regarding the social class biases of justice enforced.[73] The allegations of mass graves in Chemmani that came up during the course of the Krishanthy Kumaraswamy court case were taken up by the Sri Lankan Human Rights Commission (HRC) and the Office of the UN Commissioner for Human Rights, with the involvement of forensic experts. Some 15 bodies were exhumed in the presence of international observers in 1999. While the government claimed exoneration from the charges of mass graves, others have called for further investigation of Chemmani and other mass graves in the north (and the south).[74]

In May 1997 the Sri Lankan military began yet another major military operation to regain territory in the Vanni and Mullativu and to open a land route between Vauniya and Jaffna. This operation lasted two years, leading to massive military buildup and recruitment on both sides. The LTTE recruited thousands of young people into the Vanni through Karuna, its commander in the east, and increased its arms imports.[75] Thus strengthened, in Colombo the LTTE bombed the 39-storey twin tower World Trade Centre, Sri Lanka's tallest building, on 15 October 1997, by blowing up a truck packed with 400kg of explosives. Apparently the LTTE had intended one tower to collapse on top of the other, similar to what had been planned in the twin tower attack in New York in 1993. This attack, which raised fears of cooperation among international terrorist groups, killed 18 and injured at least 96 people including foreigners (among them US Army Green Berets providing services to the Sri Lankan armed forces). The attack came just three days after the building had been opened and eight days after the US government had designated the LTTE a terrorist organization after repeated requests by Sri Lankan Foreign Minister, Lakshman Kadirgamar, a Tamil lawyer, for controls on LTTE funding in the West.[76] On 25 January 1998, the LTTE staged yet another suicide bomb attack, this time against the sacred Temple of the Tooth (the Dalada Maligawa) in the ancient capital city of Kandy. The Temple was severely damaged, but the Buddha's tooth relic, a historical symbol of the Sinhala Buddhist state, was not. The next day, the Sri Lankan government proscribed the LTTE. Two more days later, a court in Madras,

India, sentenced 26 people, 13 Indians and 13 Sri Lankans, accused in the Rajiv Gandhi assassination. The verdict came after a seven-year investigation involving over 1,000 witnesses and extensive written and material evidence. The first accused in the case was the LTTE leader, Velupillai Prabhakaran, who continues to be on the wanted list of Interpol.[77]

The sentences for the Rajiv Gandhi assassination in India and international proscriptions of the LTTE did not stop its murderous suicide bombings and political assassinations in Sri Lanka. For example, in a suicide bomb attack on 5 March outside a school in Maradana, in Colombo, in which vans carrying school children were caught, 36 civilians were killed and 250–300 injured.[78] The LTTE also continued its practice of eliminating Tamil political dissidents and moderates, for example, Sarojini Yogeswaran, the newly elected mayor of Jaffna in May 1998.[79] Her husband, ex-TULF MP for Jaffra was killed in 1989.

What finally brought international attention to LTTE terrorism was the assassination of Neelan Tiruchelvam, the TULF politician and architect of the devolution package. He was killed on 29 July 1999 by a suicide bomber in Colombo. Fear and terror prevented the Tamil minority in Sri Lanka from mourning the death of Tiruchelvam, who had worked tirelessly for the Tamil cause. It prompted his ICES colleague, Radhika Coomaraswamy, to call for non-violence in the pursuit of Tamil nationalism:

> The Tamil leadership in all its variety has been single minded in its pursuit of ethnic Tamil nationalism through the use of armed violence. Has this strategy worked?… We (Tamils) claim that this has given us dignity. Has it? The majority of our people are now in diaspora and not in their 'homeland' … it is time for the Tamils to turn the search light inward.[80]

But the war continued its relentless course. On 19 September 54 ethnic Sinhalese were butchered in the east by suspected LTTE guerillas led by women fighters supposedly as a retaliation for an air force bombing which killed 22 Tamil civilians three days earlier.[81] In Colombo, there was an abortive LTTE suicide bombing attempt on the life of President Kumaratunga during an election rally in December 1999 resulting in the loss of her right eye and injury to several ministers and foreign journalists. There was also an assassination attempt on the life of Prime Minister Sirimavo Bandaranaike on 5 January 2000, the same day that Kumar Ponnambalam, leader of the All Ceylon Tamil Congress, was killed by an unknown gunman. On 7 June 2000, Sri Lanka's 'War Heroes Day', a senior government minister, C.V. Gooneratne, was killed along with 22 others in Ratmalana near Colombo.[82]

In the north, the LTTE was able to reverse the earlier gains of the Sri Lankan army. In November–December 1999, in what came to be known as the 'Vanni Debacle', the LTTE gained over 1,000 square kilometers of territory, causing heavy casualties for the Sri Lankan army.[83] This was followed by the 'Elephant Pass Debacle' in April 2000, when the LTTE was able to take control of the crucial military base in Elephant Pass, which joins the Jaffna Peninsula with the mainland. As 10,000 Sri Lankan troops were withdrawn, 30,000 other troops were trapped in the Jaffna Peninsula without access to the land route.[84] As military analyst Iqbal Athas and others have commented, the opportunism and bloated egos of politicians and top-level military men were responsible for the failure of conventional strategies in the guerilla war and the massive sacrifice of the lives of ordinary soldiers in debacles such as those of Vanni and Elephant Pass.[85] Though accurate figures are hard to come by, the Vanni and Elephant Pass battles had caused heavy loss of lives and casualties on both sides.[86]

The ethnic complexion of the war was underlined by developments in the south including the mob killing by Sinhalese of 27, and serious injuring of 14, Tamil detainees, all real or suspected LTTE members, in the Bindunuwewa detention facility in Badulla in the Central Province on 25 October 2000. Riots by Indian Tamils that broke out in the Nuwara Eliya and Badulla Districts a few days later, as well as the arrest of the leader of the Upcountry People's Front, Chandrasekaran, and ten Tamil youths in connection with incidents in Talawakaele on 29 October, may also have been instigated by the Bindunuwewa killings.[87] Like the communal violence of 1977 and July 1983, the Bindunuwewa massacre was initially seen as a spontaneous Sinhala outburst against the minority Tamils and was blamed on members of the poor farming community in the region. But subsequent inquiries revealed that it was an organized massacre involving outsiders, and that some of the 60 police officers who were present at the scene were also responsible. The Supreme Court's acquittal of all the defendants in the Bindunuwewa massacre in 2005 led Brad Adams, Asia Director of Human Rights Watch, to respond that 'As the victims were all Tamil, the government needs to move quickly to start fresh investigations and to prosecute the perpetrators, some of whom were police officers, or it will only further distance aggrieved Tamils'.[88]

Violent Sinhala–Muslim clashes in April 2001 in the town of Mawanella in the Central Province reinforced the perception of the Sinhala majority as oppressor and the minorities as victim. Like the infamous 1915 riots, Sinhala perception and resentment of exploitation by Muslim merchants seem to have been an underlying cause. But, here too, external instigation was a major factor. Activities of a government minister's thugs and police complicity are believed to have sparked off the communally based violence. The failure of the government to discipline the minister and those involved soured the relationship between the Sinhalese and the Muslims, leading to further anti-Muslim attacks in the outskirts of Colombo in early 2002.[89] Externally instigated incidents deflected attention from the dominant tradition of ethno-religious harmony in the island. The on-going war and worsening economic conditions created new ethnic enmities imposing suffering on all communities.

The government's negligence and the economic costs of the war became starkly evident by the LTTE's daring attack on the Katunayake Airforce base adjoining the country's international airport on 24 July 2001. A number of airmen and LTTE guerillas lost their lives in the fighting: three of the Sri Lankan Airlines commercial planes were destroyed and two damaged. The Sri Lankan

Airforce lost two helicopters, three jets, one Russian built Mig 27 attack aircraft and three Israeli built Kfir jets.[90] In addition to the military set backs, the Katunayake airport attack dealt a heavy blow to the Sri Lankan economy and the tourist industry, stunting Sri Lanka's long-term economic development.

Economics of war

Although the PA government was considered left-liberal, its economic policies were no different from that of the previous rightist UNP regime. Economic liberalization, privatization, and structural adjustment policies were continued. State enterprises and vital assets such as the national airline, telecommunications, and the container terminal of the Colombo harbor were sold or leased to foreign interests to raise revenue as the external debt, and dependence on IMF/World Bank loans and conditionalities increased. By 1998 Sri Lanka had become one of the 'mostly free' economies of the world, according to the Index of Economic Freedom compiled by the Heritage Foundation and the Wall Street Journal.[91] But critics of the 'Open Door' economic policy begun in 1977 charged that it ruined the country, turning it into a 'happy hunting ground of neocolonialism', benefiting the rich countries at the expense of Sri Lanka.[92] The peace dividend of US$600 million a year in military expenses that Kumaratunga had promised to allocate to youth employment and poverty alleviation never materialized.[93]

The war was becoming costly to Sri Lanka in both blood and treasure. Up to 1998, an estimated 50,000–60,000 people, combatants and civilians, lost their lives due to the long term conflict between the GOSL and Tamil separatists. A 2001 publication of the National Peace Council estimated that direct military expenditures of the 17-year-old war by the government and LTTE amounted to Rs.295 billion (excluding expenditure of the IPKF between 1987 and 1990). The total value of property destroyed and damaged by the war and cost of repair and replacement was estimated at Rs.137 billion in 1998 prices. Additional costs due to the war, including expenditures on displaced persons, up to 1998 was calculated at Rs.38 billion.[94] But the true costs of the war included not only direct expenditures but also the value of output and income foregone due to migration, loss of human capital, decline in tourist arrivals, and foreign investment, with the Northern and the Eastern provinces experiencing the greatest losses in output and development.[95]

There is no question that the war represented a massive misallocation of resources. But, as in all wars, there were those who benefited. To understand the full economic consequences of the war, military expenditures must be seen within the broader context of the global military economy and the dependence of large sectors of local populations on the war economy for their very livelihood. In a sad way, both average people and elites find war and its attendant sectors the only way to make a living. The expansion of the global military economy and the arms trade make it harder for peace processes to succeed in local situations, such as in Sri Lanka.

War: poverty and profit

Toward the end of the 1990s, approximately half of the Sri Lankan government's defense expenditures went for salaries and wages.[96] Youth employment was a significant problem and a major factor in the rise of both the Sinhala JVP and the Tamil separatist insurgencies. Most of the combatants of the government and the Tamil militant groups were youths in the 16–25 age group from the same social class background. While they were not forcibly recruited, as most LTTE cadres were, the Sri Lankan troops were also drawn from relatively poor rural families with little educational qualifications and few alternative means of livelihood.[97] Few members of the Sinhala elite or the Tamil elite, including the Tamil diaspora that advocate war, send their own children to the battlefield. Historically and cross-culturally, poor youth have been sacrificed for power hunger and wars of elites.

The Sri Lankan army quadrupled from 30,000 troops in 1986 to 129,000 by 1996. In 1996 the overall number of the armed forces (army, navy, and air force) had increased to 167,000.[98] The armed forces provide a regular paycheck and benefits as well as generous death benefits to families: 'the family of a soldier killed in combat not only receives the soldiers salary until the year in which he would have turned 55; it is also entitled to a gratuity and a house that, combined, total as much as Rs.100,000 (more than US$1,000).[99] By 2000, 5 percent of the Sri Lankan population, mostly rural poor, were estimated to be living on the salaries of soldiers, 400,000 urban poor were also engaged in security and other services in the private sector linked to the war economy.[100] In some of the so-called border areas such as Puttalam and Vauniya, local economies expanded due to infusion of aid from humanitarian relief agencies.[101] Despite the war, or because of the war, a thriving 'Muslim economy' emerged in the east. Although many Muslim farmers continued to be poor, wealthy Muslims were able to buy off rich agricultural land from both the Tamils and the Sinhalese, who were at war with each other.[102] Tamil demand for regional autonomy overlooks the emergence of the Muslims as the wealthiest community in the east.

The Army appealed to poor families to send their sons to the war, claiming that the shortage of personnel was the 'only obstacle to defeating the LTTE'.[103] At the same time, there were reports of massive corruption on the part of high-level army officers. For example, between US$80 million and US$120 million out of a government allocation of US$800 million for military equipment in early 2000 allegedly went to politicians and military officials as kickbacks.[104] Fraud and corruption was at an 'all time high' under the PA government.[105] Money was siphoned from the privatization of state assets.[106] The 'hidden economy of corruption' was not restricted to the highest echelons of the government and its security forces. Ordinary soldiers and LTTE cadres also made money, for example, from issuing passes allowing civilians to move about in conflict areas.[107] LTTE members engaged in extortion of Tamil and Muslim civilians in the North and the East and it is widely believed that Sri Lankan security personnel divulge security information to the LTTE in return for money.

Sri Lankan and LTTE military hierarchies are not the only ones to benefit from war. Defense being the most lucrative sector of the global economy, a host of weapons producers, exporters, middlemen and mercenaries in the legal and illegal sectors profit from the arms trade and attendant wars.[108] The global and local war economies have also spawned new administrative and intellectual fields such as relief and humanitarian assistance, human rights advocacy, and ethnic studies – 'industries' providing lucrative employment and comfortable lifestyles not only to politicians and government bureaucrats but also to international and local policy analysts and activists in the so-called civil society or 'third sector'.[109] In the Sri Lankan case, critics have suggested that a 'parasitic' class 'in the 'flourishing non-governmental activist sector with Colombo as its hub' has benefitted from the continuation of the war.[110]

War and criminal activity

The expansion of the war economy was accompanied by a massive increase in Sri Lanka's black market, valued at US$3 billion a year in 2000, or 'more than one-quarter the size of the official economy – much of it centering on the country's now booming heroin and weapons trade'.[111] The internationally banned LTTE, with its heavy involvement in the heroin and illegal weapons trades, has had an 'influential stake' in the Sri Lankan as well as the global underworld.[112] At the end of the 1990s, one out of every five Sri Lankan Tamils was living overseas, and the bulk of the LTTE war budget was raised from the diaspora in continental Europe and North America.[113] Monies thus raised were remitted outside the legal banking system through brokering systems.[114] Illegal and legal components of LTTE's finance generation overlap. The TRO (Tamil Rehabilitation Organization), for example, is known to spend money it raises both on rehabilitation and weapons procurement.[115] In 1999, Rohan Gunaratna wrote:

> Trading in gold, laundering money and trafficking narcotics bring the LTTE substantial revenue ... needed to purchase sophisticated weaponry. The SAM missiles procured from Cambodia cost the LTTE United States one million dollars apiece ... Money is invested in legitimate ventures that make it difficult for security and intelligence agencies to monitor their investments, accounts, transfers and investments.... It is believed that the LTTE transports heroin on board LTTE owned ships from Myanmar to Europe. The LTTE also has their own fleet of vehicles in many countries from Tamil Nadu to Ontario. They also play a role in providing passports, other papers, and also engage in human smuggling.[116]

The LTTE war machine

Operating like both a multinational firm and an intelligence agency with a global reach, the LTTE has allocated its money strategically for its dual military and ideological strategies to establish Tamil Eelam.[117] Operating out of the main centers of its global network in London, Toronto, New Jersey and Norway, the LTTE utilizes the vast resources extracted from the Tamil diaspora and from its illegal and legal enterprises to influence policymakers, media, academia, and other influential sections in the state and NGO sectors within the international community. Thus it has gained sympathy and support even though it has no democratic mandate from Tamils and has a long record of killing Tamil dissidents and moderates, forcible child recruitment, and other violations of human rights and democratic norms. As Clifford Bob has convincingly shown, it is not the movements with the most legitimate grievances but those that are politically savvy and market themselves effectively that gain international recognition.[118] Ironically, it is the English-language facility and professional status acquired through the free education system in Sri Lanka by Tamil doctors, lawyers, and engineers that have given the LTTE the competitive edge in the global political arena.[119] By strategically employing international public relations firms, hiring well-known lawyers, and cultivating academics, media people, and human rights organizations, the LTTE has built a sophisticated global ideological and political apparatus that is the prototype of twenty-first century terrorism.

Gunaratna has pointed out the many different ways the LTTE has used its money to build connections and gain 'access to some world leaders through powerful business friends and other connections'. It gives money and makes its supporters campaign for political candidates in countries including Australia, England, India and Canada 'so that in the event they come into power, the LTTE could use them to advance LTTE goals'.[120] It lobbies to appoint individuals who are pro-LTTE to head the Sri Lanka NGO consortium and cultivates connections with officials who decide on the yearly aid package for Sri Lanka. It has also obtained the support of academics in the West, like Peter Schalk of Uppsala University and human rights lawyers like Karen Parker to support its cause and has acquired 'excellent access to media organizations from the newspapers in Canada to the BBC in London'.[121]

Leading security analyst, Peter Chalk has shown how these efforts have succeeded in LTTE's ability to gain sympathy and support of prominent human rights groups in the West despite LTTE's ban as a terrorist organization in many of the same countries and its horrific record of violence and human rights violations:

'Peace' is a banner under which the LTTE continuously campaigns internationally. The slogan has been used effectively to attract several non-governmental organizations to side with the LTTE struggle in Sri Lanka. Prominent examples include the Canadian Relief Organisation for Peace in Sri Lanka; the International Educational Development Inc. (IED); the World Council of Churches; the Australian Human Rights Foundation; the International Human Rights Group; the International Federation of Journalists; *Pax Romana*; the International Peace Bureau; the International Human Rights Law Group; and the Robert F Kennedy Memorial Center for Human

Rights. Gaining the support of such groups by playing the 'peace card' has been extremely beneficial to the LTTE. By publicly demonstrating the support the group has received from prominent NGOs around the world, the LTTE believes it has succeeded in internationalizing their cause and legitimizing the claim for an independent state of Tamil Eelam.[122]

The relative failure of the international and local peace lobby to acknowledge the true nature of the LTTE has resulted in an overwhelming focus on the human rights violations on the part of the Sri Lankan government. The economic and ideological empowerment of the LTTE on the global scale solidified its terrorism and totalitarian hold over the Tamil people. But there was no meaningful protest from the international and local peace lobbies. Instead of supporting the few remaining Tamil dissidents, the Sri Lankan peace lobby seemed to collude with the Tigers' suppression of democratic protest with apparent knowledge of its foreign funders. Hoole from the UTHR, for example, claimed that the Tamil journals of the MIRJE and the Free Media Movement belittled those who exposed LTTE's violations of Tamil rights, invoking Sinhala–Tamil antagonism and repeatedly telling the readers that the 'Sinhalese are vile'.[123]

The UTHR also questioned the peace lobby's demand that the Sri Lankan government talk with the LTTE without acknowledging LTTE oppression of Tamils. Eelam War III strained the relations between the government and the INGO and local peace and human rights lobby, which charged Kumaratunga with pursuing a 'war for peace strategy'.[124]

Their charges resulted in the evolution of the international community's position on Sri Lanka that equates Tamil grievances with the LTTE's separatist cause.

Evolving position of the international community

Some international and local humanitarian NGOs had been functioning in LTTE-controlled areas at government request to assist with urgently needed relief work. But subsequently there were government charges against the ICRC and the MSF for siding with the LTTE and inflating civilian deaths and refugee figures to raise funding abroad.[125] A conference of the NGO Forum on Sri Lanka, which brought together 21 foreign representatives and 61 local organizations at a beach resort south of Colombo on 15–16 November 1995, to discuss the human rights situation, highlighted the growing strain. The day before the meeting, the Sri Lankan media carried reports that the conference was organized to support the LTTE, to draw attention to the large number of people displaced by the war, and to pressure the government to stop the military offensive. These reports incited protests against alleged NGO efforts to interfere in Sri Lanka's sovereignty and territorial integrity. While the degree of government involvement in the media reports was not clear, the incident reflected the break-up in the initial partnership between the PA government and the NGO community on the peace package.[126] A March 1996 report by the US Committee for Refugees called for dialogue between the Sri Lankan government and NGOs and issued a blanket endorsement of NGOs, stating that 'The Sri Lankan government should guarantee the freedom of association and expression of all NGOs'.[127]

A high level Commission of Inquiry in respect of NGOS, known as the NGO commission and appointed in 1990, had conducted proceedings until 1993, and a statutory framework requiring registration of all NGOs and supervision and monitoring of all NGO funding and activities had been put in place in 1993. But regulation of NGOs had lapsed the following year with the formation of the new PA government, which had come into power with the support of foreign funded NGOs.

On 26 February 1996, the Christian Michelsen Institute held a Conference in Bergen, Norway, on the role of the international community in Sri Lanka and reopening of the peace negotiations at a time when LTTE terrorism was killing hundreds of civilians and destroying valued property and infrastructure The conference was sponsored by the Norwegian government in cooperation with the Norwegian All Parties Solidarity Group for Sri Lanka. Its report and recommendations reveal the evolution in the position of the international community on the Sri Lankan conflict and in particular the position of Norway, which subsequently became a key actor. The conference was attended by representatives of the Norwegian Ministry of Foreign Affairs (Jan Egeland), the Tamil diaspora in Norway, the London based NGO Forum on Sri Lanka, the Sri Lankan UNP opposition party, the LTTE (V. Rudraku-maran) and the Norwegian funded NGO, the National Peace Council in Sri Lanka (Jehan Perera). Neither the democratically elected Sri Lankan govern-ment, nor the grassroots Sri Lankan NGOs participated.[128] Rudrakumaran, the international political advisor of the LTTE, began his presentation by paying homage to Christian Michelsen, the founder of the Institute and the first prime minister of Norway, who 'played an important role in the peaceful secession of Norway from Sweden'. Rudrakumaran was explicit that LTTE's interest was not in 'the distribution of power between the center and the periphery' – devolution/federalism as envisaged by the Sri Lankan government – but in the 'struggle for political power and territory' – that is, separation.[129]

The conference report, entitled 'Norwegian Peace Initiative', depicted the Sri Lankan conflict as a 'long-standing, difficult relationship between the ethnic majority and the principal minority in the island state'. It recommended three 'confidence-building measures' favorable to the Tamil separatist cause. The report called for several measures. Measure 1, 'Mutual recognition and respect between the negotiation parties', arguing that as the government starts with the advantage of 'initial monopoly on international recognition', 'in order to chal-lenge the government, a rebel movement must close some of the gap in status and international access'. The report went on to say that 'since the LTTE ... has lost some of the international sympathy it used to enjoy, the government, it seems, can afford to be generous in providing a sense of recognition for the movement so as to facilitate talks'. Measure 2, 'Humanising and De-escalating the war', called for a DMZ (De Militarized Zone) in Jaffna, which at the time was under government control, and recommended that 'The city itself would be placed under joint local–national civilian administration, and security would be provided by an international peacekeeping force'. Measure 3, 'Devolution of Power', praised the Kumaratunga Peace Proposals for annulment of Sri Lanka's unitary state:

> A very significant item in the devolution package is the proposed annulment of Article 2 of the 1978 Constitution, which states that 'The Republic of Sri Lanka is a Unitary State'. Given the original separatist nature of the conflict, the proposal is a particularly courageous initiative.[130]

Thus, the 'international community', led by Norway, called for the recognition of the terrorist LTTE and symmetry with the Sri Lankan government, and also advocated an 'internationally supervised withdrawal of the Sri Lankan army from the Jaffna city', abrogation of the unitary character of the Sri Lankan state in favor of decentralization and devolution of power, and acceptance of the 'principles of consociationalism and asymmetry [between federated regions]' as 'pillars in a stage that is reconstructed for meaningful negotiations'.[131] As preconditions for the talks, the Sri Lankan government was expected to make major concessions with regard to its sovereignty and territorial control, while the LTTE was not required to give up its demand for a separate state or its acts of terrorism, such as forcible child recruitment and political assassinations. Despite the dangers posed by the Norwegian led international position to Sri Lanka's sovereignty and territorial integrity, President Kumaratunga invited Norway to act as a peace mediator in 1999 because of Norway's reputation in international mediation and its trust by the LTTE. However, the Norwegian position exemplified in the Christian Michelsen Report was not translated into policy and implemented until the UNP won the parliamentary elections in December 2001 and Ranil Wickramasinghe became the prime minister.

Although the LTTE had reneged on negotiations and used ceasefires to build up its military strength again and again, the 'international community' and the local peace lobby prevailed upon the Sri Lankan government to accept its position that genuine grievances of Tamils had led the LTTE to take up terrorism, that the war was 'unwinnable', and that a political settlement involving devolution would lead the LTTE to give up terrorism and embrace the path of democracy and the rule of law.[132] International Christian NGOs, such as the World Council of Churches, and Churches' Commission on Mission, which worked closely with the National Council of Churches in Sri Lanka, played an active role in advocating for a negotiated settlement.[133]

Sinhala nationalists were not the only ones aghast at what seem to be an uncritical appeasement of LTTE terrorism by the international community and endorsement of the NGOs as an objective international moral authority.[134] Dissidents within the Tamil community were also critical of the biases of the INGO peace lobby. The overwhelming emphasis that left-liberal international and local human rights lobbies placed on the government's human rights violations and the relative dismissal of LTTE violations made it seem as if they were condoning LTTE terrorism. As Sumathi Rajasingham, a dissident Tamil activist, dared to state, the relative silence of the left-liberal NGO peace lobby on LTTE violations contributed to advancing the fundamentally undemocratic premise of the LTTE as the 'sole representative of Tamils'.

> [T]he Tamil problem today … is … deeply influenced … by interactions with the outside world…, some global influences, more than helping to solve the problem, have driven it into a deeper crisis…, there are powerful NGOs, linked to global counterparts,… building up the LTTE as the sole representatives of the Tamil people. In the meantime the ordinary Tamils are becoming more and more powerless and one could name several NGOs in this country that are partly to blame for that.[135]

After the 11 September 2001, attacks in the United States, the threat of international terrorism was taken far more seriously, and both the US and Britain tightened laws against terrorism. The LTTE was included among 25 other terrorist organizations whose assets were to be frozen by British financial institutions.[136] As the 'war on terror' came to the center stage of global politics, there was increased interest in the linkages between the various international terrorist groups, including connections between Al-Qaeda and the LTTE.[137] Indeed, the horrific tragedy of 11 September 2001, presented an unprecedented opportunity to the Sri Lankan government to rally international support to destroy LTTE terrorism and find a lasting solution to the conflict. As S.L. Gunasekara put it, 'We were … given the opportunity,… to gain the active support of the … "International Community" … to eradicate the incubus called the LTTE from our midst'.[138]

But the opportunity was lost. While the 'war on terror' came to the center of global geo-politics, what transpired in Sri Lanka was another attempt at political negotiation with the LTTE. Though the 'international community', led by the United States, sought to defeat terrorism militarily, the Sri Lankan government committed itself to restoring peace through negotiation. A confluence of factors – the influence of the NGO peace lobby, opportunism of Sri Lankan parliamentary politics, and LTTE savvy – culminated in a new peace initiative instead of an intensified war on terror in Sri Lanka.

8 Norwegian facilitated peace initiative, 2002–2008

In early 2001 Rauf Hakeem and his Sri Lanka Muslim Congress left the People's Alliance (PA) coalition, which had governed since 1994, and joined the opposition UNP seeking a separate Muslim administrative district in the Eastern Province. It instigated the defection of some leading government ministers. As a result, the PA government lost its parliamentary majority, parliament was dissolved, and new elections were held on 5 December 2001.

The elections brought to power the UNF (United National Front) coalition. Ranil Wickramasinghe of the UNP became the new prime minister while his rival, Chandrika Bandaranaike Kumaratunga of the PA, remained the president, creating an uneasy coexistence.[1] The defeat of the PA was due to the widespread sentiment that it had destroyed the economy and government institutions, elevated corruption in public life, mishandled the war, and caused the unnecessary slaughter of massive numbers of youths.[2]

The UNF victory was narrow; it received 46.80 percent of the votes cast, against 46.29 percent received by the PA and its ally, the JVP (which had re-entered parliamentary politics after de-proscription in 1994).[3] Since the introduction of proportional representation in the 1978 Constitution, which favored minorities, support of the communal minority parties became crucial to winning the contest between the SLFP and the UNP. The Sri Lanka Muslim Congress and the Indian Tamil CWC, which had supported the SLFP-led PA in 1994, switched allegiances to the UNP in the 2001 elections. The newly established Indian Tamils' Up-Country People's Front (UCPF) also supported the UNP in 2001.[4]

What was unusual in the 2001 elections was the support the UNP received from another unofficial communal entity, the newly formed Tamil National Alliance (TNA) comprising the TULF, ACTC, and the former militant groups, the EPRLF (Premachandran faction) and the TELO. Echoing the 1976 Vaddukoddai Resolution of the TULF, which was the first call for a separate Tamil state, the manifesto of the TNA committed itself to campaign nationally and internationally to 'mobilize the Tamil-speaking people of the northeast, in order to achieve ... the objectives of Tamil nationalism, self-determination and the 'Tamil homeland'.[5] The LTTE had brutally and systematically eliminated the leaders of the TULF, EPRLF, TELO over the years. But, out of fear and opportunism, the 'moderate' groups comprising the TNA now accepted the LTTE as 'sole representatives of Tamils', becoming what critics have called 'mindless and soulless puppets' of the LTTE.[6] Elections marred by violence and rigging in the north and the east favored the TNA, which contested exclusively in those areas.

Proportional representation designed to increase minority representation was decisive in the final outcome of the 2001 elections. The TNA, which received 3.9 percent of total votes cast, was able to secure 15 parliamentary seats, whereas the JVP, an increasingly popular Sinhala party that received 9.1 percent of the votes, only received 16 parliamentary seats. The Muslim Congress, which received 1.2 percent of the total votes, also benefited from proportional representation, receiving five seats.[7] Dependent on the minority parties for its parliamentary majority, the UNF became more beholden to their communal agendas than previous regimes had been. The LTTE was heavily involved in behind-the-scenes manipulation of the political process. It was widely believed that the LTTE had come to a secret agreement with the UNP before the elections in return for TNA support to the UNP.

The 'ethnic outbidding' for minority votes, which had replaced the outbidding for popularity with the Sinhala Buddhist majority, became a major obstacle to finding a unified solution to the separatist conflict. Lack of political unity is a problem inherent in parliamentary politics. As S.L. Gunasekara, who founded the Sinhala Urumaya (Sinhala Heritage) Party as an alternative to the UNP and the SLFP in 2000 argued, the power struggle between the two major Sinhala parties, the SLFP and the UNP has been a major cause of Sri Lanka's inability to crush LTTE terrorism.

> The 'malady' from which these two Parties ... are suffering..., is that they ... see ... the UNP or the SLFP, as the case may be, and not the LTTE as the 'Public Enemy No. 1',... and are willing to sacrifice or compromise any principle or enter into any sleazy deal,... however unsavoury ... provided that by doing so they would be able to defeat the UNP or the SLFP ... and gain for themselves the reins of political power.[8]

Although the UNF victory was narrow, it was hailed by the local and international peace lobbies as a mandate to end military operations and renew negotiations with the LTTE. Soon after the elections, the LTTE extended a month-long ceasefire to the new UNP government on 24 December 2001, which in turn led to the signing of a ceasefire agreement (CFA) between the government and the LTTE on 21 February 2002, facilitated by Norway. The ceasefire was welcomed by the war-weary Sri Lankan population and the international community eager to find a resolution to the protracted conflict.[9] The Sri Lankan government accepted the position of the international and local peace lobby that the war was 'unwinnable' and that a settlement had to be made at whatever cost for the sake of peace.[10] Norway, which became the facilitator of the 2002 peace process, played a crucial role in the drafting and acceptance of the CFA. The deepening of Norway's role in Sri Lanka led to the imposition of what has become known as the 'Norwegian Model' for global peacemaking and conflict resolution.

The Norwegian model

Norway is a relatively young nation, having emerged in 1905 after a secessionist conflict with Sweden, and a small country, with a population of 4.5 million people. Though a relatively marginal country during much of its short history, the recent discovery of offshore oil has made Norway the third biggest exporter of oil and the wealthiest country in the world in terms of per capita GNP (after the Duchy of Luxembourg).[11] In recent decades Norway has been one of the most generous foreign aid donors contributing 0.9 percent of its GDP and providing massive humanitarian and international development support.[12] Former Prime Minister Gro Harlem Bruntland stated that it was 'typical for Norwegians to be good' and Lutheran clergyman and Norwegian Prime Minister Kjell Magne Bondevik stated in 1999, 'Norway has had a reputation as a humanitarian Great Power'.[13] The image of Norway as global 'moral entrepreneur' has become a part of Norwegian consciousness'.[14]

Since brokering the 1993 Israeli–Palestinian Oslo Accords, Norway has emerged as the preeminent global 'peacemaker'. The self-image of Norway as an 'international brand name circling around the international engagement for democracy, human rights, conflict solution and peace' owes much to the work of Norwegian politician, Jan Egeland.[15] He is credited with the Norwegian strategy for 'peacemaking diplomacy' articulated in his graduate thesis in the 1980s, 'Impotent Superpower-potent Small State'.[16] His argument that as a neutral, trustworthy, and peace-loving country, Norway is in a better position than powerful countries to broker peace deals, has been embraced by the Norwegian political and policy establishment.[17] The Norwegian Ministry of Foreign Affairs identifies four elements of the so-called 'Norwegian model' invented by Egeland:

> 1) Norway is no big power; we are not any threat to other countries. 2) Norway is peaceful. We have no modern history of colonisation and warfare, but rather a history of peacemaking ... 3) The peace work builds upon a flexible combination of actors from the state and voluntary organisations. 4) Norway combines peace broking with long term humanitarian aid, in which Norway is not small, but a medium size donor.[18]

The Norwegian model has played a major role in advancing the role of the NGOs and the so-called 'third sector', and the privatization and 'outsourcing' of diplomacy and international conflict resolution.[19] It assumes that NGOs, church groups, and others can 'do things a government would not attempt, such as disguising secret talks as humanitarian or academic meetings'.[20] Norwegian Foreign Ministry officials admit that 'The Ministry is quite limited when it comes to expertise in different parts of the world, so we've been exploiting outside expertise. We have the money, they have the contacts'.[21] According to Egeland 'The purest form of the Norwegian model is the foreign ministry working in symbiosis with one or more academic or nongovernmental humanitarian organizations'.[22]

While the Norwegian Model is held in high esteem by the international community and the United Nations, Norway's neutrality and peacemaking have come under increasing questioning in recent years. Norway was the 'seventh largest exporter of arms and ammunitions ... in 2006'[23] and it has been a member of NATO since the treaty's inception. The very title of the Norwegian strategy document reveals that Norwegian 'peacemaking diplomacy' is really about Norway, 'the potent small state' serving the interests of the 'impotent superpower', the United States.[24]

The critics argue, further, that the country is not even a genuinely pluralist parliamentary democracy. Article 1 of the Constitution of Norway states, for example, that 'The Kingdom of Norway is a free, independent, indivisible and inalienable Realm. Its form of government is a limited and hereditary monarchy'. Article 2 states that 'the Evangelical–Lutheran religion shall remain the official religion of the State. The inhabitants professing it are bound to bring up their children in the same'. And Article 4 states that 'The King shall at all times profess the Evangelical–Lutheran religion, and uphold and protect the same'.[25] Continuing issues over political and territorial rights of the Sami indigenous minority have also raised concerns about Norwegian government's commitment to equality and pluralism in Norway.[26]

US anthropologist Francisco Gil White claims that Norway plays the role of agent of the 'Washington Consensus' and its neo-liberal agenda in delegitimizing, destabilizing, and dismembering existing states to maintain the hegemony of the West.[27] The Washington Consensus is generally understood as a collection of economic policies of western industrialized countries and carried out by institutions such as the IMF, the World Bank, and US Treasury Department, all based in Washington, DC. Broadly speaking, the policies which mandate often-harsh reform to expand the role of market forces constrain the role of the state, are also described as neo-liberalism or market fundamentalism.

Questions are also raised in many quarters as to whether the NGOs and international NGOs (INGOs) promoted by the Norwegian model constitute an independent third force genuinely committed to global peace and social and economic justice. For example, should NGOs and INGOs, which lack transparency and accountability, be given a free hand in important policy decisions that affect the lives of millions of people across the world? Are religious organizations, such as the Lutheran church, objective actors in all cultural contexts? The close connection between the Norwegian government aid agencies such as the Norwegian Agency for Development Cooperation (NORAD) and the NGOs has led critics like Dag Hareide to question if there is now a 'corporate power system and a closed labour market [with the same individuals moving back and forth] .. . and if non-state actors are entirely independent of state authority'.[28] While the Norwegian model treats NGOs as an independent force committed to peace, realists see NGOs either as 'front organizations thinly disguising the interests of particular states, or as potential revolutionaries, seeking to undermine national solidarity and the stability of the state system'.[29]

Sociologist Susantha Goonatilake has charged that by using Norwegian-funded NGOs, such as International Alert operating internationally and the National Peace Council operating locally, Norway has created a new form of 'NGO colonialism via a new dependent class' in Sri Lanka. Goonatilake argues further that '[t]heir [Norwegian] NGOs have stood against the sovereignty of this country such as welcoming Indian troops, and asking for foreign intervention. Norway has become a proxy ruler through such NGO fronts'.[30] Revelations of extremely high salaries being paid to NGO peace activists in Sri Lanka has strengthened these charges.[31]

Huge salaries and other benefits widen income disparities in the state and NGO sector and between social classes and aggravate grievances within the country (Table 8.1). Yet, the Norwegian model of conflict analysis continues to be founded on the assumed primordial antagonism between oppressor and victim. Its conflict resolution strategies try to promote symmetry, if not equality, between warring parties, whether they be legitimate democratic governments or internationally banned terrorist organizations like the LTTE. Francisco Gil White points to the failure of the model in the Middle East and Bosnia to argue that the flawed Norwegian model has led to legitimization of terrorism and exacerbation of conflicts rather than peaceful resolution in many situations. Applying the 'logic' of the Norwegian model to the Sri Lankan case, he predicted that:

Table 8.1 Norwegian foreign ministry funds: selected Sri Lankan recipients, 2005

Recipient	*Norwegian kroners**
Center for Policy Alternatives	446
Milinda Moragoda Institute	8,400 (USD 1.2 million)
National Christian Council	75
National Peace Council of Sri Lanka	2072 (USD 300,000)
Peace Secretariat for Muslims, Sri Lanka	1,590
Peace Secretariat of LTTE	5,676 (USD 900,000)
SCOPP, Secretariat for Coordinating the Peace Process, Sri Lanka	50
Sri Lanka Monitoring Mission	8,929
Redd Barna	13,417
Sri Lanka Press Institute	3,700 (USD 450,000)
TRO	15,000 (USD 2.3 million)
Plan International	5,000
Sewalanka	10,500

Source: Enclosure, Norwegians Against Terrorism, report of 14 January 2007, Table 4, online, available at: www.svik.org/nat1.pdf (accessed 15 February 2008).

Notes
USD conversion as given in original.
*All amounts in 1000 Norwegian kroner (Nok).

A Norwegian 'peace' process is designed to give the Tigers *more* of what they want, not less. A 'peace' process, by definition, will treat the Tiger terrorists as a political force that supposedly represents the Tamil people.... This is precisely what the Norwegian diplomatic intervention helped do for the brutal and terrorist KLA, and also for the terrorist Al-Fatah ... In other words. The Tamil Tigers will become the recognized government for the Tamils, and will be given more autonomy, because this is how the Norwegian 'peace' process works. It does not matter that ... these very Tamil Tigers ... are responsible for the oppression ... of innocent Tamils.[32]

Advancing the theory that Norway is the agent of the Washington Consensus entrusted with the task of breaking up existing nation states, Gil White also alleges that the ultimate reason behind the empowerment of the Tamil Tigers is the encouragement of South Indian secessionism and destabilization of India, which like Yugoslavia – which at the time of its breakup was an ally of Russia in Europe – is a large country with an independent foreign policy and a potential threat to the hegemony of the West. He writes:

There are 60 million Tamils in India. There is a significant secessionist movement in Tamil-Nadu (the three Tamil parties in Vajapayee's coalition- all secessionist). The 'peace process' in Sri Lanka will create a Tamil 'mini-state' or quasi-state' or 'de facto' state in Sri Lanka. This will simultaneously encourage Tamil secessionists in India and will increase the power and influence of the Tigers in India's Tamil-Nadu, which is already not insignificant.... India will be destroyed for the same reasons Yugoslavia was destroyed.... Its destruction will further an overall goal of cutting up the world into smaller pieces, made manageable for US world domination, and of preventing large power coalitions in Eurasia, which is the US's main goal.[33]

Notwithstanding the sensationalism of such claims, the neutrality and efficacy of the Norwegian intervention in the Sri Lankan conflict need close examination.

Norwegian intervention in Sri Lanka

Norway has had a 'long and close relationship with Sri Lanka', being one of Sri Lanka's biggest foreign donors.[34] But the work of NORAD and Redd Barna (the Norwegian Children's Fund) in the settlement of Indian Tamils in the north since the late 1970s has been suspected by some as aiding Tamil separatism.[35]

Why would Norway be inclined to support the Tamil separatist cause, if in fact it has? Norway's own secessionist history might lead it to be sympathetic to Tamil separatism. But a more influential factor is the Sri Lankan diaspora in Norway, which though relatively small in number, has been successful in lobbying Norwegian politicians. The LTTE is highly organized and active in Norway. Taking advantage of the good reputation of the Tamil diaspora in Norway, the

LTTE has presented its cause as synonymous with Tamil interests while at the same time using threats and intimidation to extort money and support from the diaspora, as it does elsewhere, even while interfering in domestic Norwegian politics.[36]

In 2003 Norwegians were shocked to find that the Oslo City Council elections had been rigged in favor of an LTTE activist from the Sri Lankan Tamil diaspora who won a seat as a Labour Party candidate in the Oslo Municipality through 'pre-arranged voting ballots'. Apparently, this was the first ever election rigging in Norway, which considers itself an 'impeccable democracy'. The house of the Norwegian journalist who exposed the LTTE fraud was later hit with bullets.[37] Reports by the research organization Norwegians Against Terror (NAT) have claimed that many Sri Lankan Tamils, including LTTE cadres, were able to come to Norway on documents and passports bought from corrupt employees of the Norwegian Foreign Ministry.[38] NAT has also shown that the Norwegian Foreign Ministry and the Oslo Municipality have given millions to the LTTE through front organizations, notably the TRO (Tamil Rehabilitation Organization)[39] (Table 8.1).

Others have attributed Norwegian involvement in Sri Lanka and support for the Tamil separatist cause to Norwegian politicians' interest in gaining the votes of the Sri Lankan Tamil diaspora in Norway, providing job opportunities for professionals in the significant Norwegian 'peace industry', and business for the Norwegian oil industry. Some critics have suspected that Norway may want control over the marine and off-shore mineral resources in Sri Lanka's north and east after the establishment of a separate state.[40]

Regardless of whether those motives are true, Norway has used its economic aid to pressure the Sri Lankan government to engage in political negotiations with the LTTE since the 1980s, and in the 1990s it was involved in shaping international policy on the Sri Lankan separatist conflict. Norway became the internationally recognized peace facilitator after Ranil Wickramasinghe came into power in December 2001. Norwegian parliamentarian, Erik Solheim (currently in 2008, Minister of the Environment and Minister of Development Cooperation in Norway) who was known to be personally linked to the LTTE, was appointed Special Advisor of the Norwegian Foreign Ministry to the Sri Lankan peace process. He was credited with secret drafting of the LTTE-friendly ceasefire agreement signed in February 2002. The terms of this document were based on the 'Norwegian Peace Initiative' discussed at the Christian Michelsen Institute's Conference in Bergen in 1996. But like the Indian imposed Indo-Sri Lanka Accord of 1987, the so-called 'Westborg [Norwegian Ambassador to Sri Lanka]–Wickramasinghe–Prabhakaran CFA', was anathema to much of the local population.[41]

2002 ceasefire agreement

The objective of the 2002 ceasefire agreement (CFA) was to 'find a negotiated solution to the ongoing ethnic conflict in Sri Lanka'. While it noted that other groups have also suffered the 'consequences of the conflict', it upheld the dualistic characterization of the conflict by recognizing only the government of Sri Lanka and the LTTE as the two parties to the conflict. Bypassing elected members of parliament representing non-LTTE Tamil interests and choosing to negotiate with the unelected LTTE, the Agreement accepted the LTTE as 'the sole representative of Tamils'.[42]

International euphoria notwithstanding, the legality and terms of the Agreement, the process of its acceptance, and its enforcement were highly controversial, especially among Sinhalese. It was pointed out that because the LTTE was a proscribed terrorist organization, the engagement in 'any activity, of, or connected with, or related to such proscribed organization' contravened Sri Lanka's Prevention of Terrorism Act No. 48 of 1972 making the offender, in this case the prime minister, liable to mandatory imprisonment.[43] It was also charged that the government's failure to consult and obtain approval of the

> [C]onstitutional head of the state, her Excellency the President, [Kumaratunga] has made the MOU a focus of disunity and given currency to the existence of a secret pact between the LTTE and the UNF Government to divide and rule Sri Lanka.[44]

Paul Harris, who was reporting for the London *Daily Telegraph* and *Jane's Intelligence* and was based in Sri Lanka at the time, called the CFA 'The Greatest Giveaway in History'.[45]

An examination of the CFA does reveal a disconcerting abdication of territory and sovereignty on the part of the GOSL (Government of Sri Lanka). The 2002 CFA elevated the LTTE, an internationally banned terrorist organization, to an equivalent status with the lawful and democratically elected Sri Lankan government. Article 1 stated that 'The Parties have agreed to implement a ceasefire between their armed forces', and Article 2.13 referred to the obligation of the two 'Parties' to provide family members with access to their respective 'detainees'.[46] 'Armed Forces' commonly refers to forces of a sovereign state and 'detainees' to those held in lawful custody.[47] Thus the LTTE, the oppressor of Tamils, was recognized as their representative and a legitimate entity. The Agreement did not require LTTE cadres to be disarmed. Rather, Article 1.8 dictated terms to weaken the armed forces of the GOSL and strengthen LTTE military capability by requiring the GOSL to disarm non-LTTE Tamil paramilitary groups and to offer to integrate those cadres within the GOSL armed forces 'for service away from the Northern and Eastern Province'. Article 2:1 of the CFA called for the 'Parties' to abstain from 'hostile acts against the civilian population' but did not ban child soldiering and forcible recruitment and child recruitment, routine practices of the LTTE, although Sri Lanka is a signatory to the United Nations Resolution banning Child Soldiers. The agreement also failed to specify mechanisms to monitor and enforce other serious human rights violations or to uphold pluralism and democracy.[48]

Other terms of the agreement further advanced the totalitarian and separatist ambitions of the LTTE. Article 1.5 stated that 'the status quo as regards the areas controlled by the GOSL and the LTTE, respectively on 24 December 2001 shall continue to apply pending ... demarcation'. Clause 1.6 asserted that 'The Monitoring Mission [SLMM] shall assist the Parties in drawing up demarcation lines at the latest by D-day + 30'.[49] By accepting these clauses, the GOSL not only acceded to the LTTE's right to control land areas it had usurped in the Northern and Eastern Provinces. It also agreed to a formal partition of the country under the supervision of the Scandinavian-led Sri Lanka Monitoring Mission (SLMM).[50] Furthermore, the GOSL agreed to Article 1.13, which gave unarmed LTTE cadres freedom to move in areas of the North and the East under GOSL control 'for the purpose of political work' while similar freedom of movement was not allowed GOSL troops in the areas under LTTE control. By allowing expansion of its 'political work', namely, its propaganda campaign, the agreement advanced the separatist agenda of the LTTE, which was nowhere renounced in the CFA.[51]

Despite all that the government had acceded to at the expense of Sri Lanka's sovereignty, democracy, and territory, the LTTE, for its part, was not willing to compromise its entrenched position. At a press conference in Killinochi on 2 April 2002, which was attended by 300 international and local journalists, the LTTE 'theoretician' Anton Balasingham and the 'supreme leader' Prabhakaran affirmed their commitment to separatism and the establishment of Eelam. When asked if Prabhakaran recognizes Wickramasinghe as his prime minister, Balasingham replied, 'Prime Minister Ranil Wickramasinghe is the Prime Minister of those who elected him. Here in Tamil Eelam our Prime Minister and President is Prabhakaran'.[52] When Prabhakaran was asked if the statement he had made to his cadres that he could be shot if he gave up the demand for Eelam, still stands, he replied, 'That statement stands'.[53] Notwithstanding the implications of such statements for democracy and peaceful conflict resolution, there was massive support for the CFA from the 'international community' and the local peace lobby, which dubbed it as the 'best chance to establish peace'.[54]

For those opposed to separatism and the LTTE, however, the CFA symbolized appeasement, if not outright capitulation, to terrorism. Norway, the facilitator of the peace process, and the Scandinavian countries that provided the members to the SLMM were the final arbiters and supervisors of the implementation of the agreement. Article 3:2 of the CFA stated that 'Subject to acceptance by the Parties, the Royal Norwegian Government ... shall appoint the Head of the SLMM ... who shall be the final authority regarding interpretation of this Agreement'.[55] Although this placed Norway in the dominant position, Norway and the Nordic SLMM were severely constrained by the CFA's capitulation to terms laid down by the LTTE. For example, according to Article 3:6, the SLMM, which established its headquarters in Colombo and local monitoring committees in all other districts of the north and the east, was excluded from Killinochchi and Mullativu, the LTTE strongholds where the Tamil Tigers were allowed to do as they pleased without any kind of monitoring.[56] Given the LTTE's insistence that the proscription prevented it from being 'an equal and legitimate party to engage in peace talks with the government', the Sri Lankan government lifted the proscription on the LTTE on 6 September 2002, paving the way for negotiations.[57] There was tremendous local opposition against this move since the LTTE had neither disavowed separatism nor were disarmed.

Challenges to the peace process

During the 2002–2003 negotiations the GOSL and the LTTE held six highly publicized rounds of talks in Thailand, Norway, Germany, and Japan, all facilitated by Norway. The LTTE refused to deal with the core issue – specifically the nature of the administration for the north and the east – at any of these sessions. At the second round of talks held in Oslo in December 2002, however, the LTTE delegation agreed to;

> [E]xplore a solution founded on the principle of internal self-determination in areas of historical habitation of the Tamil-speaking peoples, based on a federal structure within a united Sri Lanka. The parties acknowledged that the solution has to be acceptable to all communities.[58]

This was hailed as a major political breakthrough by the international community, but the LTTE soon disavowed its own offer.[59]

The situation on the ground became more confused, and there was little hope for long-term peace among those directly affected by the conflict. Marginalization by the peace process and fear of living under a terrorist LTTE regime radicalized many young Muslims, who began to demand a separate Muslim region in the southeast. Although Hakeem, a cabinet minister and leader of the SLMC, paid a visit to Killinochchi and signed a separate MOU with Prabhakaran shortly after the 2002 CFA, the expected protection for Muslims in the east did not come to pass. Instead, the LTTE stoked Tamil–Muslim animosities by propagating anti-Muslim rhetoric and a boycott of Muslim shops, which fuelled Muslim militancy and Tamil–Muslim clashes.[60] Alleged support from international Islamic groups gave rise to fears that an 'Osama group' with external support would arise in the east.[61] As mentioned earlier, the demand for a separate Muslim autonomous region in the south east was not new, but, now it was more clearly and vigorously articulated. On 29 January 2003, students of the South Eastern University put forward a separatist Muslim platform – the Oluvil Declaration. Echoing the landmark 1976 Tamil separatist declaration, the Vaddukoddai Resolution, it asserted that Muslims are a separate nation with claims to a 'traditional homeland', self-determination, and political autonomy apart from both Tamil and Sinhala domination:

> 1. The North-eastern Muslims are a separate political community, nationality or nation... 2. The North-eastern region is the traditional homeland of the Muslims. 3. The North-eastern Muslims have the right of self-determination... 4. In any political solution ... the territory comprising the areas predominantly inhabited by Muslims must be ... consolidated in an

autonomous political unit 5. The social, political economic and cultural rights of our Muslim brethren who live outside the North-east should be reasonably ensured.[62]

The peace process was not broadened in response to the concerns of Muslims or different Tamil and Sinhala groups. Thus the internationally driven bipolar conflict resolution model intensified the specter of a future globalized war between the LTTE and the Muslims and ethnic balkanization of the east.[63] Low caste Dalits who constitute a major portion of the LTTE cadres also felt marginalized by the peace process. Continued caste oppression could radicalize them, encouraging them to join their Indian Dalit counterparts, such as the Dalit Panthers in Tamil Nadu. During the international press conference held in Killinochchi after the signing of the CFA in April 2002, the LTTE leader said that he had invited leaders of the Muslim and hill country Tamils to discuss matters concerning their future. But as a Sri Lankan Tamil Dalit leader wrote, the press conference was

> disturbingly silent on the question of Dalit-untouchables who constitute nearly 15 percent of the Tamil population in Eelam ... the reticence of the Tamil leadership is deliberate neglect. A problem that that has been awaiting a resolution for decades was simply glossed over as if it did not even exist.[64]

It was the established practice of the LTTE to enter ceasefires and peace processes when it suited it, gain as much as possible, and leave when it wanted.[65] Despite all the advantages given to the LTTE leadership, the peace process broke down on 21 April 2003, when the LTTE unilaterally suspended the talks but not the ceasefire, on the ground that it was not invited to a preparatory aid seminar on Sri Lanka held in Washington, DC, on 14 April 2003. Although the LTTE was very active in the US and had engaged top US lawyers, such as former Attorney General Ramsey Clark, to get itself de-proscribed, it remained a banned terrorist organization in the US and hence not invited.

Still, the 2002 peace process was continued with Japan now playing a new leadership role. At a major aid conference held in Tokyo in June 2003 attended by 51 countries and 22 international organizations, the international community pledged US$4.5 billion for reconstruction and rehabilitation in Sri Lanka. The Tokyo Declaration put strict conditions on the disbursement of the funds. Its paragraph 18 called for protection of human rights, termination of child recruitment, Muslim participation in the peace process, and demilitarization and normalization necessary to arrive at a political settlement.[66]

Despite the painstaking efforts of the Sri Lankan government and the international community, the LTTE refused to rejoin the peace process. The Sri Lankan government put forward proposals in July 2003 to set up a provincial administrative structure for the north and the east to negotiate a settlement based on the Oslo Declaration of December 2002. Among other things, the government agreed to Muslim participation in discussions of the provincial administration and to a LTTE majority in the proposed Provincial Administrative Council (PAC), with weighted representation for the Sinhala and Muslim communities. The PAC was expected to take over governmental powers and functions in the regional administration, 'except the areas of police and security, land and revenue – but including rehabilitation, reconstruction, and resettlement'. The government also proposed district councils for each of the districts of the north and the east, district sub-committees and special committees of the PAC to strengthen the economy, infrastructure and essential services.[67]

The LTTE rejected the government proposals outright, and in November 2003 put forward its own proposals for an Interim Self Governing Authority (ISGA) as the basis for re-entering talks.[68] The LTTE was assisted by the International Working Group on Sri Lanka, a network of international humanitarian and advocacy groups including church based INGOs in devising the proposals. The ISGA designed to dismember Sri Lanka was drawn up by this group at a seminar held in Ireland.[69]

ISGA proposals

The ISGA is the only comprehensive proposal put forward by the LTTE to work out a political solution to the conflict up to date (May 2008). The plan provided for an internationally designed blueprint for a separate sovereign state in the north and the east of Sri Lanka rather than a formula for sharing power between the center and the region within a unitary state.[70] The opposition SLFP's statement on the ISGA proposals drafted by Lakshman Kadirgamar, a former foreign minister, pointed out that

> [T]he Preamble shows that the LTTE is getting ready for the day when it could argue that if the negotiations are unsuccessful (because they do not yield the results the LTTE wants), it will have no alternative but to go for a separate state.[71]

The 26 paragraphs of the preamble built the LTTE's legal case for separation by distorting facts and exaggerating charges against the Sinhalese and the Sri Lankan state. It asserts that the Sri Lankan government has repeatedly broken agreements with elected Tamil representatives and discriminated and used violence against Tamils, that an electoral 'mandate' was received from Tamil people to establish an independent Tamil state following the Vaddukoddai Resolution in 1976, and that the Tamil armed struggle for 'self defense and right to self determination' rose 'only after more than four decades of peaceful struggle'.[72] These assertions conveniently overlooked complex realities: agreements like the Bandaranaike–Chelvanayakam and Senanayake–Chelvanayakam pacts would not have received majority votes in parliament; Sri Lankan state 'discrimination' and violence was not entirely ethnically based; and the majority of people in the Eastern Province voted against the separatist agenda in 1977. Asserting that there are 'international precedents for establishing interim governing arrangements in war-torn countries having the force of law based solely on pacts or agreements between the warring parties recognized by the international community', paragraph 25 of the preamble attempted to establish the LTTE's right to come to a legal agreement with the UNP/UNF government outside the democratic process in violation of the Sri Lankan Constitution and Parliament.[73]

Clause 2 of the LTTE proposal called for an absolute majority of LTTE appointees in the ISGA making that the basis for representation of the Sinhala and Muslim communities in the 'NorthEast'. The chairperson of the ISGA appointed by majority vote would in turn choose the chief administrator and other officials for the 'NorthEast', thus ensuring totalitarian control of the LTTE. Clause 9 stated that 'the ISGA will have 'plenary powers' for the governance of the Northeast 'including ... law and order and over land. These powers shall include all powers and functions in relation to regional administration exercised by the GOSL in and for the NorthEast'.[74] 'Plenary' refers to absolute, unqualified power and 'governance' including security and defense.[75] Other clauses of the LTTE proposals spelled out in detail the complete abdication of Sri Lankan government authority in the north and the east. According to Clauses 10, 11, and 12, separate institutions were to be established for the administration of justice and finance in the 'NorthEast', giving the ISGA power to engage in and regulate internal and external trade, borrow and receive aid, and appoint a separate Auditor General.

Clause 16 called for ISGA control of all land in the 'NorthEast' that is not privately owned and the appointment of a Special Commission on Land Administration 'to inquire into and report on the rights of dispossessed people over land and land subject to encroachment, notwithstanding the lapse of any time relating to prescription'. Clause 17, 'Resettlement of Occupied Lands', called for immediate vacation of all land said to be illegally occupied by Sri Lankan armed forces and required of the Sri Lankan government to 'compensate the owners for the past dispossession of their land'.[76] These clauses would have allowed an LTTE Land Commission to interpret land rights according to the fallacious 'Tamil homelands' concept and drive out descendants of impoverished settlers of all communities who were granted state land since the colonial, if not the pre-colonial, period.[77] Clause 18 of the LTTE proposals on marine and offshore resources, which stated that the 'ISGA shall have control over the marine and offshore resources of the adjacent seas and the power to regulate access thereto', would have given control of almost two-thirds of the coast of Sri Lanka to an LTTE Navy.[78] This would compromise not only the sovereignty and territorial integrity of Sri Lanka, but also threaten international shipping lanes passing the East Coast and the security interests of neighboring India.[79]

Clause 22, affirming that the LTTE was preparing the legal ground for a separate state, stated that:

> In the determination of any dispute [e.g. water use] the arbitrators [e.g. the Royal Norwegian Government] shall ensure the parity of status of the LTTE

and the GOSL and shall resolve disputes by reference only to the provisions of this Agreement.[80]

The LTTE's ultimate goal was also evident in Clause 3 on elections, which states that if a final settlement has not been reached and implemented within five years after the ISGA Agreement comes into effect, an independent election commission appointed by the ISGA 'shall conduct free and fair elections in accordance with international democratic principles and standards under international observation'.[81] Concealed in this clause was the right or power to secede after five years. Under it, the LTTE could claim that an agreement has not been reached, hold an election, declare a separate state, and call for international recognition – with Norway likely to lead the approval.[82]

The ISGA represented a comprehensive blueprint for a separate Tamil state. But before the proposals could be discussed, President Kumaratunga intervened on the grounds that the LTTE military build-up during the peace process, such as armed camps established around the strategic Trincomalee harbor, presented serious threats to national security. While Prime Minster Wickramasinghe was on a visit to Washington DC, Kumaratunga took over the key Ministries of Defense, Interior, and Information and exercised her presidential prerogative to suspend parliament. Her controversial 'constitutional coup' and dissolution of parliament in February 2004, four years before the end of its term, and announcement of new elections for April 2004 destabilized the 'peace' process.[83]

Peace at any cost

There were both gains and losses under the 2002 CFA and the Norwegian facilitated 'peace at any cost' approach. The end to active hostilities was welcomed by the war-weary Sri Lankan population, and life returned to some degree of normality. Check points and security barriers were taken down, allowing people to move freely. Buddhists were able to go on pilgrimage to sacred sites in the north and the east after decades of war, and people from the north including LTTE cadres were able to travel to the south more easily. Like the average citizens, the Sri Lankan government too seemed to have equated the ceasefire with absence of war when it abandoned the successful intelligence operation of the Long Range Patrol Group compromising its secret location in January 2002. It led Paul Harris, the British military reporter, to remark that 'SRI LANKA ABANDONED ITS ONLY WINNING STRATEGY AT THE POINT AT WHICH IT WAS WORKING' (capitals in original).[84]

The government's abdication of security measures did not mean that the separatist insurgency or terrorism were over. Over the course of the ceasefire, the LTTE continued to buy arms internationally, bring in shiploads of weapons, surround the Trincomalee harbor, and recruit and train cadres, all in violation of the CFA. By mid-2002, LTTE cadres, including its 'police force' were estimated to be 30,000 – of which over 10,000, including 3,500 combat cadres, were estimated to be females.[85] And during the course of the peace process the Tamil

Tigers built an air force, becoming the first global terrorist group to have air capability.[86]

The internationally driven 2002 peace process solidified the de facto division of Sri Lanka, extending LTTE control into areas in the north and the east earlier held by Sri Lankan security forces.[87] It also spread LTTE's reach and power beyond the north and the east. Soon after the signing of the CFA, cabinet ministers A. Thondaman (grandson of S. Thondaman) and Chandrasekaran, who also represents Indian Tamils, paid visits to Prabhakaran in Killinochchi and openly expressed support for the LTTE cause.[88] LTTE's territorial ambitions were further revealed by a Tamil Pongu rally held in Nuwara Eliya in the Central Province, where Indian Tamils are a large community. Larger xenophobic anti-Sinhala LTTE rallies were held in the north and the east, where Tamil crowds raised their right arms in 'Nazi' salute to Prabhakaran, hailing his name.[89] At these LTTE rallies, maps of Tamil Eelam comprising two-thirds of the coastline and almost half of Sri Lanka's land mass were displayed and sometimes 'consecrated' by Catholic clergymen.[90] At one rally in March 2002 in Batticoloa, several speakers even envisioned a regional and global Eelam saying 'wherever there are Tamils there is Eelam'.[91]

Notwithstanding its professed role as protector of Tamils, the LTTE continued to oppress Tamil people, using the legitimacy given by the CFA as their 'sole representative'. According to SLMM statistics, the LTTE has been responsible for a disproportionately large number of the CFA violations and human rights abuses. Between February 2002 and April 2007, for example, the LTTE was responsible for 3,830 and the GOSL for 351 out of all violations ruled and reported by the SLMM.[92] Of these, LTTE was responsible overwhelmingly for human rights violations including child recruitment, torture, forced recruitment of adults, and assassinations (Table 8.2).

UNICEF, Human Rights Watch, Child Soldiers Global Report, and the local human rights group UTHR have reported that the CFA led to an increase in one of the worst aspects of the 21-year separatist conflict – the forcible recruitment of children, some as young as ten or 11 years of age.[93] As of the end of October 2004, UNICEF had documented 3,516 new cases of underage recruitment by the LTTE since the signing of the CFA in February 2002.[94] UTHR charged the Norwegian facilitators and the SLMM for putting the ceasefire before human rights.[95] A Child Soldiers Global Report in 2004 stated that '[m]any children were simply abducted. The February 2002 CFA allowed unarmed LTTE members to enter government-controlled territory, reportedly enabling child kidnappings to take place'.[96] The report also pointed out that the LTTE practice of demanding that each family give one child as part of a 'quota' system continued.

A speech given by an LTTE regional commander to Tamil expatriates in Switzerland revealed the class basis of the separatist war. He said, 'The Batticoloa people are giving their children, you must give your money'.[97] According to UNICEF, the average age of the children recruited was 15 years. In 2003, 43 percent of the recruits were girls, and 57 percent were boys.[98] Although a formal mechanism was put in place by UNICEF in mid-October 2003 to release and

Table: 8.2 CFA violations: selected human rights violations (22 February 2002–30 April 2007)

Category	LTTE		GOSL	
	Cases	%	Cases	%
Child recruitment	1,743	45.51	–	0
Abduction of adults	579	15.12	22	6.27
Abduction of children	253	6.61	3	–
Harassment	237	6.19	80	22.79
Assault	210	5.48	19	5.41
Assassinations*	119	3.11	36	10.26
Hostility to civilians	64	1.67	23	6.55
Intimidation	50	1.31	8	2.28
Forced Recruitment of adults	34	0.89	–	–
Extortion	30	0.78	–	0.00
Confiscations	18	0.47	4	1.14
Torture	13	0.34	–	–
Family denied access to detainees	3	0.08	–	–
All other violations	477	12.44	156	45.3
Total CFA violations	3,830	100.00	351	100.00

Sources: Violations Ruled by Sri Lanka Monitoring Mission, 'Secretariat for Coordinating the Peace Process', online, available at: www.peacesrilanka.com accessed 9/13/2008.

Note
* No definitions given.

reintegrate child soldiers, child recruitment and re-recruitment continued. Human Rights Watch reported that the total number of underage soldiers remaining with the LTTE in November 2004 may have been four times greater than the 1,395 figure registered by UNICEF.[99] The close cooperation of UNICEF with the TRO in running 'transit centers' is believed to have actually facilitated re-recruitment. The TRO is a front organization of the LTTE and its primary fund-raising arm. Because the TRO had been designated as a terrorist organization, its assets in the United States would be frozen in November 2007.

Just as UNICEF was relatively ineffectual in stopping LTTE's recruitment of children, the SLMM was ineffectual in controlling Sinhala–Tamil as well as Tamil–Muslim clashes which flared up in the east in the aftermath of the signing of the CFA.[100] Not only did the LTTE abduct many Tamil, Muslim, and Sinhala civilians; it also kidnapped, tortured, and murdered opponents belonging to rival Tamil groups such as the EPDP and EPRLF who had surrendered their weapons in accordance with the CFA. Political assassinations also increased after the signing of the CFA. More than 200 politicians from rival Tamil parties were reportedly killed between the signing of the CFA in 2002 and mid-January 2006. A number of Tamil media personnel who did not toe the LTTE line completely were also believed to have been eliminated by the LTTE[101] (Table 8.2). Providing long lists of names of Tamil opponents systematically eliminated by the LTTE, the UTHR blamed civil society activists, the international community and the Sri Lankan government for the 'manipulative', 'unprincipled', and costly approach to peace which yielded 'Dividends of Terror' rather than peace.[102]

Critics of the CFA

Sinhala nationalists criticized the so-called 'track two' diplomacy of INGOs and their local counterparts for compromising Sri Lanka's sovereignty and helping strengthen LTTE terrorism in the name of peace. 'Track two' diplomacy usually refers to citizen diplomacy outside official processes although in Sri Lanka the foreign-funded NGOs were closely related to international diplomatic circles and removed from grassroots citizen concerns. The activities of the German NGO, the Berghof Foundation for Conflict Studies in particular came under attack as an undue foreign interference in the state defense and security sector.[103] Berghof had been invited by the Sri Lankan government to set up an office in Sri Lanka in July 2001 to support 'constructive conflict transformation'. During the course of the ceasefire, over a period of about 18 months in 2002–2003, Berghof Foundation conducted a series of workshops on how to break the 'deadlock' over the High Security Zones (HSZs) in the north (land areas taken over by the Sri Lankan military to protect strategic interests). According to critics, Berghof propagated removing and minimizing the HSZs and advocated 'downsizing' or 'rightsizing' Sri Lanka's defense forces 'so that their strength and power will not surpass that of the LTTE'. Sinhalese critics also claimed that Berghof, along with Sri Lankan NGO partners such as the Centre for Policy Alternatives (CPA), Foundation for Co-Existence (FCE), Initiative for Political and Conflict Trans-formation (InPACT), Social Scientists' Association (SSA) promoted federalism and notions of 'shared sovereignty' in the name of peace. Berghof has denied promoting the 'division of the country', but the controversies surrounding Berghof and its partners continue to unfold.[104]

Norway, the facilitator of the peace process, and the Scandinavian peace monitors, the SLMM, came under even more criticism from Tamil dissidents, Sinhala and Muslim nationalists, and some international human rights and anti-terrorist groups. Norway has played and continues to play multiple and conflict-ing roles in Sri Lanka as peace facilitator, leader of the SLMM, and leading aid and loan provider. As Human Rights Watch observed in August 2003,

> The SLMM appears to lack both sufficient political distance from the nego-tiating process and a genuine capacity to investigate these [human rights] incidents. As a Norwegian-led initiative, the monitoring effort is too closely tied to the politics of the peace process.[105]

Critics have questioned Norway's objectivity in the Sri Lanka peace process, charging it with deliberate support of the LTTE and its separatist agenda.[106] The Norwegian Svik Organization has gone so far as to claim that Norway's liberal

immigration and other policies have made their country a 'safe haven' for terrorists from many parts of the world, especially Sri Lanka.[107] NAT claims that the
Norwegian government increased aid to the LTTE while LTTE's CFA violations were soaring, that it failed to stop LTTE fundraising in Norway, and continued funding LTTE front organizations in Norway and some LTTE-friendly
individuals and organizations including politicians, journalists, and journalist
organizations in Sri Lanka among others[108] (Table 8.1). It says that Norway
arranged and paid for LTTE propaganda trips and lobbied against terrorist
listing of the LTTE in the European Union. NAT has questioned the statement
of Erik Solheim that 'the LTTE will never be classified as a terrorist organization by Norway'.[109] NAT has also charged that Norwegian military support
and intelligence has been given to the LTTE, including a tour for a LTTE delegation to Norwegian Special Forces training camp in Rena, Norway.[110] According to the IPS news service, former members of the Norwegian Special Forces
allegedly provided military training to Tamil Tigers in Thailand, which has
become a nerve center of the LTTE international network.[111]

Norwegian impartiality was further implicated in complicity with the LTTE
when President Kumaratunga asked the head of the SLMM, retired Norwegian
Major General Tellefsen, to leave Sri Lanka after the discovery that he had provided military intelligence to the Tamil Tigers that allowed an LTTE arms
smuggling vessel to escape capture by the Sri Lankan Navy. Tellefsen had also
proposed treating the Sea Tigers and Sri Lankan Navy as equals by allocating
sea lanes to the LTTE in violation of Sri Lanka's territorial rights.[112] Tellefsen's
successor, General Furuhovde, was also accused of helping cover up LTTE
crimes by attributing them to an 'unknown third party in stolen uniform'. The
Norwegian Ambassador in Sri Lanka at the time, John Westborg, was also
charged with providing six tons of sensitive radio transmission equipment to the
LTTE, as revealed in a taped phone conversation with an LTTE leader. According to intelligence sources, the equipment was to be used in tracking phone con-
versations and locations and elimination of political opponents.[113]

Although Norwegian peace 'facilitation' in Sri Lanka continued to be viewed
positively in the international media and by LTTE supporters, there was growing
frustration and anger in Sri Lanka. Norway was seen as a new colonial ruler and
a supporter of LTTE separatist terrorism.[114] There was a growing feeling that
'our country has today become an open sieve for every white Tom, Dick and
Harry not to mention Jane to put his finger in'.[115] The Patriotic National Movement, which emerged in February 2004 with the objective of protecting Sri
Lanka's sovereignty and territorial integrity, called for the expulsion of Norwegian facilitators from Sri Lanka.[116] Effigies of Norwegian facilitator Erik
Solheim were burnt, and mass protests were organized by Sinhalese and Tamil
dissidents against what was seen as Norwegian favoritism towards the LTTE.
One rally drew over 50,000 people, considered to be the largest protest in Sri
Lankan history.[117] Frustrated by Norwegian disregard for LTTE atrocities, Tamil
dissident groups frequently protested outside the Norwegian embassy in
Colombo, bringing coffins of their politicians said to have been murdered by the

LTTE.[118] NAT has recommended that Sri Lankan victims of terrorism sue Norway for funding and supporting the LTTE, just as families of Lockerbie victims sued Libya for supporting terrorism.[119] Sinhala and Tamil critics and international security analysts convened at conferences in Oslo and Colombo in 2004 to bring international attention to the serious problems created by the Norwegian peace process. A report published by the Asia Foundation in 2005 was compelled to question the Norwegian facilitated peace process vis-à-vis the actual complex realities on the ground:

> The entire architecture of the peace process has been built around international engagement. The UNF government put its faith in the 'international security net' in order to bail them out if things went wrong. Norway was seen as an acceptable and non-threatening facilitator by the main protagonists. Although the LTTE pulled out of negotiations in April 2003, Norway continues to facilitate communication between both sides, and Track Two initiatives are ongoing. Therefore, though peace talks have stalled there is still a peace *process*. Some of the lessons to be drawn from Norway's role in this process are as follows: first, negotiations were based on a bilateral model of the conflict and sought to forge an elite pact between the main protagonists. Arguably, the exclusion of key stakeholders provoked spoiler behavior. Second, there was a constant tension between the imperatives of conflict management and human rights concerns. The perception that the international community was prepared to soft pedal on human rights issues, particularly in relation to the LTTE, played a role in undermining the credibility of the UNF government in the eyes of India and the southern electorate. Third, there was a growing perception that the peace process changed from being internationally supported to internationally driven, shaped by the priorities and timeframes of external rather than domestic actors. Yet even with an 'international tailwind', it proved impossible to 'bring peace', showing that international actors cannot simply engineer peace and complex socio political processes are not amenable to external micro management.[120]

Demise of the CFA: LTTE split and 2004 elections

The limitations of the bipolar model of conflict analysis and resolution became most apparent when the LTTE split into two in March 2004. The Northern/Wanni wing led by Prabhakaran moved against the renegade LTTE Commander in the East, Karuna (V. Muralithiran) and some 7,500 of his cadres, in violation of the CFA. But, both the SLMM and the Sri Lankan government turned a blind eye. Karuna was responsible for cold-blooded murders of Sinhalese, including some 600 soldiers who had surrendered on orders from the Premadasa government in June 1990. He was also responsible for extensive child recruitment in the east. But after the LTTE break-up, Karuna released his cadres, formed a new political party (TMVP Tamileela Makkal Viduthalai Pulikal), and joined the democratic process.

Karuna's challenge to Prabhakaran's authority was more than a personal matter. It was also driven by more deeply rooted historical, cultural, and regional differences and political-economic inequities between the Tamils of the north and the east. While the LTTE in the east had provided large numbers of cadres and sacrificed disproportionately for the separatist cause over the years, eastern leaders were not given commensurate power and authority within the LTTE hierarchy. In defecting from the LTTE, Karuna invoked the deeply held resentment of eastern Tamils toward the northern Tamils who had long dominated over them and spoken for them. The split in the LTTE into northern and eastern wings was a major blow to the LTTE claim as sole representative of the Tamils.

The LTTE split exposed the shortcomings of the bipolar conflict resolution model, which overlooked intra-ethnic, regional, and cultural differences within and across the linguistic divide. The eastern LTTE cadres felt that although they sacrificed disproportionately for the separatist war, they were left out of the benefits of the Norwegian facilitated 'peace process'. Calling for self-determination of eastern Tamils, Karuna criticized the 'unequal distribution of resources' between the LTTE north and the east: 'Eastern soldiers [LTTE] are used as cannon fodder ... We cannot understand what is happening to the money in the Wanni'.[121] The ground situation in the north and the east, became rife with internal LTTE feuding and LTTE intra-ethnic killing.

2004 elections

Mass discontent with the handling of the peace process was the primary reason for the defeat of the UNF coalition and the resurgence of Sinhala nationalist parties in the April 2004 parliamentary elections. The JVP, which was strongly opposed to the Norwegian-led peace process, gained 39 seats and became a major coalition partner of the new government. The Jathika Hela Urumaya (JHU National Sinhala Heritage), a new political party led by Buddhist monks that was founded on the eve of the elections, gained nine seats.[122] Buddhist monks have been the symbol of Sinhala Buddhist nationalism historically, but their entrance in the 2004 election was controversial. Several causes drove the JHU's emergence at this time: loss of trust in the established political parties, opposition to the internationally driven peace process, and the mysterious death in December 2003 of Venerable Soma, the Buddhist monk who had opposed Christian evangelical conversions. The SLFP-led UPFA (United People's Freedom Alliance) came to power in the 2004 elections promising to make the peace process transparent and to fine-tune the role of the peace facilitator. It rejected the LTTE's claim to be the 'sole representative of Tamils' as an undemocratic premise and the ISGA proposals as a blue print for a separate state. President Kumaratunga talked of sending the Norwegians back home because the public had lost of faith in their neutrality.

Once in power, however, the UPFA followed the same path as its predecessor. International pressure was put on the new government to return to peace talks essentially on terms laid down by the LTTE. The April 2004 elections in the north were ridden with violence and widespread fraud by the LTTE. Tamil political parties that tried to contest the elections called for new elections, but the legal case to revoke the elections in the north were not taken up in court. The situation was further complicated by the tsunami that devastated Sri Lanka in December 2004.

Tsunami and aftermath: a lost opportunity for reconciliation

In the immediate aftermath of the destructive tsunami in December 2004, there was a ray of hope that the country would unite to face the tragedy, which took the lives of some 30,000 Sri Lankans and displaced hundreds of thousands more. There were reports of Sri Lankan soldiers and LTTE cadres caught in the tsunami saving each others' lives and Sinhalese, Tamils, and Muslims coming to each others' aid afterwards.[123] But the spirit of unity did not last long as contention emerged over the disbursement of the massive international aid for rehabilitation and reconstruction of the six coastal districts of the north and the east that had been most affected by the tsunami.

Under pressure from international donors, the government secretively entered into a controversial agreement to establish the Post-Tsunami Operational Management Structure (P-TOMS). The P-TOMS Agreement, which is believed to have been devised by the LTTE and the Norwegian facilitators, gave the LTTE control over a regional committee constituted on an ethnic basis and headquartered in Killinochchi. Financial matters were to come under the authority of a regional fund managed by a multilateral agency – that is, a foreign body.[124] All political parties except the TNA (and some fringe groups) opposed the deal on the ground that it violated the territory and sovereignty of Sri Lanka. Although the LTTE was in control of less than 15 percent of the tsunami-affected coastal belt at the time, as critics pointed out, the P-TOMS was designed to give the Tigers 'a foothold in the entirety of the coastal belt extending from Mannar on the west coast to Arugam Bay in the south east coast, giving rise to many security considerations, including the policing of Sri Lanka's territorial waters'.[125] The JVP, the government's coalition partner, took the matter to the Supreme Court and stopped the implementation of the internationally supported P-TOMS.[126]

The Norwegians and the SLMM were ineffectual in making the LTTE respect the ceasefire as the Tigers continued to violate the 2002 CFA. Fratricidal killings between the LTTE northern and eastern wings intensified, as did LTTE killings of other dissident Tamil politicians, intellectuals, and Sri Lankan government intelligence operatives. Foreign Minister Lakshman Kadirgamar expressed his concern over the rapid deterioration of security and democracy in the north and the east. He suggested that

> [I]f the government of Norway is unable to plead this cause with the conviction and determination that it deserves it should stand aside and yield to other parties who could carry the flag of democracy into areas where darkness presently prevails.[127]

A few weeks later, in August 2005, Kadirgamar, a Tamil and a national leader, was assassinated, allegedly by the LTTE. Assassinations and attempted assassinations of other Tamil leaders followed. Ketheswaran Loganathan, deputy director of the national government's Peace Secretariat and a former member of the separatist EPRLF was killed in August 2006 and Douglas Devananda, leader of the EPDP managed to escape several attempts on his life by suicide bombers.[128] In effect, the CFA had become a dead letter.

A sophisticated terrorist organization

During the three years of the CFA, the LTTE established a de facto regime over a large area of territory in the north and the east of Sri Lanka strengthening its 'centralised, hierarchical organization' and its 'strategic position'. It had created one of the most sophisticated terrorist organizations in the world and emerged as one of 'the most dangerous' international terrorist organizations.[129] In addition to contributions from the Tamil diaspora and siphoned funds, the Tamil Tigers raised funds from a host of legitimate businesses. As *Jane's Intelligence Review* reported:

> Through its licit and illicit businesses and fronts, the Tamil Tigers generate an estimated USD200 to 300 million per year. After accounting for its estimated USD8 million per year of costs within the LTTE-administered Sri Lanka, the profit margin of its operating budget would likely be the envy of any multinational corporation.[130]

The financial largess has allowed the LTTE to purchase advanced weaponry for its military struggle. It has also allowed it to pursue a sophisticated propaganda campaign on electronic, print and other media and try to portray itself 'as a genuine national liberation' movement despite its continued terrorist activities.[131]

The LTTE's success in marketing its separatist cause was based not only on its sophisticated ideological strategy but also its strategic use of money to buy influence. Its vast financial resources allowed the LTTE to lobby lawmakers in western democracies by financing their election campaigns.[132] It is reported that three members of the US House of Representatives received financial support from LTTE front organizations. Through the TRO, the LTTE reportedly financed Congressmen Brad Sherman of California, a member of the powerful House Foreign Affairs Committee, who has consistently called for removal of the LTTE from the US list of international terrorist organizations and supported the creation of a separate Tamil state in Sri Lanka. Congressman Danny Davis of Illinois has admitted accepting a junket from the Federation of Tamil Sangams of North America (FeTNA), linked to the LTTE, for a trip to the LTTE stronghold in Wanni in Sri Lanka in 2005. Congressman Rush Holt of New Jersey, who has received money from the TRO coordinator in New Jersey, has 'actively touted the "Tamil homeland" concept', criticized the Sri Lankan government for human rights violations, and called for international intervention in Sri Lanka. The same TRO coordinator in New Jersey was listed as an approved fund solicitor for Senator Hilary Clinton's presidential campaign until questions were raised about LTTE infiltration, leading to removal of his name from the Clinton campaign website.[133] Influential professionals, such as, former US assistant attorney general Bruce Fein have been hired to lobby for the 'Deproscription of the LTTE, and Statehood for Tamils in the island of Sri Lanka'.[134] Tamils for Justice, believed to be an LTTE proxy organization estimates costs of its 'Bruce Fein Project' to be US$90,000 for the first three months and US$180,000 for the second phase of six months, if the project continues. Tamils for Justice openly raises contributions for this project on its Internet website.[135]

While Norway was facilitating the peace process in Sri Lanka, several of its government officials were found to have accepted bribes from the LTTE in return for information, passports, weapons, and services to the LTTE. In Thailand, three LTTE sympathizers were arrested for attempting to bribe Thai police officers.[136] As NAT says, 'What worries us is not is not all those who have been arrested, but those that still are on the LTTE payment. How many .. . politicians, police, bureaucrats and military personnel [globally] are on the LTTE payment list?'[137]

Clearly the Sri Lankan separatist war is not merely a primordial domestic conflict between the Sinhala majority and the Tamil minority. It is a highly sophisticated and globalized conflict. It benefits a handful of powerful individuals internationally while the people of Sri Lanka – Tamil, Sinhala, and Muslim, and especially the poorer classes and castes – suffer immeasurably. Failure of the CFA contributed to the defeat of Wickramasinghe in the November 2005 election and the appointment of populist SLFP leader Mahinda Rajapakse as President albeit with the narrowest of margins.

Return to war

Although the international press dubbed him as 'hawkish', upon coming into power, Rajapakse immediately affirmed his commitment to a negotiated political settlement with the LTTE. But the LTTE found excuses against negotiations and increased its terrorist activities. It accused the Sri Lankan government of using the Karuna group against it and demanded that the Sri Lankan government disband the Karuna group. In the meantime, the LTTE increased its unprovoked attacks against civilians and government security personnel. Deputy Army Commander Parami Kulatunga was killed and Army Commander Sarath Fonseka was severely injured by a pregnant suicide bomber. Sinhala civilians in so-called 'border areas' such as Kebethigollawa were brutally massacred. When the LTTE blocked access to water for Sinhala and Muslims farmers at Mavil Aru in the east targeting the Trincomalee harbor in February 2006, the government initiated a full-scale military offensive, recapturing areas in the east that had fallen into LTTE hands. Currently the government is pursuing a hard-line strategy to oust the LTTE from the north and to rout out LTTE terrorism once and for all.[138]

The government formally abrogated the CFA in 18 January 2008 and the Norwegian and SLMM monitors left the country.

There is a growing acceptance, except among those who tend to identify terrorism with Tamil grievances, that there can be no peace negotiations without eliminating the international LTTE network. In recent months there have been increased international vigilance and crack-downs on LTTE illegal financial networks and arms procurement in the US. In August 2006, 13 people connected with the LTTE, including a Tamil doctor, were arrested in New York for, among other things, attempting to use LTTE front organizations, including the TRO, to bribe US State Department officials. In 2007, four LTTE agents, including three foreign nationals, were arrested in Baltimore for attempting to illegally export arms for the LTTE.[139] In 2008 the United States froze the financial assets of the TRO, and the FBI issued a statement declaring the LTTE to be among 'the most dangerous and deadly extremists in the world'.[140]

Repeated attempts by Sri Lankan governments to negotiate with the LTTE have failed and resulted in the appeasement of LTTE terrorism, which poses a grave threat to life and liberty of all Sri Lankans regardless of ethnicity. The current Sri Lankan government has pledged to negotiate a federal administrative framework within a unitary Sri Lanka. Eelam IV is currently going on and the future is unknown. What is known, however, is that as long as separatist struggles persists even after possible demise of the LTTE, there will not be peace in Sri Lanka.

9 Globalization and conflict resolution

Separatism or pluralism?

As this book goes to press in the spring of 2008, there is a drumbeat in some quarters for a renewed international intervention on behalf of Tamil separatism and the division of the country – a result, should it occur, that would not bring peace and reconciliation. Rather, it would undermine the very strength of Sri Lankan history and Sri Lankan society – its inherent multiculturalism. To understand why a divided Sri Lanka would be a calamity, it is necessary to set the conflict in its global setting.

Globalization and conflict

Despite its promises of prosperity and democracy, the current phase of neo-liberal globalization is deepening worldwide social and economic inequalities. The global South, where 80 percent of the global population live, has access to about 15 percent of the global wealth.[1] Transnational corporations and powerful countries are acquiring global resources and advancing economically while at the same time debt, poverty, and strife are increasing in the global South. The Congo, for example, is rich in mineral resources yet utterly poor and stricken by war; an estimated 5.4 million people there have died over the past decade in a so-called protracted local conflict that has received little global media coverage.[2] Lacking education and other opportunities, the vast pool of young unemployed in the South (and increasingly in the North) must survive in any way they can in the informal or 'shadow' economy. 'Complex emergencies' resulting from the confluence of poverty, environmental destruction, and war are increasing refugee populations across the world. Many are displaced in their own lands due to so-called ethnic and religious conflicts which are largely the result of the forces of globalization.[3]

Even the meager social welfare services once provided by governments, such as those in Sri Lanka, have been dismantled by the structural adjustment, privatization, and other policies imposed by the IMF, World Bank, and western governments.[4] As the state has been displaced from its socio-economic functions, it has been reduced to an institution of patronage and corruption and a vehicle for maintaining law and order. And even that role is threatened in many countries by the privatization of security and maintenance of law and order and the rise of armed militias and criminal gangs. As economic crises worsen, ethnic cleavages sharpen, escalating into civil wars and separatist struggles.[5] Besieged states come to rely more and more on militarism and purchase of weapons from arms-exporting countries. Many international terrorist organizations, such as the LTTE, FARC in Colombia, and Hezbollah in Lebanon, have also become massive importers and exporters of weapons. They also engage in burgeoning global black market activities like human smuggling, narcotics, and money laundering, as well as legal activities such as retail business and the stock market, to raise funds for their military and ideological campaigns.

The arms trade is a lucrative business, perhaps even the most lucrative business in the global economy.[6] Even countries like Norway, considered to be global peacemakers, are involved in this nefarious business, just as the intelligence agencies of military powers further the arms trade and war by providing training to warring factions in local conflicts: Israeli Mossad has allegedly given training simultaneously to both Sri Lankan soldiers and LTTE cadres.[7] The failure of western democracies to curb the illegal export of weapons by diaspora groups has also contributed to intensification of wars in places like Sri Lanka.[8] Primordial arguments – that the conflicts are centuries old and inevitable – aside, without the proliferation of weapons, especially small arms that are manufactured and sold by a range of countries, cultural tensions and conflicts in the world would not be as bloody as they are today. In regions beset by war, guns are more readily available than food, even to children. Children raised in poverty and in a global culture of violence are susceptible to becoming child soldiers. This is sadly the case in Sri Lanka and many other Asian and African countries.[9] As long as militarism remains the growth sector of the global economy and weapons proliferate, it will be difficult to bring peace to Sri Lanka or the world.

The frustration and anger of the world's poor – the surplus population – provide fertile soil for mobilizing resentment. Today the response to oppression does not take the form of class struggle as predicted by Marx but along ethno-religious or cultural lines as defined by local and international 'ethnic entrepreneurs'. Individuals feeling alienated and marginalized are amenable to movements that promise a sense of community and social betterment by directing their anger and aggression against the religious or ethnic Other. The ensuing so-called ethno-religious conflicts create massive violence, death, and destruction, even genocide, that threaten human life and security around the world.[10]

As former British Prime Minister Tony Blair has put it, 'acts of genocide can never be a purely internal matter'.[11] Indeed, the international community has a moral responsibility to protect people whose lives are threatened by dire circumstances. It is necessary to remember, however, that international intervention has been responsible for many so-called ethno-religious conflicts, death, and destruction around the world. The Sri Lankan Tamil dissident Mutukrishana Sarvanathan has articulated a perspective widely held in the global South:

> Most of the dictators, extremist governments, and violent anti-government movements in the Third World have been protégés of one of the governments of the Western World. Ayatollah Khomeini who established the

Islamic Republic of Iran against which the entire Western World is waging a proxy war today, was France's protégé. Saddam Hussein was a protégé of many Western Governments including the USA. The United States sponsored the Mujahedin in Afghanistan that created the Taliban regime. All the foregoing extremist governments/forces have bitten the hands that once fed them. Moreover, dubious roles played by Western Governments in other countries' conflicts have now begun to nurture indigenous extremist/violent forces within their own countries (Britain is a prime example).[12]

Approaches that focus merely on surface manifestations of conflict and limited views of human rights and minority grievances do not help in finding lasting solutions. Rather, it is important to understand how the increasingly powerful 'global civil society' sector and human rights advocacy networks promote international intervention as the solution to domestic conflicts – and how they can exacerbate, rather than mitigate, conflict.

Global civil society: the third sector

The proliferation of conflicts in the post-Cold War period and the privatization of peace and security have expanded the roles of INGOs and NGOs in situations of conflict.[13] As globalization has weakened states and dismantled many of their economic and social service functions, a plethora of non-state actors – INGOs and NGOs, including faith-based organizations – have stepped into fill the vacuum. Referred to as an independent 'third sector' (separate from the state and the market), or the 'global civil society', these organizations are seen by many as an impartial moral force holding states accountable to international norms against violation of citizens' rights, especially those of ethnic minorities. But their role in Sri Lanka has not been so benign.

The 'Boomerang Pattern' conceptualized by Margaret Keck and Kathryn Sikkink has become useful in understanding the dynamics of transnational advocacy networking and political entrepreneurship.[14] It illustrates how local interest groups can enter the 'globalized political space', mobilize international support, and then turn that pressure back on their own local governments in order to further their causes. In effect, international organizations then become allies of one side in a conflict, not neutral participants. Keck and Sikkink write:

> When channels between the state and its domestic actors are blocked, the boomerang pattern of influence characteristic of transnational networks may occur: domestic NGOs bypass their state and directly search for international allies to try to bring pressure on their states from the outside. This is most obviously the case in human rights campaigns … Linkages are important for both sides: for the less powerful third world actors, networks provide access, leverage, and information (and often money)…, for the northern groups, they make credible the assertion that they are struggling with, and not only for, their southern partners.[15]

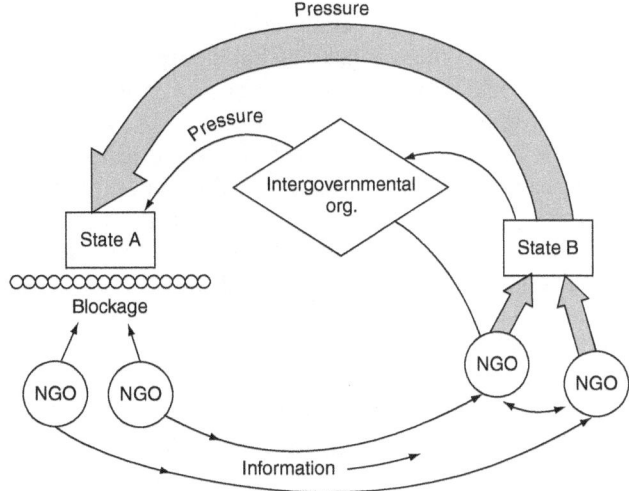

Figure 9.1 Boomerang pattern (source: Margaret E. Keck and Kathryn Sikkink, *Activists Beyond Borders: Advocacy Networks in International Politics*, Inthaca: Cornell University Press, 1998, p. 13).

Transnational advocacy networks that place human rights on the global policy agenda are widely seen as fitting a simple model: they are a force of global democratization and humanitarianism opposing repression and authoritarianism. Analyses of their organizational structures and operational procedures reveal, however, that international CSOs (civil society organizations) are 'not hampered by cumbersome democratic deliberations'.[16] As John Clark has pointed out, CSOs are not generally founded on a broad-based membership or participation; their organizational structures are 'generally vertical'. For example, Human Rights Watch, established in 1988, is a 'highly centralized, US NGO with specialist sections (Americas Watch, Asia Watch, Africa Watch, among others) and global reach'.[17] Lack of accountability and transparency allow influential, wealthy Northern NGOs to dominate their Southern affiliates and also allow southern NGOs, with 'virtually no grassroots base' to 'emerge as authorities in their field'.[18] Many of the NGOs in the peace and security sector in Sri Lanka have reproduced the hierarchical authoritarian structures of operation.[19]

Despite their lack of accountability and the contradictions in the mission of 'transnational democracy', INGOs have emerged as 'a significant source of change in international politics' and highly influential in the redefinition of sovereignty, the key organizing principle in the international system.[20] However, as Keck and Sikkink, who are themselves proponents of transnational advocacy networking, acknowledge, the selective use of international pressure and 'targeting' of weak states over others leads to serious questions about the neutrality and motivation behind international intervention on human rights grounds.[21]

Transnational human rights activism is not always a democratic humanitarian force. It can be used by dominant powers to advance their global political and economic hegemony. It can be manipulated by politically savvy, financially powerful, non-state actors, including terrorist groups, to bring pressure on democratically elected, but relatively weak, governments to advance their own questionable objectives. When the boomerang effect is directed against states with relatively little international leverage, as has been done in Sri Lanka, it can undermine local democracies and strengthen authoritarian and even terrorist forces. In other words, the 'global civil society' is not inherently a democratic force. The internationalization of conflicts in weak states such as Sri Lanka need to be understood in the context of an expanding neo-liberal economic agenda with which the global society sector is identified. In *Democracy Makers*, Nicolas Guilhot argues that the movement for global democracy and human rights has been appropriated by the US government, the World Bank, NGOs, think tanks, and other well-placed international organizations collaborating, intentionally and coincidentally, to export neoliberal economic policies around the world. Guilhot also says that the repudiation of Marxism and class analysis by the liberal left wing, especially after end of Cold War, has contributed to their embrace of a narrowly conceptualized human rights paradigm that has become aligned with maintaining the global status quo.[22] Indeed, in many parts of the world, the human rights and conflict-resolution NGOs are seen as lucrative 'industries', bringing together local and global elite class interests. Some critics in the global South have criticized them outright as 'human rights imperialism'.[23]

Looking at transnational advocacy from yet another important political-economic angle, Clifford Bob argues that it is not the groups with the most legitimate grievances who are able to make use of transnational networking to further their causes. Rather, it is the groups who are best able to 'market' themselves who succeed in obtaining INGO support and global media attention to advance their causes.[24] Well-financed terrorist groups, like the Tamil Tigers, who are the very oppressors of people they claim to represent, are able to present themselves as their liberators by winning support of international networks and powerful individuals. Thus elite ethno-class agendas can be presented as mass-based grievances even when they are contrary to the interests of the poor. Privatization of conflict resolution and international intervention in crisis regions by INGOs and NGOs has contributed to what Mark Duffield has called a 'new form of imperialism'.[25] The intervention of the International Alert in the conflicts in Sierra Leone and Sri Lanka has come under severe criticism in this regard, for alleged support of a coup in the former and active support for Tamil separatism in the latter.[26] In many places, partisan international intervention prevails even in the provision of aid, and has become a factor in exacerbating rather than alleviating inter-group conflicts.[27]

There is increasing global concern that protests rooted in real local causes is being replaced by NGOs employing highly paid professionals. These externally funded organizations, which lack transparency and accountability to local people, have taken on the power to 'judge' what causes are fair and just – and, further, to judge even democratically elected governments, for example, in Sri Lanka – all under the mantle of seeming to be unbiased and objective. But the 'global civil society' does not necessarily represent an independent political realm. Many of the INGOs have been created by, and work in close collaboration with, the governments and intergovernmental organizations that fund and direct them including the World Bank and United Nations agencies. There is a frequent rotation of personnel at the highest levels, not only between the state and civil society but also the corporate sector.[28] Given the dominant tendency of civil society organizations to interpret most local conflicts as ethnic problems, Indian political scientist Bhupinder Brar asks if 'the essentialization of ethnic groups is not a way of addressing and approaching them over the heads of states in which they are located'. Brar has called upon post-colonial societies to 'understand the "ethnic" dimension of their societies and politics from a perspective of their own' rather than from the colonial perspective of western social science.[29]

Many in the global South fear that the money and political weight behind transnational activism is further weakening poor countries whose economies and states have already been weakened by neo-liberal globalization. It is in this context that the radical charge that the Washington Consensus is simultaneously promoting global economic integration and global political fragmentation needs to be considered.[30] The argument here is that political disintegration creates more markets, thereby allowing greater external political control of local societies. In a recent article in the *Financial Times* (UK), Gideon Rachman celebrates the proliferation of new nation-states (from 45 in 1945 to 192 member states in the United Nations in 2007) as representing the emergence of more markets and more manageable political entities.[31] Conflict analysis built on the assumption of primordial hatred and conflict resolution based on the inevitability of separatism and partition divert attention from the increasing concentration of the global economy in the hands of transnational corporate interests. In the past, colonial powers pursued policies of 'divide and conquer', exacerbating, if not actually creating, local ethno-religious conflicts to meet their hegemonic needs. The continent of Africa is currently divided into some 50 separate countries, many of them rife with ethno-religious and secessionist conflicts fought by poor youth, many of them child soldiers. This internal division allows external interests to more easily control Africa's vast natural resources. Likewise, the proposed dismemberment of Iraq into three separate Shiite, Sunni, and Kurd ethno-nationalist states, it is commonly believed, is motivated by the interest of the US and its allies in gaining easier access to the Middle East and its vast oil resources.[32]

Some extraordinary situations may require partition as a solution to civil conflict. Yet, it is necessary to question if new concepts and programs, such as the UN Responsibility to Protect (R2P) program and the discipline of 'partition studies' are forces of democracy and humanitarianism or forces of global–local elite collusion for dismembering the world into smaller and weaker political units. The growing political fragmentation may allow powerful nations to maintain global control and local minority elites to become rulers of new mini-states. But current experiences of intervention and partition show that they do not necessarily lead to protection of human rights or the broader political-economic interests of the masses of people across the ethnic divides.

Intervention, partition, sovereignty

There is a growing sentiment in the international community that the idea that state sovereignty is inviolable, a concept that dates back to the treaties of Westphalia of 1648, is no longer viable in the current era of globalization.[33] In setting up a permanent UN international court to try war criminals, former United Nations Secretary General Kofi Annan declared in 1998 that 'state frontiers should no longer be seen as water-tight protection for war criminals and mass murderers'.[34] International humanitarian intervention is applauded by its proponents as a 'long overdue internationalization of the human conscience'. Reflecting on 'prospects for human security and intervention' in the twenty-first century, Annan, in his Millennium Report to the General Assembly in 2000, posed this question: 'If humanitarian intervention is, indeed, an unacceptable assault on sovereignty, how should we respond to a Rwanda, to a Srebrenica – to gross and systematic violations of human rights that offend every precept of our common humanity?'[35]

Today, the international community – that is, the powerful western countries, the United Nations, and the NGOs – are the final arbiters in contests over self-determination and sovereignty.[36] There's no doubt that the international community has strong influence, and UN decisions on humanitarian intervention get worked out through exertion of political influence. Critics fear that the new moral paradigm for human protection in the new millennium represents 'an alarming breach' of the United Nations Charter, which upholds 'sovereignty of states and the inviolability of their territory'.[37] The December 2001 'Report of the International Commission on Intervention and State Sovereignty', which advocated the 'right of humanitarian intervention' and the principle referred to as 'Responsibility to Protect' (R2P) stated:

> What has been gradually emerging is a parallel transition from a culture of sovereign impunity to a culture of national and international accountability. International organizations, civil society activists and NGOs use the international human rights norms and instruments as the concrete point of reference against which to judge state conduct. Between them, the UN and NGOs have achieved many successes.[38]

Undeniably, international humanitarian intervention may be necessary in certain cases to stop state excesses and repression. But, as critics ask, 'Is R2P simply a new name for the right to intervene?'[39] Indeed, what are the criteria for intervention? Who makes the decisions? What makes a state a 'failed state' requiring external intervention? Who holds non-state actors responsible to international humanitarian laws at a time when their financial power is growing and their violence – terrorism – is becoming an increasing threat to peace and security everywhere? International non-intervention in desperate situations, such as Rwanda in 1994 and Srebrenica in 1993 and Darfur more recently has cast doubt on the United Nations' moral authority and shown that intervention is not based on objective or neutral criteria. There is a sense that human rights and humanitarian intervention will continue to be used by the North as a weapon against targeted states, like Sri Lanka, especially in the global South. Security Council resolutions notwithstanding, international intervention can provide the basis for unilateral declaration of independence leading to dismemberment of existing states and international recognition of separate states, as seems to be happening in Kosovo right now.[40]

Self-determination

Just as R2P, backed by a combination of powerful countries, NGOs, and the United Nations, is redefining the concept of sovereignty, the concept of self-determination too is undergoing a similar transformation. The concept of self-determination first arose in the American and French revolutions to uphold the principles of individual liberty and freedom. In western Europe, self-determination was originally identified with popular sovereignty and representative government.[41] The United Nations Charter, the first international document to uphold the right of self-determination, applied the right to member *states* and not to *peoples or groups*, thus upholding the sovereignty and territorial integrity of member states and the principle of non-intervention. The 1960 UN Declaration Granting Independence to Colonial Peoples applied the right of self-determination to colonies, basing it on territory rather than ethnicity or nationality. It is only more recently that the 'right of self-determination' has come to be associated with distinct ethnic groups and peoples, although what that means remains 'unclear' and 'highly controversial'.[42] Unlike western Europe in the past, in Central and Eastern Europe and many areas of the global South today, self-determination has come to be rooted 'in an exclusive nationalism' that encourages ethnic groups to seek their own separate states.[43] Political scientist Eric Brahm has pointed out:

> Self-determination in international law takes two primary forms. One part is the developing human rights law, which is predicated on the notion of giving individuals more control over their lives. The other part, which is more contentious, involves groups that make claims to establish independent sovereign states … This conflicts with the long-standing understanding that international borders are inviolable. Legally self-determination has generally been confined to the level of the state. Empirically those movements that utilize violence and succeed tend to be recognized, thereby spreading the message that violence pays.[44]

The confluence of terrorism, minority nationalisms, and international intervention is leading to political fragmentation of the world into more and more ethnically homogeneous units and states. The dismemberment of nation-states is based on the primordialist assumption that partition is the only solution to the security dilemma and that minorities will be victimized or even face genocide unless they are physically separated.[45] Certainly, in some cases like Rwanda and Cambodia during the Pol Pot regime, international intervention should have occurred to save millions of lives. Failure to intervene in such horrific situations calls into question the very criteria for intervention in conflict situations. Is the determining factor the extent and level of human suffering? Or is it the political influence of secessionists and other interested parties? Partition has rarely been a sustainable solution; many so-called successor states, like Pakistan, Serbia, and East Timor, have had to face their own minority problems and secessionist movements.

What US political scientist Milton Esman pointed out over 30 years ago still holds true: 'The conflict regulation potential of territorial autonomy [is limited] when territorial units ... make extravagant and even incompatible demands ... which the polity cannot accommodate, thus escalating rather than regulating conflict'.[46] Chaim Kaufmann, leading proponent of partition as solution to ethnic conflict, agrees that 'Political partition without ethnic separation leaves incentives for ethnic cleansing unchanged; it actually increases them if it creates new minorities'.[47] In criticizing partition as a solution to ethnic conflict, Yale political economist Nicolas Sambanis has pointed out more recently that the important issues of 'partition theory' remain unresolved: What are the determinants of partition? Does partition create democratic/undemocratic states? Does it prevent recurrence of war? Does it end low-grade ethnic violence?[48] To these must be added the questions raised by other critics of partition theory, like Timothy Sisk, who have asked: Does rearranging majorities and minorities solve the problem in multi-ethnic societies? Who is the genuine representative of any group?[49]

In seeking answers to those questions, it is important to bear in mind the questions posed by the Report of the International Commission on Intervention and State Sovereignty, the original report creating the R2P principle. With regard to the controversial NATO intervention in Kosovo, it asks: 'Was the cause just: were the human rights abuses committed or threatened by Belgrade authorities sufficiently serious to warrant outside involvement? Did those seeking secession manipulate external intervention to advance their political purposes?'[50] These questions are, of course, highly relevant to Sri Lanka, which is currently facing massive external pressure – the full boomerang effect – to accept international intervention in response to human rights charges against the government.

The Sri Lankan case

The conflict in Sri Lanka is not a simple one. Any discussion of ethno-regional separatism as the solution must consider the growing calls for partition and

Tamil regional autonomy as well as the basic realities pertaining to human rights, demography and democracy.

Human rights: basis for intervention

Victory over LTTE terrorism, or global terrorism for that matter, is not assured. But at the time of this writing, in April 2008, the Sri Lankan government is winning the military battle against the LTTE despite the sentiment that prevailed until recently that the war is 'unwinnable'.[51] But like terrorism, the human cost of the war is heavy, and there is legitimate concern that the government's war on terror is begetting state terror.

There have been human rights violations on the part of successive Sri Lankan governments against both the Sinhala JVP and Tamil insurgent youth. Current charges of human rights violations of suspected LTTE members and supporters need to be taken seriously. In the case of the Sinhala insurgents in the 1970s and 1980s, there was relatively little, if any, support from the international human rights lobby, and the depredations against them went largely unreported. JVP leader, Somwansa Amerasinghe reminded visiting United Nations High Commissioner for Human Rights, Louise Arbour in October 2007,

> In 1989 more than hundred thousand [sic] citizens of this country were murdered ... We wrote to the UNO then. However, we didn't see any response from the UNO regarding that suppression. At least there wasn't even a statement made. The UNO can't have double standards.[52]

However, because of the ethnic interpretation of the Sri Lankan separatist struggle and the global movement supporting it, the human rights violations by successive Sri Lankan governments in the case of the Tamil insurgency has received enormous international attention. Since resumption of the armed conflict in February 2006, the government has been accused of the displacement and killing of civilians, abductions, disappearances, torture, media restrictions, and other fundamental rights violations.[53] The still unresolved killing of 17 humanitarian aid workers in a fierce battle between the government forces and Tamil Tigers in Muttur in August 2006, in particular, has caused severe condemnation of the government.[54] Against this backdrop, the international community has demanded that the government stop the military offensive and return to the negotiating table. The call for international intervention, specifically by a United Nations human rights field operation in Sri Lanka, is growing louder.[55]

While the government is refusing the presence of a United Nations human rights field operation in Sri Lanka, it has been open to visits by the International Independent Group of Eminent Persons (IIGEP), a group of 20 world leaders acting in their personal capacities, and a stream of high-powered UN and other international officials to investigate the human rights situation. The UN investigators have included Special Representative of the UN Under-Secretary for Children in Armed Conflict, Allan Rock (November 2006); UN Special

Rapporteur on Extra-Judicial Execution, Philip Alston (November 2006); UN Under-Secretary General for Humanitarian Affairs Sir John Holmes (January 2007); UN Special Rapporteur on Torture, Manfred Nowak (August–September 2007); the United Nations High Commissioner for Human Rights, Louise Arbour (September 2007), Assistant Secretary-General for Political Affairs, Angela Kane (February 2008).[56] Rock charged that both the LTTE and the LTTE break-away Karuna group were conscripting child soldiers, the latter under the patronage of the Sri Lankan armed forces.[57] Holmes stated that Sri Lanka is 'one of the most dangerous places for humanitarian workers', and Nowak reported routine use of torture by security forces to extract confessions.[58] Arbour called for ways to expand the mission of the Office of the High Commission for Human Rights (OHCHR) and to allow it an independent presence in Sri Lanka.[59] There have also been numerous human rights charges by western diplomatic missions in Colombo. The ambassadors of Germany, the UK, USA, and other countries have called on the government to cease hostilities against the LTTE and to introduce extensive regional devolution as the solution to the conflict.[60] Some international aid to Sri Lanka has been cut; for example, the US Congress passed the Leahy Amendment in October 2007, prohibiting sale or transfer of military equipment and technology from the US to Sri Lanka on human rights grounds.[61]

The government challenged Allan Rock's charge that it was aiding child conscription, pointing out that the Karuna group was not a creation of the government but of the LTTE. Sri Lankan and sections of diaspora media alleged that Rock, a Canadian politician, was connected to an LTTE group in Canada and blamed the UN Under-Secretary for Children and Armed Conflict, Radhika Coomaraswamy, for sending Rock in a calculated attempt to take attention away from the LTTE and focus on the Karuna faction and Sri Lankan armed forces.[62] Reports of UNICEF involvement with TRO activities also prompted the GOSL to request clarification from UNICEF recently.[63]

Responding to the highly critical US State Department's 2007 Country Report on Human Rights (USCR), the Sri Lankan government issued a report pointing out that USCR failed to deal with LTTE terrorism and violations in 'sufficient detail', such as the LTTE's requirement that each family in areas under its control give up one child to the terrorist cadre and the massive human rights violation it represents.[64] The government further argued that the USCR has distorted the actual human rights situation by errors, exaggerations, and unsubstantiated allegations.[65]

Disputing the USCR charges, the Sri Lankan government report pointed out that there is extensive press freedom in the country and that there is a 'domination of the news media by private news agencies' in print, radio and television and in all three languages (Sinhala, Tamil and English).[66] Many of these media outlets are opposed to the government and publish reports highly critical of the government. Responding to an attack on a Christian place of worship by 'Buddhist extremists' cited in the USCR, the Sri Lankan government report pointed to the extensive religious freedom allowed in the Sri Lankan Constitution, including the freedom to proselytize. It noted that minority religious groups have more places of religious worship than the majority per capita. Buddhists, Hindus, Muslims and Christians are 70 percent, 15 percent, 8 percent, and 7 percent of the island's total population, respectively; the number of their places of religious worship are 59 percent, 23 percent, 11 percent, and 7 percent of the total.[67]

With regard to disappearances, the Sri Lankan government report stated that the USCR had relied on 'politically motivated' and exaggerated claims of NGOs and other parties and that the USCR failed to acknowledge the 'downward trend in disappearances and killings in government-controlled areas during the second and third quarter of 2007', as reported by an international agency 'reputed for its impartiality'.[68] With regard to a list of 355 cases of disappearances given to the Sri Lankan authorities by the US Ambassador in Sri Lanka in April 2007 and reported in the USCR, the government, responded that:

> 5 names had been duplicated. 6 persons ... have left Sri Lanka or have applied for passports after the dates of their alleged disappearances. 24 persons have been traced, including a couple that had eloped! ... 4 persons have been found to have died. The inquiries into their deaths are continuing. 3 persons have been arrested by the law enforcement authorities. 106 cases had never been reported to the Police and the US Ambassador was requested to furnish more details. Such details have not been received to date, even though almost a year has lapsed. As for the rest, the Disappearance Investigation Unit of the Police is continuing its investigation with the assistance of the relevant local Police Stations ... one NGO included among the 'disappeared', six Sri Lankan security personnel who had been killed by an LTTE bomb, where their names were altered to resemble those of Tamils.[69]

The Sri Lankan government has undertaken a number of initiatives in response to human rights concerns, such as the appointments of the Presidential Commission on Abduction, Disappearances and Killings (the Tillekeratne Commission), the Ministry of Disaster Management and Human Rights, a police commission, and special police units for enforcement of human rights.[70] In its response to the 2007 USCR, the government pointed out that over 200 indictments have been served against some 700 members of the police and security forces for alleged human rights violations.[71] In a separate response, the government pointed out that the mission of the IIGEP failed because their European assistants had a hidden 'political agenda' to prove that the Sri Lankan government was at fault.[72] GOSL underlined the observation of Nowak, UN special rapporteur on torture that:

> Notwithstanding the difficult security situation the Government is faced with, Sri Lanka ... is still able to uphold its democratic principles, ensure activities of civil society organizations and media, and maintain an independent judiciary.[73]

The Sri Lankan government has argued that instead of worsening the island's conflict, its abrogation of the ineffective CFA has allowed the democratic political process to move forward and hold free elections in the East after nearly two decades. The government reports that the former LTTE faction led by Karuna and Pillayian has entered mainstream democratic politics as the TMVP and that provincial council elections will be held in May 2008, which would result in the implementation of the 13th Amendment to the constitution as a political settlement to the conflict.[74] The international community needs to support Sri Lanka's efforts to defeat terrorism and advance local democracy. If not, in the current context of decreasing western economic aid to Sri Lanka and much of the global South, western moral authority would have to be asserted more and more by threat of intervention. This in turn would make targeted countries like Sri Lanka increasingly dependent on military and financial support from China and Middle Eastern Muslim countries further shifting the geopolitical realities in Asia and the world.

This is not to deny that the Sri Lankan government, like all governments and non-state actors, must be held accountable to human rights and democratic norms. A culture of impurity must not be tolerated and the rule of law and good governance must be encouraged to the greatest extent possible. Still, it is necessary to consider the questions being posed by many people in Sri Lanka as to whether the human rights situation is being 'grossly exaggerated' by external forces in order to establish a UN monitoring mission and 'undermine the sovereignty of our nation'.[75] The neutrality of the United Nations is being questioned in light of attempts to enforce the R2P principle in Sri Lanka. Colonel Anil Amarasekara, a Sri Lankan nationalist, expressed the growing concern in the country over UN intervention as proposed by the Canadian (former) head of the UN Human Rights Commission:

> The UN agencies are also surreptitiously infiltrated by western nations and used to further their vested interests. On their recommendations a UN Peacekeeping Force is then deployed in a country where internal disputes are often even created by western nations. The situation in that country is then manipulated to achieve the interests of the western nations. The use of a UN Peacekeeping Force in Serbia and the recognition of the independence of Kosovo, by the western nations is a good example of this type of modus operandi. The UN itself is made a silent witness sans any protests, while smaller and weaker nations are thus dismembered.[76]

The INGOs, western governments, and multilateral organizations must take a critical look at its assumptions and answer several questions:

- Does the level of human rights violations in Sri Lanka warrant the kind of international intervention demanded by the UN High Commissioner for Human Rights, Human Rights Watch, and the proponent of R2P?
- How can local human rights monitors and mechanisms be strengthened

instead of calling for international intervention, which has failed repeatedly in Sri Lanka under the Indians, the Norwegians, and the Scandinavian Monitoring Mission?

- Is there a future for the country and the region without the elimination of LTTE terrorism?
- What does the international community expect the government to do in the face of relentless suicide bombings and political assassinations by the LTTE?
- Does it genuinely believe that it is possible to negotiate with the LTTE?
- Why is there a double standard on human rights?

It is interesting to note that while UN rapporteur Nowak was allowed free access to prisons and detention centers throughout Sri Lanka, he has been refused access to US prisons operating in Iraq, even after reports that conditions there had improved following the Abu Ghraib incidents.[77] These developments raise questions about the politicization of human rights and the extent to which the call for international intervention in Sri Lanka is manipulated by the international lobby for Tamil separatism.

Ignoring the grave threat to life, liberty, and human rights posed by the LTTE, 'the most ruthless terrorist organization in the world', supporters of the Tamil Tigers, moderate Tamils, and the local and international peace lobby are demanding urgent United Nations intervention to end 'genocide' of Tamils and the 'ethnic conflict' in Sri Lanka. The Swedish academic Peter Schalk, a long-time supporter of the LTTE, is demanding that the EU

[C]onsider the development of East Timor and ask … whether it is not the plight of the UN to intervene militarily and create a situation of two states [in Sri Lanka] with borders at the time of the Cease Fire Agreement in 2003.[78]

In the US, influential US attorney Bruce Fein, hired by the LTTE, congressmen Brad Sherman and Rush Holt, and other representatives who have allegedly received money from LTTE front organizations also call for a two-state solution for Sri Lanka[79] In the UK, members of the British All Party Parliamentary Group for Tamils headed by Keith Vaz and including Andrew Pelling, and others who are said to be dependent on Tamil diaspora votes and money, are also supporting a Tamil separate state in Sri Lanka.[80] Meanwhile it is reported that 'under what is called the "UK Peace Building Strategy"' the British High Commission in Sri Lanka is operating a 'monitoring centre' (for intelligence gathering on a daily basis) in the Eastern Province, 'without prior consent of the government of Sri Lanka'. The centre is said to be 'a network of support to local NGOs (many of which are known to be infiltrated by the LTTE)'.[81]

Global civil society is playing a major role in setting the stage for intervention. In the annual Neelan Tiruchelvam Memorial Lecture at the ICES in Colombo in July 2007, Gareth Evans, an Australian politician and head of the influential International Crisis Group (ICG) and one of the leading promoters of the R2P concept, warned that on-going events in Sri Lanka made international intervention a likely possibility. ICG and its reports have played an instrumental role in the secession of Kosovo.[82] In November 2007, ICG issued a report attributing the Sri Lankan conflict exclusively to 'Sinhala nationalism and the elusive southern consensus', ignoring LTTE terrorism and all other dimensions of the complex situation.[83] Evans' warning was widely seen as part of a 'well planned scheme' to make the ICES an affiliate of the New York Center for Responsibility to Protect, which promotes R2P. In a major scandal that erupted subsequently in early 2008 over behind-the-scenes efforts to enforce the R2P principle in Sri Lanka,[84] Radhika Coomaraswamy, former director of ICES and current United Nations under-secretary general for Children in Armed Conflict and Indian national Rama Mani, director of ICES, were charged with alleged attempts to use World Bank funds to enforce the R2P principle 'without the consent of the Ministry of Constitutional Affairs and National Integration [in Sri Lanka], with which ICES has a Memorandum of Understanding'.[85] Their actions are widely interpreted as efforts to undermine the country's sovereignty and create a Kosovo-like situation. Many observers are raising the very question posed in the R2P commission report: Are 'those seeking secession [or regional autonomy] manipulat[ing] external intervention to advance their political purposes?'[86]

Partition and regional autonomy

As the LTTE is being defeated by the Sri Lankan government and the latter's hold over the Sri Lankan Tamil community is being loosened, a consensus seems to be emerging among Tamil moderates that 'We, Tamils are better off without the Tamil Tigers'. The Tamil Tigers were nurtured as part of the youth wing of the moderate TULF in the early 1970s, although the LTTE ended up killing many of the TULF leaders in opposition to what was seen as the moderates' compromises with the Sinhala governments to settle the separatist issue. Tamil militant violence helped pressure the Sri Lankan state and bring global attention to the Tamil cause. But today the LTTE appears to have outlived its usefulness, and the moderates seem ready to abandon the ruthless organization. In a recent interview, S.C. Chandrahasan, son of S.J.V. Chelvanayakam, the founder of the separatist Tamil State Party ITAK, asserts that the LTTE has become 'more of a problem rather than the solution'. Arguing that 'the LTTE not being in the picture will strengthen the Tamil side', he goes on to stress that 'the struggle will go on till justice is achieved'.[87] He does not specify if justice would require the ultimate creation of a separate state, as his father had.

Despite all the human rights charges against the Sri Lankan government, most Tamils, the so-called "silent majority', are understandably relieved to get rid of the Tamil Tigers, who are believed to have killed more Tamils than the Sri Lankan armed forces.[88] The IPKF could not free the Tamils from the LTTE, nor could the Norwegians or the SLMM. In fact, they helped to solidify the LTTE's totalitarian control over the Tamils. In that respect, the Sri Lankan security forces appear to be the liberators of Tamils from the oppressive LTTE, although there is no question that Tamil civilians are also getting killed in the government's offensive against the LTTE. The defeat of the LTTE, however, would provide the basis for a non-violent solution to the terrible conflict that has caused indescribable suffering to all communities on the island. A long-term solution requires moving beyond the narrow bipolar Sinhala versus Tamil analysis. The Tamil moderates are now able to come forward as the LTTE's totalitarian power recedes due to the Sri Lankan government's military operation. However, instead of acknowledging the complex multi-ethnic realities of the island, many of them still cling to the dualistic Sinhala versus Tamil analysis of the conflict and Tamil regional autonomy as the inevitable solution. The diaspora-based Sri Lanka Democracy Forum, for example calls for 'substantial devolution to the regions' and 'state reform', meaning Tamil regional autonomy within a federal structure, as the only way out of present dilemma.[89]

But this approach is unlikely to end the separatist conflict, even if the LTTE is completely vanquished. The contradictions in the Tamil moderate position are revealed in the January 2008 statement made by V. Ananandasangaree, the head of the TULF, on the political proposals of the APRC (All Party Representative Committee) appointed by the government to explore non-military solutions:

> TULF has formed an alliance [with PLOTE and EPRLF] in the good interest of the Tamil speaking minorities. It is no secret that we had been agitating for a solution based on the Federal concept and also offered to accept the Indian Model as an alternative if the term federal is allergic to anyone. We have not changed our views in this matter and in the matter of merger of the North and the East. We assure everybody that while spurning violence we will by non-violent means and in a friendly way continue to persuade the citizens of our country to agree that no permanent solution can be found under a Unitary System. We will continue to dispel the fears of those who think that the country will be divided. We will take all steps to erase off the minds of our people the idea of separation and to strongly support the concept of a United Sri Lanka.... We call upon the 60 million Tamils living across this strait [Palk] to give their blessings and their co-operation to bring back normalcy and peace for our people ... without being misled by a handful of LTTE Leaders on both sides. We assure the Tamils living across [Tamil Nadu], that there is no attempt by anybody to annihilate the Tamils and that contrary to that, more than half of the Tamil population is living in the South happily among the Sinhalese and the Muslims reposing confidence in them, far away from their traditional places of habitation.[90]

This statement is a reiteration of the original TULF position that gave rise to the separatist conflict and the militant violence after 1972. Its claim to speak for 'Tamil speaking minorities' is likely to aggravate Muslim separatism and balkanization of the Eastern Province. The separatist demand for the merger of the North and the East comes from the recognition that 'much of the EP would have to be administered jointly with the NP if any regionalization of power and status were to be economically viable'.[91] But this demand is unlikely to be acceptable to the majority of people in the multi-ethnic Eastern Province who did not vote for the TULF separatist platform in the 1977 elections. Ananadasangaree's call for the blessings of the Tamils in South India is a further reminder that the Sri Lankan separatist conflict is not a domestic Sinhala versus Tamil issue, but a broader South Indian phenomenon. The TULF leader does not explain why there should be a Tamil autonomous federal state or provincial unit in the north and the east when, as he admits, 'more than half the Tamil population is living in the South happily among the Sinhalese and the Muslims'.[92] What are the implications for democracy in demarcating two contradictory regional systems, an exclusive Tamil north and east and a pluralist – Tamil, Sinhala, and Muslim – south? Would such an unjust division lead to forced population transfers and the attendant horrors of partition and further ethnic polarization, conflict, and violence?

Like Chelvanayakam and the original TULF, Ananadasangaree is eschewing the violent path of armed struggle. Yet his final goal, and that of his coalition – a separate autonomous region dominated by the Sri Lankan Tamil community in the north and the east – is unlikely to bring peace. PLOTE and EPRLF, the TULF's current coalition partners, were once armed terrorist groups, and the TULF has had close relations with such armed terrorist groups in the past. As the Australian Center for Sri Lankan Unity (ACSLU) points out, these groups may 'not hesitate to revert to their old tactics if they do not get what they want by following the non-violent route'.[93] The same vicious cycle could repeat itself even after a possible defeat of the LTTE. As the examples of India, Yugoslavia, Ethiopia, and East Timor have shown, it is highly unlikely that devolution and ethnically based regional autonomy for Tamils in the north and the east would end the Sri Lankan conflict. Justus Richter has pointed out that 'partition would not solve the problem because within the supposed Tamil state, particularly in the eastern province, the Muslims constitute a strategic minority'.[94] In a paper entitled 'Dangers of Devolution', Darini Rajasingham-Senanayake also concluded that given the pluralism and complex political-economic realities in the north and east, conflict and violence are likely to continue even if regional autonomy is conceded to the Tamils. As she emphasized, devolution 'should not succumb to the ethnic enclave mentality whose logical end is ethnic cleansing and ethnic absolutism'.[95]

Would government defeat of the LTTE and enforcement of the 13th Amendment to the constitution, imposed on Sri Lanka by the Indian intervention and the Indo-Sri Lanka Accord of 1987, resolve the conflict? Or would regional autonomy envisaged in a federal political structure and the Provincial Council system provide the stepping stone for eventual separation and the creation of Eelam? Chelvanayakam, the father of Sri Lankan Tamil separatism, envisaged federalism as the gradual path to separatism, 'a little now, more later'. Regional autonomy and a UN Security Council resolution against separatism did not prevent the unilateral declaration of independence by Kosovo in February 2008. Even iron-clad guarantees against separation in a final document may not be honored if international interests coalesce to recognize a new sovereign state, as many countries, including the US and 18 out of 27 countries of the EU recognized Kosovo in less than two months after its declaration of independence. As Ladduwahetty argues, federalism could lead to a Kosovo-like scenario in Sri Lanka, especially in the Northern Province.

> The Northern Province has all the characteristics of Kosovo. Even though the USA, the EU and India have assured their commitment to the territorial integrity of Sri Lanka, all these commitments are assurances. If the territorial integrity of Serbia could be violated despite Security Council Resolutions in place, clearly Sri Lanka cannot rely on such assurances ... since peripheral unit as the Province with assigned powers has the potential to influence developments as in Kosovo, it is vital that civil society reexamine the constitutionality of the procedures followed when the 13th Amendment was adopted.[96]

In Sri Lanka, the resolution of the separatist conflict requires a principled stance on the part of the island's powerful neighbor, India. In many ways, Sri Lanka has been grappling with India's southern secessionist problem sacrificing Sri Lankan lives – Sinhala, Tamil and Muslim. The Indian central government's regional hegemonic interests and reliance on Tamil Nadu political support have contributed to the perpetuation of the 'Sri Lankan' separatist conflict. Indian political scientist S.D. Muni gave voice to this contradiction when he noted that '...India could neither stand the victory of the Sinhala hegemonic state nor the establishment of a separate Tamil state...'.[97] The Indian government needs to move beyond the narrow Sinhala versus Tamil dualistic ethnic characterization, recognize its own responsibility for the origin and evolution of the conflict and help find a solution which recognizes multipolarity – the domestic complexities as well as the regional and international dimensions of the Sri Lankan conflict.

Ultimately, it is necessary to move away from what the ACSLU calls the 'Apartheid Principle', which will 'divide the country on a racial or ethnic basis', towards a 'Multicultural Principle', which will maintain the unitary basis of the country as a secular, democratic, and pluralistic nation.[98] The choice of multiculturalism over separatism, however, is not an abstract philosophical exercise. It is firmly grounded on the historical traditions of pluralism and mutual co-existence in Sri Lanka and the contemporary demographic and political realities of the island. It calls on all concerned – Sri Lankans as well as members of the international community – to transcend the static bipolar Sinhala versus Tamil analysis and accept a multipolar analysis that reflects the shifting, complex demographic and political-economic realities during the course of the war.

Pluralism: the foundation of reconciliation

Sri Lanka continues to be one of the most densely populated countries in the world.[99] The uneven population distribution was exacerbated with increased population concentration in the south, especially the metropolitan Western Province, partly due to the separatist conflict in the north and the east. In contrast, the Northern and Eastern Provinces being demanded as a separate Tamil region, which together constitute about one-third of the island and two-thirds of the coastline, have remained relatively under-populated (Table 2.2).

The previously multi-ethnic Northern Province is now an ethnically homogeneous Tamil region due to ethnic cleansing of Muslims and Sinhalese. But, the Eastern Province has remained multiethnic. It does not have an ethnic majority, but, a 'tripartite' ethnic composition. In 1981, Sri Lankan Tamils were a majority in the Batticoloa District, Muslims were a plurality in the Amapara District and the Sinhalese were a plurality in the crucial Trincomalee District bordering the Northern Province. Within each of these districts, there are pockets of minority ethnic concentration (Table 4.2 and Map 4.2). Thus, any effort to create a single contiguous region by joining the Northern and Eastern Provinces would have to sacrifice homogeneity. As US geographer, Robert Stoddard, who has examined ethnic distribution of populations in the Eastern Province concluded,

> [T]his, of course, is the very situation that is being opposed now by those who are dissatisfied with living in a pluralistic society. Thus, this can hardly be regarded as a justifiable solution ... the current distribution of ethnic populations in Sri Lanka cannot be regionalized to form a single, contiguous territory for each group. The final resolution to the ethnic conflict in the country will have to recognize this geographic reality.[100]

These observations are even more pertinent today given the changes in ethnic distribution that have taken place since the 1980s. There has been a large outmigration of Tamils, Muslims and Sinhalese from the Northern and Eastern Provinces to southern areas of the country over the course of the war. Accurate population figures are not available because the LTTE did not allow the Sri Lankan government to complete the 2001 census in most of the districts of the Northern and Eastern Provinces. The large proportion of Tamils of Indian origin in the north and their self-identification as Sri Lankan Tamils have also have made it difficult to arrive at accurate estimates of the Sri Lankan Tamil population in the country (Table 4.2). The percentage of Sri Lankan Tamils on the island in 1981 was 12.6 percent of the total population. According to Sri Lankan government estimates, Sri Lankan Tamils were 11.9 percent and Moors and Malays) were 8.3 percent and 0.3 percent of the island's population, respectively, in 2001.[101] According to other estimates, the percentage of Sri Lankan Tamils is less. For example, *The Economist*, gives an estimate of 8 percent, about the same as for the Muslims, i.e. 8 percent, about of the total population in Sri Lanka in 2002.[102] As the Sri Lankan Tamils have the lowest fertility rate (after the Burghers) and the Muslims, notably the Sri Lankan Moors have the highest fertility rate among all ethnic communities, the respective proportions of the two communities will keep decreasing and increasing if present trends continue.[103]

Since the last estimates made by the Sri Lankan Government in 2002, the out-migration from the north and the east has steadily increased due to the war and LTTE terrorism. More than half the Sri Lankan Tamil population is now believed to be living outside the north and the east although official estimates are to be made available. Certainly, when both the Sri Lankan Tamils and the Indian Tamils are counted, the majority of Tamils in Sri Lanka live amidst the Sinhalese and the Muslims in the multicultural southern areas of the island. This is particularly evident in the increasing pluralism of the capital. In 2001, the population of the Colombo Municipal Council area was 41 percent Sinhala; 29 percent Sri Lankan Tamil; 24 percent Sri Lankan Moor; 2 percent Indian Tamil and 2 percent Malay, i.e. predominantly non-Sinhala.[104] There are more Sri Lankan Tamils in Colombo than in Jaffna. In other words, the Tamil community now is more an island-wide rather than a regional minority. These multicultural demographic realities under-mine the separatist argument that an exclusive Tamil northeastern region is required for the Tamils to live in safety apart from the 'aggressive' Sinhalese.

Given the significant emigration of Sri Lankan Tamils abroad since 1983, some 800,000, that is, more than 25 percent of Sri Lankan Tamils, are now part of the diaspora.[105] Toronto is believed to be the largest Sri Lankan Tamil city in the world. The 're-drawing of the ethnic map of Sri Lanka'[106] calls into question the justice of granting one-third of the island exclusively to the small population of Sri Lankan Tamils especially when increasing numbers of them are no longer living in the areas claimed as the 'traditional Tamil homelands'. Much of the financial (about 90 percent) and ideological support for the LTTE comes from the Tamil diaspora elite and the worldwide Tamil community, making the Sri Lankan separatist struggle a transnational phenomenon increasingly removed from domestic realities.[107] The decline of the Sri Lankan Tamil population in the north and east and their increasing 'locational diversity' in Sri Lanka and world-wide status are highly relevant to a just resolution of the separatist conflict.

For most of the long history of the island, tolerance and mutual co-existence have been the predominant characteristics of inter-group relations, not enmity and conflict. During the course of the war examined in this book, two broad patterns of ethnic relations have emerged: a mono-ethnic policy in the north and ethnic pluralism in the south. Some 100,000 Muslims and a smaller number of Sinhalese were driven out of the Northern Province by the LTTE's ethnic-cleansing campaign, making it imperative that any solution to the separatist conflict take into account Muslim and Sinhala rights to the north and the east and their opposition to Tamil regional autonomy. Muslims have exceeded the Sri Lankan Tamils as the largest minority group in the island, and they are the largest and most prosperous community in the Eastern Province, the largest province in the island. Despite the most gruesome LTTE massacres of Sinhala and Muslim civilians in the Eastern Province, it has maintained its multi-ethnic – Muslim, Tamil, and Sinhala – character, but, given historical settlement patterns that enhance mutual co-existence, attempts to artificially carve out exclusive ethnic enclaves by Tamil or Muslim separatists could lead to greater upheaval and suffering (Map 4.2).

In the South, despite constant suicide bombings and killing of political leaders and thousands of civilians by the LTTE, there have been no major backlashes against Tamils since July 1983. It is also important to acknowledge the advances made in the integration of ethno-religious communities within Sri Lanka's democratic polity: proportional representation system advantageous to the minorities; making Tamil an official language equal to Sinhala throughout the island; citizenship rights to Indian Tamils; favorable university admission quotas for 'backward' regions, as well as the Jaffna district; important ministerial portfolios for members of minority communities; and official island-wide holidays on important days in Hindu, Muslim and Christian calendars – Sri Lanka may be the country with the largest number of religious holidays of any country in the world, 19 per calendar year.

In contrast to the pluralism in the rest of the country, the Northern Province has been turned into an exclusively Tamil Province. Due to the armed conflict and oppressive LTTE policies, such as extortion and forcible child recruitment, large numbers of Tamils from the north and the east have moved to the predominantly Sinhala south. The LTTE is not a mass-based populist movement, such as it presents itself to the world. Only Tamils who have not been fortunate enough to escape the LTTE remain under its totalitarian rule. Hoole has asked:

> How did a highly educated society holding out promise of better things give birth to a monstrosity beyond morality and beyond shame? ... The Sinhalese for their original sin have become the scapegoats for every wickedness committed under the guise of liberation' ... Who would be left in Eelam for bringing the transition to democracy?[108]

Of course, not all Sri Lankan Tamils were ever highly educated. It was, indeed, the highly educated who were threatened by Sinhala majoritarian politics that first took up the idea of separatism and drew lower-class and caste youth into armed struggle as the path to national liberation. But democracy cannot simply be equated with devolution and Tamil regional autonomy, as elite groups tend to do. The solution to Tamil grievances, like Sinhala and Muslim grievances, requires broadening the definition of democracy.

Common concerns across ethnic boundaries

While ethnically based dualisms such as Sinhala versus Tamil are functional for perpetuating national and international elite interests, they divert attention from widening economic inequalities shared by members of all groups and the political contradictions within ethnic groups. The responsibility for the rise of the brutal separatist conflict must be attributed largely to elites from both the Sinhala and Tamil communities – their political opportunism, hunger for power, refusal to curb violence at the outset, and collusion with external interests at the expense of the masses of people in all communities. A few leaders of the

Muslim and the Indian Tamil communities have exacerbated problems by under-mining the multicultural character of the country in supporting Tamil and Muslim separatism at different times. Today there is an acute disparity between the privileged members of the Tamil diaspora in the wealthy western countries who are funding the separatist war and their poor brethren left at home to become child soldiers and suicide bombers.[109] Among the Sinhalese, a small group of politicians and army leaders have benefitted from the war while young men from the poorest Sinhala families without other employment opportunities sacrifice their lives for the war.

The repression of the JVP insurgency against the Indian imposed Indo-Sri Lanka Accord (as with the 1971 JVP insurrection) revealed that state violence and human rights violations are not limited to Tamils. As discussed earlier, some low caste Sinhala villages were singled out for decimation because of alleged support for the JVP. Among the Tamils, the most oppressed, 'untouchable' castes have been made to sacrifice young lives disproportionately for the separatist struggle. Dalit recruitment has been extended to Tamil Nadu furthering the regional basis of the separatist conflict. Recent reports state that given the shortage of suicide cadres, Tamil Tigers are smuggling in underaged Dalit girls from Tamil Nadu: 'Tiger agents have come down from Europe and America to recruit young girls by throwing money at their families'.[110]

Given the dominant Sinhala versus Tamil dualism, few studies have explored the common political-economic issues facing youth across the different communities. An exception is the study by sociologists S.T. Hettige and Markus Meyer, which has explored the similarity of grievances and social backgrounds of the Sinhala JVP and the Tamil LTTE. Based on the findings of an island-wide National Youth Survey (including the North and the East) published in 2002, Hettige and Meyer observed that while 'ethnic tensions' exist, they have been 'exacerbated by the ongoing conflict' and that both Tamil and Sinhalese youth have 'similar major concerns'. They concluded that 'in such a case, reducing the potential of violent conflict to ethnic discrimination belies the complexities of social discrimination and the very real lack of adequate employment and livelihoods of youth both'.[111] Unlike the older generations, the younger generations of all communities who have been brought up with the promise of democracy and social mobility have refused to acquiesce to social marginalization. Educationist Siri Gamage has also pointed out the class contradictions that cut across the Sinhala versus Tamil ethnic divide:

> [T]here are important parallels between the material conditions which led to the creation of LTTE and the JVP: educational disadvantages, unemployment, poverty, landlessness, English language problems, substantial exclusion from the political and community decision making processes. Similarly, there are some ideological and political common grounds between the LTTE and the JVP, both movements promote their own linguistic and ethnic nationalisms. Both are also against the domination of Colombo-based elitist state.[112]

It is easy to agree that the formula for demobilizing soldiers and armed cadres lies in the capacity to find alternative employment.[113] But in an increasingly globalized world, this cannot be done outside the transformation of the dominant model of economic growth and its leading sector, the arms trade.

Unless elimination of terrorism is accompanied by broader and global political-economic transformation, it can result in further militarization and erosion of democracy, pluralism and human rights at the local, regional and international levels (Figure 9.2).

Ethnic interpretations of conflict deflect attention from increasing external control over local resources and cultures. The Sri Lankan separatist conflict has to be placed within the historical context of global political-economic domination and the historical divide-and-conquer strategies, dating back to British colonialism and perpetuated by ethnic elites after independence, including promotion

Levels	Actors	Strategies
International	Transnational corporations/ business sector	Economic development, redistribution, employment
	States	Consensus strategy on eliminating terrorism
	Intergovernmental organizations, e.g. UN	Human rights
	Non-state actors, e.g. diasporas, NGOs, etc.	Dialogue/reconciliation
Regional	Regional corporations/ business sector	Economic development, redistribution, employment
	States Central governments Regional governments	Consensus strategy on eliminating terrorism
	Co-ethnic and caste groups Non-state actors Diasporas, insurgency networks, etc.	Dialogue/reconciliation
Domestic	Corporations/business sector	Economic development, redistribution, employment
	Coalition of all political parties	Political and administrative decentralization/consensus strategy on eliminating terrorism Fundamental rights/civil rights legislation and enforcement
	Multiple ethnic groups Elites Ethnoclasses, regional groups Non-state actors, NGOs	Dialogue/reconciliation

Figure 9.2 Conflict resolution: levels, actors, strategies.

of conflict among local ethnic and religious groups. Amarasekara, for example, suggests that the underlying reason for international intervention in Sri Lanka at this time may not be Tamil human rights but western political and economic hegemony:

> One reason for a powerful nation to destabilize and gain control over a weaker nation may be due its strategic location. Our country for example, from a military point of view, is strategically located. It dominates the international shipping route from the west to the east ... The other reasons is the availability of very valuable natural resources ... Indians have found oil in the Kowari basin [in the Palk Strait] and it is correct to predict that the Mannar basin should also have oil deposits. Many of us are unaware that a very large deposit of Thorium and Titanium is found off the coast of Trincomalee. However, powerful western nations are well aware of this fact. This therefore is the other reason for them wanting to gain control of this country.[114]

Various external interests may be waiting for the opportunity to gain access to the vast stretches of undeveloped rich agricultural land, magnificent beaches, strategic Trincomalee harbor, and potential mineral resources in the Eastern Province. But would local, Indian, or international efforts to develop the region benefit the poor from all the communities? A sustainable solution to the Sri Lankan conflict 'must take into account issues of poverty and property rather than seek to extend the interests of international corporations'.[115] Indeed, decentralization of power needs to be carried in a way that allows local people – Tamils, Muslims, and Sinhalese – greater control over regional resources and decisions over governance. The creation of separate ethno-nationalist regions is not a panacea. A policy that only breaks up the unitary, centralized Sri Lankan state through a form of federalism and grants Tamil regional autonomy is unlikely to address these fundamental issues of economic democracy and political participation that are important to all Sri Lankans, not just a single ethnic group. Ultimately, the inherent ecological unity and integrity of the resplendent island of Sri Lanka – 'Pearl of the Indian Ocean', the 'tear drop of India' – transcend the separatist conflicts of her human inhabitants.

Notes

Introduction

1 Human Development Index (composite based on life expectancy, adult literacy and consumer purchasing power), UNDP, *Human Development Report*, 2007/2008.
2 Cecile Van de Voorde, 'Sri Lankan Terrorism: Assessing and Responding to the Threat of the LTTE', *Police Practice and Research*, vol. 6, no. 2, May 2005, p. 195.
3 *The Economist*, 7 February 2008, online, available at: www.economist.com accessed 6 May 2008.
4 South Asia Terrorism Portal, online, available at: www.satp.org/satporgtp/countries/shrilanka/terroristoutfits/LTTE.HTM accessed 6 May 2008.
5 Online, available at: www.fbi.gov/page2/jan08/tamil_tigers011008.html.
6 Paul Collier, 'Ethnic Civil Wars: Questioning the Received Wisdom', *Harvard International Review*, vol. 28 (4), winter 2007, p. 3.
7 Muttukrishna Sarvanathan, 'In Pursuit of a Mythical State of Tamil Eelam: A Rejoinder to Kristian Stokke', *Third World Quarterly*, 28(6), 2007, pp. 1185–1195.
8 Online, available at: www.globalsecurity.org/military accessed 6 May 2008.
9 Human Rights Watch, Universal Periodic Review of Sri Lanka, 5/5/2008, online, available at: http://hrw.org retrieved 6 May 2008.
10 E.g. Stanley Tambiah, *Buddhism Betrayed: Religion, Politics and Violence in Sri Lanka*, Chicago: University of Chicago, 1992; C.R. de Silva and Tessa Barthlomeuz, *Buddhist Fundamentalism and Minority Identities in Sri Lanka*, New York: SUNY Press, 1998.
11 Chelvadurai Manogaran, *Ethnic Conflict and Reconciliation in Sri Lanka*, Honolulu: University of Hawaii Press, 1987; Neil DeVotta, *Blowback: Linguistic Nationalism, Institutional Decay, and Ethnic Conflict in Sri Lanka*, Palo Alto: Stanford University Press, 2004.
12 Jeffrey Lunstead, *The United States' Role in Sri Lanka's Peace Process: 2002–2006*, Colombo: Asia Foundation, 2007, p. 5.
13 Asoka Bandarage, 'Ethno-Religious Evolution in Pre-Colonial Sri Lanka', *Ethnic Studies Report*, vol. xxi, no. 2, July 2003.
14 Susantha Goonatilake, *Anthropologizing Sri Lanka: A Eurocentric Misadventure*, Bloomington: Indian University Press, 2001, p. 91.
15 Sirima Kiribamune, 'Tamils in Ancient and Medieval Sri Lanka: The Historical Roots of Ethnic Identity', *Ethnic Studies Report*, Kandy: International Centre for Ethnic Studies, vol. iv, no. 1, January 1986, p. 1.
16 Department of Census and Statistics, Sri Lanka, 1981.
17 Stephen Steinberg, *The Ethnic Myth: Race, Ethnicity and Class in America*, Boston: Beacon Press, 2001, p. 169.
18 Asoka Bandarage, *Women, Population and Global Crisis: A Political-Economic Analysis*, London: Zed Books, 1997, pp. 314–318; Asoka Bandarage, 'Ethnic and

Religious Tension in the World', in *Global Political Economy and the Wealth of Nations*, ed., Philip Anthony O'Hara, London: Routledge, 2004, p. 287.

19 Sarvanathan, 'In Pursuit of a Mythical State', op. cit.; Norman Uphoff, 'Ethnic Cooperation in Sri Lanka: Through the Keyhole of a USAID Project', in *Carrots, Sticks, and Ethnic Conflict: Rethinking Development Assistance*, Milton J. Esman and Ronald J. Herring, eds., Ann Arbor: University of Michigan Press, pp. 120, fn. 14, p. 133.

20 Ravikumar, 'Caste of the Tiger', *Himal*, online, available at: www.himalmag.com/2002/august accessed 6 May 2008.

21 Muttukrishna Sarvanathan, 'Norwegian and British Interventions in Sri Lankan Conflict: A Sorry Tale of Misinformation and Misunderstanding', *The Island*, 19 December 2007, p. 1.

22 Ibid.

23 S.L. Gunasekara, *Wages of Sin*, Colombo: Sinhala Jathika Sangamaya, p. 47.

24 Partha S. Ghosh, *Ethnicity versus Nationalism: The Devolution Discourse in Sri Lanka*, Colombo: Vijitha Yapa Publications, 2003, op. cit., p. 237.

25 Jagath Senaratne, *Political Violence in Sri Lanka 1997–1990: Riots, Insurrections, Counterinsurgencies, Foreign Intervention*, Amsterdam: Vu University Press, 1990; Kenneth Bush, *The Intra-Group Dimensions of Ethnic Conflict in Sri Lanka: Learning to Read Between the Lines*, New York: Palgrave Macmillan, 2004; *Sri Lanka Strategic Conflict Assessment 2005*, San Francisco: Asia Foundation, 2005.

26 Nira Wickramasinghe, *Sri Lanka in the Modern Age: A History of Contested Identities*, Sri Lanka: Vijitha Yapa Publications, 2006.

27 Sarvanathan, 'Norwegian and British Interventions', op. cit.

28 Asia Foundation, *Sri Lanka Strategic Conflict Assessment 2005*, op. cit.

29 Bandarage, *Women, Population and Global Crisis*, op. cit., appendix 2.

30 Amy Chua, *World On Fire: How Exporting Free Market Democracy Breeds Ethnic Hatred and Global Instability*, New York: Anchor Books, 2004.

31 Asoka Bandarage, *Colonialism in Sri Lanka: The Political Economy of the Kandyan Highlands, 1833–1886*, Berlin: Mouton, 1983.

1 Conceptual frameworks: terrorism, ethnicity, political economy

1 Norman Uphoff, *Learning from Gal Oya: Possibilities for Participatory Development and Post-Newtonian Social Science*, Ithaca: Cornell University, Press, 1992, p. 307.

2 Council of Foreign Relations, online, available at: www.terrorismanswers.com/home.

3 Ernesto Che Guevara, *Guerilla Warfare*, Lincoln: University of Nebraska Press, 1985, pp. 62–63.

4 *Democracy and Society*, Georgetown University, vol. 5, issue 1, Fall 2007, p. 13.

5 Raymond C. Taras and Rajat Ganguly, *Understanding Ethnic Conflict: The International Dimension*, New York: Longman, 2006, pp. 1, 11.

6 Bandarage, 'Ethnic and Religious Tension', op. cit., p. 288.

7 Mahmood Mamdani, *When Victims Become Killers: Colonialism, Nativism and the Genocide Rwanda*, Princeton: Princeton University Press, 2001, p. 15; Taras and Ganguly, *Ethnic Conflict*, op. cit., p. 13.

8 Benedict Anderson, *Imagined Communities*, London: Verso, 2006.

9 Steinberg, *Ethnic Myth*, op. cit., p. 170.

10 James Petras and Henry Veltmeyer, *Globalization Unmasked: Imperialism in the 21st Century*, London: Zed Books, 2001, pp. 130–135.

11 Edward Said, *Orientalism*, New York: Vintage, 1998.

12 Yetman and Steele, *Minority and Majority: Dynamics of Race and Ethnicity in American Life*, Boston: Allyn & Bacon, 1982, preface, p. 1.

13 Cited in ibid., p. 1.

14 Ibid., p. 1.

15 Hurst Hannum, *Autonomy, Sovereignty, and Self-Determination: The Accommodation of Conflicting Rights*, Philadelphia: University of Pennsylvania press, 1990, p. 453.
16 Van de Voorde 'Sri Lankan Terrorism', op. cit., p. 198; Chaim Kaufmann 'When All Else Fails: Ethnic Population Transfers and Partitions in the Twentieth Century', *International Security* 23 (2), Fall 1998: 120–156.
17 Ibid; Nicolas Sambanis, 'Ethnic Partition as a Solution to Ethnic War: An Empirical Critique of the Theoretical Literature', World Bank, 18 September 1999, p. 2.
18 Ibid., p. 19.
19 Richard Rosencrance and Arthur A. Stein, eds., *No More States: Globalization, National Self-Determination, and Terrorism*, Lanham: Rowman & Littlefield, 2006.
20 Cited in United States Institute of Peace, US Responses to Self-Determination Movements: Strategies for Nonviolent Outcomes and Alternatives to Secessionism, *Peaceworks*, no. 16, 1997, p. 19.
21 J.S. Furnivall, *Colonial Policy and Practice: A Comparative Study of Burma and Netherlands India*, Cambridge: Cambridge University Press, 1948.
22 Edna Bonacich, 'A Theory of Middleman Minorities', in Yetman and Steele, *Majority and Minority*, op. cit., p. 270.
23 Milton Gordon, *Assimilation in American Life: Race, Religion and National Origin*, New York, Oxford University Press, 1964.
24 Steinberg, *Ethnic Myth*, op. cit., p. 261.
25 Ibid., preface, pp. ix–x.
26 Charles Keyes, ed., *Ethnic Change*, Seattle: University of Washington Press, 1981, pp. 4, 27.
27 Paul R. Brass, *Ethnicity and Nationalism: Theory and Comparison*, New Delhi: Sage, 1991, p. 3.
28 Donald L. Horowitz, *Ethnic Groups in Conflict*, Berkeley: University of California Press, 1985, p. 272.
29 Ted Robert Gurr, *Peoples Versus States: Minorities at Risk in the New Century*, Washington DC: United States Institute of Peace, 2000, pp. 70, 95.
30 Ibid., pp. 123–124.
31 Amy Chua, *World On Fire, op. cit.;* Jack L. Snyder, *From Voting to Violence: Democratization and Nationalist Conflict*, New York: W.W. Norton, 2000.
32 Benjamin R. Barber, *Jihad vs. McWorld: How Globalism and Tribalism Are Reshaping the World*, New York: Ballantine Books, 1996; Tariq Ali, *The Clash of Fundamentalisms*, London: Verso, 2003.
33 Yossi Shain, 'The Role of Diasporas in Conflict Perpetuation or Resolution', *SAIS Review*, 22:2, Summer–Fall 2002.
34 Cited in S.L. Gunasekara, *Tigers, 'Moderates' and Pandora's Package*, Colombo: Sinhala Jathika Sangamaya, 1996, p. 6.
35 Rohan Gunaratna, *Sri Lanka's Ethnic Crisis and National Security*, Colombo: South Asian Network on Conflict Research, 1998; Peter Chalk, 'Liberation Tigers of Tamil Eelam's (LTTE) International Organization and Operations – A Preliminary Analysis', Commentary no. 77, Winter 1999; Peter Leitner, 'War in Sri Lanka is the Legacy left by European Colonialism' *Asian Tribune*, 5 February 2008, online, available at: www.asiantribune.com; Van de Voorde, 'Sri Lankan Terrorism', op. cit.
36 Rohan Gunaratna, 'Special Report on Al-Qaeda', *Jane's Intelligence Review*, vol. 13, no. 8, August 2001, pp. 42–45.
37 Paul Collier and Anke Hoeffler, 'Greed and Grievance in Civil War, Paper No. 128, World Bank, 2004.
38 Paul Harris, 'The Appeasement of Terrorism: Doomed to Failure', in *Peace in Sri Lanka: Obstacles and Opportunities*, London:, WAPS, 2005 op. cit., pp. 127–128; Paul Harris, 'The Greatest Give Away in History', *Sri Lanka Express*, May 10, 2002, p. 4.
39 Darini Rajasingham-Senanayake, 'The Dangers of Devolution: The Hidden Economies of Armed Conflict', in Robert I. Rotberg, ed., *Creating Peace in Sri*

Lanka: Civil War and Reconciliation, Washington DC Brookings Institute, 1999, p. 67; Uphoff, 'Ethnic Cooperation', op. cit.

40 Ibid., p. 119.

41 Presidential Commission Report on 1977 Incidents, Sri Lanka Government Sessional Paper No. VII, 1980, p. 64.

42 Ibid., pp. 288–291.

43 Gunasekara, *Tigers, 'Moderates'*, op. cit., p. 88.

44 Ibid., p. 19.

45 Uphoff, 'Ethnic Cooperation', op. cit., p. 133, fn14.

46 Ghosh, *Ethnicity*, op. cit., p. 351.

47 G.H. Pieris, 'Prospects for a Negotiated Settlement of Sri Lanka's Ethnic Conflict', in K.M. de Silva and G.H. Pieris, eds., *Pursuit of Peace in Sri Lanka,: Past Failures and Future Prospects*, Sri Lanka, ICES and USIP, Washington DC, 2000, pp. 281, 283.

48 'No More Tears, Sister', video documentary, National Film Board Canada, 2004 Rajan Hoole, Daya Somasundaram, K. Sritharan and Rajani Thiranagama *The Broken Palmyra – The Tamil Crisis in Sri Lanka: An Inside Account*, Claremont, CA: The Sri Lanka Studies Institute, 1990.

49 Ibid.

50 Neville Ladduwahetty, 'Impact of Abrogation of CFA on Humanitarian and Human Rights Law', *The Island*, 19 January 2008, p. 4. Online, available at: www.island.lk/2008/01/19/features1.html.

51 Ibid., p. 4.

52 Ibid., p. 4.

53 Rajan Hoole, *Sri Lanka: The Arrogance of Power: Myths, Decadence and Murder*, Colombo: UTHR, 2001, p. 278.

54 *A Case Against A Federal Constitution for Sri Lanka: Report of an Independent and Representative Committee*, Colombo: The National Joint Committee, September 2003, pp. 12.

55 Ibid., pp. 19–20; see also, Nalin de Silva, *An Introduction to Tamil Racism in Sri Lanka*, Maharagama: Chintana Prashadaya, 1997.

56 Satchi Ponnambalam, *Sri Lanka: The National Question and the Tamil Liberation Struggle*, London: Zed Books, 1983, p. 12, op. cit., p. 19; TULF Election Manifesto, cited in K.M. de Silva, 'Separatist Ideology in Sri Lanka', Kandy: IICES, Occasional Paper, 4, 1995, p. 13.

57 Ibid., p. 13.

58 Online, available at: www.sangam.org/FB_HIST_DOCS/vaddukod.htm.

59 A.J. Wilson, *S.J.V. Chelvanayakam and the Crisis of Sri Lankan Tamil Nationalism, 1947–1977*, Honolulu: University of Hawaii Press, 1994, p. 128.

60 Hardgrave, 'The Riots in Tamilnad: Problems and Prospects of India's Language Crisis', *Asian Survey*, vol. 5, no. 8, 1965, p. 399.

61 Ibid., p. 396; Duncan Forrester, 'The Madras Anti-Hindi Agitation, 1965: Political Protest and its Effects on Language Policy in India', *Pacific Affairs*, 39, 1966, p. 23.

62 K.M. De Silva, *Managing Ethnic Tensions in Multi-Ethnic Societies: Sri Lanka, 1880–1985*, Lanham: University Press of America, 1988, p. 324.

63 MDMK Manifesto, online, available at: www.vaiko-mdmk.com/manifesto.html.

64 Cited in H.L. de Silva, 'Indo–Sri Lanka Peace Accord: An Appraisal', in Indo-Sri Lanka Agreement of July 1987, ed. Shelton U. Kodikara, Colombo: The International Relations Programme, University of Colombo, 1989, p. 28.

65 World Confederation of Tamils, online, available at: www.tamilnation.org.

66 Online, available at: www.tamilnation.org/books/Nationalism/guibernau.htm.

67 27 November 2007, online, available at: www.eelamweb.com.

68 Sarvanathan, 'Norwegian and British Interventions', op. cit., p. 3.

69 Norwegians; Against Terrorism, update July 2007, online, available at: www.svik.org/nat.pdf p. 13.

70 P. Rasmasamy, 'Malaysian Tamils Back the Cause of Eelam', online, available at: www.tamlcanadian.com.
71 Harris, 'Appeasement', op. cit., pp. 134–135; Sumedha, 'The Majority Politics and Abortive Military Strategies', The *Sunday Times*, 27 December 1998.
72 Kumar Rupesinghe, ed., *Negotiating Peace in Sri Lanka*, vol. 2, Colombo: Foundation for Co-Existence, 2nd edition, p. xxvii.
73 Social Scientists Association, *Ethnicity and Social Change in Sri Lanka*, Colombo, 1984, Introduction, p. 4.
74 Kumari Jayawardena, *Ethnic and Class Conflicts in Sri Lanka*, Sri Lanka: Centre for Social Analysis, 1985; International Crisis Committee; ICG, Sri Lanka: Sinhala Nationalism and the Elusive Southern Consensus, Asia Report N°141, 7 November 2007.
75 Tambiah, *Buddhism Betrayed*, op. cit.; de Silva and Bartholemeuz, *Buddhist Fundamentalism*, op. cit.
76 Hoole *Sri Lanka*, op. cit., p. 470.
77 MIRJE, *Emergency '79'*, Colombo, 1980, p. 38.
78 Sumanasiri Liyanage, 'Revisiting Thimpu Principles: A Social Democratic Perspective', in Jayadeva Uyangoda and Morina Perera, *Sri Lanka's Peace Process 2002: Critical Perspectives*, Colombo: Social Scientists Association, 2003, p. 33.
79 Panel Discussion (PICAR), Harvard University, 'A Real Chance for Peace: Sri Lanka at the Crossroads', 2 December 2002.
80 Charles Abeysekara, Rohan Edirisinghe, Sumanasiri Liyanage, Paikiasothy Saravanamuttu and Jayadeva Uyangoda eds., *Unitarianism, Devolution and Majoritiarin Elitism: A Response to the Interim Report of the Sinhala Commission*, Colombo: Social Scientists Association, 1998, pp. 2, 7, 43.
81 'Introduction', Sunil Bastian, ed., *Devolution and Development in Sri Lanka*, Colombo: International Center for Ethnic Studies, Colombo:, 1994, p. 3.
82 Charles Abeysekara, 'Political Package needed to Win Over Tamils', *Sunday Observer*, 30, July 1995.
83 Abeysekara, *et al.*, *Unitarianism*, op. cit., pp. 2, 7, 43.
84 UTHR Special Report No. 5, 15 September 1993, p. 19.
85 Radhika Coomaraswamy, 'Myths Without Conscience, Tamil and Sinhalese Nationalist Writings of the 1980s', in Charles Abeysekara and Newton Gunasinghe, *Facets of Ethnicity in Sri Lanka*, Colombo: Social Scientists Association, 1987, pp. 91, 96.
86 Ranjith Soysa, 'Sri Lanka: Open Letter to the Donor Country Leaders', SPUR, *Asian Tribune*, 14, March 2007.
87 L. Piyadasa, *Sri Lanka: The Holocaust and After*, London: Marram Books, 1984, p. 25.
88 Amita Shastri, 'Material basis for separatism: the Tamil Eelam Movement in Sri Lanka', *The Journal of Asian Studies*, February 1990, (49) 1, pp. 56–77; Patrick Peebles, 'Colonization and Ethnic Conflict in the Dry Zone of Sri Lanka', *The Journal of Asian Studies*, February 1990 (49) 1, p. 32.
89 Kapferer, B. *Legends of People, Myths of State: Violence, Intolerance, and Political Culture in Sri Lanka and Australia*, Washington: Smithsonian Institute of Press, 1988; William McGowan, *Only Man Is Vile*, New York: Farrar, Strauss & Giroux, 1992.
90 Hoole, *Sri Lanka* op. cit., p. 278, *passim*.
91 Ghosh, *Ethnicity versus Nationalism*, op. cit., 2003, p. 26.
92 Siri Hettige, 'Economic Liberalization, Social Class and Ethnicity' in Siri Gamage and I.B. Watson, eds., *Conflict and Community in Contemporary Sri Lanka*, Colombo: Vijitha Yapa, 1999, p. 308.

2 Prelude: the British colonial period and early years of independence

1 Bandarage, *Colonialism*, op. cit., chapter 8.
2 Ghosh, *Ethnicity*, op. cit., p. 47.
3 Vaddukoddai Resolution, op. cit.
4 Gunasekara, *A Tragedy of Errors*, Colombo: Sinhala Jathika Sangamaya, 2001, p. 34.
5 De Silva, *Separatist Ideology*, op. cit., pp. 9, 83.
6 Ibid., p. 9.
7 Ibid., p. 10.
8 Bandarage, *Colonialism*, op. cit., chapter 6; Fred Halliday, *The Ceylonese Insurrection*, online, available at: http://members.tripod.com/~jvp_srilanka/history/ pp. 1, 3, 5.
9 Ibid.
10 Eric Meyer, 'Labor Circulation between Sri Lanka and South India in Historical Perspective', in Claude Markovitz, Jacques Pouchepadas and Sanjay Subramaniyam, eds., *Society and Circulation: Mobile People and Itinerant Cultures in South Asia, 1750–1950*, pp. 73–74.
11 Bandarage, *Colonialism*, op. cit., chapter 5.
12 B.H. Farmer, *Pioneer Peasant Colonization in Ceylon*, London: Oxford University Press, 1957, p. 209.
13 Ibid, p. 91; Bandarage, *Colonialism*, op. cit., chapter 9.
14 Michael Roberts. *Caste Conflict and Elite Formation: The Rise of the Karava Elite, 1500–1931*, Cambridge: Cambridge University Press, 1982, p. 316, table 12.
15 S.J. Tambiah, *Sri Lanka: Ethnic Fratricide and the Dismantling of Democracy*, Chicago: University of Chicago Press, 1986, p. 155; Jane Russell, *Communal Politics and the Donoughmore Constitution, 1931–1947*, Dehiwala: Tissara Publishers, 1982, op. cit., p. 21.
16 Ibid., pp. 13–14; Murugar Gunasingham, *Sri Lankan Tamil Nationalism: A Study of its Origins*, Sydney: MTVP Publications, 1999, pp. 88–89.
17 Ananada Wickremaratne, *The Roots of Nationalism: Sri Lanka*, Colombo: Karunaratne and Sons, 1955, pp. xv–xvi.
18 Stanley J. Thambiah, 'Ethnic Representation in Ceylon's Higher Administrative Services, 1870–1946', *University of Ceylon Review*, (13) 2 and 3, April–July 1955, p. 129.
19 Thangarajah, 'Youth Conflict and Social Transformation', op. cit., p. 176; University Teachers for Human Rights (Jaffina), *Broken Palmyra*, 1988, online, available at: www.uthr.org/BP/content.htm. 6.2.5, 6.2.11.
20 Elizabeth Nissan and R.L. Stirrat, 'The Generation of Communal Identities', in Jonathan Spencer, ed., *Sri Lanka: History and the Roots of Conflict*, London: Routledge, 1990, p. 29.
21 Government of Sri Lanka, Thesawalami Pre-Emption Ordinance, 1960, Article 2; Savitri Gunasekara, *Introduction to the Laws of Sri Lanka*, Colombo: Open University, 1997, pp. 47, 61.
22 Nira Wickramasinghe, *Ethnic Politics in Colonial Sri Lanka*, New Delhi: Vikas, 1996, p. 36.
23 Ibid., p. 30.
24 Cited in ibid., p. 31.
25 C.Y. Thangarajah, 'The Genealogy of Tamil Nationalism in Post-Independent Sri Lanka', in S.T. Hettige and Markus Mayer, eds., *Dilemmas and Prospects After Fifty Years of Independence*, Delhi: Macmillan, 2000, p. 120.
26 R.A. Ariyaratne, 'Communal Conflict and the Formation of the Ceylon National Congress', in *Ceylon Journal of Historical and Social Studies*, vol. 7, New Series, no. 1, Jan–June 1977, pp. 58–59.

27 Wickramasinghe, *Ethnic Politics*, op. cit., p. 29.
28 Thangarajah, 'Genealogy', op. cit., p. 121.
29 University of Ceylon, *History of Ceylon*, vol. 3, op. cit., p. 283.
30 Cited in Ghosh, *Ethnicity*, op. cit., p. 60.
31 Wickramasinghe, *Ethnic Politics*, op. cit., pp. 32–33.
32 Ghosh, *Ethnicity*, op. cit., p. 61.
33 University of Ceylon, *History of Ceylon*, vol. 3, op. cit., p. 394.
34 Wickramasinghe, *Ethnic Politics*, op. cit., p. 33.
35 Michael Roberts, 'Noise as Cultural Struggle: Tom-Tom Beating, the British, and Communal Disturbances in Sri Lanka, 1880s-1930s', in Veena Das, ed., *Mirrors of Violence, Communities, Riots and Survivors in South Asia*, Delhi: Oxford, 1990.
36 P.T.M. Fernando, 'The British Raj and the 1915 Communal Riots in Ceylon', *Modern Asian Studies*, 111, 1969, pp. 249.
37 *History of Ceylon*, Vol. 3, op. cit., pp. 396–403.
38 P.T.M. Fernando, 'British Raj', op. cit., p. 254.
39 Samaraweera, 'The Muslim Revivalist Movement, 1880–1915', in Michael Roberts, ed., *Collective Identities, Nationalisms and Protest in Modern Sri Lanka*, Colombo: Marga Institute, 1979, p. 269.
40 A.P. Kannangara, 'The Riots of 1915 in Sri Lanka: A Study in the Roots of Communal Violence', *Past and Present*, no. 102, 1984, p. 147; Anagarika Dharmapala, *Return to Righteousness*, ed. by Ananada Guruge, Colombo: Ceylon Government Press, 1965, p. lxi
41 K.M. de Silva, *A History of Sri Lanka*, Delhi: Oxford University Press, 1981, p. 367.
42 University of Ceylon, *History of Ceylon*, vol. 3, op. cit., p. 394.
43 Ibid., p. 398.
44 Ibid., p. 399; A. Jeyratnam Wilson, *The Break-up of Sri Lanka: The Sinhalese-Tamil Conflict*, Honolulu: University of Hawaii Press, 1988, p. 8.
45 Thangarajah, 'Genealogy', op. cit., p. 122.
46 Partha Ghosh, 'Colonial Origins of Sinhala–Tamil Ethnic Conflict in Sri Lanka', in Ramakan and B.C. Upreti, eds., *Nation-Building in South Asia*, vol. 2, New Delhi: South Asian Publishers, 1991, p. 316; Pfaffenberger, 'The Cultural Dimension of Tamil Separatism', *Asian Survey*, vol. 21, no. 11, November 1981.
47 University of Ceylon, *History of Ceylon*, vol. 3 op. Cit., p. 396.
48 Ibid., p. 401.
49 Wickramasinghe, *Ethnic Politics*, op. cit., p. 15.
50 University of Ceylon, *History of Ceylon*, vol. 3, op. cit., pp. 364, 402.
51 Ibid., pp. 396–398.
52 Ibid., p. 400.
53 Gunasingham, *Sri Lankan Tamil Nationalism*, op. cit., p. 217.
54 Wilson, *Break-up*, op. cit., p. 8.
55 Robert L. Hardgrave, 'The DMK and the Politics of Tamil Nationalism', *Pacific Affairs*, vol. 37, no. 4, Winter 1964/65, pp. 397–398.
56 Kiribamune, 'Tamils in Ancient and Medieval Sri Lanka', op. cit., p. 1; R.A.L.H. Gunawardena, 'The People of the Lion: Sinhala Consciousness in History and Historiography', in SSA, *Ethnicity and Social Change*, op. cit., p. 38.
57 University of Ceylon, *History of Ceylon*, vol. 3, op. cit., p. 402.
58 Ibid., p. 494.
59 De Silva, *Managing Ethnic Tensions*, op. cit., pp. 52–55.
60 Halliday, *The 1971 Insurrection*, op. cit., p. 5; vol. 3, p. 493; Ravikumar, 'Caste of the Tiger, op. cit., p. 2.
61 University of Ceylon, *History of Ceylon*, vol. 3, op. cit., p. 495.
62 Wickramasinghe, *Ethnic Politics*, pp. 105, 113.
63 Ibid., p. 99.
64 K.N.O. Dharmadasa, *Language, Religion and Ethnic Assertiveness: The Growth of*

Sinhalese Nationalism in Sri Lanka, Ann Arbor: University of Michigan Press, 1995, p. 239; *History of Ceylon*, vol. 3 op. cit., p. 487.

65 Sunil Bastian, 'Liberalised Policies and Regional Autonomy', in Bastian, ed., *Devolution and Development*, op. cit., p. 187.

66 Wickramasinghe, *Ethnic Politics*, op. cit., p. 104.

67 Ibid., pp. 185–187.

68 Cited in National Joint Committee, Sinhala Commission Report, vol. 1, 1998, pp. 120–121; Russell, *Communal Politics*, op. cit.

69 De Silva, *Managing Ethnic Tensions*, op. cit., pp. 80–81.

70 Dharmadasa, *Language, Religion*, op. cit., p. 258.

71 Wickramasinghe, *Ethnic Politics*, op. cit., p. 196.

72 Ibid., pp. 105, 199.

73 Ibid., p. 190.

74 Ghosh 'Colonial Origins', op. cit., p. 323.

75 Wickramasinghe, *Ethnic Politics*, op. cit., pp. 215–216.

76 K.M. de Silva, *A History*, op. cit., p. 511.

77 De Silva, *Managing Ethnic Tensions*, op. cit., p. 155.

78 Thangarajah, 'Genealogy', op. cit., p. 130.

79 Kumari Jayawardena, *Ethnic and Class Conflicts in Sri Lanka*, op. cit., p. 76.

80 De Silva, *Managing Ethnic Tensions*, op. cit., p. 153.

81 W. Howard Wriggins, *Ceylon: The Dilemmas of a New Nation*, Princeton, NJ: Princeton University press, 1960, pp. 145, 146.

82 Wilson, *Chelvanayakam*, op. cit., p. 6.

83 Ibid., pp. 24–25.

84 Ibid., p. 30; Wilson, *The Break-up of Sri Lanka*, op. cit., p. 73.

85 Cited in Gunasekara, *Tigers*, op. cit., p. 35.

86 Wilson, *Chelvanayakam*, op. cit., p. 32.

87 S. Arasaratnam, 'Nationalism in Sri Lanka and the Tamils', in Roberts, *Collective Identities*, op. cit., p. 501.

88 Robert L. Hardgrave, Jr, 'The Riots in Tamilnad: Problems and Prospects of India's Language Crisis', *Asian Survey*, 1973, p. 399; Hardgrave, 'The DMK', op. cit., p. 396; Duncan B. Forrester, 'The Madras Anti-Hindi Agitation, 1965: Political Protest and its Effects on Language Policy in India', *Pacific Affairs*, Spring–Summer 1966, 39, p. 22.

89 Wilson, *Chelvanayakam*, op. cit., p. 1.

90 Ibid., pp. 3, 25, 35.

91 Robert N. Kearney, *Communalism and Language in the Politics of Ceylon*, Durham: Duke University press, 1967, p. 96.

92 Ibid., pp. 91, 96.

93 Wilson, *Chelvanayakam*, op. cit., p. 42.

94 Ibid., p. 42; Gunasekara, *Tigers*, op. cit., p. 32.

95 Wilson, *Sri Lankan Tamil Nationalism*, op. cit., p. 83.

96 Cited in de Silva, 'Separatist Ideology', p. 6.

97 Kearney, *Communalism*, op. cit., pp. 93–94.

98 Ibid., p. 95.

99 Wilson, *Chelvanayakam*, op. cit., p. 33.

100 Ibid., p. 136.

101 Ibid., p. 33.

102 De Silva, *Separatist Ideology*, op. cit., p. 7.

103 UTHR, Special Report No. 5, 15 September 1993, p. 19.

104 Ibid., pp. 7–8.

105 Gunasekara, *Tigers*, op. cit., p. 33.

106 Wilson, *Chelvanayakam*, op. cit., pp. 30–31.

107 Justus Richter, 'The Conflict Between Sinhalese and Tamils in Sri Lanka: An

Antagonistic Ethnic Cleavage', in *Regional Security, Ethnicity and Governance*, Justus Richter and Christian Wagner, eds., Delhi: Manohar, 1998, p. 110.

108 Kearney, *Communalism*, op. cit., pp. 90–91; Wriggins, *Ceylon*, op. cit., p. 146.

109 De Silva, *Managing Ethnic Tensions*, op. cit., p. 155; Wilson, *Break-up*, op. cit., p. 35.

110 K.M. de Silva, *A History*, op. cit., p. 517.

111 Halliday, *The 1971 Insurrection*, op. cit., p. 8.

112 Dharmadasa, *Language, Religion*, op. cit., p. 270; de Silva, *A History*, op. cit., p. 512.

113 Gananath Obeysekara, 'Comments on the Social Background of the April 1971 Insurgency in Sri Lanka', *Journal of Asian Studies*, (33)3, 1974, p. 381; Wriggins, *Ceylon*, op. cit., pp. 105, 192–196.

114 Tarzie Vittachi, *Emergency '58 – The Story of the Ceylon Race Riots*, Deutsch, 1958, p. 19.

115 Wriggins, *Ceylon*, op. cit., p. 80.

116 Ibid., pp. 61, 245.

117 Ibid., pp. 249–253; Kearney, *Communalism*, op. cit., pp. 72–74.

118 Wilson, *Chelvanayakam*, op. cit., p. 50.

119 Gunasekara, *Tigers*, op. cit., pp. 38–39.

120 Kearney, *Communalism*, op. cit., p. 73.

121 Ibid., p. 78; Buddha Sasana Commission Report, 'The Betrayal of Buddhism', Ceylon: Dhamavijaya Press, 1956 op. cit., *passim*.

122 Vittachi, *Emergency '58*, op. cit., pp. 16–18.

123 Kearney, *Communalism*, op. cit., p. 70.

124 Wriggins, *Ceylon*, op. cit., pp. 361, 364, 369.

125 Kearney, *Communalism*, op. cit., pp. 82, 84, Appendix 1.

126 De Silva, *A History*, op. cit., p. 511.

127 DeVotta, *Blowback*, op. cit., pp. 90–91; Ghosh, *Ethnicity*, op. cit., p. 76.

128 Vittachi, *Emergency '58*, op. cit., p. 16.

129 De Silva, *Managing Ethnic Tensions*, op. cit., p. 233.

130 Ibid., pp. 172–173.

131 Kearney, *Communalism*, op. cit., pp. 112–113.

132 C.Y. Thangarajah, 'Youth, Conflict and Social Transformation in Sri Lanka', in Hettige and Mayer, eds., *Sri Lankan Youth: Challenges and Responses*, Colombo: Friedrich Stiftung, 2002, p. 176.

133 D.R.L. Fernando, *The Big Bluff*, Sydney: D.R.L. Fernando, 1985, pp. 45, 79.

134 Hoole, 'The Tamil Secessionist Movement', op. cit., p. 12.

135 Mahindapala, 'The Revolt of the Oppressed', *The Sunday Times*, 22 September 1996.

136 DeVotta, *Blowback*, op. cit., p. 94.

137 Wilson, *The Break-up*, op. cit., p. 108.

138 De Silva, *Reaping the World Wind*, op. cit., p. 121.

139 Manogaran, *Ethnic Conflict*, op. cit., pp. 48, 93; Vittachi, *Emergency '58*, op. cit., p. 20.

140 Ranjani Obeysekara, 'The Transformation of Buddhism and the Ethnic Question', unpublished paper, op. cit., p. 16; Vittachi, *Emergency '58*, op. cit., p. 37.

141 Thangarajah, 'Genealogy', op. cit., p. 132; Norman Uphoff, 'Ethnic Cooperation', op. cit., p. 116; Gananath Obeysekara, 'Political Violence and the Future of Democracy in Sri Lanka', online, available at: genocide.org.uk/genocide/?page_id=42.

142 In Olcott Gunasekara, 'The Implementation of the Official Language Policy', in K.N.O. Dharmadasa, ed., *National Language Policy in Sri Lanka, 1956–1996*, Kandy: International Centre for Ethnic Studies, 1996, p. 34.

143 Thangarajah, 'Genealogy', op. cit., p. 133.

144 G.H. Peiris, *Development and Change in Sri Lanka: Geographical Perspectives:* New Delhi: Macmillan, 1996, p. 205.

145 Wilson, *Chelvanayakam*, op. cit., p. 21.
146 Roberts, *Collective Identities*, op. cit., p. 75.
147 C.W. Nichols, 'Historical Topography of Ancient and Medieval Ceylon', cited in de Silva, *Separatist Ideology*, op. cit., p. 42; Dennis McGilvray, 'Arabs, Moors and Muslims: Sri Lankan Muslim Ethnicity in Regional Perspective, *Contributions to Indian Sociology*, vol. 32, no. 2, 1998, p. 459.
148 Malinga H. Gunaratna, *For a Sovereign State*, Ratmalana: Vishva Lekha, 1998, pp. 27, 201, 242.
149 '1981 – The year of Racial Violence' Kandy: Movement for Inter Racial Justice and Equality, 1983, p. 24.
150 Ceylon, Department of Census and Statistics, 1986.
151 Anula Attanayake, *Sri Lanka: Constitutionalism, Youth Protest and Political Violence*, Matara: Department of History, University of Ruhuna, 2001, p. 76.
152 Ibid., p. 72.
153 Tissa Balasuriya, 'Minority Problems – a Socio-Economic Perspective', *Logos*, vol. 16, no. 2, August 1977, p. 7.
154 Kearney, *Communalism*, op. cit., p. 95.
155 The 'Bandaranaike–Chelvanayakam Pact (1957)', cited in DeVotta, *Blowback*, op. cit., pp. 209–210.
156 K.M. de Silva, *Reaping the World Wind: Ethnic Conflict, Ethnic Politics in Sri Lanka*, New Delhi: Penguin, 1998, op. cit., p. 54.
157 DeVotta, *Blowback*, op. cit., pp. 110, 157.
158 Ibid., pp. 110–111.
159 De Silva, *Reaping*, op. cit., p. 122.
160 Vittachi, *Emergency '58*, op. cit., pp. 61–62.
161 Ibid., p. 37.
162 Ibid., pp. 60–62.
163 Ibid. pp. 21, 88–89, 116.
164 De Silva, *Reaping*, op. cit., p. 54.
165 Kearney, *Communalism*, op. cit., p. 88; Hoole, *Sri Lanka*, op. cit., p. 3.
166 M.R. Narayan Swamy, *Tigers of Sri Lanka: From Boys to Guerillas*, Delhi: South Asia Books, 1995, p. 24.
167 Ibid., p. 24.
168 Mark P. Whitaker, 'Tigers and Temples: The Politics of Nationalist and Non-Modern Violence in Sri Lanka', in Gamage and Watson, *Conflict and Community*, op. cit., p. 186; de Silva, *Managing Ethnic Tensions*, op. cit., p. 324.
169 The Tamil Language (Special Provisions) Act, No. 28 of 1958 and The Tamil Language (Special Provisions) Regulations (1966) Appendices III and IV in Kearney, *Communalism*, op. cit., pp. 146–150.
170 Agreement Between Dudley Senanayake and S.J.V. Chelvanayakam(1965) in DeVotta, *Blowback*, op. cit., p. 212, Appendix E.
171 De Silva, *Managing Ethnic Tensions*, op. cit., pp. 133, 192–193.
172 Halliday, *1971 Insurrection*, op. cit., p. 10.
173 Ibid., p. 2.
174 De Silva, *Managing Ethnic Tensions*, op. cit., p. 239.
175 De Silva, *Reaping*, op. cit., p. 124.

3 From class struggle to ethnic separatism, 1971–1977

1 Saman Kelegama, *Development Under Stress: Sri Lankan Economy in Transition*, Sri Lanka: Vijitha Yapa, 2006, pp. 43, 48.
2 Obeysekara, '1971 Insurgency', op. cit., p. 380.
3 D.L. Jayasuriya, 'Developments in University Education: The Growth of the University of Ceylon', *University of Ceylon Review*, April 1965, Table 111, p. 148.

4 K.M. de Silva, 'Affirmative Action Policies: The Sri Lanka Experience', *Ethnic Studies Report*, vol. xv, no. 2, July 1997, p. 248.

5 Ibid., p. 250; C.R. de Silva, 'The Politics of University Admissions', op. cit., *passim*.

6 S.W.R. de A. Samarasinghe, 'The Dynamics of Separatism: The Case of Sri Lanka', in Ralph Premdas, S.W.R. de A. Samarasinghe and Alan B. Anderson, eds., *Secessionist Movements in Comparative Perspective*, London: Pinter Publishers, 1990, p. 52.

7 Ibid., p. 90; de Silva, 'Affirmative Action Policies', op. cit., p. 250.

8 C.R. de Silva, 'The Politics of University Admissions: A Review of some Aspects of the Admission Policy in Sri Lanka, 1971–1978', *Sri Lanka Journal of Social Sciences*, 1978, 1 (2), p. 90.

9 Ibid., pp. 89–90.

10 Kearney, 'Educational Expansion and the Political Volatility in Sri Lanka', *Asian Survey*, (XV)9, p. 742.

11 Obeysekara, '1971 Insurgency', op. cit., p. 383.

12 A.C. Alles, *The J.V.P. 1969–1989*, Colombo: Lake House Publishers, 1990, First Introduction.

13 Obeysekara, '1971 Insurgency', op. cit., p. 380.

14 Ibid., p. 83; Attanayaka, *Sri Lanka*, op. cit., p. 95.

15 Ibid., p. 4.

16 Alles, *J.V.P.*, op. cit., p. 333.

17 Halliday, *1971 Insurrection*, Prins Gunasekara, *Sri Lanka in Crisis: The Lost Generation – The Untold Story*, Colombo: S Godage & Brothers, 1998, p. 28.

18 Halliday, *1971 Insurrection*, op. cit., pp. 8, 19.

19 Ibid., p. 6.

20 Ibid., p. 7.

21 Gunasekara, *Lost Generation*, op. cit., p. 6.

22 Ibid, p. 29.

23 Ibid., pp. 100, 116.

24 Cited in Halliday, *1971 Insurrection*, op. cit., op. cit., p. 9.

25 Rohan Gunaratna, *Sri Lanka: A Lost Revolution? The Inside Story of the JVP*, Sri Lanka: Institute for Fundamental Studies, 1990, p. 105.

26 Robert N. Kearney and Janice Jiggins, 'The Ceylon Insurrection of 1971', *The Journal of Commonwealth and Comparative Politics*, vol. XII, no. 1, March 1975, pp. 45–46, p. 62 fn19; C.A. Chandraprema, *Sri Lanka: The Years of Terror: The JVP Insurrection 1987–1989*, Colombo: Lake House Bookshop, 1991, pp. 129–130.

27 Gunaratna, *Sri Lanka*, op. cit., p. 115.

28 Ibid., pp. 196, 199, 213; Gunasekara, *Lost Generation*, op. cit., p. 40.

29 Gunaratna, *Sri Lanka*, op. cit., pp. 115–116.

30 Ibid., p. 96.

31 De Silva, *Managing Ethnic Tensions*, op. cit., pp. 241–242, 249.

32 Ibid., p. 251.

33 Attanayaka, *Sri Lanka*, op. cit., pp. 104–105.

34 Peebles, 'Colonization', op. cit., p. 38.

35 A.D.V. de S. Indraratna, 'Economic Development and Policy', in *Fifty Years of Sri Lanka's Independence: A Socio-Economic Review*, Colombo: Sri Lanka Institute of Social and Economic Studies, 1998, p. 6.

36 Ibid., p. 7.

37 C.R. de Silva, 'Politics of University Admissions', op. cit., p. 91.

38 Ibid., p. 93.

39 Ibid., p. 92; K.M. de Silva, 'Affirmative Action', op. cit., pp. 251–252.

40 Meghan O'Sullivan, 'Conflict as Catalyst: The Changing Politics of the Sri Lankan Muslims', in Gamage and Watson, *Conflict and Community*, op. cit., pp. 255–257.

41 Mansoor Mohamed Fazil, 'The Muslim Factor in the Sri Lankan Conflict', in

George Frerks and Bart Klem eds., *Dealing With Diversity: Sri Lankan Discourses on Peace and Conflict*, Clingendael: Netherlands Institute of International Relations, 2005, p. 170.

42 Ibid., pp. 170–171.
43 De Silva, 'University Admissions', op. cit., pp. 92–94.
44 Ibid., pp. 92–94; Bikas Sanyal, 'University Education and Graduate Employment in Sri Lanka', UNESCO/The Marga Institute, Colombo: Sri Lanka, 1983, p. 141.
45 Ibid., p. 93.
46 Ibid., p. 94; K.M. de Silva, 'Affirmative Action', op. cit., p. 250.
47 Thangarajah, 'Youth, Conflict', op. cit., p. 176.
48 Ibid., pp. 96–97; K.M. de Silva, 'Affirmative Action', op. cit., 252–254.
49 Abeysekara, 'Ethnic Representation in the Higher State Services', in Social Scientists Association, *Ethnicity and Social Change in Sri Lanka*, Colombo, 1984, pp. 184–187, 193.
50 Thangarajah, 'Youth Conflict and Social Transformation', op. cit., p. 176.
51 Cited in K.M. de Silva, *Sri Lanka: Ethnic Conflict, Management and Resolution*, Kandy: ICES, 1999, p. 21.
52 Thangarajah, 'Youth, Conflict', op. cit., p. 176.
53 Wilson, *Tamil Nationalism*, op. cit., p. 116.
54 Fazil, 'The Muslim Factor', op. cit., pp. 170–171.
55 Asoka Bandarage, 'College Degrees Bear Bitter Fruit in Sri Lanka', *Chronicle of Higher Education*, 18 December 1998.
56 P.V.J. Jayasekara and Y.R. Amerasinghe, 'The Economy, Society and Polity from Independence to 1977', in David Dunham and Charles Abeysekara, eds., *The Sri Lankan Economy: 1977–1983*, Colombo: Social Scientists Association, 1987, pp. 47–48.
57 Ibid., p. 48.
58 De Silva, *Managing Ethnic Tensions*, op. cit., p. 327.
59 Ibid., pp. 241–242, 249; Ponnambalam, *Sri Lanka*, op. cit., p. 161; Attanayaka, *Sri Lanka*, op. cit., pp. 95–96.
60 S.L. Gunasekara, *A Tragedy of Errors*, Colombo: National Joint Committee, 2001, p. 30.
61 Constitution of the Republic of Sri Lanka adopted, 22 May 1972.
62 De Silva, *Ethnic Conflict, Management*, op. cit., p. 12; Bandarage, *Colonialism*, op. cit., p. 49.
63 Articles 2 and 4, The Constitution of the Kingdom of Norway.
64 De Silva, *Managing Ethnic Tensions*, op. cit., p. 253.
65 Chapter VI, Constitution of the Republic of Sri Lanka, 1972.
66 Ibid.
67 Chapter 1, Clause 2, Constitution of the Republic of Sri Lanka, 1972.
68 De Silva, *Managing Ethnic Tensions*, op. cit., pp. 253–254.
69 Ibid., p. 251; Ponnambalam, *Sri Lanka*, op. cit., pp. 157–167.
70 Ibid, p. 162; de Silva, *Managing Ethnic Tensions*, op. cit., pp. 251–252.
71 Ibid., pp. 256–257.
72 Wilson, *Chelvanayakam*, op. cit., p. 117.
73 Hoole, 'The Tamil Secessionist Movement: A Case of Secession by Default?', online, available at: www.uthr.org/Rajan/selfdet.htm, p. 8.
74 De Silva, *Managing Ethnic Tensions*, op. cit., pp. 329–330.
75 Ibid., p. 324.
76 K.M. de Silva, 'Indo-Sri Lanka Relations, 1975–89: A Study in the Internationalization of Ethnic Conflict', in K.M. de Silva and R.J. May, eds., *Internationalization of Ethnic Conflict*, Kandy: ICES, 1991, p. 77.
77 Wilson, *Chelvanayakam*, op. cit., p. 20 fn. 16 and p. 118 fn. 8.
78 Ibid., pp. 3, 118 fn. 8.

79 Ibid., p. 118 fn. 8; see also, S.U. Kodikara, 'The Separatist Eelam Movement in Sri Lanka: An Overview', *India Quarterly*, April–June 1981, New Delhi, p. 202.

80 Purnaka L. de Silva, 'The Growth of Tamil Paramilitary Nationalisms', in Gamage and Watson, eds., *Conflict and Community*, op. cit., p. 93.

81 Ibid., p. 258.

82 Wilson, *Tamil Nationalism*, op. cit., p. 20.

83 M.R. Narayan Swamy, op. cit., p. 25.

84 Wilson, *Tamil Nationalism*, op. cit., p. 20.

85 Swamy, *Tigers*, op. cit., p. 24.

86 Ibid., p. 31; Rohan Gunaratna, 'Internationalisation of the Tamil Conflict (and its Implications', in Gamage and Watson, *Conflict and Community*, op. cit., p. 110; Wilson, *Sri Lankan Tamil Nationalism*, op. cit., pp. 124–125.

87 Gunaratna, *Sri Lanka*, op. cit., p. 127; MIRJE, *Emergency '79*, 1980, p. 7.

88 Report of the Presidential Commission on 1977 Incidents, Sessional Paper, no. vii, 1980, pp. 3, 4, 33.

89 Ibid., p. 33; de Silva, *Managing Ethnic Tensions*, op. cit., p. 261.

90 Presidential Commission on 1977, op. cit., p. 26; Wilson, *Tamil Nationalism*, op. cit., p. 125.

91 Hoole, *Sri Lanka*, op. cit., p. 449.

92 Ibid., p. 125.

93 Presidential Commission on 1977, op. cit., pp. 1–2.

94 Ibid., pp. 1–2; Gunaratna, *Sri Lanka*, op. cit., 127; Edgar O'Ballance, *The Cyanide War: Tamil Insurrection in Sri Lanka, 1973–88*, London: Brassey's, 1989, p. 16.

95 *Broken Palmyrah*, op. cit., chapter 2: 2.

96 Ibid.

97 Swamy, *Tigers*, op. cit., p. 26.

98 Presidential Commission on 1977, op. cit., p. 2; O'Ballance, *Cyanide War*, op. cit., p. 14; see also Reports of UTHR.

99 Swamy, *Tigers*, op. cit., pp. 29, 31; Wilson, *Tamil Nationalism*, op. cit., p. 12; Presidential Commission on 1977, op. cit., p. 33.

100 O'Ballance, *Cyanide War*, op. cit., p. 30.

101 Swamy, *Tigers*, op. cit.

102 Purnaka de Silva, 'Growth of Tamil Paramilitary Nationalisms: Sinhala Chauvinism and Tamil Responses', in Gamage and Watson, *Conflict and Community*, op. cit., pp. 92–93.

103 *Broken Palmyra*, Chapter 2: 3.

104 Ibid.

105 Swamy, *Tigers*, op. cit., p. 29.

106 Presidential Commission on 1977, op. cit., pp. 29, 39.

107 Ibid., pp. 23, 39.

108 Gunaratna, *International and Regional Security Implications of the Tamil Insurgency*, St Albans, UK: International Foundation of Sri Lankans, 1997, p. 8.

109 Presidential Report on 1977, op. cit., p. 23.

110 De Silva, *Managing Ethnic Tensions*, op. cit., p. 269; Balasuriya, 'Catastrophe '83', op. cit., p. 39.

111 Presidential Commission, op. cit., pp. 4, 33–34.

112 *Emergency '79*, op. cit., p. 7; Wilson, *Sri Lankan Tamil Nationalism*, op. cit., p. 125.

113 *Emergency '79*, op. cit., p. 18.

114 Presidential Commission on 1977, op. cit., pp. 33–34.

115 Attanayaka, *Sri Lanka*, op. cit., p. 107.

116 Presidential Commission on 1977, op. cit., p. 33.

117 De Silva, *Managing Ethnic Tensions*, op. cit., p. 256.

118 Hoole, *Sri Lanka*, op. cit., p. 216.

119 Swamy, *Tigers*, op. cit., p. 29, Presidential Commission of 1971, op. cit., pp. 25–26.

120 Ibid., p. 33; Swamy, *Tigers*, op. cit., p. 30.
121 Ibid., pp. 30–31; see also, Presidential Commission, op. cit., pp. 53–56.
122 Swamy, *Tigers*, op. cit., p. 31.
123 Ibid., p. 3; Wilson, *Tamil Nationalism*, op. cit., p. 125.
124 De Silva, *Managing Ethnic Tensions*, op. cit., 259.
125 Thangarajah, 'Youth Conflict', op. cit., p. 182.
126 Vaddukoddai Resolution, op. cit.
127 Report of the Presidential Truth Commission, Sessional Paper No. III, 2003, p. 19; see also, Jayasekara and Amerasinghe, 'Economy, Society', op. cit., p. 48.
128 Mohameed Ismail, Rameez Abdullah, Mansoor Mohamed Fazil, 'The Other Side of the Muslim Nation', in Georg Frerks and Bart Klem, eds., *Dealing With Diversity*, op. cit., p. 196; Fazil, 'The Muslim Factor', op. cit., pp. 170–171.
129 De Silva, *Managing Ethnic Tensions*, op. cit., 259.
130 Presidential Commission of 1977, op. cit., pp. 40–41.
131 TULF, General Election Manifesto, July 1977, Colombo: Modern Printers, 1977.
132 Bandarage, 'Ethno-Religious Evolution' op. cit.
133 TULF, Election Manifesto, 1977, op. cit.
134 UNP Election Manifesto cited in Presidential Truth Commission, op. cit., pp. 21–22.
135 De Silva, *Managing Ethnic Tensions*, op. cit., pp. 288–289; Thangarajah, 'Youth Conflict', op. cit., p. 183.
136 Ibid., pp. 287–288.
137 Balasuriya, *Sri Lanka's Crisis of National Unity*, Colombo: Centre for Society and Religion, 1979, op. cit., pp. 23, 33.
138 Ibid., op. cit., p. 39.
139 Hoole, *Sri Lanka*, op. cit p. 21.
140 Thangarajah, 'Youth Conflict', op. cit., p. 183.
141 De Silva, *Managing Ethnic Tensions*, op. cit., p. 327.
142 Balasuriya, *Sri Lanka's Crisis*, op. cit., pp. 58, 8, 21.
143 Ibid., p. 29.
144 Hoole, *Sri Lanka*, p. 145.
145 Kodikara, 'The Separatist Eelam Movement', op. cit., p. 210.
146 Ibid., p. 210; Report of the Presidential Truth Commission, op. cit., p. 20.
147 De Silva, *Managing Ethnic Tensions*, op. cit., p. 325.
148 Tissa Balasuriya, 'Catastrophe '83', *Logos*, vol. 22, no. 4, December 1983, pp. 10, 27.
149 MIRJE, *1981– The Year of Racial Violence*, Kandy: MIRJE, 1983, pp. 51–52.
150 Kodikara, 'Eelam Movement', op. cit., p. 210.
151 Presidential Commission on 1977, op. cit., pp. 280–284.
152 Ibid., *passim*; see also Report of Presidential Truth Commission, op. cit., p. 20.
153 Kodikara, 'Eelam Movement', op. cit., p. 210.
154 Ibid., p. 210; de Silva, *Managing Ethnic Tensions*, op. cit., p. 288.
155 Balasuriya, 'Catastrophe '83', op. cit., p. 28.
156 Ibid., p. 210; Presidential Commission of 1977, op. cit., p. 280.
157 de Silva, *Managing Ethnic Tensions*, op. cit., p. 305.

4 Liberalization, authoritarianism, and communal violence, 1977–1983

1 Ronald J. Herring, 'Making Ethnic Conflict: The Civil War in Sri Lanka', in Esman and Herring, *Carrots, Sticks and Ethnic Conflict*, op. cit., p. 145.
2 Asoka Bandarage, 'Women and Capitalist Development in Sri Lanka: 1977–1987, *Bulletin of Concerned Asian Scholars*, (20)2, 1988, p. 78.
3 Ibid., p. 78.
4 Ibid., p. 111.

5 Ibid., p. 75; W.D. Lakshman, 'Income Distribution and Poverty', in *Dilemmas of Development: Fifty years of Economic Change in Sri Lanka*, Colombo: Sri Lanka Association of Economists, 1997, p. 193.

6 Bandarage, *Colonialism*, op. cit., chapter 8.

7 Lakshman, 'Income Distribution', op. cit., pp. 196–197.

8 David Dunham and Sisira Jayasuriya, 'Is all so well With the Economy and with the Rural Poor?', *Pravada*, vol. 5, no. 11, 1998, p. 23.

9 Lakshman, 'Income Distribution', op. cit., p. 193.

10 Siri T. Hettige, 'Economic Policy, Changing Opportunities for Youth, and the Ethnic Conflict in Sri Lanka', in Winslow and Woost, eds., *Economy, Culture and Civil War in Sri Lanka*, Bloomington: Indiana University Press, 2004, op. cit., p. 127.

11 Tambiah, *Ethnic Fratricide*, op. cit., Appendix, 3, p. 152.

12 Ministry of Plan Implementation and the Department of Census and Statistics, 1983 cited in Tambiah, *Ethnic Fratricide*, op. cit., p. 152.

13 C.Y. Thangarajah, 'Youth, Conflict', op. cit., p. 176.

14 Nira Wickramasinghe, *Civil Society in Sri Lanka: New Circles of Power*, New Delhi: Sage Publications, 2001, p. 78.

15 Siri Hettige, 'Economic Liberalization, Social Class and Ethnicity: Emerging Trends and Conflicts', in Gamage and Watson, *Conflict and Community*, op. cit., p. 310.

16 Ibid., pp. 313–314.

17 Ibid., pp. 77–78; Richardson, 'Violent Conflict and the First Half Decade of Open Economy Policies', in Winslow and Woost, *Economy*, op. cit., pp. 56–57; Lakshman, 'Income Distribution', op. cit., p. 176.

18 Ibid., p. 193.

19 R.M.K. Ratnayaka, 'Poverty in Sri Lanka: Incidence and Poverty Reduction Strategies', in A.D.V. de Indraratna eds., *Fifty Years of Sri Lanka's Independence*, Colombo: Si Lanka Institute of Social and Economic Studies, 1998, p. 590.

20 Herring, 'Making Ethnic Conflict', op. cit., p. 157.

21 Richardson, Violent Conflict, op. cit., pp. 55; see also, Newton Gunasinghe, 'The Open Economy and Its Impact on Ethnic Relations in Sri Lanka', in Winslow and Woost, *Economy*, op. cit., pp. 107–114.

22 Richardson, 'Violent Conflict', op. cit., p. 55; Tambiah, *Ethnic Fratricide*, op. cit., p. 51.

23 Gunasinghe, 'Open Economy', op. cit., p. 108.

24 Tambiah, *Ethnic Fratricide*, op. cit., p. 161; Herring, op. cit., Richardson, 'Violent Conflict', op. cit., p. 60.

25 Sri Lanka 1981 Census of Population.

26 Vidyamali Samarasinghe, 'The Tyranny of Space: A Socio-Economic Analysis of the Spatial Dimensions of the Ethnic Conflict in Sri Lanka', in Paul Groves, ed., *Economic Development and Social Change in Sri Lanka*, Delhi: Manohar, 1996, pp. 238–239.

27 Gunasinghe, 'Open Economy', op. cit., p. 108.

28 O'Sullivan, 'Conflict as Catalyst' op. cit., p. 267.

29 Ibid., p. 267.

30 Ibid., p. 267.

31 Bandarage, 'Ethnic and Religious Tension', op. cit., *passim*.

32 Mick Moore, 'Economic Liberalization', Growth and Poverty', Institute of Development Studies, discussion paper 274, March 1990, pp. 373–374.

33 Ibid., p. 375.

34 Hettige, 'Economic Liberalization', op. cit., p. 314.

35 David Gillies, 'Principal Intervention: Canadian Aid, Human Rights and the Sri Lankan Conflict', in Robert Miller, ed., *Aid as Peacemaker: Canadian Development*

Assistance and Third World Conflict, Ottawa: Carleton University Press, 1992, p. 64.

36 Ibid., p. 64; Herring, 'Making Ethnic Conflict', op. cit., p. 149.
37 Ibid., Bandarage, *Women and Capitalist Development*, op. cit., p. 64.
38 Ibid., p. 64.
39 N. Shanmugaratnam, 'The "Open Economy" Strategy and Agriculture', in Dunham and Abeysekara, *The Sri Lankan Economy*, op. cit., pp. 206–207.
40 Richardson, 'Violent Conflict', op. cit., p. 55; Tambiah, *Ethnic Fratricide*, op. cit., pp. 50–51.
41 Hoole, *Sri Lanka*, op. cit., p. 74.
42 Peebles, 'Colonization', op. cit., p. 45.
43 Manogaran, *Ethnic Conflict*, op. cit., p. 107.
44 Peebles, 'Colonization and Ethnic Conflict', op. cit., pp. 32, 39.
45 Thayer Scudder, 'Constraints to the Development of Settler Incomes and Production Oriented Participatory Organizations in Large-Scale Government Sponsored Projects: The Mahaweli Case', in S.T. Hettige and H.P. Muller, eds., *Blurring of A Vision – The Mahaweli*, Ratmalana: Sarvodaya, 1995, p. 156.
46 Samarasinghe, 'Tyranny of Space', op. cit., p. 235.
47 Gillies, 'Principled Intervention', op. cit., p. 55.
48 Ibid., p. 55; see also, Gunaratna, *Sovereign State*, op. cit., pp. 53, 63.
49 Gillies, 'Principled Intervention', op. cit., p. 56.
50 Gunaratna, *Sovereign State*, op. cit., pp. 55–56.
51 Manogaran, *Ethnic Conflict*, op. cit., p. 91.
52 Gillies, 'Principled Intervention', op. cit., pp. 55–56.
53 Frerks and Klem, *Dealing With Diversity*, op. cit., Part iii.
54 Balasuriya, *Sri Lanka's Crisis*, op. cit., p. 33.
55 Senaratna, *Political Violence*, op. cit., p. 25.
56 Berghof Foundation, 'Control over land: Competing Claims and Fuzzy Property Rights in the North-East of Sri Lanka', 21 March 2003, cited in http:/sangam.org/ taraki retrieved 23 April 2008; Amita Shastri, 'Material Basis', op. cit., p. 11.
57 Balasuriya, *Sri Lanka's Crisis*, op. cit., p. 7; Presidential Commission of 1977, op. cit.
58 Senaratna, *Political Violence*, op. cit., p. 25.
59 Ibid., pp. 8, 21.
60 Bandarage, *Colonialism*, op. cit., chapter 7.
61 Peebles, 'Colonization', op. cit., p. 45.
62 Indra Gajanayake, 'Ethnic Conflict in Sri Lanka: A Demographic Perspective', paper prepared for UNU/WIDER project on social change and social conflict in contemporary Sri Lanka, 30 March 1989, table 11.
63 Ibid.
64 Robert N. Kearney, 'Territorial Elements of Tamil Separatism in Sri Lanka', *Pacific Affairs*, vol. 60, no. 4, winter 1987–1988, table 7.
65 De Silva, *Managing Ethnic Tensions*, op. cit., p. 356.
66 Presidential Commission of 1977, op. cit., p. 122.
67 Peebles, 'Colonization', op. cit., p. 45.
68 Hoole, *Sri Lanka*, op. cit., pp. 50–51, 310.
69 Gunaratna, *Sovereign State*, op. cit., p. 106.
70 Ibid. p. 119.
71 Ibid., p. 119; MIRJE, '1981', op. cit., pp. 52–54.
72 Peebles, 'Colonization', op. cit., p. 45.
73 Gunasekara, *Tigers*, op. cit., p. 189; Gunaratna, *Sovereign State*, op. cit., p. 36.
74 Peebles, 'Colonization', op. cit., p. 45; Hoole, *Sri Lanka*, op. cit., pp. 51, 125.
75 MIRJE, '1981', op. cit., pp. 55–65;. Presidential Truth Commission, op. cit., pp. 30–31.

76 Ibid., p. 31.
77 Roberts, *Collective Identities* op. cit., p. 74; Manogaran, *Ethnic Conflict*, op. cit., p. 93.
78 G.H. Peiris, 'An Appraisal of the Concept of a Traditional Tamil Homeland in Sri Lanka', *Ethnic Studies Report*, 9(1), Jan. 1991, pp. 33–34.
79 K. Sivathamby, 'Some Aspects of the Social Composition of the Tamils of Sri Lanka', in Social Scientist Association (SSA), *Ethnicity and Social Change*, op. cit., pp. 134–135.
80 P.K. Balachandran, *Hindustan Times*, online, available at: www.island.lk/ 2003/11/11.
81 De Silva, *Managing Ethnic Tensions*, op. cit., p. 312.
82 Ibid., p. 258.
83 Ibid., p. 257; S.W.R. de A. Samarasinghe, 'Dynamics of Separatism', in R.R. Premdas, S.W.R. de Semarasinghe, A.B. Anderson (eds.), *Secessionist Movements*, New York: St Martin's Press, 1990, p. 52.
84 Ibid., pp. 293–303; Constitution of the Democratic Socialist Republic of Sri Lanka, 31 August 1978.
85 Ibid., Chapter IV; see also, de Silva, 'Affirmative Action Policies', op. cit., p. 272.
86 Laksiri Jayasuriya, *The Changing Face of Electoral Politics in Sri Lanka, (1994–2004)*, Nugegoda: Sarasavi Publishers, 2005, pp. xix, 18.
87 De Silva, *Managing Ethnic Tensions*, op. cit., pp. 301–302.
88 Ibid., p. 301, *Sri Lanka Strategic Conflict Assessment*, op. cit., vol. 3, p. 1.
89 De Silva, *Managing Ethnic Tensions*, op. cit., p. 320.
90 Ibid., p. 320.
91 Ibid., pp. 318–319.
92 Fazil, 'The Muslim Factor', op. cit., p. 175.
93 Ibid., p. 161.
94 Ibid., p. 260.
95 A. Jeyaratnam Wilson, *The Gaullist System in Asia: The Constitution of Sri Lanka (1978)*, London: MacMillan Press, 1980, p. 17.
96 Ibid., p. 116.
97 De Silva, *Managing Ethnic Tensions*, op. cit., pp. 302–303; MIRJE, *Emergency '79*, op. cit., pp. 10–14.
98 De Silva, *Managing Ethnic Tensions*, op. cit., p. 289.
99 Ibid., p. 293; MIRJE, *Emergency '79*, op. cit., pp. 10–11.
100 Cited in de Silva, *Managing Ethnic Tensions*, op. cit., p. 294.
101 Ibid., p. 303.
102 MIRJE, *Emergency '79*, op. cit., p. 14.
103 Ibid., pp. 290–291, 319.
104 Ibid., p. 316.
105 Balasuriya, *Catastrophe '83*, op. cit., p. 119.
106 Bastian, 'Liberalised Policies', op. cit., p. 194.
107 Ibid., p. 195; Tissa Balasuriya, 'Economic and Social Justice, Democracy and Ethnic Harmony', in Indo–Sri Lanka Peace Accord 29 July 1987, *Logos*, vol. 26, nos. 1, 3, 4, December 1987, p. 150; see also, Moore, 'Economic Liberalization', op. cit., p. 346.
108 Ibid., p. 371.
109 Balasuriya, 'Economic and Social Justice', op. cit., p. 150; Moore, 'Economic Liberalization', op. cit., p. 359; 'A Crisis of Civilisation': The Human Rights Situation in Sri Lanka, Centre for Society and Religion, Colombo: Human Rights Day, 1983.
110 Wilson, *The Gaullist System*, op. cit., p. 157.
111 Ibid., pp. 150–154.
112 Ibid., p. 154.
113 Moore, 'Economic Liberalization', op. cit., p. 360.

114 Balasuriya, 'Catastrophe '83', op. cit., p. 67; Tambiah, *Ethnic Fratricide*, op. cit., p. 51.
115 Ibid., p. 151.
116 Moore, 'Economic Liberalization', op. cit., p. 361; Balasuriya, 'Economic and Social Justice', op. cit., pp. 360, 151.
117 Hoole, *Sri Lanka*, op. cit., p. 68.
118 Jayasekara and Amarasinghe, 'The Economy', op. cit., pp. 52–53.
119 Moore, 'Economic Liberalization', op. cit., p. 364; Balasuriya, 'Economic and Social Justice', op. cit., p. 155; Hoole *Sri Lanka*, op. cit., p. 155.
120 Ibid., pp. 364; Balasuriya, 'Economic and Social Justice', op. cit., p. 155; Hoole, *Sri Lanka*, op. cit., p. 68.
121 Bandarage, 'Ethnic and Religious Tension', op. cit., *passim*.
122 Moore, 'Economic Liberalization', op. cit., p. 381; Sasanka Perera, Political Violence in Sri Lanka, Centre for Women's Research, 1998, p. 20.
123 O'Ballance, *Cyanide War*, op. cit., p. 12.
124 Ibid., op. cit., pp. 17–18.
125 Ibid., p. 15.
126 De Silva, *Managing Ethnic Tensions*, ibid., p. 328.
127 O'Ballance, *Cyanide War*, op. cit., p. 16.
128 De Silva, *Managing Ethnic Tensions*, op. cit., p. 327.
129 *Broken Palmyrah*, chapter 3: 2–7, 1982.
130 Rohan Gunaratna, *International and Regional Security*, op. cit., p. 8.
131 De Silva, *Managing Ethnic Tensions*, op. cit., p. 330.
132 Ibid., p. 97.
133 De Silva, *Managing Ethnic Tensions*, op. cit., p. 330.
134 *Emergency '79*, op. cit., pp. 19–20.
135 O'Ballance, *Cyanide War*, op. cit., p. 15.
136 Gunaratna, *Sovereign State*, p. 282.
137 K.M. de Silva, 'Indo-Sri Lanka Relations', op. cit., pp. 77–78.
138 Gunaratna, *International and Regional Security*, op. cit., p. 17.
139 O'Ballance, *Cyanide War*, op. cit., pp. 14–15.
140 Balasuriya, 'Economic and Social Justice', op. cit., p. 164; Hoole, *Sri Lanka*, op. cit., p. 59.
141 O'Ballance, *Cyanide War*, op. cit., pp. 19.
142 Ibid., pp. 14–15; Gunaratna, *International and Regional Security*, op. cit., pp. 17–18.
143 Balasuriya, 'Economic and Social Justice', op. cit., pp. 164–165; K.M. de Silva, 'Indo-Sri Lanka Relations', op. cit., pp. 77–78.
144 Gunaratna, *War and Peace in Sri Lanka*, Sri Lanka: Institute of Fundamental Studies, 1987, p. 50.
145 Ibid., pp. 48–50; de Silva, 'Indo-Sri Lanka Relations', op. cit., pp. 77–78.
146 Balasuriya, 'Economic and Social Justice', op. cit., p. 165.
147 *Emergency '79*; *Sunday Observer*, 15 July 1979.
148 *Emergency '79*, op. cit., pp. 23–25.
149 Ibid., p. 25.
150 Ibid., '1981', MIRJE, p. 22.
151 MIRJE, '1981', Appendix II, p. 47: de Silva, *Managing Ethnic Tensions*, op. cit., 331; O'Ballance, *Cyanide War*, op. cit., p. 19.
152 MIRJE, 1981 op. cit., p. 8; de Silva, *Managing Ethnic Tensions*, op. cit., p. 332.
153 Ibid., p. 333; MIRJE '1981', op. cit., p. 39.
154 Ibid., p. 33.
155 Ibid.
156 Ibid., pp. 39–40.
157 Balasuriya, 'Catastrophe '83', op. cit., pp. 39–40.
158 O'Ballance, *Cyanide War*, op. cit., p. 19.

159 Peebles, 'Colonization', op. cit., p. 45.
160 Tissa Balasuriya, 'Youth Insurrection and Democracy in Sri Lanka: 1971–1987', in Democracy in Sri Lanka, *Logos*, vol. 26, no. 2, August 1987, pp. 52–54.
161 Gunaratna, *Sri Lanka*, op. cit., p. 179.
162 Indo–Sri Lanka Peace Accord 29 July 1987, Logos, vol. 26 Nos. 1, 3 and 4, Dec. 1987, p. 159.
163 De Silva, *Managing Ethnic Tensions*, op. cit., 335.
164 'Referendum '82: Eclipse of Parliamentary Democracy in Sri Lanka', *Logos* vol. 22, no. 1, March 1983, p. 92.
165 Ibid., pp. 90–105.
166 Ibid., p. 105; Gunaratna, *Sri Lanka*, op. cit., p. 181.
167 Tissa Balasuriya, 'Economic and Social Justice', op. cit., p. 159.
168 Ibid., p. 159.
169 Ibid., p. 160.
170 Gunaratna, *Sri Lanka*, op. cit., p. 184.
171 Balasuriya, 'Economic and Social Justice', op. cit., p. 160.
172 Hoole, *Sri Lanka*, p. 105.
173 Gunaratna, *Sri Lanka*, op. cit., pp. 184–188.
174 Hoole, *Sri Lanka*, op. cit., p. 66.
175 Ibid., p. 68.
176 Ibid., p. 68.
177 Balasuriya, 'Catastrophe '83', p. 47.
178 Balasuriya, 'Economic and Social Justice', op. cit., p. 163.
179 Hoole, *Sri Lanka*, op. cit., p. 105.
180 Ibid., p. 123.
181 Piyadasa, *Sri Lanka*, op. cit., pp. 90–91; see also, Anita Pratap, *Island of Blood*, London: Penguin, 2001, p. 53.
182 Quoted in S.L. Gunasekara, *Tigers*, op. cit., p. 9.
183 Piyadasa, *Sri Lanka*, op. cit., p. 98.
184 Ibid, p. 84; Gunasinghe, 'The Open Economy', op. cit., p. 99; Hoole, *Sri Lanka*, op. cit., pp. 107–113.
185 Piyadasa, *Sri Lanka*, op. cit., p. 81.
186 American Heritage Dictionary, Boston: Houghton Mifflin Co., 1973.
187 Hoole, *Sri Lanka*, op. cit., pp. 109, 111; Tambiah, *Ethnic Fratricide*, op. cit., p. 25.
188 Ibid., p. 112, Balasuriya, 'Catastrophe '83', op. cit., p. 46.
189 Ibid., pp. 113, 131, 135, 139, 143.
190 Piyadasa, *Sri Lanka*, op. cit., p. 99.
191 Gunasinghe, 'Open Economy', op. cit.
192 Tambiah, *Ethnic Fratricide*, op. cit., pp. 132, 160.
193 Ibid., pp. 23, 113.
194 Anita Pratap, *Island of Blood*, op. cit., p. 53.
195 *India Today*, 31 August 1983, cited in Tambiah, *Ethnic Fratricide*, op. cit., p. 23.
196 Hoole, *Sri Lanka*, op. cit., p. 157.
197 Piyadasa, *Sri Lanka*, op. cit., p. 103.
198 Caluwadewage Cyril Mathew, An Appeal to UNESCO to Safeguard and Preserve the Cultural Property in Sri Lanka Endangered by Racial Prejudice, Unlawful Occupation and Willful Destruction, Colombo: Ministry of Industries and Scientific Affairs, 1983.
199 Hoole, *Sri Lanka*, op. cit., pp. 173–174.
200 Piyadasa, *Sri Lanka*, op. cit., p. 108.

5 Internationalization of the secessionist struggle, 1983–1987

1 Gamini Samaranayake, 'The Changing Attitude Towards the Tamil Problem Within the Janatha Vimukthi Peramuna' in Abeysekara and Gunasinghe, *Facets of Ethnicity*, op. cit., pp. 283–284.
2 Rohan Gunaratna, *Sri Lanka's Ethnic Crisis and National Security*, Colombo: South Asian Conflict on Conflict Research, 1998, p. 127.
3 Gunasekara, *A Lost Generation*, op. cit., pp. 13–14.
4 Tambiah, *Ethnic Fratricide*, op. cit., pp. 44–45.
5 S.D. Muni, *Rings of Proximity*, Oslo: PRIO, 1993, p. 186.
6 Gunaratna, *Ethnic Crisis*, op. cit., p. 111; Hoole, *Sri Lanka*, op. cit., pp. 455–456.
7 Ibid., pp. 68, 111–112.
8 Ibid., p. 112.
9 De Silva, *Managing Ethnic Tensions*, op. cit., p. 344.
10 Muni, *Proximity*, op. cit., p. 186.
11 Ibid., pp. 53–54.
12 Ibid., p. 187.
13 Ibid., p. 71.
14 Ibid., p. 71.
15 Cited in Pratap, *Island of Blood*, op. cit., p. 51.
16 Dayan Jayatilleka, 'The Indian Intervention in Sri Lanka: 1987–1990: The NEPC and Devolution of Power', *Occasional Paper 7*, Kandy: ICES, 1999, p. 54.
17 Hoole, *Sri Lanka*, op. cit., p. 63.
18 Muni, *Proximity*, op. cit., p. 71.
19 Ibid., p. 188; O'Ballance, *Cyanide War*, op. cit., p. 27; Hoole, *Sri Lanka*, op. cit., pp. 123, 178.
20 Muni, *Proximity*, op. cit., Appendix I, pp. 185–203.
21 Ibid., p. 63.
22 Ibid., pp. 61–62.
23 De Silva, *Managing Ethnic Tensions*, op. cit., p. 346.
24 Muni, *Proximity*, op. cit., p. 68; see also, Michael Roberts, *Narrating Tamil Nationalism: Subjectivities and Issues*, Sri Lanka: Vijith Yapa Publications, 2004, *passim*.
25 Gunaratna, *For A Sovereign State*, op. cit., p. 294.
26 'Annexure C' reproduced in Appendix II, in Muni, *Proximity*, op. cit., pp. 204–205.
27 Ibid., p. 205; de Silva, *Managing Ethnic Tensions*, op. cit., p. 345.
28 Muni, *Proximity*, op. cit., p. 189; de Silva, *Managing Ethnic Tensions*, op. cit., p. 346.
29 Ibid. p. 72.
30 Gunaratna, *Sri Lanka's Ethnic Crisis*, op. cit., p. 115.
31 Ibid., p. 72.
32 *Broken Palmyra*, vol. 2, 6.2.
33 Gunaratna, *Ethnic Crisis*, op. cit., p. 113, Jayatilleka, 'Indian Intervention', op. cit., p. 13.
34 O'Ballance, *Cyanide War*, op. cit., p. 31, de Silva, *Managing Ethnic Tensions*, op. cit., p. 347.
35 O'Ballance, *Cyanide War*, op. cit., p. 31.
36 Jayatilleka, 'Indian Intervention', op. cit., p. 13.
37 Ibid; Goonatilake, *Recolonisation*, op. cit., pp. 88–89.
38 Gunaratna, 'Internationalisation', op. cit., pp. 116–117.
39 Hoole, *Sri Lanka*, op. cit., p. 213.
40 De Silva, *Managing Ethnic Tensions*, op. cit., p. 351.
41 Madduma Bandara, *Lionsong: Sri Lanka's 'Ethic Conflict'*, Sri Lanka: Sanadruuan Madduma Bandara, 2002, p. 166.
42 Gunaratna, *Sri Lanka's Ethnic Crisis*, op. cit., p. 113.

43 De Silva, *Managing Ethnic Tensions*, op. cit., pp. 349–350.
44 O'Ballance, *Cyanide War*, op. cit., p. 44.
45 Ibid., p. 214.
46 Ibid., p. 39.
47 Thomas Abraham, 'The Emergence of the LTTE and the Indo-Sri Lanka Agreement of 1987', in Rupesinghe, *Negotiating Peace in Sri Lanka*, op. cit., p. 22.
48 De Silva, *A History of Sri Lanka*, Colombo: Vijitha Yapa Publications, 2005, p. 698.
49 Muni, *Proximity*, op. cit., p. 188.
50 O'Ballance, *Cyanide War*, op. cit., p. 37.
51 Muni, *Proximity*, op. cit., pp. 54–55; Hoole, *Sri Lanka*, op. cit., pp. 348–349.
52 Gunaratna, *Sri Lanka*, op. cit., p. 255.
53 Sivarajah, *Politics of Tamil Nationalism*, op. cit., p. 185.
54 Stewart Bell, 'The Snow Tigers: The Canadian Tamil Tigers Network', in SPUR, *Road Maps to Peace in Sri Lanka*, 20 August 2004, p. 3; Gunaratna, *Sri Lanka's Ethnic Crisis*, op. cit., p. 21.
55 Gunaratna, *International and Regional Security*, op. cit., p. 11.
56 Bell, 'The Snow Tigers', op. cit., p. 3.
57 Gunaratna, *International and Regional Security*, op. cit., p. 11.
58 Hoole, *Sri Lanka*, op. cit., pp. 413–414.
59 Gunaratna, *International and Regional Security*, op. cit., p. 11; O'Ballance, *Cyanide War*, op. cit., p. 37.
60 F. Rovik, 'Norway: A Terrorist Safe Haven', in *Peace in Sri Lanka: Obstacles and Opportunities*, London: WAPS, 2005, p. 7.
61 Gunaratna, 'Internationalisation', op. cit., p. 109; see also Rohan Gunaratna, 'Impact of the Mobilized Tamil Diaspora on the Protracted Conflict in Sri Lanka', in Kumar Rupesinghe ed., *Negotiating Peace in Sri Lanka*, vol. 1, Colombo: Foundation for Co-Existence, 2006, op. cit., pp. 269–302.
62 Peebles, 'Colonization', op. cit., p. 45; Gillies, 'Principled Intervention', op. cit., pp. 55–56; Gunaratna, *Sovereign State*, op. cit., pp. 62–94.
63 Ibid., pp. 69, 89.
64 Ibid., pp. 93–94, 225.
65 Gillies, 'Principled Intervention', op. cit., pp. 57, 65.
66 Ibid., p. 62.
67 Ibid., pp. 63–64.
68 Gillies, 'Principled Intervention', op. cit., p. 55.
69 Herring, 'Making Ethnic Conflict', op. cit., p. 151.
70 Gilles, 'Principled Intervention', op. cit., p. 55.
71 Uphoff, 'Ethnic Cooperation', op. cit., p. 133, fn 14.
72 Gunaratna, *Sovereign State*, op. cit., p. 37.
73 UTHR, Special Report No. 5, op. cit.
74 Ibid; MIRJE, 1981, op. cit., p. 66; 'Exodus of Buddhist Monks and Closure of Temples in NCP', *Island*, 30 September 2002.
75 Thayer Scudder, 'Constraints to the Development of Settler Incomes and Production Oriented Participatory Organizations in Large-Scale Government Sponsored Projects: The Mahaweli Case', in Hettige and Mayer, eds., *Blurring of A Vision*, op. cit., p. 155.
76 Ibid., p. 155; see also, Thawalama Foundation, Draft for Discussion Submitted by UNHCR, 2005.
77 Gunaratna, *Sovereign State*, op. cit., p. 193.
78 UTHR, Report No. 5, op. cit., p. 8; Gunaratna, *Sri Lanka's Ethnic Crisis*, op. cit., p. 20.
79 Ibid., p. 20; UTHR, Report No. 12, chapter 3, pp. 1–2.
80 Peebles, 'Colonization', op. cit., p. 46.
81 Gunaratna, *Sovereign State*, op. cit., p.200; Hoole, *Sri Lanka*, op. cit., pp. 196, 213.

82 Gunaratna, *Sovereign State*, op. cit., pp. 187–200.
83 Rameez Abdullah, 'Ethnic Harmony in Eastern Sri Lanka', in Frerks and Klem, *Dealing With Diversity*, op. cit., p. 187.
84 Fazil, 'The Muslim Factor in the Sri Lankan Conflict', op. cit., p. 171.
85 Ibid., p. 172; Karthigesu Sivathamby, 'The Sri Lankan Ethnic Crisis and Muslim–Tamil Relationships – A Socio-Political Review', Abeysekara and Gunasinghe, *Facets of Ethnicity*, op. cit., p. 192.
86 Rubin and Grossman, 'Accounting for "Disappearances"', in Sri Lanka: An Excerpt from an Asia Watch Report, *South Asia Bulletin*, vol. 8, 1988, p. 81, op. cit., p. 75.
87 Ladduwahetty, 'The Impact of Abrogation of CFA', op. cit., p. 3.
88 Vinay Lal, 'The Imperialism of Human Rights', *Focus on Law Studies*, 8, 1, Fall 1992.
89 Ladduwahetty, 'The Impact of Abrogation of CFA', op. cit., p. 4.
90 Sivarajah, *Tamil Nationalism*, op. cit., p. 185.
91 Ibid., pp. 28–29.
92 Virginia A. Leary, Ethnic Conflict and Violence in Sri Lanka, International Commission of Jurists – with a supplement by the ICJ staff for the period 1981–1983, August 1983.
93 Gunaratna, *Sri Lanka's Ethnic Crisis*, op. cit., pp. 20–21; Hoole, *Sri Lanka*, op. cit., p. 330.
94 Ibid., p. 330; O'Ballance, *Cyanide War*, op. cit., p. 78.
95 Ibid., p. 44; Hoole, *Sri Lanka*, op. cit., p. 213.
96 Ibid., pp. 212–213.
97 Asia Watch, *Cycles of Violence*, op. cit., p. 23.
98 Ibid, p. 1.
99 Ibid. p. 23.
100 Amnesty International, 'Sri Lanka: Disappearances', New York, 1986.
101 Ibid., pp. 19–21; O'Ballance, *Cyanide War*, op. cit., p. 45.
102 Tilak Ratnakara, Chairman, Media Centre, A Reply to the Report Entitled 'Disappearances in Sri Lanka' issued by the Amnesty International, Department of Information, 25 September 1986, pp. 1–12; Asoka Weerasinghe, 'Amnesty International's Reports of "Disappearances" in Sri Lanka Biased', *The Whig-Standard*, Canada, 15 January 1987.
103 Amnesty International, AI Index: ASA 37/17/86, Distr: SC/CC, Sri Lanka Disappearance Campaign, Update no. 2, 23 October 1986.
104 Sivarajah, *Politics of Tamil Nationalism*, op. cit., p. 186; Goonatilake, *Recolonisationop*, New Delhi: Sage Publications, 2006, pp. 251, 104–116; see also, International Alert, 'Prospects for Peace in Sri Lanka: Report of Seminar Held in Oslo', 24 October, 1986, Oslo: International Peace Research Institute, 1986.
105 O'Ballance, *Cyanide War*, op. cit., p. 87.
106 Hoole, *Sri Lanka*, op. cit., p. 214; Gunaratna, *Sri Lanka's Ethnic Crisis*, op. cit., p. 21.
107 Barnett Rubin and Patricia Gossman, 'Accounting for "Disappearances" in Sri Lanka, p. 81.
108 Hoole, *Sri Lanka*, op. cit., p. 331.
109 Gunaratna, *Sri Lanka's Ethnic Crisis*, op. cit., p. 22; see also, International Centre for Ethnic Studies, Ethnic Conflict in Sri Lanka: Time Line, online, available at: www.ices.lk/sl_database/ethnic_conflict/time.line.
110 United States Committee for Refugees, *Sri Lankan Tamils' Search for Asylum: An Update*, Washington DC: United States Committee for Refugees, March 1987, p. 8.
111 Ghosh, *Ethnicity versus Nationalism*, op. cit., p. 29; see also The Thimpu Declaration, online, available at: www.tamilnation.org.
112 Gunasekara, *Tigers*, op. cit., p. 88.
113 Ibid., p. 54.

114 Sumansiri Liyanage, 'Rereading Thimpu Principles: An Integrative Perspective', in Rupesinghe, *Negotiating Peace in Sri Lanka*, op. cit., p. 7.
115 Bandara, *Lionsong*, op. cit., p. 143.
116 O'Ballance, *Cyanide War*, op. cit., p. 51.
117 Ambalavanar Sivarajah, *Politics of Tamil Nationalism in Sri Lanka*, New Delhi: South Asian Publishers, 1996, p. 178.
118 Ibid., p. 179.
119 'Thimpu Talks – Struggle for Tamil Eelam', online, available at: www.tamilnation.org; Hoole, 'The Tamil Secessionist Movement', op. cit., p. 1.
120 Thomas Abraham, 'The Emergence of the LTTE', op. cit., p. 22.
121 Muni, *Proximity*, op. cit., pp. 81–82, 198; O'Ballance, *Cyanide War*, op. cit., p. 88, International Centre for Ethnic Studies, 1995, p. 10.
122 Muni, *Proximity*, op. cit., p. 81, 83.
123 *Broken Palmyrah*, 5:6.
124 Ibid., 5:6.
125 Chandraprema, *Sri Lanka*, op. cit., p. 106.
126 Gunaratna, *Sri Lanka* op. cit., p. 233.
127 Muni, *Proximity*, op. cit., pp. 82, 200; Sivathamby, 'Ethnic Crisis', op. cit., p. 200.
128 Gunaratna, *Sri Lanka's Ethnic Crisis*, op. cit., pp. 22.
129 Muni, *Proximity*, op. cit., p. 193.
130 Ibid., p. 82.
131 Gunaratna, *Sri Lanka's Ethnic Crisis*, op. cit., p. 22; O'Ballance, *Cyanide War*, op. cit., pp. 55, 71.
132 Hoole, *Sri Lanka*, op. cit., p. 215.
133 Ibid., p. 214.
134 Gunasekara, *Wages of Sin*, p. 53.
135 Ibid., p. 77; Hoole, *Sri Lanka*, op. cit., p. 340; Gunaratna, *Sri Lanka's Ethnic Crisis*, op. cit., p. 22.
136 Jayatileka, *The Indian Intervention in Sri Lanka, 1987–1990*, Kandy: International Center for Ethnic Studies, 1999, p. 10.
137 Hoole, 'The Tamil Secessionist Movement', op. cit., p. 20.
138 O'Ballance, *Cyanide War*, op. cit., p. 71.
139 Ibid., pp. 68–69, 71–72.
140 Ibid., pp. 73, 76.
141 Muni, *Proximity*, op. cit., p. 198; O'Ballance, *Cyanide War*, op. cit., pp. 86–87.
142 Ibid., pp. 76, 90.
143 Ibid., pp. 75–76; Muni, *Proximity*, op. cit., pp. 199–200.
144 Ibid., p. 200.
145 O'Ballance, *Cyanide War*, op. cit., pp. 81–84.
146 Bandara, *Lionsong*, op. cit., p. 181.
147 Jayatilleka, *Sri Lanka: The Travails of a Democracy, Unfinished War*, Kandy: ICES, 1998, p. 10; Hoole, *Sri Lanka*, op. cit., p. 214.
148 Ibid., p. 84.
149 Ibid., p. 84.
150 O'Ballance, *Cyanide War*, op. cit., p. 85.
151 Ibid., p. 85.
152 J.N. Dixit, 'IPKF in Sri Lanka', text of a talk given on 10 March 1989 to members of the USI, *U.S.I. Journal*, p. 262.
153 Muni, *Proximity*, op. cit., pp. 200–201; O'Ballance, *Cyanide War*, op. cit., 85.
154 Ibid., pp. 85–86; Muni, *Proximity*, op. cit., p. 201.
155 Ibid., p. 201.
156 Ibid., pp. 201–202.
157 Shelton U. Kodikara, ed., *Indo-Sri Lanka Agreement of July 1987*, Colombo: University of Colombo, 1989.

158 O'Ballance, *Cyanide War*, op. cit., p. 90.
159 Ibid., p. 92.
160 Ibid., p. 92.
161 Muni, *Proximity*, op. cit., p. 202; O'Ballance, *Cyanide War*, op. cit., p. 90.
162 Ibid., p. 83.
163 Ibid., pp. 90–91.
164 Hoole, *Sri Lanka*, op. cit., p. 217.
165 O'Ballance, *Cyanide War*, op. cit., p. 91.

6 Indian intervention, Indo–Sri Lanka Accord, and intensification of violence, 1987–1994

1 Indo–Sri Lanka Agreement and annexure, in Muni, *Pangs of Proximity*, op. cit., Appendix IV.
2 Online, available at: www.constitution.gov.lk; Bandara, *Lionsong*, op. cit., pp. 207–208.
3 Muni, *Proximity*, op. cit., appendix iv.
4 Sinhala Samiti Niyojana Mandalaya, 'The Indo–Sri Lanka Agreement and Exchange of Letters: An Analysis', Colombo: Bauddaloka Mawatha, n.d., p. 26.
5 Cited in Kodikara, *Indo–Sri Lanka Agreement*, op. cit., p. 147.
6 Ibid., p. 66.
7 Shelton U. Kodikara, ed., *South Asian Strategic Issues: Sri Lankan Perspectives*, New Delhi: Sage Publications, 1990, p. 161; Sinhala Samiti Niyojana Mandalaya, 'The Indo–Sri Lanka Agreement', op. cit., pp. 11–12.
8 Goonatilake, *Recolonisation*, op. cit., pp. 98–99.
9 Chandraprema, *Sri Lanka*, op. cit., pp. 179–180.
10 Gunaratna, *Sri Lanka*, op. cit., p. 235.
11 Ibid., pp. 233–234; Alles, *The JVP*, op. cit., p. 287.
12 Gunaratna, *Sri Lanka*, op. cit., p. 235.
13 Ravinatha P. Ariyasinghe, 'The Follies of a Small State: The Political Response to the Indo–Sri Lanka Accord in Sri Lanka', in Kodikara, *Indo–Sri Lanka Agreement*, op. cit., pp. 116, 137; Bandara, *Lionsong*, op. cit., pp. 188–189.
14 Ibid., p. 116; Shelton U. Kodikara, 'The Continuing Crisis in Sri Lanka: The JVP, the Indian Troops, and Tamil Politics', *Asian Survey*, vol. xxix, no. 7, July 1989, p. 719; Sinhala Mandalaya, 'The Indo–Sri Lanka Agreement', op. cit., p. 27.
15 K.M. de Silva, *A History*, op. cit., p. 701.
16 Ariyasinghe, 'The Follies', op. cit., p. 129.
17 Cited in Ketheshwaran Loganathan, 'Indo–Sri Lanka Accord and the Ethnic Question: Lessons and Experiences', in Rupesinghe, *Negotiating Peace in Sri Lanka*, op. cit., p. 80.
18 Goonatilake, *Recolonisation*, op. cit., pp. 97–103; Hettige, 'Economic Liberalization', op. cit., p. 300.
19 International Alert, 'Political Killings in Southern Sri Lanka', London: 1989; Goonatilake, 'Norway, a 2 Year Odyssey: From Sympathizer to Colonial Intruder', in WAPS, *Peace in Sri Lanka*, op. cit., pp. 23–25.
20 Godfrey Gunatilleke, 'The Peace Accord: Problems and Prospects', in 'Indo–Sri Lanka Peace Accord', *Logos*, op. cit/. pp. 2, 14–15 and *passim*.
21 Loganathan, 'Indo–Sri Lanka Accord', op. cit., p. 80; see also, Jayadeva Uyangoda, 'The Indo–Sri Lanka Agreement of July 1987 and the State in Sri Lanka', in Kodikara, *Indo–Sri Lanka Agreement*, op. cit., *passim*.
22 Gunasekara, *Tigers*, op. cit., pp. 96–97.
23 Ariyasinghe, 'The Follies' op. cit., p. 81; *Broken Palmyrah*, vol. 1, chapter 9:1.
24 Ibid., vol. 1, chapter 8:2.
25 Shastri, 'The Material Basis', op. cit., pp. 56–77.

26 Bandara, *Lionsong*, op. cit., p. 192.
27 Cited in 'Indo–Sri Lanka Peace Accord', 29, July 1987, *Logos*, vol. 26, nos. 1, 3 and 4 December 1987, pp. 44–47.
28 Ibid., pp. 8–9; M.H.M. Ashroff, 'The Muslim Community and Peace Accord', in 'Indo–Sri Lanka Peace Accord', *Logos*, op. cit., pp. 48–75.
29 *Broken Palmyrah*, vol. 1, chapter 8:3.
30 Ashroff, 'The Muslim Community', op. cit., pp. 63–64; Fazil, 'The Muslim Factor', op. cit., p. 176.
31 Ashroff, 'The Muslim Community', op. cit., p. 57; Abdullah and Fazil, 'The Other Side of the Muslim Nation', op. cit., pp. 196.
32 Fazil, 'The Muslim, Factor', op. cit., p. 176; Abdullah and Fazil, 'The Other Side of the Muslim Nation', op. cit., pp. 193–194.
33 Fazil, 'The Muslim, Factor', op. cit., pp. 177–178.
34 *Broken Palmyrah*, vol. 1, chapter 8:2.
35 Gunaratna, *Sri Lanka*, p. 209; Bush, *Intra-Group Dimensions*, op. cit., pp. 112–113.
36 Gunaratna, *Sri Lanka*, pp. 208–212.
37 Ibid., pp. 199, 205, 208.
38 Cited in Premachandra, *Sri Lanka*, op. cit., p. 105.
39 Ibid., p. 212.
40 Ibid., pp. 212–213, 219.
41 Ibid., pp. 224, 267; see also Amnesty International, 'Sri Lanka: Extra Judicial Executions, "Disappearances" and Torture, 1987–1990', p. 7; A.C. Alles, *The J.V.P.*, op. cit., appendix vi, p. xviii.
42 International Alert, 'Political Killings in Southern Sri Lanka', London: 1989, Part 1, p. 2.
43 Chandraprema, *Sri Lanka*, op. cit., p. 134.
44 Gunaratna, *Sri Lanka*, op. cit., p. 257.
45 Ibid., pp. 246–247; International Alert, "Political Killings", op. cit., part 3.
46 Gunaratna, *Sri Lanka*, op. cit., p. 224; Kodikara, 'The Continuing Crisis', op. cit., p. 716; Chandraprema, *Sri Lanka*, op. cit., pp. 144–148, 163; Alles, *The J.V.P.*, op. cit., p. 332.
47 Kodikara, 'The Continuing Crisis', op. cit., p. 717; Gunaratna, *Sri Lanka*, op. cit., p. 261.
48 Chandraprema, *Sri Lanka*, op. cit., pp. 125–132.
49 Lakshman, 'Income Distribution and Poverty', op. cit., p. 197.
50 Bush, *Intra-Group Dimensions*, op. cit., p. 105.
51 Alles, *The J.V.P.*, op. cit., p. 343.
52 Gunaratna, *Sri Lanka*, op. cit., p. 361.
53 Chandraprema, *Sri Lanka*, op. cit., p. 180.
54 Ibid., p. 184.
55 Ibid., p. 184.
56 Bandara, *Lionsong*, op. cit., p. 194.
57 Ariyasinghe, 'The Follies of a Small State', op. cit., pp. 116, 137; Chandraprema, *Sri Lanka*, op. cit., p. 299.
58 Ibid., p. 181.
59 Ibid., pp. 299–300.
60 Ibid., p. 173.
61 Ibid., pp. 173, 176, 177.
62 Cited in ibid., p. 176.
63 Gunaratna, *Sri Lanka*, op. cit., p. 273.
64 Chandraprema, *Sri Lanka*, op. cit., p. 201.
65 Kodikara, 'The Continuing Crisis', op. cit., p. 716.
66 Alles, *The J.V.P.*, op. cit., p. 332; Gunaratna, *Sri Lanka*, op. cit., pp. 293–294.
67 Ibid., pp. 267, 293.

68 Alles, *The J.V.P.*, op. cit., Appendix VI, pp. xix. pp. 292–293, 317.
69 Amnesty International, Sri Lanka: Extrajudicial Executions, 1987–1990, op. cit., p. 10.
70 Ibid., p. 10; International Alert, 'Political Killings', op. cit., part 1, p. 5.
71 Chandraprema, *Sri Lanka*, op. cit., p. 254.
72 Gunaratna, *Sri Lanka*, op. cit., p. 298;Alles, The *J.V.P.*, op. cit., p. 290.
73 Ibid., p. 290.
74 Ibid., p. 298.
75 Ibid., p. 303.
76 Ibid., pp. 304–305.
77 Ibid., p. 305; Hoole, *Sri Lanka*, op. cit., p. 247.
78 Gunaratna, *Sri Lanka*, op. cit., p. 268.
79 Ibid., p. 268.
80 Gunaratna, *Sri Lanka's Ethnic Crisis*, op. cit., p. 23; International Alert, 'Political Killings', op. cit., part 4, p. 7; Alles, *The J.V.P.*, op. cit., p. 317.
81 Chandraprema, *Sri Lanka*, op. cit., p. 184.
82 Amnesty International, 'Extrajudicial Executions, 1987–1990', op. cit., p. 10.
83 Ibid., p. 10.
84 Gunaratna, *Sri Lanka's Ethnic Crisis*, op. cit., p. 24; Chandraprema, *Sri Lanka*, op. cit., p. 312;Bandara, *Lionsong*, op. cit., p. 225.
85 Gunaratna, *Sri Lanka's Ethnic Crisis*, op. cit., p. 24; Gunaratna, *Sri Lanka*, op. cit., p. 335.
86 Chandraprema, *Sri Lanka*, op. cit., p. 296.
87 Ibid., pp. 296–297; Amnesty International, 'Sri Lanka: Reports of Extrajudicial Killings', December 1989, *passim.*
88 Ibid, p. 37; Chandraprema, *Sri Lanka*, op. cit., p. 238.
89 Hoole, *Sri Lanka*, op. cit., p. 255.
90 Ibid., pp. 240–241; Hoole, *Sri Lanka*, op. cit., pp. 262–263.
91 Ibid., pp. 249, 252, 267; *The Hindu*, 23 August 2000.
92 Barnett Rubin and Patricia Gossman, 'Accounting for 'Disappearances', op. cit., p. 75; International Alert, 'Political Killings', op. cit., part 4, p. 11; Amnesty International, 'Sri Lanka: Extra Judicial Killings', op. cit., p. 2; Asia Watch, 'Asia Watch Condemns Killings of Civilians by Sri Lankan Forces and JVP', 5 September 1989. Campaign for the Release of Political Prisoners, June 9, 1986, p. 1.
93 Asia Watch, 'Asia Watch Condemns', op. cit., p. 2; Asia Watch, 'Sri Lanka: Emergency Re-imposed as Killings Continue', 18 July 1989, p. 5; Amnesty International, 'Sri Lanka: Repeal of Indemnity Legislation Sought', AI Index: ASA 37/01/89 January 1989.
94 Amnesty International, 'Sri Lanka: Reports of Extra Judicial Killings', op. cit., p. 19.
95 Ibid., pp. 1, 19, 39.
96 Amnesty International, 'Sri Lanka: Reports of Extra Judicial Killings', op. cit., pp. 13–14; Hoole, *Sri Lanka*, op. cit., p. 237.
97 Chandraprema, *Sri Lanka*, op. cit., pp. 304–311; Gunaratna, *Sri Lanka*, op. cit., p. 341.
98 Ibid., p. 260.
99 Ibid., p. 272.
100 Amnesty International, 'Extrajudicial Executions', op. cit., pp. 22–24.
101 Hoole, *Sri Lanka*, op. cit., p. 261; Amnesty International, 'USA: Action Alert on Death Threats to Manorani Sarvanamuttu', 5 June 1990.
102 Hoole, *Sri Lanka*, op. cit., p. 255.
103 Subhash Wickramasinghe, *Under Attack: A Collection of Articles on Political Activities in the Face of LTTE Terrorism*, Ratmalana: Vishva Lekha Publishers, 2007, pp. 29–30.

104 Clifford Bob, *The Marketing of Rebellion*, Cambridge: Cambridge University Press, 2005, *passim*.
105 Gunaratna, *Sri Lanka*, op. cit., p. 359.
106 13th Amendment to the Constitution (1987) cited in ICES, *Sri Lanka: The Devolution Debate*, Colombo: ICES, 1996, appendix k; de Silva, *Reaping the World Wind*, op. cit., p. 239; Dayan Jayatilleka, *The Indian Intervention*, op. cit., Appendix, p. 76; Bastian, *Devolution and Development in Sri Lanka*, op. cit., p. 1.
107 De Silva, *Reaping the World Wind*, op. cit., p. 239; Jayatilleka, *Indian Intervention*, op. cit., Appendix, p. 76.
108 Harkirat Singh, *Intervention in Sri Lanka: The IPKF Experience Retold*, Colombo: Vijitha Yapa Publications, 2006, p. 133.
109 Ibid., p. 7.
110 Kodikara, 'Indo–Sri Lanka Agreement: Retrospect', op. cit., p. 174.
111 De Silva, *Reaping the World Wind*, op. cit., p. 236; Bandara, *Lionsong*, op. cit., pp. 195–197.
112 Gunaratna, *Sri Lanka's Ethnic Crisis*, op. cit., pp. 318–319.
113 Hoole, *Sri Lanka*, op. cit., pp. 403, 456.
114 Ibid., p. 410.
115 *Broken Palmyrah*, op. cit., second preface, February 1990, p. 2.
116 Hoole, *Sri Lanka*, op. cit., pp. 226–227.
117 Asia Watch, *Cycles of Violence*, op. cit., pp. 51–52; Hoole, *Sri Lanka*, op. cit., p. 227; Asia Watch, News From Sri Lanka, op. cit., January–April 1988, p. 4.
118 Hoole, *Sri Lanka*, op. cit., p. 226.
119 Ibid., p. 228.
120 Asia Watch, *Cycles of Violence*, op. cit., December 1987, p. 52.
121 Ibid., p. 57.
122 Asia Watch, News From Sri Lanka, op. cit., January–April 1988, p. 4.
123 Hoole, *Sri Lanka*, op. cit., p. 226.
124 Harkirat Singh, *Intervention*, op. cit., pp. 54, 76.
125 Asia Watch, News From Sri Lanka, op. cit., January–April 1988, p. 4; International Alert, 'Political Killings', op. cit., part 1, p. 3.
126 Asia Watch, News from Sri Lanka, January–April 1988, op. cit., pp. 4–5.
127 Hoole, *Sri Lanka*, op. cit., p. 218; Bandara, *Lionsong*, op. cit., pp. 197–198.
128 Hoole, *Sri Lanka*, p. 219.
129 Bandara, *Lionsong*, op. cit., pp. 199–200; Singh, *Intervention*, op. cit., pp. 62–64, 75–76.
130 Ibid., p. 81; Bandara, *Lionsong*, op. cit., pp. 199–200.
131 Bandara, *Lionsong*, op. cit., p. 210.
132 Asia Watch, *Cycles of Violence*, op. cit., December 1987, p. 52.
133 Bandara, *Lionsong*, op. cit., p. 210; Singh, *Intervention*, op. cit., pp. 123.
134 Asia Watch, 'Sri Lanka: Emergency Reimposed as Killings Continue', 18 July 1989, pp. 7–8; Asia Watch, News from Sri Lanka, Jan-April 1988, op. cit., p. 4.
135 Ibid., p. 3.
136 Amnesty International, 'Sri Lanka: Briefing', September 1990, p. 16; see also, Amnesty International, 'Sri Lanka: Reports of Extrajudicial Executions', December 1989, pp. 11–13.
137 Canada–Asia Working Group's Report submitted to the United Nations Commission on Human Rights in Geneva, February 1990, *Currents*, vol. 1 and 2, nos. 1 and 2; see also, Amnesty International, Sri Lanka: Continuing Human Rights Violations', May 1989, *passim*; *Broken Palmyra*, op. cit., vol. 2, *passim*.
138 Ibid., pp. 53, 55.
139 Singh, *Intervention*, op. cit., pp. 50, 133.
140 Ibid., p. 75.
141 Bandara, *Lionsong*, op. cit., p. 217.
142 Ibid., p. 217.

143 Ibid., p. 218.
144 Jayatilleka, *Indian Intervention*, op. cit., p. 45.
145 Ibid., pp. 44–45.
146 De Silva, *Reaping*, op. cit., p. 240; Bandara, *Lionsong*, op. cit., p. 218.
147 Canada–Asia Working Group's Report submitted to the UNCHR in Geneva, February 1990, *Currents*, vol. 1 and 2, nos. 1 and 2, op. cit., p. 55; Swamy, *Tigers*, op. cit., pp. 304–308.
148 Ibid., p. 55; Jayatilleka, *Indian Intervention*, op. cit., pp. 53, 77; *Broken Palmyra*, op. cit., appendix 1, 1:4.
149 *Broken Palmyra*, op. cit., appendix 1, 1:4; second preface, February 1990, p. 3.
150 Ibid., p. 53; Bandara, *Lionsong*, op. cit., p. 226.
151 Jayatilleka, *Indian Intervention*, op. cit., p. 53, 57–60.
152 G.D.C. Weerasinghe, 'Conflict Resolution: Lessons for Sri Lanka', Colombo: Lake House Publishers, 2007, p. 38.
153 Cited in Bandara, *Lionsong*, op. cit., p. 213.
154 Asia Watch June'89, op. cit., p. 3; Bandara, *Lionsong*, op. cit., p. 221, 223.
155 Sarath Munasinghe, *A Soldier's Version*, Colombo: Market Information Systems, 2000, pp. 38–39; Gunaratna, *Sri Lanka's Ethnic Crisis*, op. cit., p. 24.
156 Ibid., p. 318.
157 Gunasekara, *Tigers*, op. cit., pp. 96–97.
158 Singh, *Intervention*, op. cit., p. 137; Bandara, *Lionsong*, op. cit., pp. 232–233.
159 Gunasekara, *Tigers*, op. cit., p. 96; Munasinghe, *Soldier's Version*, op. cit., p. 98.
160 Ibid., p. 101; Bandara, *Lionsong*, op. cit., p. 232.
161 Ibid., p. 233; Munasinghe, *Soldier's Version*, op. cit., p. 102.
162 'Gaps in the Krishnathy Kumaraswamy Case: Disappearances and Accountability', *Special Report No. 12*, UTHR, p. 36.
163 Bandara, *Lionsong*, op. cit., p. 236; Gunasekara, *Wages of Sin*, op. cit., pp. 34; Gunaratna, *Sri Lanka's Ethnic Crisis*, op. cit., p. 24.
164 Munasinghe, *Soldier's* Version, op. cit., p. 192, Report of the Presidential Truth Commission, op. cit., p. 31; Fazil, 'The Muslim Factor', op. cit., pp. 173–174.
165 De Silva, *Reaping*, op. cit., p. 245.
166 Gunaratna, *Sri Lanka's Ethnic Crisis*, op. cit., p. 25.
167 De Silva, *Reaping*, op. cit., p. 245.
168 Swamy, *Inside An Elusive Mind – Prabha Karam*, Sri Lanka: Vijitha Yapa Publications, 2003, p. 281.
169 Gunaratna, *Sri Lanka's Ethnic Crisis*, op. cit., pp. 25–27; see also Gunaratna, 'Internationalisation of the Tamil Conflict', op. cit., p. 123.
170 Gunaratna, *International and Regional Security*, op. cit., p. 32.
171 Gunaratna, *Sri Lanka's Ethnic Crisis*, op. cit., pp. 25–26.
172 Hoole, *Sri Lanka*, op. cit., p. 449.
173 Ibid., p. 26; Bandara, *Lionsong*, op. cit., p. 250.
174 Cited in Swamy, *Inside an Elusive Mind*, op. cit., p. 249.
175 Ibid. p. 252; Gunaratna, *Sri Lanka's Ethnic Crisis*, op. cit., p. 121.
176 Munasinghe, *A Soldier's Version*, op. cit., pp. 132–134; Gunaratna, *Sri Lanka's Ethnic Crisis*, op. cit., pp. 26, 27, 121.
177 Hoole, *Sri Lanka*, op. cit., pp. 406–407, 432, 449.

7 A peace package, war, and the international community, 1994–2001

1 Report of the Sinhala Commission, Part II, Colombo: NJC, 2001, op. cit., pp. 74–75; Udan Fernando, *NGOs in Sri Lanka: Past and Present Trends*, Sri Lanka: Waslaa Publications, 2003, p. 38; Camilla Orjuela, 'Building Peace in Sri Lanka?', *Journal of Peace Research*, vol. 40, no. 2, 2003, p. 199.

2 Ghosh, *Ethnicity*, op. cit., p. 158.
3 K.M. de Silva, 'Affirmative Action Policies', op. cit., p. 267.
4 INFORM, Situation Report, Colombo: Sri Lanka Information Center, February 1995, p. 7.
5 Ghosh, *Ethnicity*, op. cit., p. 159; ICES, *Sri Lanka: The Devolution Debate*, Appendices A, B, C, D.
6 Neelan Tiruchelvam, 'Devolution of Power: The Problems and Challenges', in ICES, *The Devolution Debate*, op. cit., pp. 39, 41.
7 Political Proposals, INFORM, Sri Lanka Information Center, Special Dossier on Devolution Package, September 1995, pp. 1–2.
8 Ibid., p. 4; see also Text of President Kumaratunga's Speech to the Nation, 3 August 1995, ibid., pp. 5–6.
9 'Basis for New Lanka', *Sunday Leader*, 6 August, 1995.
10 '30 NGOs Appeal for Peace Consensus', *Daily News*, 7 August, 1995.
11 'Promise of a New Dawn', The *Hindu*, 5 August, 1995; 'Proposals Evoke Appreciative Comments in Leading Indian Newspapers', *Daily News*, 7 August, 1995; 'Package Deserves to Succeed', *Daily News*, 8 August 1995; 'Canada Welcomes Peace Initiatives', *Daily News*, 11 August, 1995.
12 'Resolution Supporting Sri Lanka Govt. Before US Congress', *The Island*, 10, August 1995.
13 INFORM, Situation Report, Colombo: Sri Lanka Information Center, February 1995, p. 7.
14 Udan Fernando, *NGOs*, op. cit., p. 38.
15 Camilla Orjuela, 'Building Peace', op. cit., p. 200.
16 Miriam A. Young, 'Report on Trip to Sri Lanka for the NGO Forum on Sri Lanka, February 20–March 10, 1995', Southern Asia Office, United Church Board for World Ministries, Division of Overseas Ministries, pp. 1, 12.
17 Ibid., p. 3.
18 Ibid.
19 Report of the Sinhala Commission, Part 2, op. cit., pp. 70–71, 93–95; Joint Statements by NGOs at 47th and 50th sessions of the UN Sub Commission on Human Rights, online, available at: www.tamilnation.org/unitednations.
20 'The Unity and Sovereignty of Sri Lanka', *The Island*, 13 August, 1995.
21 Buddhadasa Hewavitharana, *Economic Consequences of the Devolution Package*, Colombo: Sinhala Weeta Vidhana, 1997, pp. 87, 207.
22 'MEP Calls for Withdrawal of Devolution Proposals', *Daily News*; 11 August 1995, 'YMBA and other Organizations Reject Devolution Proposals'*, Daily News*, 14 August 1995.
23 'SLES Wants Govt. to Abandon the "Devolution Package"', *Daily News*, 2 August 1995.
24 Ibid.
25 ICES, *The Devolution Debate*, op. cit., Appendix C.
26 Gunasekara, *Tigers*, op. cit., pp. 119, 127, 195.
27 Ibid., pp. 112–114, 127.
28 Ibid., p. 240.
29 Ibid., p. 238.
30 Ibid., pp. 237–238.
31 Ibid., p. 240.
32 Report of the Sinhala Commission, op. cit., parts 1 and 2.
33 National Joint Committee, Interim Report, op. cit., p. 25.
34 Ibid., pp. 60–97; Ghosh, *Ethnicity*, pp. 206–208.
35 National Joint Committee, Interim Report, op. cit., p. 49.
36 Ghosh, *Ethnicity*, op. cit., p. 210.
37 Ibid., p. 212.

38 Abeysekara *et al.*, *Unitarianism*, Colombo: Social Scientists Association, 1998, pp. 2, 7, 43.
39 Ibid., pp. 15–17; see also, Ghosh, *Ethnicity*, op. cit., p. 212.
40 Bastian, ed., *Devolution and Development*, op. cit., p. 3.
41 Online, available at: www.manthree.com/docs/1997.
42 Neil DeVotta, op. cit., *Blowback, passim.*
43 Ibid., p. 159; INFORM, Situation Report, Colombo: Sri Lanka Information Center, January 1996.
44 Ghosh, *Ethnicity*, op. cit., p. 358.
45 Ibid. p. 376.
46 Young, 'Report on Trip', op. cit., p. 11; Gunaratna, *Sri Lanka's Ethnic Crisis*, op. cit., p. 27.
47 Ghosh, *Ethnicity*, op. cit., p. 376.
48 Ibid., p. 376.
49 M.R. Narayan Swamy, *Inside an Elusive Mind*, op. cit., p. 248.
50 UTHR Information Bulletin No. 7, 4 September 1995.
51 Gunasekara, *Wages of Sin*, op. cit., p. 18; Bandara, *Lionsong*, op. cit., p. 259.
52 Gunasekara, *Tigers*, op. cit., pp. 107–108.
53 Ibid., pp. 110–111.
54 Ibid., p. 358; Gunaratna, *Sri Lanka's Ethnic Crisis*, op. cit., p. 28.
55 Gunasekara, *Tigers*, op. cit., pp. 109–110.
56 Letter to LTTE International Secretariat, from Deputy Secretary General, Amnesty International, 11 September 1995, in Amnesty International 'Correspondence with the Liberation Tigers of Tamil Eelam on Human Rights Abuses', September 1995, p. 1.
57 Letter from the LTTE International Secretariat to Amnesty International, 10 July 1995, in Amnesty International Correspondence with the Liberation Tigers of Tamil Eelam on Human Rights Abuses', September 1995, p. 3.
58 Movement for Inter Racial Justice and Equality, Update, November 1995, p. 3.
59 Ibid., pp. 1, 4; Swamy, *An Elusive Mind*, op. cit., pp. 255–256.
60 US Committee for Refugees, 'The People in Between: Sri Lankans Face Long-Term Displacement', Washington DC, March 1996, pp. 1, 5; MIRJE, Update, November 1995, p. 2.
61 Rajasingham-Senanayake, 'Dangers of Devolution', op. cit., p. 62.
62 UTHR, Information Bulletin No. 7, 4 September 1995, p. 10.
63 Human Rights Watch/Asia, 'Sri Lanka: Stop Killing of Civilians', July 1995, vol. 7, no. 11, pp. 6–7; UTHR, 4 September 1995, pp. 2–3; Human Rights Watch, 'Sri Lanka, Stop Killing Civilians', vol. 7, no. 11, op. cit., p. 1.
64 Ibid., p. 7; Amnesty International, 'Appeal for Full Implementation of Commitment to Human Rights', July 1995, *passim*; see also, Jim McDonald, New AI Report on Sri Lanka, 3 February 1996.
65 Amnesty International, 'Sri Lanka: Under Scrutiny by the Human Rights Committee', ASA 37/2/95, December 1995, *passim.*
66 MIRJE, Update, op. cit., pp. 1–3.
67 Rajasingham-Senanayake, 'Dangers of Devolution', op. cit., p. 67; Gunaratna, *Sri Lanka's Ethnic Crisis*, op. cit., p. 28.
68 Ghosh, *Ethnicity*, op. cit., p. 358; Bandara, *Lionsong*, op. cit., p. 266; Swamy, *Inside an Elusive Mind*, op. cit., p. 256.
69 Ibid., p. 257; Gunaratna, *Sri Lanka's Ethnic Crisis*, op. cit., p. 28.
70 Ibid., pp. 29, 121, 285; Swamy, *Elusive Mind*, op. cit., pp. 258–259; Bandara, *Lionsong*, op. cit., pp. 269–270.
71 'Gaps in the Krishanthy Kumaraswamy Case: Disappearances and Accountability', UTHR, Special Report No. 12, op. cit., p. 27.
72 Ibid, p. 5.

73 Ibid., pp. 5–6, *passim*; Hoole, *Sri Lanka*, op. cit., p. 441.
74 *New York Times*, 29 August 2001; 'Chemmani Exhumations – Positive First Steps Towards Truth and Justice', Amnesty International, AI, 22 June 1999; Human Rights Watch, Sri Lanka Country Report, 1999, p. 2.
75 Bandara, *Lionsong*, op. cit., pp. 273–274, 279.
76 Gunaratna, *Sri Lanka's Ethnic Crisis*, op. cit., p. 282.
77 Ibid., p. 29.
78 Ibid., p. 30, Bandara, *Lionsong*, op. cit., p. 283.
79 Hoole, *Sri Lanka*, op. cit., p. 439.
80 'UN Official Warns of War Crimes Charges Against Tamil Rebels', *AFP* 22 September 1999, pp. 1–2.
81 Ibid., p. 2.
82 Bandara, *Lionsong*, op. cit., pp. 304, 315.
83 Ibid., p. 301; S. Sathnanathan 'Elections, Meditation and the Tamil National Movement', 4 November 1999, online, available at: www.tamilnation.org.
84 M.V.S. Sambandan, *Frontline*, vol. 17, issue 09, April 29–May 12, 2000.
85 Bandara, *Lionsong*, op. cit., pp. 309–310.
86 Ibid., pp. 312, 316.
87 Ibid., p. 324; Hoole, *Sri Lanka*, op. cit., pp. 459–462.
88 'Sri Lanka: Failure of Justice for Victims of Massacre', Human Rights Watch, 2 June 2005; Written Statement Submitted by the Asian Legal Resource Centre, Commission on Human Rights, 57th Session, Economic and Social Council, 30 January 2001, E/CN.4/2001/NGO/70.
89 Bandara, *Lionsong*, op. cit., p. 334; 'Sri Lanka Government in a Minority as Key Coalition Partner Quits', World Socialist Web Site, 26 June 1001, online, available at: www:wsws.org.
90 Bandara, *Lionsong*, op. cit., pp. 340–341.
91 Asoka Bandarage, 'Women and Social Change in Sri Lanka: Towards a Feminist Theoretical Framework', working paper no. 11, Center for Women's Research, Sri Lanka, 1998, pp. 1–3.
92 Cited in D.M.P. Dissanayake, 'Is the JVP Intransigent?', *Sri Lanka Express*, June 30, 2006.
93 Bulletin of the NGO Forum on Sri Lanka, FOCUS, no. 2, September 1994, pp. 1–3; Ghosh, *Ethnicity*, op. cit., pp. 150–152.
94 National Peace Council, 'Cost of War: Economic, Social and Human Cost of the War, Sri Lanka', Colombo, 2001, pp. 1–2; 40; Saman Kelegama, 'Economic Costs of Conflict in Sri Lanka', in Robert I. Rotberg, *Creating Peace in Sri Lanka*, Washington DC: Brookings Institution Press, p. 79.
95 National Peace Council, 'Cost of War', op. cit., p. 2.
96 Kelegama, 'Economic Costs', op. cit., p. 73.
97 Ibid., p. 83.
98 Ibid., pp. 75, 79.
99 Roland Edirisinghe, 'Colombo Dispatch: War Effort', *The Economist*, 3 August 2000.
100 Ibid.
101 Rajasingham-Senanayake, 'Dangers' op. cit., p. 63.
102 Denis McGilvray, 'Tamils and Muslims in the Shadow of War', in Gamage and Watson, eds., *Conflict and Community*, op. cit., p. 226.
103 Bandara, *Lionsong*, op. cit., p. 309.
104 Ibid., pp. 309–310.
105 Gunasekara, *Wages of Sin*, op. cit., p. 55.
106 Edirisinghe, 'Colombo Dispatch', op. cit.
107 Rajasingham-Senanyake, 'Dangers', op. cit., pp. 61.
108 Bandarage, *Women, Population and Global Crisis*, op. cit., chapter 7.

109 Rajasingham-Senanyake, 'Dangers', op. cit., pp. 62–63; Hoole, *Sri Lanka*, op. cit., p. 433.
110 Ibid., p. 433; see also, Jonathan Goodhand, *Aiding Peace?: The Role of NGOs in Armed Conflict*, Boulder: Lynne Renner, 2006.
111 Edirisinghe, 'Colombo Dispatch', op. cit.
112 Hoole, *Sri Lanka*, op. cit., p. 429.
113 Gunaratna, 'Internationalisation', op. cit., p. 127.
114 Ibid., p. 109.
115 Ibid., p. 121.
116 Ibid., pp. 120–121.
117 Ibid., p. 130.
118 Clifford Bob, *Marketing Rebellion*, op. cit., *passim*.
119 Gunaratna, 'Internationalisation', op. cit., p. 125.
120 Ibid., pp. 130–131.
121 Ibid, pp. 130–131.
122 Peter Chalk, 'Liberation Tigers of Tamil Eelam's (LTTE) International Organization and Operations – A Preliminary Analysis', Commentary no. 77, Winter 1999.
123 Hoole, *Sri Lanka*, op. cit., p. 450.
124 Pancras Jordan, 'Speaking Truth Into Power: The Human Rights Situation in Sri Lanka', Pax Christi Australia, Ref. AP. 29. E. 97.
125 US Committee for Refugees, 'The People in Between', op. cit., pp. 12–13.
126 Ibid., pp. 12–13; Udan Fernando, *NGOs*, op. cit., p. 50; Hoole, *Sri Lanka*, op. cit., p. 385.
127 US Committee for Refugees, 'The People in Between', op. cit., p. 15.
128 'Norwegian Peace Initiative', Report of Christian Michelsen Institute Conference, sponsored by the Norwegian Government, Bergen, Norway, 26 February, 1996, pp. 1–2; The Military Column, The *Sunday Times*, 17 March 1996.
129 V. Rudrakumaran, presentation at seminar on the Sri Lankan Conflict in Bergen, TamilCanadian, online, available at: www.tamilcanadian.com/page.
130 Christian Michelsen Institute, 'Norwegian Peace Initiative', op. cit., p. 5.
131 Ibid., p. 6.
132 Sinhala Commission Report, part 2, op. cit., pp. 46, 49.
133 Elizabeth Harris, 'Sri Lanka: Making Peace Possible', April 2001; Kai Funkschmidt, Report on a WCC Sri Lanka Meeting, Sri Lanka Relations Committee, Churches' Commission on Mission, Geneva, 6 December 2002.
134 Report of the Sinhala Commission, part 2, op. cit., pp. 40–100.
135 Sumathi Rajasingham, 'Open Forum of Globalization' in Rajan Philips, ed., *Sri Lanka: Global Challenges and National Crises*, Colombo: Ecumenical Institute for Study and Dialogue, 2001, pp. 171–172.
136 Bandara, *Lionsong*, op. cit., p. 344.
137 Online, available at: www.svik.org; see work of Rohan Gunaratna, op. cit.
138 Gunasekara, *Wages of Sin*, op. cit., p. 45.

8 Norwegian facilitated peace initiative, 2002–2008

1 Sisira Ediripullige, *Sri Lanka's Twisted Path to Peace*, Sri Lanka: Resource Management Foundation, 2004, pp. 48–56.
2 Gunasekara, *Wages of Sin*, op. cit., p. 55.
3 Ibid., p. 54.
4 Gunasekara, *Wages of Sin*, op. cit., pp. 51–52.
5 Manifesto of the Tamil National Alliance, 21 November 2001, online, available at: www.tamilnation.org.
6 Gunasekara, *Wages of Sin*, op. cit., pp. 52–53.
7 2001 Sri Lankan Parliamentary Election, online, available at: http://en.wikipedia. org accessed 5 February 2008.

8 Ibid., p. 47.
9 'Secretary General Welcomes Ceasefire Agreement in Sri Lanka', Press Release, SG/SM/8136.
10 Gunasekara, *Wages of Sin*, op. cit., pp. 56–57.
11 Online, available at: http://internationaltrade.suite101.com/a retrieved 4 February 2008.
12 Doug Mellgren, 'The Descendants of Vikings Are Now Raiders for Peace', *Washington Post*, 21 April 2002, p. 3.
13 Ibid., p. 2; Simen Saetre, 'A Humanitarian Great Power's Growth and Fall', *Morgenbladet*, 12 November 2004, p. 2.
14 Ibid., p. 1; Robin Webber, 'This is the Way – Vikings are Coming Again', *World News and Prophecy: Biblical Perspectives on Current Events*, July 2000, online, available at: www.ucgstp.org/bureau/wnp/ wnp0020, p. 3.
15 Saetre, 'A Humanitarian Great Power', op. cit., p. 2.
16 Francisco Gil White, 'The Oslo War Process', 29 October 2005, online, available at: www.hirhome.com/yugo/olo3.htm; Mathew Continetti, 'Relief Pitcher', online, available at: www.weeklystandard.com/ accessed 5 March 2008; Peter Ford, 'Norway as Peacemaker', *Christian Science Monitor*, 1 May 2000.
17 Ibid.
18 Cited in Dag Hareide, 'Peace Mediator – The New Norwegian Missionary?: A Critical View of "The Norwegian Model"', Nordisk Forum for Megling Og Konnflikthandering, online, available at: www.n-f-m.org/infokategori.asp?.
19 Hareide, 'Peace Mediator', op. cit.; 'Robin Webber, 'This is the Way', op. cit., p. 2.
20 Mellgren, 'Descendants of Vikings', op. cit., p. 2.
21 Cited in Gil White, 'Norwegian International "Meditation": in "Oslo war Process"', op. cit., p. 2.
22 Ibid., p. 2.
23 Christine Kieppe, 'Record Export of Weapons', online, available at: www.ssb.no/english/magazine.
24 Gil White, 'Norwegian International "Meditation": in "Oslo war Process"', op. cit., p. 4. Hareide, 'Peace Mediator, op. cit., p. 2.
25 Constitution of the Kingdom of Norway.
26 Oystein Steinlein, 'The Sami Law: A Change of Norwegian Government Policy Toward the Sami Minority?', Tromso University, Norway, n.d.
27 Gil White, 'Oslo War Process', op. cit., *passim*.
28 Hareide, 'Peace Mediator', op. cit., p. 1; Gil White, 'The Oslo Peace Process', op. cit., *passim*.
29 Josselin and Wallace, 'Non-State Actors', cited in op. cit., in Gil-White, 'Norwegian International "Meditation": in "Oslo war Process"', op. cit., 6.
30 Goonatilake, 'Norway', op. cit., pp. 22–23; Goonatilake, *Recolonisation*, op. cit., *passim*; Goonatilake, *Anthropologizing Sri Lanka*, op. cit., chapter 12.
31 Wijitha Nakkawita, 'Kumar Rupesinghe paid Rs. 1.1 mn a Month', online, available at: www.lankaweb.com/news/items07/230707–1.html accessed 3 May 2008.
32 Gil White, 'Oslo War Process', op. cit., section 6, epilogue, pp. 2–3.
33 Ibid., pp. 3–4.
34 Norwegian Peace Initiative, Christian Michelsen Institute, 26 February 1996, op. cit., p. 7.
35 'Save the Children' Before PSCI, 18 October 2007, online, available at: www.-lankatruth-com/.
36 F. Rovik, 'Norway: A Terrorist Safe Haven?' in *Peace in Sri Lanka*, WAPS, op. cit., 2005, p. 7.
37 *Asian Tribune* July 7, 2006.
38 'The Norwegian Peace Facilitators in Sri Lanka', report prepared by Norwegians Against Terrorism (NAT), Oslo, 13 January 2006, p. 30.

39 Rovik, 'Norway', op. cit., p. 3; see also, online, available at: ww.svik.org/TC.pdf; NAT, 'The International Fight Against the LTTE', 1/14/2007Enclosures; Goonatilake, 'Norway', op. cit., 'Role of Erik Solheim Questioned by Norwegian Anti-Terrorists', *Asian Tribune*, 4, 21, 2007.

40 NAT, July 2007 Update, op. cit.

41 'Role of Erik Solheim', op. cit., p. 1, Swaris, 'Between Blinds: Norwegian Game Plan', *The Island*, 6 July 2005, p. 3.

42 Agreement on a Ceasefire between the Government of the Democratic Socialist Republic of Sri Lanka and the Liberation Tigers of Tamil Eelam Signed on 21 February 2002.

43 Gunasekara, *Wages of Sin*, op. cit., p. 58.

44 Joint Statement From Sri Lankan Organizations in Australia on the Memorandum of Understanding (MOU) Signed by Sri Lanka Government with Tamil Tigers, 14 March 2002, p. 1.

45 Paul Harris, 'The Greatest Giveaway in History', *Sri Lanka Express*, 10 May 2002, p. 4.

46 Agreement on a Ceasefire, op. cit., 21 February 2002.

47 Gunasekara, *Wages of Sin*, op. cit., p. 59.

48 Agreement on a Ceasefire, 21 February 2002; Joint Statement From Sri Lankan Organizations, Australia, op. cit., p. 2.

49 Agreement on a Ceasefire, 21 February 2002.

50 Gunasekara, *Wages of Sin*, op. cit., p. 60.

51 Ibid., p. 60.

52 Ibid., p. 77; *The Island*, 12 April 2002.

53 Ibid., p. 77, *Sunday Times*, 14 April 2002.

54 Ediripullige, *Twisted Path*, op. cit., op. cit., p. 4.

55 Agreement on a Ceasefire, 21 February 2002.

56 Ibid.; Gunasekara, *Wages of Sin*, op. cit., p. 64.

57 Ediripullige, *Twisted Path*, op. cit., p. 140.

58 Ambassador Bernard Goonatilake, 'The Ceasefire Agreement, The Peace Process and the International Community', Address at Capitol Hill, Washington DC, 25 January 2008.

59 NAT, 'Norwegian Peace Facilitators', op. cit., p. 5.

60 UTHR, Bulletin 32, pp. 14–15; UTHR, Bulletin 31, pp. 11–13.

61 Harris, 'Appeasement of Terrorism', op. cit., p. 137.

62 Ismail, Abdullah and Fazil, 'The Other Side', in Frerks and Klem, *Dealing With Diversity*, op. cit., p. 193.

63 Harris, 'Appeasement of Terrorism', op. cit., p. 137.

64 Ravikumar, 'Caste of the Tiger', op. cit., p. 1.

65 Ediripullige, *Twisted Path*, op. cit., pp. 141, 265–266; Gunasekara, *Wages of Sin*, op. cit., pp. 87, 89, 90.

66 Foreign Ministry of Japan, Tokyo Declaration on Reconstruction and Development of Sri Lanka, 19 June, 2003, cited in Ediripullige, *Sri Lanka's Twisted Path*, op. cit., Appendix IV, p. 333.

67 Ibid., Appendix II, p. 313.

68 The Proposals by the Liberation Tigers of Tamil Eelam on Behalf of the Tamil People for an Agreement to Establish an Interim Self-Governing Authority for the Northeast of the Island of Sri Lanka'.

69 Liz Philipson and Yuvi Thangarajah, 'The Politics of the North-East', in *Sri Lanka Strategic Assessment*, San Francisco: Asia Foundation, 2005, p. 18 and fn 10; see also 'Human Rights Development in Sri Lanka', 11 December 1998, online, available at: www.tamilnation.org.

70 Ediripullige, *Twisted Path*, op. cit., p. 170; Sri Lanka Freedom Party's Statement on the LTTE's proposals for an Interim Self Governing Authority for the North and East of Sri Lanka, 4 November 2003, p. 1.

71 Ibid., p. 2.
72 The Proposals by the Liberation Tigers for an ISGA, op. cit.
73 Ibid., Sri Lanka Freedom Party's Statement on ISGA, op. cit., p. 3.
74 LTTE ISGA Proposals, op. cit.
75 Sri Lanka Freedom Party's Statement on ISGA, op. cit., p. 3.
76 LTTE ISGA Proposals, op. cit.
77 Sri Lanka Freedom Party's Statement on ISGA, op. cit., p. 5; WAPS, Media Release on 31 May 2004 on ISGA Proposals.
78 LTTE ISGA Proposals, op. cit.
79 Sri Lanka Freedom Party's Statement on ISGA, op. cit., p. 4.
80 Ibid., p. 4; LTTE ISGA Proposals, op. cit.
81 Ibid.
82 Sri Lanka Freedom Party's Statement on ISGA, op. cit., p. 4.
83 William Clarence, *Ethnic Warfare in Sri Lanka and the UN Crisis*, London: Pluto Press, 2007, p. 221; WAPS, Media Release on ISGA Proposals, op. cit.
84 Paul Harris, 'The Appeasement of Terrorism', op. cit., p. 126; Special Report, online, available at: www.pnmsrilanka.com accessed 5 March 2008.
85 Bandara, *Lionsong*, op. cit., pp. 352, 353.
86 Van de Voorde, 'Sri Lankan Tamil Terrorism', op. cit.
87 Ibid., p. 136.
88 Gunasekara, *Wages of Sin*, op. cit., pp. 96–99.
89 Ibid., pp. 94–95 and cover.
90 Trinco Declared Eelam Capital at Rally that had State Support', *Sri Lanka Express*, 22 March 2002, p. 8.
91 Harris, 'Appeasement of Terrorism', op. cit., pp. 134–135.
92 SLMM statistics cited, online, available at: www.peaceinsrilanka.com/peace accessed 5 March 2008.
93 Human Rights Watch, 'Living in Fear: Child Soldiers and the Tamil Tigers in Sri Lanka', 2004, *passim*.
94 Ibid., p. 2.
95 UTHR, Bulletin 30, December 2002, 3:3, 9.
96 Child Soldiers Global Report, 2004, 'Sri Lanka', p. 2; see also, UTHR, Bulletin 31, p. 2.
97 Child Soldiers Global Report, 2004, 'Sri Lanka', pp. 1–2.
98 Ibid., pp. 1–2.
99 Ibid., p. 2.
100 UTHR Bulletin 29, October 2002.
101 NAT, 'Norwegian Peace Facilitators', op. cit., pp. 7–8, 13.
102 UTHR, Bulletin 32, p. 12; UTHR, Bulletin 31, p. 2; UTHR Bulletin 30, December 2002.
103 Goonatilake, *Recolonisation*, op. cit., pp. 121–123; Janaka Perera, 'Berghof Foundation Allegations of Defamation: A Response', *Asian Tribune*, 29 August 2006.
104 'Frequently Asked Questions', online, available at: www.berghof.foundation.lk.
105 Human Rights Watch, 'Sri Lanka: Political Killings During the Ceasefire', 7 August 2003, online, available at: http:/hrw.org/backgrounder/asia/srilanka.
106 NAT, Norwegian Peace Facilitators, op. cit., *passim*; Gil White, 'Oslo War Process', op. cit.; online, available at: www.pnmsrilanka.com.
107 Rovik, 'Norway', op. cit.
108 Report of Toronto Meeting, 10 March 2007, online, available at: www.svik.org/TC.pdf.
109 'Role of Erik Solheim Questioned by Norwegian Anti-terrorists', *Asian Tribune*, 21 April 2007.
110 Report of Toronto Meeting, 10 March 2007, online, available at: www.svik.org/TC.pdf.

111 Ibid; Walter Jayawardhana, 'Norway Allegedly Trained Sea Tigers', online, available at: www.lankaweb.org.
112 Ibid.
113 NAT, 'Norwegian Peace Facilitators', op. cit., pp. 11, 21; Rovik, 'Norway', op. cit., p. 4; Lanka Truth, 'Save the Children', op. cit.
114 Swaris, 'Between the Blinds', op. cit.
115 Susantha Goonatilake, 'Have Open Conference on Traitors Inc?', *Daily News*, 20 January 2006.
116 Online, available at: www.pnmsrilanka.com.
117 NAT, 'Norwegians Against Terror', op. cit., p. 12.
118 Ibid.
119 Report of Toronto Meeting, 10 March 2007, online, available at: www.svik.org/TC.pdf.
120 Asia Foundation, 'Aid, Conflict and Peace Building in Sri Lanka, 2000–2005', op. cit., Executive Summary, pp. 10–11.
121 K. Ratnayaka, 'A Split in the LTTE Heightens Danger of War in Sri Lanka', online, available at: www.wsws.org, 18 March 2004, p 2.
122 Online, available at: www.eueomsrilanka.org/EUEOMSriLanka2004-FinalReport. pdf.
123 Online, available at: http://www.npr.org/rundowns/rundown.php?prgId=5&prg Date=5-Jan-2005.
124 Memorandum of Understanding for the Establishment of a Post-Tsunami Operational Management Structure, 27 June 2005, online, available at: www.peceinsrilanka.com.
125 Mahinda Gunasekara, Sri Lanka United National Association of Canada, Media Release, 6 July 2005, online, available at: http://webhome.idirect.com/sluna, p. 3.
126 *Asian Tribune*, 15 July 2005.
127 Bandula Jayasekara, ''Leading Norwegian Newspaper Reveals Tigers get Millions from Norway', *The Island*, 6 July 2005; Swaris, 'Between the Blinds', op. cit., p. 3.
128 Online, available at: youtube.com/watch?v=sUdUEOVdEuc.
129 John Solomon and B.C. Tan, 'Feeding the Tiger: How Sri Lankan Insurgents Fund the War', *Jane's Intelligence Review*, 1 September 2007.
130 Ibid., p. 2; also online, available at: www.fbi.gov/jan08/tamiltigers.
131 Chalk, Peter, 'The Tigers Abroad: How the LTTE Diaspora Supports the Conflict in Sri Lanka', *Georgetown Journal of International Affairs*, 9:2 Summer/Fall 2008, pp. 97–104.
132 Peter Leitner, 'War in Sri Lanka is the Legacy left by the European Colonialism', *Asian Tribune*, 5 February 2008.
133 Hassina Leelarathna, 'US Lawmakers with ties to LTTE Money', *The Island*, 11 February 2008, online, available at: http://www.island.lk/2008/02/11/features1.html.
134 Online, available at: www.tamilsforjustice.org/project.htm accessed 3 May 2008.
135 Ibid.
136 NAT, Update, July 2007, p. 17.
137 Ibid.
138 Rohitha Bogollagama, Minister of Foreign Affairs, Sri Lanka, 'Sri Lanka Looking Beyond Terrorism: A Road Map to Peace', Johns Hopkins University – School of Advanced International Studies, 4 October 2007.
139 Ibid.
140 Online, available at: http:www.fbi.gov/page2/jan08/tamil_tigers011008.html accessed 15 January 2008.

9 Globalization and conflict resolution: separatism or pluralism?

1 Bandarage, *Women, Population and Global Crisis*, op. cit., pp. 1–4; see also, www.grossmont.edu/toddmyers/globalsouth.ppt.

2 Report on the Congo, Democracy Now, Pacifica Radio, 24 January 2008.
3 Refugees, UNHCR, vol. 1, no. 126, 2002, p. 7.
4 Bandarage, *Women, Population and Global Crisis*, op. cit., pp. 198–204.
5 Bandarage, 'Ethnic and Religious Tension', op. cit., pp. 286–301.
6 Bandarage, *Women, Population and Global Crisis*, op. cit., p. 206: www.global
   issues.org/Geopolitics/ArmsTrade/BigBusiness.asp accessed 5/5/2008.
7 Swamy, *Elusive Mind*, op. cit., p. 268; Victor Ostrovsky, *By Way of Deception*, New
   York: St Martin's Press, 2002.
8 Gunaratna, 'Internationalisation', op. cit., p. 130.
9 Neil G. Boothby and Christine M. Knudsen, 'Children of the Gun', Special Report,
   Scientific American, June 2000, pp. 60–65.
10 Bandarage, 'Ethnic and Religious Tension', op. cit., *passim*.
11 Roger Cohen, 'A Change to Believe In', *New York Times*, 21 February 2008.
12 Sarvanathan, 'Norwegian and British Interventions', op. cit., p. 3; Bandarage,
   Women, Population and Global Crisis, op. cit., chapter 7.
13 Thomas G. Weiss, 'Nongovermental Organizations and Internal Conflict', in
   Michael E. Brown, ed., *The International Dimensions of Internal Conflict*, Cambridge, MA: The MIT Press, 1996, chapter 13; John Clark, ed., *Globalizing Civic
   Engagement: Civil Society and Transnational Action*, London: Earthscan, 2003,
   Introduction, Conclusions.
14 Keck and Sikkink, *Activists Beyond Borders: Advocacy Networks in International
   Politics*, Ithaca: Cornell University Press, 1998, pp. 12–13.
15 Ibid., p. 13.
16 Clark, *Globalizing Civic Engagement*, op. cit., p. 9.
17 Ibid., p. 10.
18 Ibid., pp. 17, 26.
19 Orjuela, 'Building Peace', op. cit., p. 201.
20 Keck and Sikkink, *Activists Beyond Borders*, op. cit., p. 79.
21 Ibid., p. 117.
22 Nicolas Guilhot, *The Democracy Makers: Human Rights and the Politics of Global
   Order*, New York: Columbia University Press, 2005.
23 Lal, 'Imperialism of Human Rights', op. cit.; G.H. Pieris, 'Appeal to All Sri
   Lankans – The R2P Threat to Sri Lanka', online, available at: http://www.protectsri-
   lanka.org/Archives.
24 Clifford Bob, *Marketing Rebellion*, op. cit.
25 Mark Duffield, *Global Governance and the New Wars: The Merging of Development and Security*, London: Zed Books, 2001; Goonatilake, *Recolonisation*, op. cit.,
   p. 112.
26 Ibid., pp. 104–116.
27 Mary B. Anderson, *Do No Harm; How Aid Can Support Peace – Or War*, Boulder:
   Lynne Renner, 1999; Jonathan Goodhand, *Aiding Peace? The Role of NGOs in
   Armed Conflict*, Boulder: Lynne Renner, 2006.
28 Guilhot, *Democracy Makers*, op. cit.
29 Bhupinder Brar, *Tribune*, India, 8 January 2000.
30 Gil White, 'Oslo War Process', op. cit.
31 Gideon Rachman, 'For Nations, Small is Beautiful', *The Financial Times* (UK) 12
   April 2007.
32 Peter Galbraith, *The End of Iraq: How American Incompetence Created a War
   Without End*, Washington DC: Middle East Policy Council, 2005.
33 Roger Cohen, 'A Change to Believe In', *New York Times*, 21 February 2008.
34 Cited in G.H. Pieris, 'Responsibility to Protect: A Critique', online, available at:
   www.protectsrilanka.org/Archives.
35 'Responsibility to Protect', Report of the International Commission on Intervention
   and State Sovereignty, December 2001, p. 2.

36 Erik Voten, 'International Organizations and the Allocation of Legitimacy', Moratara Center for International Studies, Georgetown University, Working Paper C-01–0708.

37 'Responsibility to Protect', op. cit., Foreword, pp. vii, 2.

38 Ibid., p. 14.

39 Ibid., p. 11.

40 Thomas Walkom, 'Problems with Kosovo Recognition', The *Toronto Star*, 20 March 2008; Lt Col A.S. Amarasekara, 'The United Nations and Responsibility to Protect?', online, available at: www.prtectsrilanka.org/Archives/325789 (4/7/2008); Asoka Weerasinghe, 'Caution: Tamil Lobby for a Kosovo like Eelam', unpublished manuscript.

41 Eric Brahm, 'Self Determination Procedures', Knowledge Based Essay, September 2005, online, available at: http://conflict-frontiers.beyondintractability.org/essay/self_determination/?nid=6711.

42 United States Institute of Peace, 'U.S. Responses to Self-Determination Movements: Strategies for Nonviolent Outcomes and Alternatives to Secessionism', *Peaceworks*, no. 16, 1997, p. 21.

43 Brahm, 'Self Determination', op. cit.

44 Ibid.

45 Chaim Kaufmann, cited in USIP, 'U.S. Responses to Self-Determination Movements', op. cit., p. 19.

46 Milton Esman, 'The Management of Communal Conflict', *Public Policy*, XXI, Winter, 1972, p. 64.

47 Chaim Kaufmann, 'Possible and Impossible Solutions to Ethnic Civil Wars', *International Security*, 20:4 (Spring 1996), 136–175.

48 Nicolas Sambanis, 'Ethnic Partition as a Solution to Ethnic War: An Empirical Critique of the Theoretical Literature', World Bank, 18 September 1999, p. 5.

49 Sisk cited in USIP, 'U.S. Response to Self Determination', op. cit., p. 19.

50 'Responsibility to Protect', Report of the International Commission, op. cit., p. 1.

51 'Impossible Dream', *The Economist* 2 April 2008, online, available at: economist.com.

52 Asian Tribune, vol. 7, no. 1,18 October, online, available at: www.asntribune.com.

53 'Sri Lanka', US Department of State, Country Reports on Human Rights Practices, 2007; Human Rights Watch, 'Recurring Nightmare: State Responsibility for Disappearances and Abductions in Sri Lanka', March 2008; John Peter, 'Stop War on Journalists in Sri Lanka says World Press Freedom Community', online, available at: www.tamileelamnews.com/publish/tns_9580.shtml.

54 See, recent reports of UTHR; 'Sri Lanka Aid Workers Demand Justice on Anniversary of 17 Workers', *International Herald Tribune*, 6 August 2007; and 'Sri Lanka Democracy Forum': Setting the Latest UTHR Report on Mutur in Context', SCOPP, 1 April 2008.

55 Human Rights Watch Sri Lanka: "Disappearances" by Security Forces a National Crisis', 6 March 2008; Sri Lanka Democracy Forum, 7 March 2008, online, available at: www.lankademocracy.org.

56 G.H. Pieris, 'An Appeal to All Sri Lankans', online, available at: www.protectsrilanka.org/Archives.

57 Daya Gamage, 'U.N. Secretary General Rocks to Alan's Melody to Accept Unauthentic Data on Sri Lanka's Child Soldiers', 1 February 2007, online, available at: www.asiantribune.com.

58 US Department of State Report, 2007, op. cit., pp. 3, 10.

59 Ibid., p. 10.

60 Pieris, 'An Appeal to All Sri Lankans', op. cit.

61 Ibid.

62 Gamage, 'U.N. Secretary', op. cit.; Walter Jayawardhana, 'United Nations Diplomat

was Involved in Waterloo Suresh's Pro-Terrorist Student Body, Allegations Say', online, available at: http://lankapage.wordpress.com; 'Rock in Ms. Radhika Coomaraswamy's Head', asiantribune.com, 18/12/2006; 'Radhika Coomaraswamy clarifies sending Ambassador Allan Rock for Investigation', asiantribune.com, 19/12/2006.

63 News Reports, 13 November 2007 and 7 December 2007, online, available at: www.lankanewspapers.com/news/2007.

64 Response of the Government of Sri Lanka to the US State Department's Country Report on Human Rights 2007 on Sri Lanka, Ministry of Foreign Affairs, Sri Lanka, 31 March 2008, pp. ii, 13, online www.slmfa.gov.lk

65 Ibid., p. 31.

66 Ibid., pp. 21–22.

67 Ibid., pp. 29–30.

68 Ibid., pp. 8–9.

69 Ibid., pp. 8, 10.

70 Online, available at: http://hrw.org/reports/2008/srilanka0308/srilanka0308 cases.pdf.

71 Response of the Government of Sri Lanka to the US State Department's Country Report on Human Rights 2007 on Sri Lanka, Ministry of Foreign Affairs, Sri Lanka, 31 March 2008, p. 31.

72 Rajiva Wijeingha, 'The International Eminent Persons and their Assistants', Sri Lanka Secretariat for Coordinating the Peace Process (SCOPP), 2 April 2008.

73 Manfred Nowak, Report of the Special Rapporteur on Torture, Mission to Sri Lanka, United Nations General Assembly, 26 February 2008.

74 Ibid., pp. 32–33.

75 Amarasekara, 'United Nations and R2P', op. cit., p. 5.

76 Ibid., p. 3.

77 Online, available at: http://jurist.lw.pitt.edu/paperchase/2008.

78 'U.N. Enforced Two States Solution will end the Possible Genocide in Sri Lanka – Professor Peter Schalk', online, available at: www.tamileelamnews.com/news/publish, 1 April 2008 (accessed 15 April 2008)

79 Leelarathna, 'U.S. Lawmakers', op. cit.

80 Sarvanathan, 'Norwegian and British Interventions', op. cit., p. 3.

81 Pieris, 'An Appeal to All Sri Lankans', op. cit.

82 ICG, A Kosovo Roadmap (I): Addressing Final Status, Europe Report no. 124, 1 March 2002; A Kosovo Roadmap (II): Internal Benchmarks, Europe Report no. 125, 1 March 2002.

83 ICG, Sri Lanka: Sinhala Nationalism and the Elusive Southern Consensus, Asia Report no. 141, 7 November 2007.

84 H.L. de Silva, 'Responsibility to Protect and the Sovereignty of the State, online, available at: www.protectsrilanka.org/Archives, p. 1.

85 H.L.D. Mahindapala, 'Peace Secretariat Calls for UN Inquiry into Radhika Coomaraswamy, UN Under Secretary General, Stuck in NGO Scandal', *Asian Tribune*, 29 January, 2008.

86 'Responsibility to Protect', Report of the International Commission, op. cit., p. 1.

87 'We Tamils are Better Off Without the Tamil Tigers', online, available at: www./rediff.com/news/2008/March 24, p. 5.

88 Sarranathan, 'In Pursuit of a Mythical State', op. cit., p. 1193.

89 Sri Lanka Democracy Forum, 14 January 2008, online, available at: www.lankademocracy.org.

90 Speech of V. Anandasangaree at Submission of APRC Proposals, 27 January 2008 in Blog ID 8.05 of ACSLU (Australian Center for Sri Lankan Unity).

91 Amita Shastri, 'Material Basis', op. cit.

92 27 January 2008 in Blog ID 8.05 of ACSLU, op. cit., p. 3.

93 Ibid., p. 3.
94 Justus Richter, 'The Conflict Between Sinhalese and Tamils in Sri Lanka: An Antagonistic Ethnic Cleavage?', in Justus Richter and Christian Wagner eds., Regional Security, *Ethnicity and Governance: The Challenges for South Asia*, Manohar, 1998, p. 110.
95 Darini Rajasingham-Senanayake, 'The Dangers of Devolution: The Hidden Economies of Armed Conflict', in Rotberg, ed., op. cit., p. 68.
96 Neville Ladduwahetty, 'Kosovo's Independence and Sri Lanka', online, available at: www.protectsrilanka.org/Archives.
97 Muni, *Pangs of Proximity*, op. cit., p. 83.
98 27 January 2008 in Blog ID 8.05 of ACSLU op. cit., p. 3.
99 Sri Lanka Government Census of Population; CIA World Factbook – Sri Lanka, 2008.
100 Robert Stoddard, 'Regionalization and Regionalism in Sri Lanka', Lincoln: Department of Geography, University of Nebraska, 1986, pp. 9–10.
101 Sri Lanka Population and Housing Census, 2001; compare G.H. Peiris, *Sri Lanka: Challenges of the New Millennium*, Kandy: Kandy Books, 2006, p. 344.
102 'Smiles that Conceal the Worries', *The Economist*, 20 July 2002, US Edition.
103 P. Puvanarajan and W. Indralal de Silva, 'Fertility Decline in Sri Lanka: Are All Ethnic Groups Party to the Process?', *Asia-Pacific Population Journal*, vol. 16, no. 3, September 2001, pp. 31, 39.
104 Sri Lanka 2001 Census of Population and Housing.
105 Peiris, 'New Millennium', op. cit., pp. 343–344; online, available at: http://en.wikipedia.org/ retrieved 7 March 2008.
106 *The Economist*, 20 July 2002, op. cit.
107 NAT, 'The International Fight Against the LTTE', op. cit., 14 January 2007.
108 Hoole, *Sri Lanka*, op. cit., pp. 431–432.
109 UTHR Reports, See also *Broken Palmyrah*.
110 *Asian Tribune*, 7 January 2007, online, available at: www.asaintribune.com accessed 5 June 2008.
111 S.T. Hettige and Markus Mayer, eds., *Sri Lankan Youth: Challenges and Responses*, Colombo: Friedrich Ebert Stiftung, 2002, pp. 242–243.
112 Siri Gamage, 'Post Independent Political Conflicts in Sri Lanka: Elites, Ethnicity, and Class Contradictions', in Gamage and Watson, eds., Conflict and Community, op. cit., p. 333.
113 Saman Kelegama, 'Economic Costs of Conflict in Sri Lanka', in Rotberg, *Creating Peace*, op. cit., p. 83.
114 Amarasekara, 'United Nations and RP', op. cit., pp. 3–4.
115 Darini Rajasingham-Senanayake, 'Sri Lanka and the Violence of Reconstruction', *Development*, vol. 48, no. 3, September 2005, p. 117.

Selected bibliography

Abeysekara, C., Edirisinghe, R., Liyanage, S., Saravanamuttu, P. and Uyangoda, J. (1998) *Unitarianism, Devolution and Majoritarian Elitism: A Response to the Interim Report of the Sinhala Commission*, Colombo: Social Scientists Association.

Anderson, B. (2006) *Imagined Communities: Reflections on the Origin and Spread of Nationalism*, London: Verso Books.

Asia Foundation (2005) *Sri Lanka Strategic Conflict Assessment 2005*, 4 vols. San Francisco: Asia Foundation.

Bandara, M. (2002) *Lionsong: Sri Lanka's 'Ethnic Conflict'*, Sri Lanka: Sandaruwan Madduma Bandara.

Bandarage, A. (1983) *Colonialism in Sri Lanka: The Political Economy of the Kandyan Highlands, 1833–1866*, Berlin: Mouton.

Bandarage, A. (1993) 'Peace in Sri Lanka: Obstacles and Opportunities', *The Island*: 10–11 August.

Bandarage, A. (1997) *Women, Population and Global Crisis: A Political-Economic Analysis*, London: Zed Books.

Bandarage, A. (2002) 'Broadening the Prospects for Peace in Sri Lanka', The *Hindu*, 8 December.

Bandarage, A. (2003) 'Ethno-religious Evolution in Pre-colonial Sri Lanka', *Ethnic Studies Report*, vol. XXI, No. 2, July 2003.

Bandarage, A. (2004) 'Ethnic and Religious Tension in the World', in P. O'Hara (ed.) *Global Political Economy and the Wealth of Nations*, London: Routledge.

Bastian, S. (ed.) (1994) *Devolution and Development in Sri Lanka*, Colombo: International Center for Ethnic Studies.

Bob, C. (2005) *The Marketing of Rebellion*, Cambridge: Cambridge University Press.

Bush, K. (2004) *The Intra-Group Dimensions of Ethnic Conflict in Sri Lanka: Learning to Read Between the Lines*, New York: Palgrave Macmillan.

Chalk, P. (1999) 'Liberation Tigers of Tamil Eelam's (LTTE) International Organization and Operations – A Preliminary Analysis', Commentary No. 77 Winter.

Chandraprema, C.A. (1991) *Sri Lanka: The Years of Terror: The JVP Insurrection 1987–1989*, Colombo: Lake House Bookshop.

Chua, A. (2004) *World on Fire: How Exporting Free Market Democracy Breeds Ethnic Hatred and Global Instability*, New York: Anchor Books.

Clark, J. (2003) *Globalizing Civic Engagement: Civil Society and Transnational Action*, London: Earthscan Publications Ltd.

Collier, P. and Hoeffler, A. (2004) 'Greed and Grievance in Civil War', Oxford Economic Papers, 56: 563–595.

Coomaraswamy, R. (1987) 'Myths Without Conscience, Tamil and Sinhalese National Writings of the 1980s', in Abeysekara, C. and Gunasinghe, N. (eds.) *Facets of Ethnicity in Sri Lanka*, Colombo: Social Scientists Association.

DeVotta, N. (2004) *Blowback: Linguistic Nationalism, Institutional Decay, and Ethnic Conflict in Sri Lanka*, Palo Alto: Stanford University Press.

Dharmadasa, K.N.O. (ed.) (1996) *National Language Policy in Sri Lanka*, Kandy: International Centre for Ethnic Studies.

Duffield, M. (2001) *Global Governance and the New Wars: The Merging of Development and Security*, New York: Zed Books.

Farmer, B.H. (1957) *Pioneer Peasant Colonization in Ceylon: A Study in Asian Agrarian Problems*, Oxford: Oxford University Press.

Frerks, G. and Klem, B. (eds.) (2005) *Dealing with Diversity: Sri Lankan Discourses on Peace and Conflict*, Clingendael: Netherlands Institute of International Relations.

Gamage, S. and Watson, I.B. (1999) *Conflict and Community in Contemporary Sri Lanka: 'Pearl of the East' or the 'Island of Tears'*, Colombo: Vijitha Yapa.

Ghosh, P. (2004) *Ethnicity Versus Nationalism: The Devolution Discourse in Sri Lanka*, Colombo: Vijitha Yapa Publications.

Goodhand, J. (2006) *Aiding Peace?: The Role of NGOs in Armed Conflict*, Boulder: Lynne Renner.

Goonatilake, S. (2006) *Recolonisation: Foreign Funded NGOs in Sri Lanka*, New Delhi: Sage Publications.

Guilhot, N. (2005) *The Democracy Makers: Human Rights and the Politics of the Global Order*, New York: Columbia University Press.

Gunaratna, M.H. (1988) *For a Sovereign State: A True Story on Sri Lanka's Separatist War*, Sri Lanka: Vishva Lekha.

Gunaratna, R. (1997) *International and Regional Security Implications of the Sri Lankan Tamil Insurgency*, UK, International Foundation of Sri Lankans.

Gunaratna, R. (1998) *Sri Lanka's Ethnic Crisis and National Security*, Colombo: South Asian Network on Conflict Research.

Gunaratna, R. (2001) 'Special Report on Al-Qaeda', *Jane's Intelligence Review*, 13: 42–45.

Gunasekara, S.L. (1996) *Tigers, 'Moderates' and Pandora's Package*, Sri Lanka: Sri Lanka Freedom Press.

Gunasekara, S.L. (2001) *Wages of Sin*, Colombo: Sinhala Jathika Sangamaya.

Gunasingham, M. (1999) *Sri Lankan Tamil Nationalism: A Study of its Origins*, Sydney: MTVP Publications.

Gurr, T. (2000) *People Versus States: Minorities at Risk in the New Century*, Washington DC: United States Institute of Peace.

Hannum, H. (1990) *Autonomy, Sovereignty, and Self-Determination: The Accommodation of Conflicting Rights*, Philadelphia: University of Pennsylvania Press.

Harris, P. (2002) 'The Greatest Giveaway in History', *Sri Lanka Express*, Los Angeles, 23 April.

Hettige, S.T. and Mayer, M. (eds.) (2002) *Sri Lankan Youth: Challenges and Responses*, Colombo: Friedrich Ebert Stiftung.

Hoole, R. (2001) *Sri Lanka: The Arrogance of Power: Myths, Decadence, and Murder*, Jaffna: University Teachers for Human Rights.

Horowitz, D.L. (1985) *Ethnic Groups in Conflict*, Berkeley: University of California Press.

International Commission on Intervention and State Sovereignty (2001) Report on

'Responsibility to Protect', Report of the International Commission on Intervention and State Sovereignty, December.

Jayatilleka, D. (1999) *The Indian Intervention in Sri Lanka, 1987–1990: The North East Provincial Council and the Devolution of Power*, Kandy: International Center for Ethnic Studies.

Jayawardena, K. (1985) *Ethnic and Class Conflicts in Sri Lanka*, Sri Lanka: Center for Social Analysis.

Kaufmann, C. and Sambanis, N. (1992) 'Ethnic Partition as a Solution to Ethnic War: An Empirical Critique of the Theoretical Literature', World Bank Policy Research Working Paper no. 2208.

Kearney, Robert N. (1967) *Communalism and Language in the Politics of Ceylon*, Durham: Duke University Press, 1967.

Keck, M. and Sikkink, K. (1998) *Activists Beyond Borders: Advocacy Networks in International Politics*, Ithaca: Cornell University Press.

Mahindapala, H.L.D. (1996) 'The Revolt of the Oppressed', The *Sunday Times*, 22 September.

Manogaran, C. (1987) *Ethnic Conflict and Reconciliation in Sri Lanka*, Honolulu: University of Hawaii Press.

National Joint Committee (1998 and 2001) *Reports of the Sinhala Commission, Parts 1 and 2*, Colombo: National Joint Committee.

National Joint Committee (2003) The *Case Against A Federal Constitution for Sri Lanka: Report of an Independent and Representative Committee'*, Colombo: The National Joint Committee.

Peiris, G.H. (1991) 'An Appraisal of the Concept of a Traditional Tamil Homeland in Sri Lanka', Ethnic Studies Report, Kandy 9(1) January.

Peiris, G.H. (2000) 'Prospects for a negotiated settlement of Sri Lanka's ethnic conflict', in de Silva, K.M. and Pieris, G.H. (eds.) *Pursuit of Peace in Sri Lanka, Kandy: Past Failures and Future Prospects*, Washington: ICES and USIP.

Piyadasa, L. (1984) *Sri Lanka: The Holocaust and After*, London: Marram Books.

Rajasingham-Senanayake, D. (1999) 'The Dangers of Devolution: The Hidden Economics of Armed Conflict', in Rotberg, R.I. (eds.) *Creating Peace in Sri Lanka: Civil War and Reconciliation*, Washington DC: Brookings Institution Press.

Richardson, J. (2005) *Paradise Poisoned: Learning About Conflict, Terrorism and Development from Sri Lanka's Civil Wars*, Colombo: International Center for Ethnic Studies.

Roberts, M. (1979) (eds.) *Collective Identities, Nationalisms and Protest in Modern Sri Lanka*, Colombo: Marga Institute.

Rupesinghe, K. (2006) (ed.), *Negotiating Peace in Sri Lanka: Efforts, Failures, and Lessons*, Colombo: Foundation for Co-Existence.

Sambanis, N. (1999) 'Ethnic Partition as a Solution to Ethnic War: An Empirical Critique of the Theoretical Literature', Public Economics: The World Bank.

Sarvanathan, M. (2007) 'In Pursuit of a Mythical State of Tamil Eelam: A Rejoinder to Kristian Stokke', *Third World Quarterly*, 28: 1185–1195.

Shastri, A. (1990) 'Material Basis for Separatism: The Tamil Eelam Movement in Sri Lanka', *Journal of Asian Studies*, 49: 56–77.

Silva, C.R. de and Barthlomeuz, T. (1998) *Buddhist Fundamentalism and Minority Identities in Sri Lanka*, New York: SUNY Press.

Silva, K.M. de (1988) *Managing Ethnic Tensions in Multi-ethnic Societies: Sri Lanka, 1880–1985*, Lanham: University Press of America.

Silva, K.M. de (1996) *Separatist Ideology in Sri Lanka: A Historical Appraisal*, Colombo: ICES.

Spencer, J. (1990) (eds.) *Sri Lanka: History and the Roots of Conflict*, London: Routledge.

Sri Lanka Government, (1980) *Report of the Commission of Inquiry*, Sessional Paper no. VII, July.

Steinberg, S. (2001) *The Ethnic Myth: Race, Ethnicity and Class in America*, Boston: Beacon Press.

Swamy, M.R.N. (2003) *Inside an Elusive Mind, Prabhakaran*, Sri Lanka: Vijitha Yapa Publications.

Tambiah, S. (1986) *Sri Lanka: Ethnic Fratricide and the Dismantling of Democracy*, Chicago: University of Chicago Press.

Thangarajah, C.Y. (2002) 'Youth, Conflict and Social Transformation in Sri Lanka', in Hettige S.T. and Mayer, M. (eds.) *Sri Lankan Youth: Challenges and Responses*, Colombo: Friedrich Ebert Stiftung.

University of Ceylon (1959) *History of Ceylon*, Colombo: University of Ceylon Press Board.

Uphoff, N. (2000) 'Ethnic Cooperation in Sri Lanka: Through the Keyhole of a USAID project', in Herring R.J. and Esman, M.J. (eds.) *Carrots, Sticks and Ethnic Conflict: Rethinking Development Assistance*, Ann Arbor: University of Michigan Press.

Weiss, T.G. (1996) 'Nongovernmental Organizations and Internal Conflict', in Brown, M.E. (ed.) *The International Dimensions of Internal Conflict*, Cambridge, MA: MIT Press.

Wickramasinghe, N. (1996) *Ethnic Politics in Sri Lanka*, New Delhi: Vikas.

Wilson, A.J. (1988) *The Break-Up of Sri Lanka: The Sinhalese-Tamil Conflict*, Honolulu: University of Hawaii.

Wilson, A.J. (1994) *S.J.V. Chelvanayakam and the Crisis of Sri Lankan Tamil Nationalism, 1947–1977*, Honolulu: University of Hawaii Press.

Winslow, D. and Woost, M.D. (eds.) (2004) *Economy, Culture, and Civil War in Sri Lanka*, Bloomington: Indiana University Press.

World Alliance for Peace in Sri Lanka (WAPS) (2005) *Peace in Sri Lanka: Obstacles and Opportunities*, London: WAPS.

Index